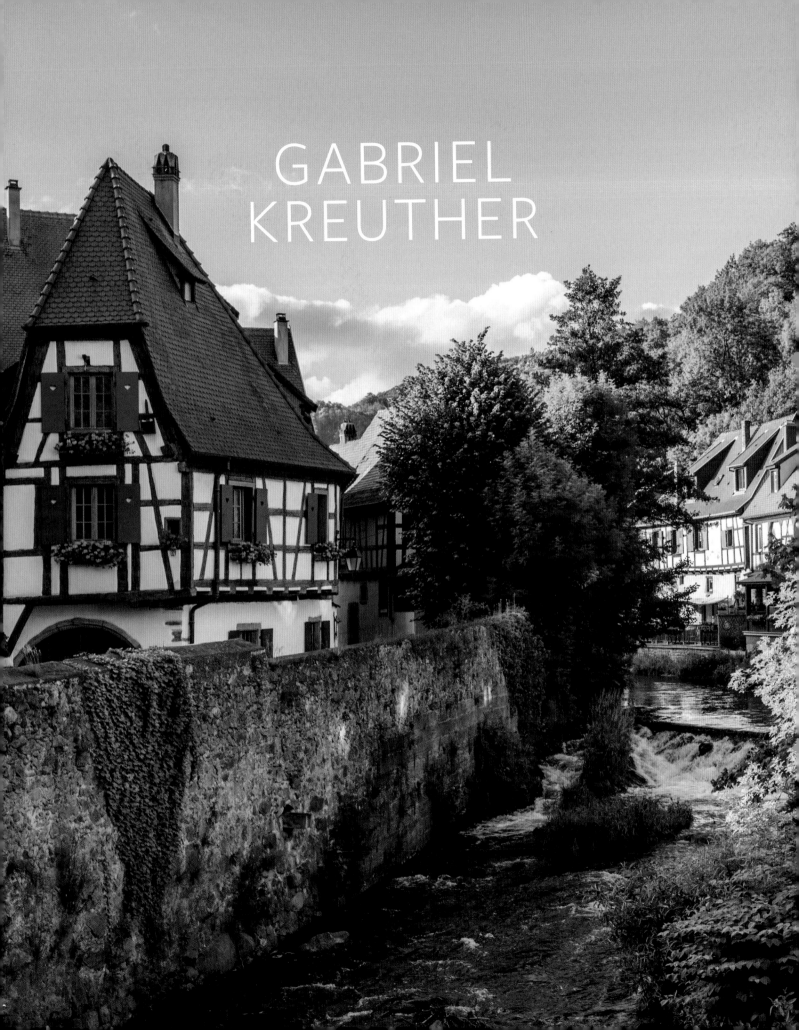

GABRIEL
KREUTHER

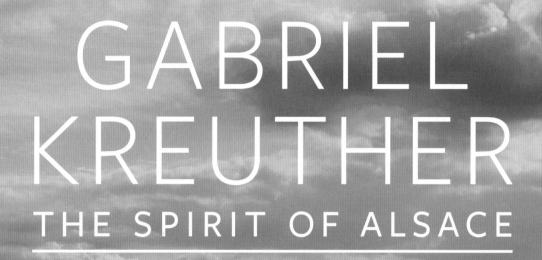

GABRIEL KREUTHER

THE SPIRIT OF ALSACE

A COOKBOOK

GABRIEL KREUTHER

with Michael Ruhlman

and with contributions from Genevieve Ko

Foreword by Jean-Georges Vongerichten

Photographs by Evan Sung

ABRAMS, NEW YORK

To my mother, Gabrielle

To my daughter, Margaux, who inspires me every day

And to young cooks everywhere. Never give up on your dreams.

CONTENTS

FOREWORD

BY JEAN-GEORGES VONGERICHTEN

I can't tell you how wonderful it is to see my past, my homeland, so beautifully and thoroughly represented in this book, and also to see how Gabriel Kreuther has brought Alsatian cuisine into the contemporary dining room. It's time.

Of course, I'd heard of Gabriel Kreuther shortly after he arrived in the 1990s—a new cook from Alsace in New York. I knew he'd be a great chef. He's from Alsace!

At the time, good cooks were hard to come by. I'd heard he worked at La Caravelle, the French fine-dining institution in Manhattan. He'd worked at Michelin-starred restaurants throughout Europe, so I expected him to be solid. After speaking with the owners of La Caravelle, I reached Gabriel in the kitchen during midday prep and said, "I've got a *chef poissonier* position available, but there's room to move up." Even though he was far more experienced than was required for that position, he took it.

Gabriel was very shy, like me. So I saw myself in him, as I was when I arrived in New York. He was a very good cook, I could see right away, with a great foundation. But more, he was a great teacher to all the chefs around him, and in a very short time he moved up to sous chef and eventually became my number-one guy at Restaurant Jean-Georges. And to me, he became almost like my brother.

He showed enormous patience with the younger chefs. He was also a great leader. He took the time to teach every *chef de partie* every dish. And he was also an innovator in my kitchen. At one point 25 percent of the dishes on my menu were his. He always cooked with great flavor and great balance, and his dishes were always founded on great fundamental technique. I would travel to Asia and pick up new flavors, and I knew the kitchen was in good hands with Gabriel in charge. He was exactly the kind of person I needed to surround myself with. He's sensitive, and, most important, he was *reliable*. When he said he'd do something, you knew it was going to get done. He was and is a great communicator and brought the team together, as he does at Restaurant Gabriel Kreuther.

I always knew someone was going to come in and take him away from me. When that happened, Gabriel was a gentleman. He would not accept the job without talking to me first. But I knew it was time for him. He really was like a younger brother, and the opportunity to open Atelier at the Ritz was one that wasn't likely to come around soon for him again. I could see in his heart he wanted to do it. So I told him, "Go for it. I know you're going to do a great job. You're going to make it." He was ready. He'd *been* ready.

And since then, opening the Modern brilliantly, winning best chef awards, and then opening his own restaurant, he's proven me right.

He's a great, original chef and very humble. Bringing sauerkraut to New York City fine dining is amazing! The tarte flambée. He's more traditional in his roots than I am—more in the vein of André Soltner, an Alsatian legend in the chef world—but it was the right time to bring these Alsatian flavors to New York. Gabriel uses his own deep nostalgia for Alsace in his cuisine in New York, so people can really enjoy the flavors of that region. People think that French cuisine is only Escoffier, *sole avec sauce vin blanc*. But Alsatian cuisine is more rustic. You've got the German influence, the Swiss influence. It's a *fascinating* region. Bringing those flavors to New York in a modern way is amazing to me. I want to try everything in this book!

Gabriel is a true Alsatian in New York. It's been amazing to watch him grow from a cook in the basement of La Caravelle, to poissonier at Jean-Georges, to today, when he's at the top of his game. Only in New York. How I love this city.

Aerial view of the center of Sélestat. Notice the extraordinary green shingles on the roof of St. George's Church, common in Alsace on important structures and houses of wealthy residents. The church dates to the early sixteenth century, replacing a chapel for Charlemagne, who visited it in 775 CE.

See page 350 for additional information on the photography of Alsace found throughout the book.

INTRODUCTION

BY MICHAEL RUHLMAN

I'm a lifelong Francophile and since my teens have been fascinated by various regions of France: The Loire Valley, famed for its wines and chateaux. The amazing, rugged region of southwestern France known as Gascony, revered for its cassoulet and foie gras and Armagnac. Having studied at the Culinary Institute of America to write about it, I developed a love of, even devotion to, classical French technique.

This set me up beautifully to work with Thomas Keller at the French Laundry, an American whom Michel Richard once called the best French chef in America. I would go on to work with Eric Ripert, at Le Bernardin, equally Michelin-starred and devoted to classical technique. And, most recently, Jean-Georges Vongerichten, who gained world renown for blending classical French technique with Asian ingredients. More importantly, though, this French chef was from a region of France called Alsace, in the very easternmost part of the country, bordered by Germany and Switzerland, a part of France I knew almost *nothing* about.

During our conversations for a memoir, Jean-Georges would grow all but misty-eyed recalling the *kougelhopf*, or cake, baked on Sunday mornings and the *baeckeoffes*, a peasant meat-and-potato casserole, of his youth, the powerful vinaigrettes his mother would make, the choucroutes his region was famous for. But we weren't *making* any of these dishes, and I found myself intensely curious.

In the fall of 2019, my editor, Michael Sand, asked if I'd be interested in working on a book with Gabriel Kreuther, chef and co-owner of Restaurant Gabriel Kreuther, a Michelin two-star restaurant on Forty-Second Street across from Bryant Park in New York City. When Michael noted that Kreuther, like Jean-Georges (his former boss, as it turned out), hailed from Alsace, I took it as a sign. Kreuther would be cooking not only the food of his fine-dining restaurant but *also* the food of his country, and his home, a farm in rural Alsace, the baeckeoffes and choucroutes I'd only heard about, because it was such a fundamental part of who he was.

I'd now have the opportunity to make a deep dive into an unfamiliar but fascinating regional cuisine, that of Alsace, a melding of the cuisines of France, Germany, and Switzerland, and also into the mind of a chef intent on translating that cuisine into the city of New York and the world of fine dining.

While Kreuther had been in New York City for more than twenty years, he hadn't hit my radar until, famously, he opened the Modern in 2004 with Danny Meyer in the Museum of Modern Art and received rave reviews. Never before had this caliber of restaurant opened in a museum. It was a fantastic restaurant. When he won best chef in New York City from the James Beard Foundation, I knew to keep my eye on him.

I entered his restaurant on a bright chilly morning to meet the chef for the first time. Restaurant Gabriel Kreuther is both modern and rustic, with white tablecloths, fine crystal, and giant wooden beams. A large bar, both elegant and casual, is set apart from the circular dining room, which leads to the main kitchen.

Chef Gabriel was easygoing and relaxed, comfortable with himself, among his staff, and in his dining room. He laughed easily and often during our first talk. He was passionate about fine dining. But he also talked about how important basic technique was. Importantly to me, his core staff—Joe Anthony, Robert Pugh, Jake Abbott, Justin Borah, executive pastry chef Marc Aumont, Priscilla Scaff-Mariani, Angela Borah, Agustin Garcia, Rodrigo Colin, Joseph Yi, Will Cesark, and others—had all been with him for years, most since the Modern, more than a decade earlier. This is one definitive sign of a good chef. Another: The kitchen, uncommonly spacious for Manhattan, was immaculate, and all the chefs at their stations worked and greeted one another with a kind of professional comportment commensurate with the aspirations of the restaurant.

As we drank our coffee, Chef Gabriel explained that he wanted to explore the food of Alsace, the *baeckeoffes* and *choucroutes* and *kougelhopfs* of his youth on a small Alsatian farm. And he wanted to show how this food, of which he was so proud, country food, could be transformed, conjoined with the globalism all around him in New York City, into extraordinarily fine cuisine worthy of Michelin stars.

"They said I couldn't put sauerkraut on the menu of a fine-dining restaurant!" he said, laughing. "Watch me!"

Happily, I did.

Quai de la Poissonnerie, in the town of Colmar, in the "Little Venice" quarter

ON BECOMING A CHEF

BY GABRIEL KREUTHER

LEARNING TO COOK

As far back as I have memories, I wanted to be a chef. From age three or four, I never desired anything else.

Chefs were in my family, and, growing up on a farm in rural Alsace, near the German border, I was surrounded everywhere by food and cooking. One uncle was a pastry chef. One was a butcher. Another was the chef-owner of a country inn known for its cuisine. My maternal grandfather raised ducks and geese for foie gras. My father worked for Feyel, one of the biggest producers and distributors of foie gras in the world. And my mother was, and remains, an amazing cook and baker.

We kept up to three hundred rabbits, as well as ducks, chickens, pigs, turkeys, and dairy cows, on our five-acre farm. We'd slaughter a chicken on Friday, pluck it on Saturday, and cook coq au vin on Sunday. We'd kill a pig only once a year. We'd smoke hams, stuff sausages, and cure bacon. We also fermented our own sauerkraut from our cabbage harvest to eat with those meats in dishes such as the great Alsatian Baeckeoffe (page 61), meat and potatoes layered in a big, covered, earthenware casserole, or of course a big choucroute garnie, sauerkraut with an assortment of meats and sausages. It was all old-school. We didn't even have plumbed bathrooms until the late 1970s, just an outhouse.

In the summer, my mother kept hundreds of tomato plants. I'd walk up and down the rows, picking the ripe fruit and eating the juiciest ones, hot from the sun, like apples along the way. The smell of those vines and the flavor of those tomatoes are engraved in me.

Growing up on the farm, I was always more attracted to the kitchen than the fieldwork. I remember spending time with my grandfather when I was a little boy, drying prunes in the old wood oven in the kitchen, making apple cider with him during apple season, and grating wild horseradish that we got from the outdoors. Working with food has always been a fundamental pleasure—as has been enjoying the fruits of our labor.

During meals, on occasion, when prompted, my grandfather would tell us stories about what happened in our village during World War II. The dining room in which we were eating had been used as a makeshift hospital for wounded American soldiers. The small city of Haguenau was only three miles away, and a lot of heavy fighting had been done in the fields behind our farm. While telling these stories, my grandfather would always eat his soup course with an American GI spoon. Talk about culinary history.

My father's brother, Michel Kreuther, and his wife, Noëlle, owned and ran the Hotel Restaurant du Rocher, in Dabo, France, an hour west of us in the northern Vosges mountains. Though it was a simple country inn, people such as President François Mitterrand of France and Chancellor Helmut Kohl of Germany would meet there, halfway between their two capitals, because of its beauty, its seclusion, and its cuisine. It sat at the top of a mountain with panoramic views and had a small chapel and exquisite food. Former president Charles de Gaulle was also a frequent guest as a private client, mostly for Sunday lunch, which he took with his wife and children in a secluded room, normally my aunt and uncle's own private dining quarters. His car was kept in the garage so that no one knew they were there.

In summer, my parents sent me there, and I would spend my days in the kitchen, helping my uncle and his staff—peeling potatoes, picking parsley, cleaning the bathrooms, cooking for the dogs of hotel patrons, and scraping beef bones to get every bit of meat off them for a staff meal Bolognese, before they were roasted for stock. Michel would receive quartered animals, which also ingrained their bone structure in my mind. I loved every moment.

By the time I was fourteen, I told my teachers that I wanted to do a cooking apprenticeship (the way teenagers had generally moved into cooking in France—this would have been 1983). They told me they did not recommend an apprenticeship, a path that was going out of vogue at that time. They wanted me to do two more years of regular school and then go to culinary school. My grades were too good to warrant becoming a chef, they believed.

They were mystified when my grades started going down and down. I simply stopped doing any schoolwork.

Unlike my teachers and my friends (it was not prestigious to be a chef back then), my parents encouraged me. They'd been watching me cook since I was six years old (and making a lot of mistakes, but learning from them). We discussed the situation with Uncle Michel, who didn't want to take me on as an apprentice. Michel resisted the idea, because he'd have to be too hard on me. And he adored me. No, Michel concluded, I needed to find another kitchen, one with Michelin stars, and begin there.

And so I began taking jobs at Michelin-starred restaurants. Their dining rooms were so beautiful, the service so refined, the food amazing. But in the kitchen it was a whole other world. First thing in the morning, I'd be sent out to the bar to fill a stockpot with beer—to make the *pâte à frire*, fritter batter, they told me with a chuckle. But they weren't making fritter batter; they were dipping their ladles into it and drinking it all morning. By lunch they were drunk.

The yelling and the fighting scared me. I saw chefs in the walk-ins come to blows, emerging with their chef coats torn. The verbal abuse was appalling. I'm not going to name the places, but they were well known. Plates were thrown; pans were thrown. Apprentices were burned on purpose (once, I saw a hand dunked in hot fry oil). I got so scared at one restaurant I ran away from it in the middle of service. I had to walk four miles through fields, lost, before I came to a town where I could call my parents.

When I told my parents and others what was happening in these kitchens, no one would believe me—it was too outrageous.

But my uncle believed me. When, as an apprentice, he'd failed to clean a pan properly, leaving a film of oil on the bottom, the chef had heated the pan until that oil got hard and sticky, then scraped it off the pan with a spatula and put it on my uncle's cheek.

He certainly didn't want me working in a place like the ones I'd described. It seems the only truly fine kitchen was Paul Haeberlin's Auberge de l'Ill (where Chef Jean-Georges Vongerichten had gone through his apprenticeship). But the time was never right for me to work for Monsieur Paul. So my uncle at last agreed to take me on.

APPRENTICESHIP

I loved it. He ran a good kitchen. At the beginning, I learned more about cleaning than anything else. Cleaning pots and pans that piled up after service, making sure that even the crevices around the handles were cleaned, which I did with a toothbrush. Cleaning all the garbage cans after collection; the stove hoods once every three weeks or so by myself after being shown how to do it; and, of course, the stove, the floors of the kitchen, the walk-in fridges, and all the bathrooms. At the time the shelves in the walk-ins were made from wood and needed a lot of attention because of the humidity. I had to bleach them once every ten days, or they'd get moldy.

As the months went by, I came to understand that all this cleaning was to show me that there is a whole other side to this business that is not glamorous but needs to be done well in order to even think about becoming a successful chef. Rather than being put off by this dirty grunt work, I embraced it as a necessary step in following my dream.

Uncle Michel would take me to dinner at other restaurants, and before ordering a drink or looking at the menu, he would use the bathroom. If the bathroom wasn't clean, you could be sure the kitchen wasn't any better. Both require hygiene and discipline—and if you can't keep a small bathroom clean, how will you keep a large kitchen? Today, I know that a spotlessly clean

My father, Léon Kreuther, in front of the family farm at 10, Rue des Hirondelles in the town of Niederschaeffolsheim in 1968. It had to have been a Sunday, because he is wearing a suit. During World War II, the two ground-floor windows with the white shutters to his right looked into what had been turned into an American infirmary. In the attic, we had a chamber connected to the chimney of the wood-burning stoves of the house, to smoke hams and bacon. At the far end of the hay barn was a type of grape resembling the Concord grape, and the vine by the drainpipe was spinning double roses my grandfather planted.

This is the Hotel du Rocher, in Dabo, France, where I did my apprenticeship for four years. The Dabo rock rising out of the Vosges forest was once a Celtic worshipping ground. The chapel was built on the grounds of a castle destroyed in the seventeenth century. The two other buildings are the hotel: one from the beginning of the twentieth century, the other built in the 1950s. The terrace in the newer building is where my uncle had his restaurant, but sadly the roof was destroyed in a fire in 2015.

kitchen, a spotless bathroom, and an impeccable dining room set the stage for all the food to come. (Every time the New York City health department makes its surprise visits and gives us an A, I have Uncle Michel to thank.)

Perhaps the most important thing he did for me was always to make me learn a new technique or recipe by hand, even if we had a machine to make the work faster and easier. Everything from using a whisk to whip cream or Hollandaise, to kneading small batches of dough by hand instead of using a mixer, to julienning celeriac with a knife rather than a mandoline.

I would work two weeks at the restaurant and go to school for one week, which was standard in the French apprentice system. What the school didn't know was that because Hotel Restaurant du Rocher was on top of a mountain, and therefore seasonal, it was closed from late fall to spring! I failed to alert the school about this fact, and so, from age fifteen on, I only went to school once every third week all winter long.

At home, I practiced cooking, mainly from *Escoffier*—making fondant and *oeufs en gelée* with pot-au-feu and learning how to clarify a stock. I made bûche de Noël, foie gras terrines and pâté de campagne, buttercream, meringue mushrooms, and pâte à choux.

Midway through my apprenticeship, when I was sixteen, my father was diagnosed with liver cancer. He died three months later, at age fifty-four. I was devastated. To lose your father on the cusp of adulthood is impossible to describe. Also, for my mother, it was a tragedy to lose her husband when he was so young. They had no life insurance, and now she was alone with a farm to run and three teenage boys (I was the oldest, Hervé was fifteen, Marc fourteen) and our little sister, Patricia, who was just six, to raise. Getting through this was one of the biggest challenges and struggles of my life, but looking back on it, I see that the hardship gave me the power of believing in myself and working even harder toward my dream of becoming a chef.

It was also at this time, ages sixteen and seventeen, when my relatives and friends were socializing, going out to clubs having fun, buying mopeds for themselves, while I was working. I worked holidays and weekends, and they laughed at me. "Why would you work so hard?" they asked. Why didn't I work at a factory for the same pay so that I could enjoy my weekends and holidays? Now that I think about it, the first club I ever went to was in America, when I was nineteen years old.

I put my head down and focused all my energy into pursuing what I loved more than anything in the world: cooking and doing it to the fullest. I spent four years in all with my uncle. When I wasn't cooking, I spent my free time studying, especially when I was at my uncle's hotel. There was no access to TV and, of course, no internet during that era. Since I was on the top of a mountain, there was nothing else to do, so I read any good cookbook I could get my hands on. One of the most meaningful for me was *Larousse Gastronomique*.

I finished my apprenticeship in June 1987, and in the middle of summer I was surprised to get a letter from Académie de Strasbourg, where I'd studied, informing me that my grades had earned me the chance to compete for best apprentice in eastern France, the winner of which would go on to compete in Paris, for best apprentice in the country. I didn't even know that such a competition existed, so I figured I had nothing to lose. I was one of eight apprentices to compete for the regionals, many of them coming from two- and three-star restaurants, including the apprentice from Paul Haeberlin at Auberge de l'Ill. Haeberlin himself would be one of the judges, all six of whom were Michelin-starred chefs. I'd never cooked for such royalty.

We all knew the dishes we'd be presenting (Filet de Barbue D'Antin, Pigeonneau en Cocotte Grand-Mére, and Riz a L'Impératrice), and I practiced and practiced them in my mother's kitchen (the hotel was closed), and paid for the food myself, while the other apprentices practiced with their chefs at their restaurants. At the competition, everyone cooked the same dishes and used the same platters. You could not personalize anything. You had to follow the guidelines given, and then the chefs tasting the food had no idea who had cooked the dish they were eating.

And I won.

No one could believe that this nobody from a small mountain inn with a little-known chef, his nephew, no less, had *won* for all of eastern France. They thought it was a fluke. And so to make sure our region was properly represented in Paris for the national championship, they decided to send the Haeberlin apprentice as well.

My best friend's mother had an aunt who lived outside Paris in the northeastern suburb of Bondy. I slept on her living room floor in a sleeping bag during the three-day contest. No one from my family could come to cheer me on.

Since the judges could only taste so many dishes in one day, the organization split the twenty-four apprentices from throughout the country into two groups of twelve. On the first day, I cooked Truite au Bleu, Sauce Hollandaise, Pommes Vapeur and Salmis de Pintadeau, and Croûtons à la Farce a Gratin along with the other eleven contestants in my group; then on the second day I had to stand by while the other group cooked. At the end of that day, during the proclamation of the results, I found out that I had placed sixth, good enough to earn a spot in the finals. That evening, there was a wonderful dinner in our honor at La Grande Cascade in the Bois de Boulogne. This famous, beautiful restaurant in the woods surrounded by the city of Paris dates back to the nineteenth century and is still in business today. I went straight to sleep that night knowing that the group had been winnowed to ten.

The next day, the day of the finals, I prepared Brochet Poché Beurre Blanc (poached pike with beurre blanc). Then Tournedos Grillé served with Pommes Soufflées followed by dessert, Île Flotante (poached egg whites with vanilla sauce). While these dishes sound straightforward, each dish is highly technical in its preparation. For the fish, rather than simply opening the belly and gutting it, as it's usually done, to prepare it in the classical way, it needed to be gutted by removing all of the guts through the gills through a small 1½-inch (4 cm) incision on the back end, while leaving the whole fish, including the head, intact. It was then to be poached whole and served standing on a platter, as if it were actually swimming. The sauce itself was also highly technical. Ordinarily a cook would use a blender to emulsify the vinegar, butter, and stock. In our case, it had to be done by hand with a whisk to make it creamy and frothy—a classical beurre blanc. This was not an easy task, and the sauce had to stay stable, and not break, throughout the long judging. As for the Tournedos Grillé, each one needed to be cooked at a different temperature, and the pommes soufflées were tricky, too, because they need to be cooked twice in order to puff up like a pillow and stay that way. It seems easy, but it's hard to do. Usually you get one good pomme soufflé out of three, and it's very time-consuming to make them, and I had to prepare five or six per judge. Lastly, while the dessert was relatively simple, since the other two dishes were so time-consuming, it required striving for a creamy but not too sweet crème anglaise and a stable egg white meringue.

That same evening, the results of the competition were announced at the famous and fortuitously named Pavillion Gabriel on the Champs-Élysées. Little did I know, the association timed the contest in December to coincide with Congrés Annuel des Maîtres Cuisiniers de France, so that the gala dinner was attended by all the best chefs in the country. I had never been in such a beautiful setting with such esteemed company, surrounded by journalists and cameras everywhere. It was a heady experience. When it came time to call the winners, unbeknownst to the contestants (or at least to me), they started with the individual dishes such as Best Dessert, Best Meat, and so on. I won for Best Fish Dish, so I thought that was it. I was pretty happy about that. They called me up onstage and gave me a diploma. Then, from there, they started announcing the overall placements. They started with number five, then number four, and so on, until they announced my name as the winner.

I was stunned. I was eighteen years old, and I'd won for best apprentice in the country out of 170 competitors. It wasn't until I got back home that it sunk in. Suddenly I realized the potential for my future.

It gave me, a poor farm boy from rural France, opportunities I'd never have dreamed of. I got so many gifts of knives, I wouldn't need to purchase my own for years. I won a trip to Morocco, my first time on a plane and first time out of Europe, where I was able to experience an entirely different cuisine. I was invited to dine at Michelin-starred restaurants, including the best of the best, Auberge de l'Ill.

But perhaps the biggest opportunity was soon to come. When I returned from Paris, I was celebrated in Strasbourg, and the dean of my school asked if I would like to take a job at Le Caprice in Washington, DC, where his friend Edmond Voltzenlogel was executive chef. Cook in America? Of course! I loved my brief experience in America. I couldn't have been luckier, because this chef, who had been a cooking teacher, knew all the "whys" of cooking. When I had a question, he didn't answer "Because that's the way we do it"; he could tell me *why* we did it this way, *why* an emulsion broke, *why* egg whites clarify a consommé.

After eighteen months cooking in America, my first kitchen beyond my uncle's, I returned to France.

As a result of winning a national competition among apprentices, I was given the opportunity to live in Washington, DC, and work at the restaurant Le Caprice, under chef Edmond Voltzenlogel. Here I am, in 1988, nineteen years old, in its kitchen.

THE POST-APPRENTICE YEARS

Obligated to spend a year in the military, as was required, I decided to get it out of the way at this time, training in a tank division (this taught me teamwork, discipline, organization, and the importance of respect).

When I got out, I was twenty-one years old, and my next goal was to continue to learn in great kitchens where I knew I would not make much money. To ensure I could accept the positions I needed in order to achieve my dream, I'd require some financial stability. I landed a job at a meat manufacturing plant in Germany, working the third shift, where we butchered between twelve and fifteen hundred pigs from midnight to eleven A.M. Not only did this job pay really well, but it also kept me in the food world, and taught me lessons in organization, health safety, and temperature guidelines. I banked my paychecks until I found the best kitchens I could.

Those kitchens would begin with that of Franz Keller at the Kronenschlösschen in Hattenheim, Germany. On my first day of work, Chef gave me a pig and said it was mine to do with what I wished. Growing up, we slaughtered a hog each fall, making sausage and bacon, salting hams, and making pâtés. This was common on any small farm. My uncle was a butcher—so I'd picked up some butchery from him. Not to mention, I'd worked for a butcher during the months I waited for the papers I needed to travel to and work in America (always staying in food, even when not in a kitchen). And I'd just spent three months helping to break down thousands of pigs a week. I knew pigs!

Colmar, arguably one of the most beautiful towns in all of France, at Christmastime. The two connected buildings to the left are Le Fer Rouge. Its chef, Patrick Fullgraff, had such a reputation I took a step down from sous chef to work for him here.

So I set to work, breaking down the hog. The head was removed and split in half. I first removed the leaf lard, that valuable fat, which is hanging inside the pig. I then removed the kidneys, followed by the tenderloins, next separating the shoulder from the belly at the sixth rib, then the loin, then the ham. The prime cuts, the loin and the tenderloin, I reserved for the patrons in the restaurant, and the rest I used to make the pâtés, sausages, and headcheese.

Everyone was ignoring me. I worked alone for three days. No one would talk to me. I thought, "OK, fine, I'll just go about my business then." When I'd done all I could with the animal and the chef was impressed, I realized the pig had been a test! Chef Keller had been a butcher himself, and this was how he judged me. I got along very well in that kitchen, ultimately rising to sous chef.

During that time, a chef named Patrick Fullgraff was earning a lot of attention at Le Fer Rouge in Colmar. He was really thinking outside the box, creating new ways of exploring the regional cuisine of rural Alsace in a fine-dining restaurant. I knew working there would

be invaluable, so I took a step down from sous chef to accept a job as chef de partie, in order to learn more. Indeed, translating the regional cuisine of my beloved Alsace into Michelin stars would be one of the hallmarks of my career.

Next I moved on to work for Bernard Ravet at L'Ermitage, a small, family-run Relais & Châteaux hotel and Michelin two-star restaurant near Lausanne, Switzerland, where I would rise again to sous chef. We were lucky to have an early nineteenth-century wood-fired brick oven. Ravet made twelve to fifteen different kinds of breads, baked daily, and so I learned breads there. We also had a large garden and grew many vegetables, berries, and herbs, and it was part of the cooks' duty to maintain the garden. We chopped our own wood, made our own vinegars—everything was done the old farm way. We made sauerkraut, marmalades, and jams. We picked linden blossoms to make linden blossom ice cream; used the wood from the bread we baked to smoke the salmon; cured our own sausages; and made homemade verjus from the juice of unripe grapes. We plucked our own pheasants, partridges, and woodcocks, and received whole lambs. It was an amazing and humbling learning experience for me, because virtually every single thing we made was done in the artisanal way—from scratch.

COMING TO AMERICA

When I turned twenty-eight, I decided it was time to see another part of the world besides central Europe, where I'd spent all but eighteen months of my life. I wanted to return to America, to the epicenter of the restaurant world, New York City. I answered an ad in a trade paper from a restaurant in Manhattan that was looking for a sous chef. I was intrigued and sent my résumé, which at that time was done by fax. The restaurant happened to be La Caravelle on West Fifty-Fifth Street, one of the city's French haute cuisine classics and considered one of the best overall restaurants in the city. In its heyday, guests like Jackie Kennedy and Salvador Dalí frequently dined there.

I arrived in July 1997, and it was hot as hell. The city stank. I walked past piles of garbage on the way to work each day. Coming from the beautiful countryside of Alsace, Switzerland, and Germany, I was unprepared for this concrete jungle. A true culture shock!

The basement kitchen was cramped, steaming hot, and often flooded. One evening in August, there was a thunderstorm, and we found ourselves working in eight inches of water. We had to stack bricks and lay wood planks down the line in order to work. Of course, I was used to hot kitchens; what got to me was the lack of space and natural light. I was spoiled by the kitchens we had at L'Ermitage. They were on the second floor of the building, air-conditioned, with large windows overlooking the garden.

As summer turned to autumn, though, the buzz and energy of New York took hold of me and I knew I wanted to stay. I found here an astonishing mix of food cultures, a restaurant clientele open to new ideas, and I knew it would be a place where I could be creative and not be prejudged (as was so often the case in the more traditional European fine-dining restaurants). Also, I'd fallen in love. That was another reason I wouldn't be leaving New York (within four years, Patricia Jalbert, a native of New Hampshire, would become my wife).

Everyone is always intrigued about how we met, because people in this business are working so many long hours that most find a relationship with someone in the industry. Patricia studied in Paris at the Sorbonne for her junior year abroad and has a minor in French,

so people who knew her thought we met in France. It so happens we met in the kitchen at La Caravelle. Chef Cyril Renaud's wife, Brigette, and Patricia were college friends at the University of New Hampshire, so she made an introduction right away.

I knew I'd never be happy in a basement kitchen at La Caravelle, respected though it was, and called my mother the week I arrived to send me my résumé materials to apply to other restaurants in the city. I didn't know the chefs of the *New York Times* three- and four-star restaurants, but I applied to them all: Daniel, Le Bernardin, Lespinasse, Jean-Georges. But no one had a position for me.

I kept on at La Caravelle, having no other recourse. One afternoon, someone told me I had a call, which was strange. Who would call the *kitchen* line of La Caravelle? Who would even know how to get that number? The voice greeted me in rapid-fire French in an accent I knew so well. It was my fellow Alsatian Jean-Georges Vongerichten. He was talking so fast! He said he only had a fish cook's position, *chef de partie poissonier*, a chef de partie position, but he assured me something would eventually open up.

Not only was JG a fellow countryman, but he had about six months earlier opened his eponymous restaurant and flagship on Columbus Circle. Ruth Reichl of the *New York Times* had given it four stars straight out of the gate, just three months after it opened, making it at the time the fifth four-star restaurant in the city.

I said yes immediately. And Jean-Georges had been right. Very soon I became sous chef in that beautiful open kitchen. And about fifteen months later I was his chef de cuisine.

LIFE HAPPENS

I was very happy at Restaurant Jean-Georges, cooking and working with that excellent crew in that bright kitchen. As JG began to open more restaurants, I had the autonomy to be creative within the rubric of JG's restaurant and style of cuisine. Patricia and I had decided to marry. Life was good.

But in the spring of 2001—I still remember where I was. It was in the middle of the afternoon and I was working in the downstairs kitchen. Someone from the offices came up to me and told me I had an emergency phone call from France. I was surprised to hear my brother Hervé's voice. Our brother Marc had committed suicide. Marc had long suffered from depression and had worked through two previous bouts of it, but could not make it through the third. The office at Jean-Georges is glass-enclosed, and I broke down, weeping in front of the whole kitchen. It was tragedy for me, for our whole family, but especially for our dear mother, who had lost her husband far too early and now a child. One thing that means so much to me to this day is that Jean-Georges's parents attended the funeral on his behalf.

In the fall of that same year, terrorists attacked and destroyed the World Trade Center in downtown Manhattan, devastating our city and the nation. Along with many others in the industry, we were part of cooking for the first responders who came from all over the country and the world to help, making meals to feed those heroes.

As much as a year earlier, Patricia and I had set our wedding date for the third Saturday in October. Amid the chaos of 9/11 and its aftermath, not to mention the

Top: With Jean-Georges Vongerichten in 2002, when I was chef de cuisine of his restaurant, at a staff party celebrating the New Year

Bottom: At a dinner with Anthony Bourdain, January 2003, at Les Halles, where he had been for many years its executive chef

anthrax scare one month later at NBC in Rockefeller Center, across the street from our wedding and reception sites, Patricia and I decided to maintain our wedding date at St. Patrick's Cathedral, October 20, the day, by chance, that my brother would have turned thirty.

AFTER JEAN-GEORGES

In 2002 a headhunter contacted me. I told them I was happy where I was, still cooking the dynamic food that had made JG the phenom that he was ever since arriving at Lafayette in Manhattan in 1986. He'd been a good friend and mentor to me. I had no intention of leaving him.

But the headhunter was persistent and finally revealed the offer. It was from the Ritz-Carlton, which was opening a new hotel on one of the most prestigious streets in the city, Central Park South. They wanted me to open a new restaurant in their hotel called Atelier. This was a tempting offer—my own restaurant. But I felt that I couldn't abandon Jean-Georges, who'd been so good to me, giving me my footing in New York City and the opportunity to lead his kitchen.

I told them I'd have to think about it. JG had been out of town, and when he returned I nervously asked to sit down and talk with him. He said, "Sure, let's go sit in the dining room." I didn't intend to take the position, but I didn't want him to find out I'd been talking to them behind his back or was thinking of leaving. I figured it would be a five-minute talk.

It lasted three hours.

Jean-Georges was full of questions. What were the details; what was the room going to look like; what kind of say would I have in design of the room, of the kitchen; who were the people involved? JG had been working with hotel restaurants since he was in his early twenties, when he'd opened a restaurant in Bangkok for his boss, three-star chef Louis Outhier, in 1980. He was very smart, and I listened to him. In the end JG said, in effect, "Look at that address—you'll never find a better one. Look at what you'll be able to do—create a new restaurant. You won't likely have this opportunity again. I think you *have* to take it."

And this is how a good chef de cuisine and a good chef work together. He was grateful to me for my loyalty and honesty, but he wanted what was best for me and my career. That's a good chef. I'm truly grateful for my years there.

And JG was right. Atelier was a hit, and here I began to receive recognition of my own. During my tenure, I earned a three-star review from the *New York Times*, a *Food & Wine* Best New Chef Award, and a nomination for Best Chef New York City from the James Beard Foundation.

One fond memory I have of that time was an evening in which Billy Joel, with his daughter by his side, sat at the piano in the lounge to play one song for someone's birthday, but suddenly this turned into a concert in which he played for more than an hour. Guests who were sitting there already called their fellow guests to come down from their rooms, and they sat on the floor anywhere there was space, listening to him and using their cigarette lighters to urge him to continue playing.

My success at Atelier caught the attention of legendary restaurateur Danny Meyer, who had agreed to open a fine-dining restaurant and bar in the Museum of Modern Art. He approached me, and after many, many meetings, I decided to do the project.

I love art, and I could not resist the opportunity to combine my cooking with these incredible works in this internationally renowned museum. I'm particularly drawn to sculpture, and it was exciting to learn that part of the design was to have the fine dining room facing the sculpture garden. It was truly inspiring. Creating a destination restaurant in a museum was unheard of at the time.

I furthermore loved the fact that we would be creating a dual concept next to each other—a restaurant and a bar—within the same space, and it was important that I was involved from the start. I loved to figure out a place and all of its challenges and opportunities. It needed to be designed and laid out like the back of house for a huge hotel restaurant and bar. Ultimately, I had a team of sixty cooks, twenty pastry cooks, and thirty-six stewards and porters—a massive team for a massive operation.

I remember visiting when concrete was poured. It was just a big hole in the ground. There is a picture of my wife and me standing next to the construction. It was a major step in my career as well as in the history of Union Square Hospitality Group. This single venture required Danny to double the staff of his company.

The Modern opened in November 2004—the first time that a great restaurant would open in an iconic museum—and I would remain there for ten years, earning three stars from the *New York Times* for both the dining room and the barroom. It was the first time, if I'm not mistaken, that the *Times* gave two distinct reviews for the same venue. It earned a Michelin star in its first year. It won restaurant of the year from *Esquire*, and I won Best Chef New York City in 2009.

The great recession at the end of 2008 and throughout 2009 was the worst blow to restaurants in my entire career as a cook and a chef thus far. Business at

My wife, Patricia, and me during construction of the restaurant and the sculpture garden at the Modern, September 2, 2004, just before Labor Day weekend. The private dining room is to the left, and the main dining room is where the columns are in the back. We created an outside lounge where guests could have an aperitif before dinner.

high-end restaurants plummeted. Danny Meyer had his flagship, Union Square Cafe, and an entire fleet of restaurants to worry about. I, as part of that group, had to face my own reality, that I might have to lay off many of our 280 staff members. My wife had lost her position in magazine ad sales that July, so those days were hard and stressful for me. Photos show how much weight I'd gained and the stress in my face. But we must learn from hard times, and the fact that I made it through without laying off a single employee told me that I could make it on my own. So that is what I set out to do.

In 2015, with the economy and fine dining stronger than ever, I met an extraordinary investor group and together we were able to open Restaurant Gabriel Kreuther, on West Forty-Second Street, across from beautiful Bryant Park. We earned the first Michelin star within three months of opening, and our second Michelin star in November 2018. We are a member of Relais & Châteaux and were recently inducted into Les Grandes Tables du Monde, an association comprising just 179 members worldwide.

Throughout the opening of RGK, Patricia and I struggled with what we now look back on as "the final chapter" of a complex fertility story. We badly wanted a child, but Patricia suffered two miscarriages, one of them at twenty-two weeks. We were at the edge of losing hope, and doctors counseled against further efforts and offered other options. But I find it very hard to give up—it's not in me, or in Patricia. We made one

The copper panels behind the bar at Restaurant Gabriel Kreuther were chosen to evoke the beer halls throughout Alsace, and the chairs are modeled after Alsatian farm chairs. The heart-shaped cutout on the bar chairs is the symbol of hospitality in Alsace.

more attempt. And on that infamous, but to us now also glorious day, September 11, 2017, we welcomed our beautiful daughter, Margaux, into the world, named for Patricia's late mother, Margaret, the French derivation, and for my love of the great Bordeaux wines Château Margaux!

FROM ALSACE TO NEW YORK

As I move into my early fifties, and with my team at Restaurant Gabriel Kreuther solid and thriving, it's been the perfect time for me to reflect on my life and my career. I hope that some of what I've learned will be useful to other cooks and chefs. I'm grateful to be able to offer to a broader audience a view of the food of an important culinary region and to be able to document the food of my restaurant, the culmination of four decades of reading, training, and cooking at restaurants throughout the world.

We are completing this book in the midst of a global pandemic that has, among other things, closed or greatly restricted restaurants throughout the country and the world. That impact has been especially powerful in New York City, a city uncommonly dense with restaurants and where entire neighborhoods have been direly affected. As this may be the hardest time of my professional life, and those of my colleagues, it's important, as I've said, to learn what we can. Certainly one big lesson we can take away from this is how important restaurants are to our culture and our lives. We've seen the impact of lockdowns and social isolation on us as a community, and we have a new appreciation for how important being social, connecting with people, truly is, and how restaurants encourage and facilitate connection by bringing people together over food—whether over onion soup at a corner bistro or a *torchon de foie gras* at a Michelin-starred restaurant. This book celebrates both of those culinary traditions.

This is foremost a book about Alsatian cuisine, about which so little has been written. This underappreciated regional cuisine is so important to me personally, but it also offers so many valuable contributions to our culinary world generally. Just as with the food of Catalonia in Spain, say, or the cuisine of Emilia-Romagna in Italy, Alsace has definitive dishes that I present in these pages, cuisine that, like all cuisines, arises from what grows in the ground, from what animals flourish on its land and in its surrounding waters.

Choucroute garnie, that celebration of pork and sauerkraut, is a staple of the region, where so much cabbage grows that we must preserve it to use year-round. Pretzels and beer and sausages are also local favorites and are important to this book. We even make a beer soup (page 45). And because I came from a poor farm, I include a recipe for flour soup (page 47)—just flour and stock and seasonings—and ways to turn it into a three-star dish. Liverwurst—mine is simply the best and I beg you to try it, if you love this sausage as I do. Baeckeoffe, the layered meat-and-potatoes casserole, and pot-au-feu—you'll find the classic preparations from my family here, as well as the sweet cakes and cookies my mother was famous for in our town.

And from this anchor of French-German country farm food, I developed my own cuisine while working in the multicultural and dynamic food scene of New York. In the Alsatian section of the book, for instance, I share a very common preparation for apple cider and cumin pickled trout (page 50). (Alsace is landlocked, so our fish dishes almost always use freshwater creatures, such as trout, eel, and crayfish.) But I also, in the section of recipes from my restaurant, present Slow-Cooked Rainbow Trout with Seasonal Farm Vegetables and Chicory Emulsion (page 269). The first is a traditional preparation using ingredients from the region. The latter takes those same main ingredients and reimagines them for fine dining—slowly baking the fish, serving it with baby vegetables and, most important, an elegant chicory sauce. Chicory, whose root is cooked and ground for its coffee-like flavors, is an herbaceous plant found throughout Alsace, and therefore an important part of its cuisine. You'll see this dynamic of traditional recipes and more elevated versions throughout the book.

There are preparations that stretch back to my years working under my fellow Alsatian Jean-Georges, from my first post as executive chef, at Atelier in the Ritz-Carlton, to my days as chef of the Modern, and of course from Restaurant Gabriel Kreuther. I have cooked in New York City for more than twenty years, but I cook as an Alsatian at heart.

All of it, and all of me, is reflected in this book, with great thanks for the help, hard work, and intelligence of my amazing chefs, and the leaders in the dining room who serve the food with such grace and care.

A NOTE ABOUT INGREDIENTS AND MEASUREMENTS

Unless otherwise noted, all eggs are large, all salt is coarse kosher salt, and all butter is unsalted.

When it comes to flour (and ingredients for baked goods and desserts in general), it's most accurate to use the metric/weight measurements rather than imperial/volume amounts. Measuring by the cup is inexact. If you do prefer to use volume, your measurement will be most exact if you use the "scoop and sweep" method, scooping the flour into the cup (not packing it) and sweeping the extra off the top.

Note that for the sections on pâte de fruit and desserts, we've included weight measurements only, as precision is especially important in those recipes.

At the restaurant we find it easier and more consistent to use metric measurements by weight. The recipes were developed using metric weights, so if you are able to use a scale, I urge you to use metric weights when making recipes from this book. But we have also included imperial measurements where appropriate for home cooks who prefer them.

CLASSIC DISHES OF ALSACE

ALSACE IS A RICH GREEN LAND WITH THE VOSGES mountains rising to the west, dotted with ancient castles and churches, and Germany's Black Forest looming to the east. Vineyards and farms cascade through the rich, fertile land, surrounding charming country villages. Its western border runs along the edge of the upper Rhine river on the border of Germany; its shorter southern border along Switzerland. Alsace has always been spiritually its own place, neither French nor German, nor Swiss, but a mixture of all. It has no official border. We like to say that, from a culinary standpoint, it combines the finesse and subtlety of French cuisine with the discipline of German and Swiss cuisines, and it shares the comfort and rusticity of all in that region with its love of sausages and pâtés, of pigs, duck, and geese, and of the hearty vegetables that grow in the region—cabbage and sunchoke and horseradish.

There is an earthiness to the cuisine, which has been influenced by the small farms that dominated the region until just recently, growing a little bit of everything. There were eighty-odd farms in my town thirty years ago. Now there are four.

I grew up on a farm in Niederschaeffolsheim, a small village about fifteen miles north of Strasbourg, the cultural capital of Alsace, just miles from the German border and the Black Forest. With the opening of Switzerland's St. Gotthard Pass in the late nineteenth century, the area also ended up situated at the north-south axis of continental Europe. That's why the regional capital of Strasbourg is known as "the crossroads of Europe" and was chosen to be the parliamentary capital of the European Union. It's also why Alsatian cuisine has German, Austrian, Swiss, and French influences.

My simple upbringing was what many food lovers of today spend a lifetime chasing. We grew and raised so many different vegetables and animals, we were almost completely self-sufficient. We even grew our own wheat to bring to the miller for our flour. We kept hundreds of rabbits, as well as ducks, chickens, and pigs. We fermented our own sauerkraut from our cabbage harvest to eat with those meats in dishes like baeckeoffe, which I still make now.

What we couldn't eat right away, we sold or preserved. We peddled potatoes at the market, wheat at the mill, and hops at the breweries. My favorite job as a kid was to climb our cherry trees and pick the sweet and sour fruit off the branches. I'd help pack up the cherries, then bring them to the fresh market where we had a stand. As a kid, I'd give some to the butcher and he'd give me a slice of liverwurst or a knackwurst to snack on in return. During village carnivals, I'd pluck walnuts from our trees and give them to the ticket vendors for a turn on the rides.

At the end of each harvest season, my family would preserve whatever remained. My mother loved to make jams and marmalades from our

Previous spread: Vineyards at the foot of Mont Sainte-Odile, one of the most visited landmarks in all of Alsace, for its historical convent at the top and superb 360-degree views. Above: A farmers' market in the old quarter of Colmar

cherries, peaches, raspberries, and currants. My grandfather pressed hard cider to drink throughout the year (and fresh juice for us kids to enjoy right away). We'd all set whole plums into egg-carton-like dishes over the wood-fired stove to dry.

Deeper in the fall, my father and I would hike into the woods and dig up horseradish. Back home, my grandfather would sit at the kitchen table and grate it, then cover the grated root with vinegar so it'd keep all year. I loved hunting mushrooms with my father, chanterelles and hen-of-the-woods. Late autumn also meant collecting dried branches to build fires. We'd gather around, sticking our homemade sausages through more branches to turn them over the flames.

All this formed my culinary soul. All this created the framework for my Alsatian cuisine. Here you will find all the common dishes, noted above, that are so prevalent in what remains a largely rural part of France. This is farmhouse cooking that uses the vegetables and livestock that thrived here, heavy on pork and sauerkraut, but offering a diversity of preparations, from savory to sweet, emphasizing economy and thriftiness in a food culture that wasted nothing and could even make soup using just chicken stock and toasted flour (page 47). The recipes in the pages to follow are the dishes of my homeland and my youth, and they form the backbone of all my cooking, both at home and in restaurants.

STARTERS

TARTE FLAMBÉE

(Flatbread with Fromage Blanc, Onions, and Bacon)

Makes four 7-by-12-inch (17 by 30.5 cm) tarts or four 11-inch (28 cm) pies

This iconic staple of Alsace is a signature dish of my restaurant—something we can serve at the bar as well as in the dining room. It's that universally appealing, both casual and elegant. This deeply satisfying dish looks like a small rectangular pizza but has a very thin, crackly crust. To achieve the crust's crisp snap and slight chew, you need a blazing hot oven. In Alsace, this was the dish that bakers slid into wood-burning ovens to test the flame's heat. If you have a pizza oven, use it here. Otherwise, heat a pizza stone, or heavy iron surface, on your oven's highest setting until it's thoroughly heated.

As for the topping, start with this classic combination of sweet onions and salty bacon over a mix of tangy and fresh cheese. Then, you can play and experiment. I top mine with everything from peekytoe crab with trout roe and horseradish to hen of the woods mushrooms with Comté cheese and nutmeg. The quality of the bacon is the key to the flavor and the success of this dish.

FOR THE DOUGH

2½ cups (325 g) all-purpose flour, plus more as needed
2¼ teaspoons (7 g) fresh active dry yeast
¼ teaspoon fleur de sel
¾ cup (175 ml) water, at room temperature

FOR THE TOPPING

1 cup (240 ml) crème fraîche
1 cup (240 ml) sour cream
½ cup (120 g) fromage blanc
Pinch freshly grated nutmeg
Salt and freshly ground white pepper
8 ounces (225 g) dry cured and smoked slab bacon, cut into ⅛-inch-thick (3 mm) matchsticks
1 yellow onion, thinly sliced

Note: For each rectangular tart, use 4½ ounces (130 g) of topping; use 5 ounces (150 g) for each round pie.

Make the dough: Combine the flour, yeast, and fleur de sel in the bowl of a standing mixer fitted with the dough hook. Mix on low speed until blended. With the machine running, add the water slowly. Continue mixing, scraping the bowl and hook occasionally, until the dough is smooth and starts to pull away from the sides of the bowl.

Turn the dough into a lightly oiled bowl and cover with plastic wrap. Let rest at room temperature until doubled in size, about 1 hour.

Uncover, punch down the dough, and cover again. Let rest for 1 hour longer. Put a pizza stone on the center rack of the oven. Preheat your oven to 500°F (260°C) during the hour the dough rests.

Make the topping: Mix the crème fraîche, sour cream, fromage blanc, nutmeg, and a pinch each of salt and white pepper in a large bowl until smooth. Cover and refrigerate until ready to use.

Bring a medium saucepan of water to a boil. Fill a large bowl with ice and water. Add the bacon to the boiling water and cook for 1 minute to prevent the matchsticks from sticking and to remove excess salt. Drain well and immediately transfer to the ice water. When cool, drain well.

Put the sliced onion in a bowl, sprinkle with salt, and toss. Let stand until wilted, about 5 minutes.

Turn the dough out onto a lightly floured work surface. Lightly flour your hands and knead the dough for 2 minutes. Divide the dough into four even pieces. Roll each piece into a small ball. With a lightly floured rolling pin, roll each piece into a 7-by-12-inch (17 by 30.5 cm) rectangle, about ⅛ inch (3 mm) thick. Or, if you prefer a round pie, roll each ball into an 11-inch (28 cm) disc. Either way, keep in mind that the thickness of the dough is most important, and if the pie or square is too large, trim it down as necessary.

Divide the cheese mixture evenly among the dough pieces and spread, leaving a ½-inch (1.25 cm) rim. Scatter the bacon and onion on top.

Slide a tarte onto a floured pizza paddle or thin cookie sheet and then slide onto the hot pizza stone. Bake until the bottom blisters and the crust crisps, 3 to 4 minutes. Serve hot. Repeat with the remaining tartes.

BIBELESKAES
(Fromage Blanc with Chives)

Serves 8

This is a dish I grew up with—a classic farmhouse summer lunch on hot summer afternoons. A very, very cold fromage blanc mixture. Fromage blanc, a fresh, spoonable country cheese, common in Alsace, is mixed with sour cream, shallots, and chives and is so satisfying in so many ways. A toasted slice of rye or country bread slathered with *bibeleskaes* is delicious—you often see this at county fairs in Alsace. Sometimes it's topped with onion and bacon, and served open faced.

I like to top the *bibeleskaes* with thinly sliced bacon and raw white onions that have been thinly sliced, well salted, and then rinsed and dried (to season them and reduce the acidity), and to serve them beside or on top of roasted or boiled potatoes.

Remember the garlic flavor takes some time to come out in the cheese, so this should sit for 20 minutes or so before serving. You can find fromage blanc at Whole Foods or other good cheesemongers.

1 pound (500 g) fromage blanc
⅔ cup (150 g) sour cream
6 tablespoons (90 ml) heavy cream
Salt and freshly ground white pepper
1 to 3 tablespoons very finely chopped shallot
1 clove garlic, peeled, smashed, and chopped
6 tablespoons chopped chives

In a mixing bowl, combine the fromage blanc and the sour cream, and stir in 1 tablespoon of heavy cream at a time to reach the desired consistency. It should be smooth and creamy but gently hold its shape when spooned onto a plate. Season with salt and pepper to your taste. Start with a half teaspoon of salt and 20 grinds of pepper and adjust as necessary. Add the shallots, garlic, and 4 tablespoons of the chives. Mix thoroughly with a rubber spatula and chill for at least 20 minutes to allow the flavors to meld, or until you're ready to serve it. Garnish with the remaining 2 tablespoons of chives.

TRADITIONAL PRETZELS
WITH HORSERADISH MUSTARD DIP

Makes 10 medium pretzels

Alsace is a region that, while physically part of France, is culturally neither France nor Germany but a spiritual mixture of both. Here, as in Germany, we love our pretzels and beer—and horseradish, a flavorful but underused aromatic root.

Pretzels are simple to make. The amazing transformation that happens when the leavened, shaped dough is dipped into a base solution (using lye or baking soda) is so satisfying, fun, and delicious, it's especially great to do with kids. Although if you're using food grade lye (easily available online), you'll need to be careful, as when it combines with water it is as caustic as sulfuric acid. Lye reacts with carbon dioxide and, in the heat of the oven, forms a carbonate, making the food safe to eat. When cooking with children, just use baking soda. I like the taste of lye-dipped pretzels and the deep brown color the lye creates. But baking soda is an acceptable substitute and completely safe.

While the classic pretzel shape is my favorite, with its twists and the increased surface area that allows for more browning and flavor, you can also make fabulous hamburger buns, pretzel rolls, or a braided pretzel loaf with this dough.

We eat pretzels with a dipping sauce—horseradish, sour cream, and mustard. Fresh horseradish is best, but some brands of prepared horseradish, such as Atomic and Gold Brand, are acceptable.

FOR THE PRETZEL DOUGH

½ cup (125 ml) warm water
½ cup (125 ml) warm milk
2 tablespoons sugar
4 teaspoons fresh yeast (10 g) or
    1½ teaspoons (5 g) active dry yeast
4 cups (500 g) all-purpose flour
1 teaspoon salt
⅓ cup (75 g) butter, melted
Fleur de sel or any large coarse salt

FOR THE LYE DIPPING LIQUID

2 quarts/liters water
2 tablespoons (30 g) food grade lye

FOR THE BAKING SODA DIPPING LIQUID (USE THIS IF YOU DON'T HAVE LYE)

1½ quarts/liters water
1 teaspoon salt
¼ cup (50 g) baking soda

FOR THE BAKING SODA-DIPPED PRETZELS

1 egg yolk, mixed with 1 tablespoon milk
    or water

recipe continues

Combine the water, milk, and sugar in the bowl of a standing mixer fitted with a dough hook. Sprinkle (or crumble) the yeast on top and mix it in. Allow the yeast to multiply, 10 to 15 minutes. Add the flour, salt, and butter and mix on low speed until well combined. Change to medium speed and let the machine knead the dough until it is smooth and pulls away from the side of the bowl, 8 to 10 minutes. Cover the bowl with plastic wrap or a damp towel. Let it double in size, about an hour.

Preheat your oven to 425°F (220°C).

Prepare the dipping liquid of your choice by combining all the ingredients and bringing them to a simmer, then turn off the heat. Again, be careful when using lye, which can burn. You can wear gloves if you're concerned, but they're not strictly necessary if you're careful with it.

As the dipping liquid is coming to a boil, turn the dough out onto a work surface (you should have about 30 ounces/900 g of dough). Divide it into ten equal pieces, so ten 3-ounce (90 g) pieces. Roll out each piece of dough into about a 2-foot (about 65 cm) rope of dough.

For a pretzel shape, make a horseshoe shape, bottom toward you. Cross the two ends once and then twice, leaving about an inch or two of tip above the curl. Pull the tips toward you and press down on the bottom of the "horseshoe." Adjust the shape to your liking and place it on a Silpat-lined baking sheet. Repeat with the other pieces.

Once the pretzels are made, you can freeze them; this way they are easier to handle when you have to dip them into the lye solution. It also gives you the possibility to make more and keep half frozen for an alternate day.

Using a large, flat, slotted spatula, carefully place each pretzel into the hot dipping water (15 seconds for the lye solution, 30 seconds for the baking soda solution). If they're not fully submerged, flip them. Return them to the lined baking sheet and repeat the process for the remaining pretzels. If you are using baking soda, brush the pretzels with egg wash for a deeper color. Sprinkle with coarse salt.

Bake for 10 to 12 minutes, until golden brown and starting to show the hallmark signs of pretzel crackling. Remove the pretzels from the oven and, using the flat spatula again, transfer them from the baking sheet to a cooling rack. Let cool for about 5 minutes, then enjoy them with the dip.

HORSERADISH MUSTARD DIP

Makes about 1 cup (240 ml)

Generous ¾ cup (200 g) sour cream
3 tablespoons freshly grated horseradish, or more to taste
1 tablespoon Dijon mustard
Salt and a few grinds pepper

In a medium bowl, whisk all the ingredients together and chill in the refrigerator until needed.

CHICKEN LIVER TERRINE

Makes 10 to 15 portions

This is a very elegant chicken liver terrine that, if you season it right and cook it perfectly, can almost be mistaken for a foie gras mousse. This was something my mother would make now and then, certainly if she had a surplus of fresh chicken livers. We also used to make this at my uncle's restaurant where I apprenticed—easy enough for home, elegant enough for a fine-dining restaurant. It's important to find very good chicken livers—preferably from a butcher or at your farmers' market. The fat back makes a lovely interior garnish. I poach it lightly in heavy cream to set its color, so that it's very white, allowing for a lovely pop of color when you slice into the terrine. I like this served simply, with mustard and cornichons, paired with a green salad with a sharp vinaigrette, and always with toasted bread.

14 ounces (400 g) pork fat back, very cold, even partially frozen for easy dicing

½ cup (120 ml) heavy cream

18 ounces (500 g) chicken livers, halved and cleaned of any veins and fat

2 eggs, beaten

Scant ¼ cup (50 ml) port wine

1 to 2 tablespoons kirsch

2 teaspoons salt

30 grinds pepper, or to taste

20 gratings nutmeg, or to taste

3 sprigs thyme

2 fresh bay leaves, halved

Put the terrine mold you're using in a roasting pan (we use a standard 1½-quart/liter terrine mold), and fill the pan with water to come three-quarters of the way up the mold. Remove the terrine mold and put the roasting pan into your oven and preheat it to 250°F (121°C).

Small dice the fat back. Combine half of it with the cream in a small saucepan over medium-high heat. Just before it comes to a simmer, remove the pan from the heat.

Puree the other half of the fat back in a food processor until it's smooth, then pass it through a tamis or sieve. In the same processor bowl (no need to clean it), puree the livers. Pass them through a tamis or sieve. Combine the liver and back fat in a mixing bowl. Mix well together with a whisk and then add the warm cream with the poached diced fat to the liver mixture. Stir again, then add the beaten eggs, port, kirsch, salt, pepper, and nutmeg. Mix very well with a whisk and double check the seasoning (yes, I taste it

raw—if your livers are high quality, they should taste very neutral), adjusting as necessary.

Line the terrine mold with plastic wrap. (Try to make sure to smooth out as many of the wrinkles as possible. The best way to do this is to roll out one piece of plastic wrap on your kitchen counter, then roll out a second layer the same size to place on top; smooth out any bubbles or wrinkles with a dry paper towel. This method reduces the static.) Add the liver mixture. Smooth it out with a small spatula. Decorate the top with the thyme and bay leaves. Cover the terrine. Place it in the water bath in the oven for 1½ hours.

Remove the terrine from the water bath. When it's cool enough to handle, refrigerate it until thoroughly chilled. It's best if it rests for a couple of days before you unmold, slice, and serve it. Leftovers can be wrapped in plastic and refrigerated for up to a week.

OUR FARM'S LIVERWURST

Serves 10 to 15

We are very proud of our liverwurst in Alsace. It's so popular that some old timers have it on toast with their coffee, sometimes even dipping the liverwurst smeared toast into the coffee! Everyone has their own version that is similar but for the seasonings. Everyone will insist that theirs is the best. Naturally. But ours really is! This is our farm's recipe, which calls for equal parts calf's liver, pork belly, and pork butt, along with a heady dose of seasonings common to the region, especially nutmeg, clove, and cardamom. Serve it with crusty toasted or grilled bread and some cornichons.

2 cups (300 g) thinly sliced yellow onions

2 tablespoons vegetable or grapeseed oil

1 to 1¼ pounds (550 g) calf's liver, cut into 3- to 4-inch (7.5 to 10 cm) pieces

1 to 1¼ pounds (550 g) pork belly, cut into 2-inch (5 cm) pieces

1 to 1¼ pounds (550 g) pork shoulder butt, cut into 2-inch (5 cm) pieces

2 tablespoons salt, or to taste

½ teaspoon pepper, or to taste

½ teaspoon ground ginger

¼ teaspoon ground mace or nutmeg

¼ teaspoon ground marjoram

⅛ teaspoon ground cloves

¼ teaspoon ground cardamom

¼ teaspoon ground bay leaf

¼ teaspoon ground thyme

½ cup (120 ml) hot milk

1 (2-foot/60 cm) natural beef or hog middle casing or synthetic casing, about 3 inches (7.5 cm) wide (this can also be rolled into a roulade in plastic wrap, but it's very liquidy, so a casing is recommended)

In a medium sauté pan over medium heat, cook the onions in the oil until they are golden brown, 10 to 15 minutes. Refrigerate the onions until they're chilled.

Bring a large pot of water to boil to blanch the liver and the meat. Add the liver and blanch for 30 seconds or so. Remove to a towel-lined plate. Add the pork belly and pork shoulder butt. Simmer the meat for 5 minutes or so. Remove the meat to the plate with the liver.

While the meat is simmering, mix all the spices together.

Combine the liver, pork belly, pork shoulder butt, and onions in a food processor and puree until they're smooth. You may need to do this in batches, depending on the size of your food processor, to achieve a perfectly smooth puree. While you're pureeing the meat, add the spice mixture to the puree so that it's uniformly combined with the meat. Remove the mixture to a large bowl. Add the hot milk and mix the meat again very well with a stiff spatula or wooden spoon until everything is well combined. Pipe or spoon this mixture into the casings (or shape into a 3- to 4-inch/7.5 to 20 cm log using plastic wrap, tying the ends tightly).

Bring a pot of water to 170°F to 180°F (77°C to 82°C) and cook the liverwurst for 1½ hours. Remove it and let cool at room temperature for 2 hours. Then refrigerate (preferably hanging to maintain the shape) for 2 days before serving.

CELERIAC SALAD

A book on Alsatian cooking would not be complete without a recipe for celeriac salad, a refreshing, crunchy salad of grated celery root that is served throughout France but is unparalleled in my homeland, Alsace. This is the simple way I make it: grated celery root (*celeriac* in French), oil, vinegar, and crème fraîche (or mayonnaise). It's a great side dish for virtually any meal, such as a terrine or the onion tart on page 81, and it's fabulous with a pot-au-feu.

Serves 8

Juice of 1 lemon

3 tablespoons grapeseed oil

2 tablespoons white wine vinegar or apple cider vinegar

2 tablespoons Dijon mustard

3 tablespoons crème fraîche (or mayonnaise)

Salt to taste

½ teaspoon white pepper

2 pounds (900 g) celeriac

In a bowl, combine the lemon juice, grapeseed oil, white vinegar, Dijon mustard, crème fraîche or mayonnaise, salt, and white pepper, and whisk well till it's thoroughly combined.

Peel and shred the celeriac (it can oxidize if you do this too far in advance). Add it to the vinaigrette and toss. It's best to wear a pair of latex gloves and press and squeeze and fluff the celery root so that it absorbs the vinaigrette.

TRADITIONAL PRESSKOPF D'ALSACE
(Cured Headcheese)

Makes about 15 portions

Headcheese, perhaps the easiest and best use of the pig's head, is classic farmhouse cooking. While it might seem intimidating, it's easy if you have a big enough pot. This recipe calls for half a pig's head. You'll need to special order this through a good butcher. Ask the butcher to halve it for you. Or use a whole head for twice the yield (same brine recipe, double amounts for the headcheese itself). The work of brining, cooking, and chilling is spread out over several days. It's a way to use all of the meat and connective tissue, creating a flavorful gelée that holds the diced meat, parsley, and cornichons together. This is my family's version. Serve it either with a salad, or with hard-boiled eggs and tomatoes, mustard, grilled bread, and thinly sliced red onion.

FOR THE BRINE
1 pound (450 g) salt, preferably gray sea salt

2 tablespoons pink curing salt

⅓ cup (100 g) sugar

2 bay leaves

2 sprigs rosemary

2 tablespoons coriander seeds

1 tablespoon black peppercorns

FOR THE HEADCHEESE
½ pig's head (4 to 5 pounds/2 to 2.5 kg)

3 medium carrots

1 large yellow onion, spiked with 5 cloves

2 medium leeks

1 stalk celery

4 sprigs thyme

2 bay leaves

2 tablespoons coriander seeds

1 tablespoon juniper berries, lightly smashed

1 bunch parsley

2 cloves garlic

TO FINISH
Salt and freshly ground black pepper

Fresh grated nutmeg

Generous ¾ cup (200 ml) dry white wine, such as Sylvaner or Riesling

4 tablespoons chopped parsley

2 cups (200 g) diced cornichon

First make the brine by combining all the brine ingredients in a pot with 1 gallon (4 liters) of water. Bring it just to a simmer to dissolve the salts and sugar and infuse the water with the aromatics. Allow it to cool. Put the pig's head in the smallest container it will fit in. Pour the brine over the pig's head. Weigh it down with a plate to ensure it is fully submerged. If you need to add more water to cover, do so. Refrigerate for 3 to 4 days.

Remove the pig's head from the brine and rinse it well under cold water, then soak the head in cold water for 3 hours, changing the water twice during that time.

In a large stockpot, combine all the ingredients for the headcheese and cover with cold water. Bring it to a boil, then reduce heat to a simmer, skimming any foam that rises to the top. Cook for 2 to 2½ hours. You will know it is done when a paring knife can be inserted into the meat without resistance. Remove the head to a platter, reserving the cooking liquid. When the pig's head is cool enough to handle, take off all the meat from the bones, making sure to remove and discard the cartilage and sinew (retain the skin and as much of the fat as you like). Put all the meat in a large container or bowl and cover with plastic wrap, pressing the wrap down onto the surface of the meat. Put a weight on top to compress the meat and refrigerate overnight.

Pass the cooking liquid through a fine-mesh strainer into a clean pot and reduce the liquid by three-quarters. Pass it through the strainer again. Taste it and add salt, pepper, and nutmeg as needed. Allow it to cool in the refrigerator for at least 24 hours; 48 hours is best (it should be very gelatinous).

On the day you remove it, unmold the meat and cut it in ½-inch (1.25 cm) dice. Bring the reduced cooking liquid to a simmer in a pot big enough to also contain the meat. Add the wine. When it returns to a boil, add the diced meat, chopped parsley, and diced cornichon. Bring it back to a boil for 1 minute. Taste for seasoning and adjust as necessary.

Line a 1½-quart (1.5 liters) enameled cast-iron terrine mold with plastic wrap, leaving a few inches of the wrap overhanging on each side, enough to fold over and cover the terrine. Ladle the meat into the mold and pour the cooking liquid over it until the mold is full. Fold the overhanging plastic wrap over the top and refrigerate for 36 hours, or up to 1 week. Unmold and slice to serve.

FARMER'S BEER SOUP

Serves 6 to 8

This is a favorite soup in Alsace, where we use a lot of beer in cooking, but it was a hit when I was chef of the Modern as well, where we made it by the gallon because it was so popular. A mix of beer and chicken stock forms the base of this hearty soup. I love the yeastiness that comes from the beer, especially as it combines with sour cream, pork, and onions. Beer is also a great braising liquid for chicken, rabbit, and pork. It's best to use a pilsner-style beer, rather than a hoppy beer, which can be bitter when used as a cooking medium.

3 cups (400 g) diced onions, from about 4 small onions

4 cups (400 g) leeks, white and light green parts only, cleaned and cut into ½-square-inch (1.25 cm) pieces

2 tablespoons (30 g) butter

1 teaspoon salt, plus more to taste

1½ quarts/liters good beer (nice and malty, like a pilsner)

1 quart/liter White Chicken Stock (page 251)

1 small smoked pork knuckle or ham hock (available from the butcher or grocery stores, where it's sometimes labeled "pork hock"; be sure to buy smoked not fresh)

Sachet d'épices (3 sprigs thyme, 2 bay leaves, 1 tablespoon black peppercorns, 1 clove, and 1 cardamom pod, tied together in cheesecloth)

1 cup (240 ml) sour cream

2 tablespoons sugar

½ small nutmeg, grated

Slurry (2 tablespoons cornstarch mixed with about 3 tablespoons cold water; it should be the consistency of cream)

In a large saucepan, combine the onions, leeks, and butter over medium-high heat and sweat them until they are translucent, giving them a teaspoon of salt as you do. Do not allow the onion to brown. Add the beer, bring it to a simmer, and cook gently until it has reduced by half.

Add the chicken stock, pork knuckle, and the herb sachet, and bring back to a simmer. Partially cover the pan, about three-quarters of the way, and continue to simmer for 45 to 60 minutes.

Remove the pork knuckle and sachet. While the pork knuckle is still warm, carefully separate the meat from the bone, the fat, and the gristle and discard them. Break down the meat by cutting it into smaller pieces or shred it by hand. Set aside until the soup is ready to serve; refrigerate if not serving right away.

Add the sour cream, sugar, and nutmeg to the soup. Taste and adjust seasoning as necessary.

Stir the slurry into the soup, and continue to simmer until it's thickened. This soup can be made ahead, cooled at this point, covered, and refrigerated for up to 3 days, then reheated when ready to serve. Garnish with the reheated meat before serving.

ON NUTMEG

Most chefs will have a ramekin of coarse kosher salt and a pepper mill at their station. Their station wouldn't be complete without them, nor would mine. But I also must have a nutmeg or two and a Microplane. Nutmeg is every bit as important to my cooking as pepper.

This, too, is part of the cuisine of my homeland: nutmeg. And so are the many other spices common in the cuisines of Alsace, Germany, and Austria: ginger, cloves, cardamom, and cinnamon. These originally entered the region from the spice route and the Roman and German empires. Nutmeg became an important commercial spice in Europe by the 1600s. Now they are a part of our culinary DNA. Of course, I use these so-called sweet spices in cookies, tarts, and breads, but they can be used to beguiling effect in savory dishes as well. I love seasoning seafood with cardamom (see page 260). I use ground ginger and cinnamon in pâtés, liverwurst, and sausages for intense seasoning.

And there's an art to blending them, making them work in concert.

But they can also be used à la minute for subtle effects, especially the nutmeg, which is why I always have it at my station. It adds what we call a *je ne sais quoi* to a dish—that note of flavor that makes you squint and think, "What is that?"—that something you can't quite place.

Notice it in my hearty greens—kale (page 74) and Brussels sprouts (page 75). But I also use it to season foie gras. I grate it into meat stuffing and dumplings, sweetbread-mushroom ravioli, and spaetzle batter, and I use it in beef, chicken, and venison recipes.

If there's a seasoning that defines me, it's nutmeg.

Joe Anthony, chef de cuisine, and behind us, executive sous chef Justin Borah, at the pass during service

TOASTED FLOUR SOUP

Serves 6 to 8

When you live on a farm, sometimes you have to make do with what you have. This is a poor man's soup, composed of nothing more than flour, fat, chicken stock, and seasoning, served with toasted bread. I include it here because we scarcely think to make a soup with such simple ingredients, and yet the simple flavors of toasted flour make this surprisingly satisfying and comforting. It's excellent finished with cream, and you could give it a buzz with a hand blender to make it frothy. Of course, you could also add mushrooms, truffle, or diced foie gras and it'll become a very special soup indeed.

5 tablespoons (60 g) butter or schmaltz
½ cup (60 g) all-purpose flour
1½ quarts/liters White Chicken Stock
    (page 251)
Salt
20 gratings nutmeg, or to taste
Freshly ground black pepper
1 to 2 teaspoons lemon juice or vinegar
1 cup (240 ml) heavy cream (optional)
Celery leaves, roughly chopped,
    for garnish

In a saucepan over medium heat, melt the butter and whisk in the flour. Cook the flour gently until it is lightly browned and nutty. Add the chicken stock and bring the soup to a simmer. Simmer for about 15 minutes, until it has thickened. Add salt (start with 2 teaspoons and adjust as necessary). Add the nutmeg, several grinds of pepper, and the lemon juice. Taste and adjust the seasoning. Finish with the cream, if using. Serve garnished with celery leaves.

Variation: This soup can also be made with ⅔ cup (120 g) semolina flour (coarse hard wheat flour).

MAIN COURSES

APPLE CIDER AND CUMIN PICKLED RAINBOW TROUT

Serves 8

We ate a lot of freshwater fish in Alsace. Salmon used to be plentiful in the rivers, as were crayfish, frog legs, and eel. This is a classic Alsatian way to prepare trout, though we could use many different freshwater fish, including perch, sandre (in the perch family), and pike.

Here a vinegar-based brine, heavily seasoned with spices common to the region—coriander, cumin, fennel—is poured hot over whole trout that has been floured and sautéed until nicely browned. And then it sits in the brine to pickle for a week before being served. It can be served cold from the fridge (it will keep for 3 weeks) with potato salad, a green salad, or whatever you have on hand.

My favorite way to enjoy this is to thicken some of the pickling liquid with a roux, and serve the trout, drizzled with the thickened pickling liquid, beside leek vinaigrette—a classic side dish made from the white part of the leeks, which have been boiled in salted water until soft and are served warm, topped with chopped hard-boiled eggs, parsley, and vinaigrette (page 77).

FOR THE PICKLING LIQUID

1 tablespoon white peppercorns

1 tablespoon coriander seeds

1 tablespoon fennel seeds

4 tablespoons (32 g) cumin seeds

1½ quarts/liters water

1 quart/liter apple cider vinegar

1½ cups (130 g) sugar

1 tablespoon salt

2 shallots, sliced

2 bay leaves

Make the pickling liquid: Combine the peppercorns and coriander, fennel, and cumin seeds in a tall pot over high heat. Swirl the seeds around in the pan to toast them for a minute or so, until they smell fragrant. Add 1½ quarts/liters of water followed by the cider vinegar, sugar, salt, shallots, and bay leaves, bring the liquid to a boil, and then remove it from the heat.

FOR COOKING THE TROUT

4 whole dressed rainbow trout, 10 to 14 ounces (300 to 360 g) each, heads removed

All-purpose flour, for dusting

Grapeseed oil or other neutral oil for sautéing

Cook and pickle the trout: Dredge the trout in flour and shake and pat the fish to allow the excess to fall off.

Add ¼ inch (6 mm) of oil to a large sauté pan over medium-high heat. When the oil is hot, add the trout, cooking them until they are golden brown on one side, then flipping them and browning the other side.

Remove the trout to a nonreactive container (plastic or glass). When the pickling liquid has dropped below 140°F (60°C), pour it over the trout. If there is not enough liquid to submerge them, flip the trout after 10 minutes to finish cooking the other side.

Let cool to room temperature for 1 hour uncovered, then carefully turn the trout over and put the whole dish in the refrigerator, covered. Refrigerate for 1 week before serving.

Note: To make a roux, melt 2 tablespoons of butter in a saucepan. Whisk in 2 tablespoons of flour and cook it until it smells like a pie crust, and allow it to cool. Next, whisk in ¾ cup (180 ml) of hot pickling liquid to the roux, bring it up to a boil, and let simmer for about 30 seconds to 1 minute. Let cool before serving. As a rule, the roux and the liquid it is intended to thicken should be opposite temperatures.

POT-AU-FEU À L'ALSACIENNE

Serves 6

Pot-au-feu can be a weeknight meal, a Sunday feast, or even a celebration. Like Choucroute Garnie (page 59), it's a shared meal, with everyone tailoring their plate to their own tastes. Except the marrow—almost everyone fights over this delicacy. Part of the greatness of a pot-au-feu is that it uses rudimentary ingredients, tough meats, root vegetables, and water to create a deeply nourishing meal for many.

Serving this dish is almost ritualistic, and in the ritual, there is a reminder to appreciate both the food, its economy and deliciousness, and those with whom you are sharing it. First, the broth is presented, with slices of marrow, or marrow dumplings, and toasted croutons rubbed with garlic as a first course. Then a variety of crudités are served (see pages 54–55), followed by the meat and the vegetables and perhaps some roasted potatoes, accompanied by horseradish sauce, fortified with more of the broth. If you are lucky you'll have leftover meat, which can be put to use in many delicious ways, including Stuffed Potatoes (page 64) and *Fleischschnacka* (page 87).

8 meaty short ribs on the bone
(3 to 3½ pounds/1.5 kg)
2 pounds (900 g) beef shoulder or
top round
3 tablespoons salt, plus more to taste
30 grinds pepper, or to taste
3 large (3-inch/7.5 cm) marrow bones
2 large carrots
1 large leek, white and pale green parts
only, cut into 2-inch (5 cm) pieces,
halved lengthwise and washed well
2 medium turnips, peeled
1 small green cabbage
1 small celery root, peeled
Sachet d'épice (8 sprigs parsley, 5 sprigs
chervil, 8 sprigs thyme, and 2 bay
leaves, tied together in cheesecloth)
1 onion pique (see Note)
1 onion brûlée (see Note)
2 cloves garlic, peeled

FOR THE SOUP GARNISHES

18 cooked Bone Marrow Quenelles
(optional; page 83)
2 tablespoons roughly chopped celery
leaves
6 slices country bread or baguette,
toasted or grilled
2 cloves garlic, peeled and halved

FOR SERVING

Freshly grated nutmeg
2 tablespoons coarse salt
2 tablespoons chopped parsley
Horseradish Sauce (page 94)

Fill a large stockpot with 6 quarts/liters of water. Put it over high heat, and add the short ribs and beef shoulder. Add the salt and pepper. When the water comes to a simmer, skim the foam that rises to the top. Add the marrow bones, carrots, leek, turnips, cabbage, and celery root along with the herb bundle, onion pique, onion brûlée, and garlic. When the water returns to a simmer, skim again if necessary. Partially cover the pot with a lid by three-quarters. Maintain a gentle simmer, not a boil, to ensure a clear bouillon, for about 3 hours. The pot-au-feu is done when the meat is fork tender.

Remove the meat and vegetables to a plate or bowl and cover with plastic wrap. Discard the herb bundle. Serve the broth, strained if you wish, in bowls with some of the marrow or bone marrow quenelles, if using, garnished with roughly chopped celery leaves. Rub the freshly toasted or grilled bread with garlic.

When you've enjoyed the soup and are ready to serve the meat, slice it, and cut the vegetables into bite-sized pieces. Make a seasoning salt by combining the nutmeg, coarse salt, and parsley in a bowl for the table. Serve the meat and vegetables with the finishing salt mixture and horseradish sauce (add more beef broth to this for more flavor if you wish).

Note: An onion pique is an onion studded with cloves and 1 or 2 bay leaves. It makes a difference to the flavor. I peel a medium onion, rest it on its side, and make a slice halfway through the equator. Into this cut I slip one or two bay leaves. I then press four whole cloves diagonally into the onion, two on either side, right next to the bay leaves so that the cloves puncture the bay leaves to secure them in the onion.

An onion brûlée is an onion that is halved through the equator. Either end is also cut off, so that you have two flat slides to the onion halves. Put them flat side down in a dry saucepan over medium-high heat and let them cook until blackened. Then turn them over and blacken the other cut side. This will add yet another layer of flavor to the pot-au-feu broth or any kind of broth you're making.

A SELECTION OF CRUDITÉS FOR THE TYPICAL ALSATIAN POT-AU-FEU

Not to be confused with Americans' notion of crudités, these are five traditional accompaniments, more like salads of shredded vegetables than simply raw vegetables, to a pot-au-feu dinner, typically served family style after the broth—two cabbage salads (which can be refrigerated for 2 to 3 days), a cucumber salad, a black radish salad, and a tomato salad. The cabbage salads can be made a day ahead and refrigerated (I think they taste better the next day). They may seem rustic, but I featured them regularly when I was chef at the Modern in New York City. They are appropriate for a weeknight meal with any charcuterie, terrine, pâte, liverwurst, head cheese, etc., or a pot-au-feu celebration. Note: See also the Celeriac Salad on page 41.

GREEN CABBAGE AND AGED GRUYÈRE

Serves 8

1 small green cabbage, outer leaves removed
Salt
½ small red onion, thinly sliced and soaked in ice water for 20 minutes or so
½ cup (120 ml) grapeseed oil
1 teaspoon Dijon mustard
4 to 5 tablespoons (60 to 75 ml) cider or sherry vinegar
Pepper
Pinch ground coriander
4 ounces (120 g) aged Gruyère, shredded or coarsely grated

Cut the cabbage in half through the core. Remove the core from each half. Thinly slice the cabbage, by hand or use a mandoline. Put it in a mixing bowl and season with salt. Allow it to sit for 5 minutes or so, then press the cabbage between your hands to drain it, in order to get rid of the excess water and to concentrate the flavor. Drain the onions and add them to the cabbage.

Make a vinaigrette by mixing the oil with the mustard, vinegar, salt, pepper, and coriander. Toss the cabbage with the vinaigrette, then add the Gruyère. This can be refrigerated, covered, for 3 to 4 days.

RED CABBAGE SALAD

Serves 8

1 small red cabbage, outer leaves removed
Salt
1 tablespoon vegetable or grapeseed oil
1 medium onion, small diced
2 small cloves garlic, smashed and chopped
½ cup (120 ml) dry white wine
¼ cup (60 ml) cider vinegar
½ cup (120 ml) grapeseed or vegetable oil
1 teaspoon Dijon mustard
1 tablespoon mayonnaise or sour cream
20 gratings nutmeg, or to taste
Generous pinch ground cumin
Pinch ground coriander
Pepper

Cut the cabbage in half through the core. Remove the core from each half. Thinly slice the cabbage, by hand or use a mandoline. Put it in a mixing bowl and season with salt. Allow it to sit for 5 minutes or so, then press the cabbage between your hands to drain it.

In a saucepan over medium heat, add the oil and cook the onions in it, until they are translucent, a couple minutes, giving them a generous pinch of salt, then add the garlic, cook it for a minute more, then deglaze the pan with the white wine and reduce by half. Remove the pan from the heat and add the vinegar and Dijon mustard. Whisk it well and pour it over the cabbage. Toss the cabbage well. Then add mayonnaise or sour cream, nutmeg, cumin, coriander, and pepper. Mix well, pressing it between your hands. This salad can be kept, covered and refrigerated, for 3 to 4 days.

CUCUMBER SALAD

Serves 8

4 cucumbers
1 tablespoon salt, plus more to taste
1 tablespoon Dijon mustard
1 tablespoon mayonnaise or sour cream
¼ cup (60 ml) cider or sherry vinegar
¼ cup (60 ml) grapeseed oil
½ onion, small diced
Pepper
2 tablespoons chopped chives

Peel the cucumbers, halve them, and scrape out the seeds (if they're seedless, they can be used whole). Cut the cucumber into about ¹⁄₁₀-inch-thick (2 to 3 mm) slices. Put them in a colander, add in the salt, and let them sit to disgorge for about 2 hours, pressing down on them to help extract the water. Rinse them well under cold water and press them in your hands to squeeze out the excess water.

Put the cucumbers in a bowl. Add the mustard, mayonnaise, vinegar, oil, and onion and mix well. Season with salt and pepper and top with the chives.

BLACK RADISH SALAD

Serves 8

6 black radishes
1 tablespoon salt, plus more to taste
1 tablespoon Dijon mustard
2 small shallots, minced
¼ cup (60 ml) cider or sherry vinegar
⅓ cup (75 ml) grapeseed or vegetable oil
Pepper

Wash and trim the radishes. Shred them on a vegetable shredder or in a food processor with a shredder blade. Put them in a bowl, sprinkle them with the salt, and let them sit for an hour or so, pressing on them occasionally, three or four times, to help extract the water.

Rinse them well, squeezing out any residual water. Combine them in a bowl with the mustard, shallots, vinegar, and oil and season with salt and pepper to taste.

TOMATO AND HARD-BOILED EGG SALAD

Serves 8

4 to 6 vine-ripe tomatoes, at room temperature
4 to 6 hard-boiled eggs, peeled and cut into wedges
Salt and freshly ground black pepper
⅓ cup (75 ml) sherry vinegar
½ cup (120 ml) grapeseed or vegetable oil
1 tablespoon Dijon mustard
3 small shallots, minced
2 tablespoons chopped parsley

Core each tomato and make an x on the bottom with a paring knife. Bring a large pot of water to a boil, blanch them for 30 to 45 seconds, and then remove them to an ice bath. Peel the tomatoes. Pat them dry with a paper towel, then cut them crosswise into ¼-inch-thick (6 mm) slices.

In a casserole dish or on a serving platter, layer the tomatoes and eggs, alternating one then the other. Season the tomato and egg with salt and pepper.

Make the vinaigrette by combining the vinegar, oil, and mustard, blending well with a whisk (or shaken in a jar). Spoon the vinaigrette over the tomatoes and eggs. Top them with the shallot and parsley. Let sit for 20 to 30 minutes before serving.

To understand Alsatian cuisine, one must understand the life and death of pigs. These animals bring together our families and communities while sustaining us in all seasons, especially in rural France, where so many small farms flourished. We treasure pigs by raising them with care, killing them humanely, cooking each part carefully to bring out the best flavor and texture, and using every bit of the animal. To learn how to cook each part properly, you need to know how difficult it is to care for, slaughter, and prepare the animal for that cooking.

I was lucky enough to grow up on a farm where we slaughtered a pig each year. I say that now. As a kid, I didn't feel lucky at all. Farms are endless chores with no time off for fun. I wasn't afraid of hard work, but while my friends were out biking, I was cleaning stables. I only appreciated my upbringing when I left the country for big cities. Some people I met there didn't even know which cuts of pork come from which part of the pig.

So now I'm glad I was raised on a farm, even if it wasn't easy. As a kid, I got attached to the animals: the rabbits, pigs, sheep, all of them. They were friends. When you have to kill them, it's hard. Sometimes I cried a little bit because I was close to a particular lamb or chicken. But I also understood that it needed to happen for us to eat, and I developed a deep respect for the process of the natural world. Taking a life away to make food is normal in nature's cycle. What isn't normal is hiding that connection. Today, no one has to see the slaughter anymore or engage with the process. And when people don't put one and one together in the supermarket's meat case, they can lose respect for the animals who deserve it. When people do witness it, they take care to cook every part with attention and without waste.

Everyone in my village took part in the pig slaughter. It was a community affair. Each family killed one pig a year. They'd keep half and give the other half to a neighboring farm family. Six months later, the neighbor would hand over half of the pig they'd just killed. Before this semi-annual barter, the families gathered to decide what they would want: more bacon and sausage or more fresh meat. The farmer then would choose an animal of the right age, size, and quality. With a plan in place, the butcher arrived.

In my family, that was my mother's brother. He'd come with his butcher friends and invited me to participate for the first time when I was ten years old. But he asked me to step back for the first part, which he handled alone. Butchers know how to kill. He said, "You want the pig to die fast." In that simple statement—along with the swift slaughter—I learned the importance of respecting the animal's life, especially in death.

Immediately afterwards, everyone worked rapidly to preserve the best of the pig. The neck was slit over a bucket to collect the blood, which was mixed with vinegar and continuously stirred with a wooden paddle until cooled. If the stirring stopped, the blood would coagulate, making it unusable in blood sausage.

A group would lower the body into a tub as big as a dining table, filled with hot water. Five of us would kneel at the edges, shaving the hair off underwater. We felt connected, razors in hand, arms scalding. We concentrated on getting the closest shave, knowing that smoother skin produced better bacon. After that, the trotters were taken off, the nail caps clipped. The butcher then sawed the pig cleanly down the middle and hung the halves on a ladder in the farm's courtyard to cool.

Finally, the butcher would cut the pieces for traditional Alsatian cooking. One ham for smoking, one for using fresh. Thin slices of raw ham meat often end up pounded and fried into schnitzel. One side of belly for salting and smoking into bacon, the other for brining to eat with sauerkraut. The loins, chops, ribs, shoulders, and cutlets would be prepared for freezing to cook later. The same for the shanks, hocks, ears, and feet, all of which would be braised. The head, jowl, offal, fatback, and caul fat would be set aside for sausages. And then there were the intestines.

My mother cleaned the intestines so we could turn them into sausage casings. It's ugly work. She'd squeeze them out by hand to empty them. Once deflated, she'd pull the tubes inside out, then scrape

The town of Ungersheim's Alsatian heritage museum, a collection of more than eighty classic farm buildings dating from the fifteenth to the nineteenth century, moved to and rebuilt on 37 acres. In summer, it becomes a living village where costumed staff work and dress as people did in their respective eras. Note the stork nesting on top of the building. Storks are the iconic symbol of Alsace and can be viewed throughout the region. Visit www.ecomusee.alsace.

off the inner mucous with a soup spoon. The process was exactly as disgusting as you would imagine. Finally, she'd wash, wash, and wash them until they were pure and clean.

The stomach was almost as difficult to clean, but at least we got to eat it right away. It's the delicacy of slaughter day. We'd stuff it with potatoes, sauerkraut, bacon, and onions, then sew it tightly. It'd look like a giant kidney bean. It'd be poached, then roasted. The rubbery stomach would turn into a crisp-tender shell around the salty, tangy, sweet, funky filling. It cut into beautiful porchetta-like slices and was the best way to celebrate a day of working with family and friends.

On those slaughter days, I felt like I touched life. I tasted it too. The trueness of pork became ingrained in me. I recognize now that there was an authenticity of life in those experiences, an authenticity that's

disappearing. My village modernized over the years. We transitioned from sharing a pig with the neighbor, to selling parts to whomever wanted to buy some, to supermarket shopping. There are only four farms of what used to be eighty.

I miss my country roots, but I'm looking forward to the future of farming too. Of course, it's hard for me to find the same true tastes I experienced as a child. But I've come close. We work with many small sustainable farms and the dedicated farmers who want to do the right thing and connect us to the roots of our food. They're bringing back heritage breeds, letting them eat from nature, giving them stress-free lives in the open, keeping them healthy without antibiotics. That's the pork you need to find and cook. When you do, remember that it represents a life worthy of respect.

UNCLE MICHEL'S CHOUCROUTE GARNIE

Serves 6

When people come to Alsace, they often seek out the most famous specialties of the region—Alsatian onion tart (page 81) and choucroute garnie. Alsace is one of the great charcuterie centers of Europe, and we use this (sliced pork belly, ham, sausages) to "garnish" or top our sauerkraut. And my uncle, Michel Kreuther, catered to a lot of tourists at his restaurant and hotel in the mountain town of Dabo. Like the pot-au-feu (page 53), it can be a simple weeknight meal or it can be a great celebration, depending on the variety of meats and sausages you serve. He would serve a great one, with five different sausages, a smoked bacon, an unsmoked bacon, liver quenelles, ham hocks, and potatoes. It was a huge meal. One that I like to serve with boiled new potatoes and whole grain mustard. Leftover sauerkraut (flavored by all the meats) could be the center of a meal of spaetzle or schmaltz dumplings the next day. For all the recipes in this book that call for sauerkraut, use the method described below, with the exception of adding the bacon and the baby back ribs.

This dish is the heart and soul of Alsace.

2 pounds (900 g) sauerkraut, or more as desired (homemade as shown on page 60, or store-bought)

⅓ cup (80 g) butter, plus more for sautéing the blood sausages

2 onions, finely chopped (about 1½ cups/500 g)

3 large cloves garlic, smashed and chopped

1 (750-ml) bottle dry white wine, such as Riesling

4 whole cloves

12 whole juniper berries

2 bay leaves

Salt and freshly ground black pepper

12 ounces (350 g) applewood-smoked slab bacon

1 rack baby back ribs (preferably submerged in a 5% salt brine for 4 hours; see Note)

White Chicken Stock (page 251) or water, as needed

4 knackwurst sausages, cooked as desired (roasted, sautéed, or boiled)

4 bratwurst sausages, cooked as desired (roasted, sautéed, or boiled)

4 morcilla sausages or blood sausages

Note: To prepare the brine, heat 6 cups (1.5 liters) water in a nonreactive pan, add ¼ cup (75 g) salt, and stir until dissolved. Cool thoroughly before using. (It needs to be ice cold, so it's best to prep the brine a day ahead and cool it in the refrigerator before submerging the baby back ribs in it.)

Preheat your oven to 325°F (165°C).

Rinse the sauerkraut in a colander under cold water and a second time under warm water. Squeeze the excess water from it.

In a large stockpot over medium-high heat, melt the butter. Add the onions and garlic and cook until they're translucent. Add the wine. Then add the sauerkraut, making sure you loosen it up while you add it to the pot. Add the cloves, juniper berries, and bay leaves. Add 1 tablespoon of salt and about 30 grinds of pepper. Stir the pot well. Add the bacon and baby back ribs to the sauerkraut and bury them in it. The liquid should come up just to the level of the sauerkraut. If the wine is not sufficient, add chicken stock or water. Bring the liquid to a simmer. Press a parchment lid down onto the surface of the sauerkraut, then put a lid on the pot and put it in the oven for 45 minutes. (To make a parchment lid, cut a square of parchment that's just slightly larger than the diameter of the pot. Fold the

square in half, then in half again. Now fold this smaller square in half to make a triangle and repeat to create a small wedge. Trim the wedge to match half of the pot's radius, cut off the tip to allow steam to escape, unfold, and you will have a parchment cover to fit the interior of your pot. Press it directly onto the surface of the food.)

Remove the pot from the oven. Remove the ribs and bacon from the sauerkraut and keep warm. Stir the sauerkraut well. Taste it and add more salt and pepper as needed. Place the ribs and bacon back into the center of the pot, making sure the meats are submerged in the kraut and the juices. Re-cover with the parchment lid and pot lid and return it to the oven for 30 minutes, or until the meat is fork tender.

Just before the sauerkraut is done, reheat your knackwurst and bratwurst in simmering water or by sautéing them in a pan. Sauté the blood sausage in butter until browned and heated through.

Slice the bacon about ¼ inch (6 mm) thick. Cut the ribs into two- or three-bone pieces. Slice the sausages in two. Mound the sauerkraut in the center of a platter. Arrange the meats around it.

HOW TO FERMENT YOUR OWN SAUERKRAUT

The door to an Alsatian root cellar

I'd wager that virtually every household in Alsace had, and still has, a big crock of sauerkraut fermenting in the root cellar. We make six to eight large batches, divided in two 10-gallon earthenware or Cambro plastic containers every year at the restaurant. Not only is it incomparable in flavor when you make your own, it's also an enormously satisfying task. All you need is cabbage and salt. Our basic ratio uses minimal salt, just 12 to 15 grams per kilo, 1.5 percent of the weight of the cabbage, or about 1 tablespoon of Morton's kosher salt for every 2 pounds (910 g) of cabbage (Morton's is the one salt that has a close volume-to-weight ratio; Diamond Crystal is about 40 percent lighter). It's then weighted down to help force the water from the cabbage, which creates the fermenting brine. The following method is how we make it at the restaurant. Feel free to make more or less. We also flavor ours a little with juniper berries, another common aromatic of the region, and pepper. If possible, use the metric weights given here for the most consistent results. Also, if you have a mandoline, use it to slice the cabbage so that it's cut uniformly, which results in a better fermentation.

Makes about 3¾ pounds (1.7 kg)

**4½ pounds (2 kg) very thinly sliced
   white cabbage**
**2¼ tablespoons (30 g) coarse
   kosher salt**
**2 tablespoons juniper berries and
   1 tablespoon black peppercorns,
   loose or tied in cheesecloth**

Put the cabbage in a large bowl. Sprinkle the salt over it and thoroughly toss the cabbage, working the salt into it (wash your hands well before or wear gloves to avoid unwanted bacteria getting into the mix).

Pack half the sauerkraut into a nonreactive container (plastic, glass, or earthenware), add the juniper berries and black peppercorns in the center, then cover with the rest of the cabbage. Using a heavy lid or piece of wood or plastic, put as much weight as possible on the sauerkraut. Allow the sauerkraut to start to ferment at room temperature (around 70°F/22°C) and after 1 week move it to a slightly cooler, dark place (65°F/18°C is ideal) for 15 to 20 days, checking every few days to ensure no mold is developing and that the sauerkraut is submerged in its liquid; if there is not enough liquid to cover the cabbage, add tepid water to it, just to cover when it is weighted down.

Store the finished sauerkraut in a covered, nonreactive container for up to 4 months in the refrigerator.

TRADITIONAL BAECKEOFFE

(Wine-Marinated Meat and Potato Stew)

Serves 6

Baeckeoffe translates as "baker's oven," because that's where this dish was traditionally cooked in Alsatian villages. Before the advent of individual home ovens, everyone in town shared the bread baker's huge wood-fired oven. They'd marinate their meats and vegetables overnight, drop their casseroles off in the morning, and pick them up at the end of the day, along with a loaf of bread. To keep their stews from drying out, they'd seal the lids to the pots with a strip of dough (just around the rim that's discarded after cooking). I still do. That simple step keeps all the juices in the meat and vegetables. Of course, I also serve this with freshly baked bread for sopping up all those juices. A nice green salad is all you need to complete the meal.

Most butchers and Latin and Asian markets sell pig's trotters. When slow-cooked, they release their collagen into the cooking liquid, giving it a velvety richness. Ask the butcher to cut the trotter into pieces for you.

14 ounces (400 g) pork shoulder, cut into 6 even chunks

14 ounces (400 g) lamb shoulder, cut into 6 even chunks

14 ounces (400 g) beef roast, such as London broil, cut into 6 even chunks

1 pig's trotter, cut into pieces

2 small onions, sliced

2 medium carrots, sliced

1 small leek, split lengthwise and cleaned

4 cloves garlic, peeled

2 cups (500 ml) Sylvaner or other dry white wine, plus more if needed

5 parsley sprigs

5 thyme sprigs

1 bay leaf

18 whole black peppercorns

10 whole juniper berries

2 whole cloves

Salt and freshly ground black pepper

3 pounds (1.5 kg) potatoes, peeled and cut into ⅛-inch-thick (3 mm) slices

7 tablespoons (100 g) butter

1 cup (150 g) all-purpose flour

recipe continues

Combine the pork, lamb, beef, trotter, onions, carrots, leek, garlic, and wine in a large bowl. Make a sachet d'épices by wrapping the parsley, thyme, bay leaf, peppercorns, juniper, and cloves in cheesecloth and tying tightly. Add to the bowl. Season everything generously with salt and pepper, then mix until evenly coated. Cover tightly with plastic wrap and refrigerate for 24 hours.

Preheat your oven to 350°F (175°C).

Transfer all of the meat to another bowl. Add the potatoes to the vegetables, season with salt and pepper, and fold to mix well. Use some of the butter to generously coat the inside of a large Dutch oven or casserole. Spread half of the vegetables in an even layer across the bottom. Top with all of the meat in an even layer, then spread the remaining vegetables on top. Pour in the marinade. The liquid should come three-quarters of the way up the sides of the solids. If it doesn't, add more wine as needed. Scatter the remaining butter in bits over the top.

Cover the Dutch oven tightly with foil, then put on the lid. Stir the flour and ¼ cup (60 ml) water in a large bowl to form a dough. If the mixture doesn't come together, knead in more water, 1 tablespoon at a time. Knead the dough until smooth, then roll into a rope the length of the circumference of the Dutch oven. Wrap the dough around the rim of the Dutch oven, pressing it between the lid and base to seal it shut.

Bake for 2 hours and 45 minutes. Let rest for 15 minutes, then crack open the dough seal and uncover. Discard the dough and sachet. Season to taste with salt and pepper and serve.

TRADITIONAL STUFFED POTATOES

Serves 6

Nothing is wasted on a farm in Alsace. This is one of my favorite ways to put leftover pot-au-feu meat to use, making a stuffing for hollowed-out potatoes. You can also use any cooked poultry, like chicken or turkey, that you happen to have on hand. One way to make this is to stuff two halves of a potato then tie them together with string to bake them whole. This makes for a fun presentation and eating experience, finding the surprise inside, like a gift! But here I'll simply stuff them and bake them open-faced, topped with cheese. You can puree the meats rather than grind them; the texture will be a little smoother. This mixture can also be used to stuff tomatoes or zucchini.

With a salad or some sauerkraut, this is satisfying dinner. And if you are thinking like an Alsatian, you will save the trimmings from hollowing out the potato to make potato pancakes (page 91) or a potato and leek soup later in the week!

FOR THE STUFFING

1 pound (450 g) cooked meat (leftover from pot-au-feu, page 53, or any cooked leftover meat)

10 ounces (300 g) cured bacon

2 small yellow onions, finely chopped (about 1 cup/160 g)

1 tablespoon butter

Salt

4 or 5 slices (3½ ounces/100 g) dry bread, soaked in warm milk

2 eggs

2 tablespoons chopped parsley

20 grinds pepper

20 gratings nutmeg

2 tablespoons red wine vinegar

12 medium potatoes, peeled and held in water until you're ready to work with them

TO COOK THE POTATOES

6 tablespoons (90 g) butter

1 onion, sliced

1 teaspoon salt

3 to 4 sprigs thyme

1 bay leaf

8 ounces (240 g) Gruyère, grated

2 cups (450 ml) White Chicken Stock (page 251)

Make the stuffing: Grind (or puree) the cooked meat. Grind or puree the bacon. Combine them in a bowl.

Combine the onions and butter in a sauté pan over medium heat, give them a good pinch of salt, and cook them until they are translucent. Remove the onions to a plate to cool to room temperature or chill in the refrigerator.

Wring out the bread and add it to the meat, along with the cooled onion, eggs, parsley, 1½ tablespoons salt, the pepper, nutmeg, and vinegar. Mix by hand (as if making meatloaf) until all ingredients are thoroughly combined. Taste some and adjust the seasoning as necessary.

To cook the potatoes, halve them lengthwise. Using a Parisienne scoop or a spoon, scoop out as much potato as you can and still have a solid potato to work with, ⅜ inch (9 mm) or so. (Reserve the potato trimmings in water, refrigerated for another use, such as to make soup or mashed potatoes.)

Preheat your oven to 425°F (220°C).

Stuff each potato half so that it is heaping. (If you have extra stuffing, save it to stuff tomatoes or zucchini, or make fried patties or meatballs, which would go perfectly with the potato soup you'll be making.)

In a casserole dish, melt the butter, add the sliced onion and salt (if you wish, you can cook them on the stovetop or in the oven before adding, for a softer texture). Top the onions with the thyme and bay leaf. Rest the potatoes on the onion and top each with the grated cheese. Pour in the chicken stock; it should reach about three-quarters the height of the potatoes. Bring to a simmer on the stovetop, then move to the oven and bake for 1 hour or until the potatoes are completely tender.

Serve immediately with some of the onion from the bottom of the pan spooned on the side.

STUFFED VEAL BREAST

Serves 8 to 10

This is an elaborate meal, meant to feed a lot of people, and therefore it has a celebratory feel, in the making, slicing, and sharing of it with a group. A rich, delicious stuffing is made from bread, liver, meat, and seasoning. You'll need a big enough veal breast to contain the stuffing. It's cooked low and slow, browned in a pan, and then braised in liquid and aromatics. It's served sliced with a sauce made from the braising liquid. After living in the United States for almost twenty-five years now, I can see this being a wonderful alternative for a Thanksgiving feast. It's a great way to serve a lot of people economically and deliciously.

If you don't have a grinder, you can puree the liver and meat in a food processor, but everything should be very cold, even partially frozen, a good rule when grinding any meat but especially important if using a food processor. The pureed meat is mixed with bread and sautéed onion and parsley.

This dish requires the veal to be sealed or wrapped. My mother would create a pocket at one end and fill the pocket with stuffing, then sew it shut. We use Activa, often called meat glue, which binds the protein, but you could also tie it securely with butcher's twine.

FOR THE STUFFING
4 or 5 slices (200 g) of a fresh Pullman-
  style bread loaf
Milk, as needed
1½ cups (200 g) minced onions 2 tablespoons (30 ml) duck fat, foie gras fat,
  or butter
2 teaspoons salt, plus more for the
  onions and veal breast
½ cup (50 g) chopped parsley
6 ounces (180 g) fatty veal meat from
  the breast

6 ounces (180 g) chicken or duck liver
2 eggs
30 grinds pepper
¼ of a nutmeg, grated
⅛ teaspoon ground ginger
1 boned veal breast (3 to 3½ pounds/
  about 1.5 kg), cut to 13 by 7 inches
  (33 by 7 cm), then butterflied (ask
  your butcher to do this, or butterfly or
  cut a pocket yourself, as described in
  the method)
1 tablespoon Activa (meat glue), if veal is
  butterflied

FOR THE BRAISING LIQUID
2 medium onions, chopped
2 carrots, chopped
2 ribs celery, chopped
2 tablespoons (30 g) butter or grapeseed oil
½ to 1 bottle (375 to 750 ml) dry
  white wine
White Chicken Stock (page 251),
  as needed
Pinch salt
Several grinds pepper
1 bay leaf
Slurry (2 tablespoons cornstarch mixed
  with 2 tablespoons water)

Make the stuffing: Soak the bread in milk, then press out the excess.

In a saucepan over medium heat, add the onion and foie gras fat or butter, and cook the onion until it's soft, adding a teaspoon of salt as you do. Remove it from the heat, stir in the parsley, and refrigerate until chilled.

Grind the meat and the livers through a small die on a meat grinder, then puree it in a food processor (if you don't have a meat grinder, put the liver and meat in the freezer until they are stiff with cold and puree them in a food processor).

In a mixing bowl, combine the bread, onion mixture, meat puree, eggs, pepper, nutmeg, ginger, and 2 teaspoons of salt, and mix it until it is thoroughly combined. Sauté a couple tablespoons of the stuffing, if you wish, to cook through and taste for seasoning and adjust as necessary.

Trim the veal breast to measure 13 by 7 inches (33 by 17 cm). With a sharp knife, make a pocket, or simply butterfly the breast. Season with salt and pepper. For the pocket version, fill the entire cavity with the stuffing using a spoon, packing it in gently, making sure there are no air pockets. Close the opening by sewing it

with a large sewing needle and butcher's twine (see photos below). For the butterfly version, shape the stuffing in the middle, dust the edges of the breast with Activa (meat glue), and fold the meat over the stuffing, pressing the edges together.

Wrap the veal breast tightly in several layers of plastic wrap, sealing the ends well with butcher's twine (it will be poached in the plastic wrap the next day), and refrigerate overnight so the stuffing harmonizes and the Activa is activated.

The next day, take the plastic-wrapped veal breast and wrap it in two layers of aluminum foil, securing it well at the ends with butcher's twine so that it resembles a large candy wrap.

Bring a large pot of water to a boil and drop in the wrapped veal breast. As soon as the meat is placed into the pot, the water temperature will drop dramatically. Using a thermometer, bring the temperature back up to between 190°F and 200°F (85°C to 90°C) degrees. Poach for 2 hours, maintaining that temperature range. Cool the veal in cold water from the faucet for about 2 hours, then remove it from the water and refrigerate it overnight.

The next day, carefully unwrap the veal breast from the aluminum foil and plastic wrap. Reserve all the gelatinous juices in a plastic container for the braising liquid. With a paper towel, dry it well so that when searing, it doesn't splatter too much.

To finish the veal: Preheat your oven to 335°F (165°C). In a large saucepan, sweat the onion, carrot, and celery in the butter. Transfer the vegetables to the pan in which you will braise the veal. Unwrap the veal, and sear both sides in hot oil in a large pan. Put the veal on the sautéed vegetables in your braising pan. Add enough wine and chicken stock to come halfway up the side of the breast. Add the salt, pepper, and bay leaf and put it in the oven for 90 minutes; the internal temperature should be at or above 150°F (65°C).

Remove the breast from the pan to rest. Strain the braising liquid and thicken it with a slurry to use as a sauce.

Cut the veal into ¾-inch (2 cm) slices and serve with the sauce and your selected garnishes.

Braised Kale
(page 74)

Schmaltz Knepfle
(page 95)

Stuffed Veal Breast
(previous spread)

TRIPE AU RIESLING AND CURRY

Serves 6

This dish is something that would have been made as long ago as the Middle Ages in Alsace—tripe braised in wine. There's nothing like tripe—it has a barnyard-y flavor and chewy texture that is absolutely unique and delicious. Most grocery stores carry tripe, the stomach of the cow, or you can order it from a good butcher. Ask for honeycomb tripe and make sure that it has been cleaned and blanched (this is how it's typically sold). It should be bright white, unblemished, and have virtually no odor.

Here tripe is blanched again, cut into thin strips, and cooked in wine with aromatics and curry powder for 2½ to 3 hours (you can undercook tripe and it will be rubbery, but you really can't overcook tripe). It's finished with some cream and served topped with fresh gratings of nutmeg and freshly chopped parsley. It's terrific with boiled or roasted potatoes or spaetzle (page 89). The Riesling used to cook the dish can be enjoyed along with the dish.

This is a good recipe to double; a second dinner can be frozen and reheated later in the month.

4 tablespoons (30 g) salt, plus more
   as needed
1 cup (240 ml) white vinegar
1¾ pounds (800 g) tripe, well-rinsed
2 tablespoons (30 g) butter, plus more
   (optional), for finishing
1 tablespoon grapeseed oil
2 medium onions, finely chopped
2 cloves garlic, smashed and chopped
4 tablespoons (40 g) all-purpose flour
1 cup (240 ml) dry Riesling
Pepper
⅓ cup (150 ml) White Chicken Stock
   (page 251) or White Veal Stock
   (page 253)
½ teaspoon freshly grated nutmeg,
   plus more for serving
1 tablespoon curry powder
½ to 1 cup (120 to 240 ml) heavy cream,
   as needed (optional)
2 tablespoons red wine vinegar
Parsley, for garnish

To blanch the tripe, combine the salt and white vinegar in a pot with 1 gallon (3.8 liters) of water. Add the tripe, bring the pot to a boil, then reduce to a low boil for 1½ hours. Drain and rinse thoroughly under cold running water. Cut the tripe into ½-inch (1.25 cm) strips and wring them to squeeze off excess liquid.

Preheat your oven to 350°F (150°C).

In a large Dutch oven over medium-high heat, combine the butter and oil. When the butter starts crackling, add the tripe. Stir to coat the tripe with the fat, and cook for 3 to 4 minutes. Add the onion and garlic and continue to cook another few minutes, stirring regularly. Sprinkle the tripe with the flour and stir to distribute it. Add the wine and season the tripe with 2 tablespoons of salt and 60 grinds of pepper.

In a small bowl, combine the stock, nutmeg, and curry powder, mix it well, and pour it over the tripe. Stir to combine. It's best to make a parchment lid (see page 59) and press it down onto the surface of the tripe, but this is optional. Cover the Dutch oven with the lid and bake for 1½ to 2 hours.

Remove the tripe after 1 hour and give it a stir. Taste the tripe—who knows, maybe it will be tender and therefore done. If not, return the tripe to the oven until it is cooked, typically 2½ to 3 hours in all.

Put the pot on the stove over medium heat. Taste for seasoning and adjust. Bring it to a simmer. Then, just before serving, add cream, if using, to your taste and finish it with the red wine vinegar. Taste one last time for seasoning. If you like, you can also finish the dish with a couple of knobs of fresh butter.

Serve in bowls, garnishing with fresh parsley and more freshly grated nutmeg. This can be stored in the refrigerator for up to a week (it will be very gelatinous when cold), or frozen for up to 3 months.

VEGETABLES AND SIDE DISHES

BRAISED KALE OR COLLARD GREENS

Serves 4 to 6

This is the best way I know to cook kale—it results in a very moist, almost-sauced kale—creamy and satisfying. I believe the key is blanching the kale, or any braising green such as collards, first. This begins their cooking, sets their color, and reduces the bitterness of the greens. The coconut oil makes it rich and creamy. And here I hold back on the pepper—green vegetables require less of it, I find. Finish it with some bright lemon juice and colorful pomegranate seeds. It's a fabulous side dish.

Salt

1 pound (450 g) kale or collard greens, all stems trimmed and removed

1 tablespoon raw coconut oil (optional but recommended)

1 to 2 tablespoons (15 to 30 g) butter

¼ cup (50 g) minced shallot

1 cup (100 g) small-diced onion

1 cup (240 ml) White Chicken Stock (page 251) or turkey stock/jus

Slurry (1 tablespoon cornstarch mixed with 4 tablespoons/60 ml cold water)

10 grinds black pepper

20 gratings nutmeg

Juice from ½ lemon, or to taste

3 to 4 tablespoons pomegranate seeds (optional)

Bring a large pot of salted water to a boil and blanch the kale or collard greens for 3 to 4 minutes, then shock it in ice water. When it is completely cold, drain the kale in a colander and, in small batches, squeeze the leaves to extract excess water. Set aside on a paper towel–lined plate.

In a medium saucepan over medium-high heat, add the coconut oil, if using, and the butter (if not using coconut oil, use 2 tablespoons/30 g) of butter). When the butter has melted, add the shallot and onion, sweating them until they are translucent. Add the chicken stock and bring to a simmer. Add half the cornstarch-water slurry, adding more to thicken if necessary (it should be a loose-sauce consistency), and continue to simmer for 4 to 5 minutes. Season the liquid with salt, the pepper, and the nutmeg.

Roughly chop the kale and fluff it to separate the leaves. Add the kale to the chicken stock. Stir very well with a wooden spoon or rubber spatula. Cover the pot and lower the heat to simmer the kale gently for 15 to 20 minutes, stirring periodically.

Taste for seasoning and add a teaspoon or two of lemon juice, stirring it in and then tasting again for seasoning. Serve sprinkled with the pomegranate seeds.

MY BRUSSELS SPROUTS

Serves 8

A creamy sauce, seasoned with bacon, onion, and garlic, turns Brussels sprouts into a rich, delicious side dish. The key with this and any strong green vegetable is to blanch them first, and then cook them well in sauce. It has become a family tradition for me here in the States to serve this as a side dish at Thanksgiving.

2 pounds (900 g) Brussels sprouts, halved
Salt
6 ounces (175 g) applewood-smoked
    slab bacon, cut into thin strips
1 cup (160 g) finely chopped onion
½ to 1 teaspoon chopped (into a paste)
    garlic

1 cup (240 ml) half-and-half
Slurry (1 tablespoon cornstarch mixed
    with 2 tablespoons cold water)
10 grinds pepper
20 gratings nutmeg
2 tablespoons chopped chives

Make a lengthwise cut into the core of each Brussels sprout (this facilitates their cooking). Bring a large pot of salted water to a boil and blanch the Brussels sprouts for about 5 minutes. Taste one at the 5-minute mark to see if they are cooked enough—they should be tender but not mushy. Strain them in a colander.

In a large saucepan over medium heat, cook the bacon until the fat is rendered and the bacon is cooked. Add the onions and sweat them until they're translucent. Add the garlic paste and cook 1 minute longer. Add the half-and-half, turn the heat to medium high, cover the pan, and simmer for about 5 minutes. Thicken with the slurry to a nappé consistency.

Season the half-and-half with salt, pepper, and nutmeg. Add the Brussels sprouts and mix well with a wooden spoon or rubber spatula, lightly smashing the Brussels sprouts to further tenderize them and release their flavor into the sauce. Simmer for another minute or two, then serve in a bowl or casserole dish, topping them with the chives.

RED WINE–BRAISED RED CABBAGE
WITH APPLES AND/OR CHESTNUTS

Serves 6

This is a very popular side dish in Alsace. It couldn't be more basic or delicious. Apples are added towards the end and should still have some bite when served. I also love to add peeled, halved chestnuts when they're available. They could be added instead of the apples or in addition to them. It makes a great fall dish to accompany roasted duck, goose, pork, or stuffed veal breast (page 66). If you have one, cook this in an enameled cast-iron Dutch oven.

¼ cup (60 ml) schmaltz, duck fat, or butter

2 cups (220 g) sliced onion

6 to 8 ounces (200 g) bacon, cut into thin strips or ¼-inch lardons

1 red cabbage, core removed and thinly sliced

Salt (start with 3 teaspoons)

30 grinds pepper, or more to taste

1 cup (240 ml) red wine

3 tablespoons red wine vinegar

1 tablespoon sugar

1 bay leaf

2 apples (I love Honeycrisp), peeled, cored, and cut into 12 slices per apple

24 cooked, peeled chestnuts (optional)

Preheat your oven to 350°F (175°C).

In a heavy-bottomed pot or Dutch oven over medium heat, add the fat and onions. Cook until the onions are softened, then add the bacon and continue cooking until it's lightly browned.

Add in the cut red cabbage in three layers, seasoning each layer with 1 teaspoon of salt and 10 grinds of pepper. Add 1 cup (240 ml) of water, the red wine, vinegar, sugar, and bay leaf. Cover the pot and bake for 60 minutes, less if you like the cabbage to have a bite. Remove the pot from the oven and stir in the apples and/or chestnuts. Return the pot, covered, to the oven and cook for 30 more minutes to finish. Take out of the oven, stir, and taste, adjusting the seasoning if necessary.

VINAIGRETTES

Powerful flavors offset with very acidic ingredients are a common trait of Alsatian cuisine. And so we prize our vinaigrettes. When I was growing up, we made big batches of a base vinaigrette—vinegar and oil in the traditional ratio of 1 part to 3 parts respectively plus salt and pepper—and poured it into a plastic water bottle. We could just shake it up throughout the week to emulsify it and add aromatics and other ingredients à la minute for numerous vinaigrettes. (Once you've added herbs, the dressing should be used that day as the herbs don't hold well.)

Of course, the quality of the vinegar is paramount. My favorite vinegar to reach for is an aged sherry vinegar (available at good grocery stores). But you can use any good vinegar (the only vinegar I don't like, and rarely use, is balsamic vinegar). Remember, a vinaigrette should be strong so that you don't have to use much. You should dress the greens lightly—you shouldn't be able to eat a vinaigrette and greens like soup.

Here is the base, a traditional 3 parts oil, 1 part vinegar, for an herb vinaigrette, a shallot and garlic vinaigrette (vinegar softens these alliums), and a creamy vinaigrette. And please note that any vinaigrette is really elevated by a small addition of a nut oil, such as walnut—I love finishing vinaigrettes this way.

FOR THE BASE VINAIGRETTE

Salt (start with ½ teaspoon, as the vinegar should taste salty)

2½ to 3 tablespoons aged sherry vinegar, sherry, or red wine vinegar

Pepper

½ cup (120 ml) grapeseed oil or other neutral oil

Combine the salt and vinegar in a mixing bowl and whisk to dissolve the salt, then add the pepper. Whisk in the oil. This can be stored for a week in the fridge.

HERB VINAIGRETTE

This is a vinaigrette to use with delicate lettuces. The addition of a nut oil, while optional, adds one more layer of flavor that I really love. Our hands-down favorite brand is J. LeBlanc—expensive but really delicious.

Add 1 tablespoon each of chopped parsley, chervil, and chives to ½ cup (120 ml) of the vinaigrette base and whisk to combine. Finish, optionally, with a tablespoon of nut oil—walnut, hazelnut, or pistachio. The dressing should be served the same day it is made.

GARLIC AND SHALLOT VINAIGRETTE

This is a great vinaigrette for heartier, crunchy lettuces such as frisée, escarole, and romaine. It is perfect for leeks; just braise some leeks in water or vegetable stock until tender, pour vinaigrette over them and top with chopped, hard-boiled egg.

Add ¼ teaspoon garlic paste and 1 tablespoon minced shallot to the vinaigrette base, whisking to combine. Allow the vinaigrette to rest for 20 to 30 minutes so that the shallot and garlic temper and infuse the dressing. The dressing should be served the same day it is made.

CREAMY VINAIGRETTE

Use this vinaigrette for a tomato or endive salad. Again, as for all vinaigrettes, the addition of just a little nut oil adds great nuance to the dressing's flavor.

Whisk 1 teaspoon Dijon mustard, 1 tablespoon sour cream or mayonnaise, 2 tablespoons finely minced onion, and 1 to 2 tablespoons water into the vinaigrette base. Allow the vinaigrette to rest for 20 to 30 minutes, so that the onion tempers and infuses the dressing. The dressing should be served the same day it is made.

MUNSTER CHEESE SOUFFLÉ

Serves 8

Here is a traditional cheese soufflé—a béchamel sauce enriched with egg yolk and cheese, combined with meringue to make it rise—using the wonderful cheese from the Alsatian town of Munster. Don't confuse it with the American version of Muenster cheese. Try to find actual Munster or some of the good American versions that have recently become available, such as Oma.

When I was a kid, my mother would make soufflés like this when she had leftover cheese. You could also serve it as a cheese course in a longer menu or as a meal with a simple green salad. I created this version because a friend was convinced he hated Munster cheese. I served him this, he ate every bit, and pronounced it excellent. He couldn't believe it when I told him what cheese it was. People who don't like strong cheeses think they don't like Munster because it's so strong smelling—but really it's a mild, wonderful cheese.

A great way to cook any soufflé is using a cast-iron pan. Put the pan in the oven while the oven is preheating. Ramekins set directly on the iron surface will conduct the heat more efficiently for a better rise in the soufflé. And a note about the roux: As a rule, the roux and the liquid it is intended to thicken should be opposite temperatures. For small amounts of liquid, it's easiest to add cold liquid to hot roux. If you're thickening big batches of liquid, it's more efficient to bring the liquid to a simmer first and add cold roux.

2 tablespoons (30 g) butter, plus a little more for preparing the ramekins
⅓ cup (40 g) all-purpose flour, plus a little more for preparing the ramekins
1½ cups (360 ml) milk
Salt and freshly ground black pepper
Freshly grated nutmeg
5 ounces (150 g) real Munster cheese (or, if unavailable, Munster-style cheese such as Oma), cut into large chunks
4 eggs, separated

Preheat your oven to 350°F (175°C).

In a saucepan over medium heat, melt the butter, then stir in the flour, cooking it for 3 to 4 minutes, or until the flour smells like pie crust and the roux is bubbling (*fleurir*, in French, or flowering). Turn the heat to medium high and add in the cold milk slowly, whisking continuously to avoid lumps, until incorporated. Bring the milk to a simmer, then reduce the heat. Season the béchamel with salt, pepper, and nutmeg. Continue to cook the béchamel for a few more minutes. This should be a very thick sauce. Add the cheese, whisking until it's melted. Again taste for seasoning. Then whisk in the yolks. Transfer the sauce to a bowl and press plastic wrap onto its surface to prevent a skin from forming. Allow it to cool to room temperature or put it in the refrigerator to cool it faster.

Prepare 8 ramekins or baking cups (they should hold about 6 ounces/180 ml) by buttering their insides and rolling some flour inside, until the entire inside of each ramekin is coated with flour and butter.

When the cheese mixture is cool, beat the egg whites with a pinch of salt to soft peaks. Gently fold a quarter of the egg whites into the cheese mix, then add the remaining whites, folding gently until they are all incorporated. You can use a whisk by gently lifting the batter into the air with it and spinning it to allow the batter to fall off. The point is to maintain as many bubbles in the meringue as possible. Divide the batter among the ramekins, filling them three-quarters full (the soufflés should more than double in height).

Bake the soufflés for 15 minutes, and serve immediately.

MY ONION TART

Serves 6 to 8

This is a highlight of Alsatian farm cuisine—a simple onion tart, with bacon and cheese. It's like a thin quiche. It uses only the simplest ingredients but when properly cooked is a supreme dish. I intensify the traditional recipe by using a puree of steamed onions as part of the custard or flan for more onion flavor and sweetness. This was a regular feature of my childhood. My mother usually served it with a green or celeriac salad.

FOR THE DOUGH

2 cups (250 g) all-purpose flour
1 stick plus 1 tablespoon (130 g) cold
    butter, diced
Salt
⅓ cup (75 ml) cold water

FOR THE FILLING

3½ to 4 pounds (1.75 kg) onions
Salt
4 ounces (125 g) applewood-smoked
    slab bacon, cut into thin strips
4 eggs
1 cup (240 ml) heavy cream
¾ cup plus 2 tablespoons (200 ml) milk
2 tablespoons chopped parsley
50 grinds pepper, or to taste
30 gratings nutmeg, or to taste
3 ounces (100 g) grated Gruyère
    (or enough to sprinkle liberally over
    the tart)

To make the dough: Blend together the flour, butter, and salt in a mixing bowl with your fingertips just until the mixture resembles coarse meal with some roughly pea-sized lumps. Add most of the ⅓ cup (75 ml) of water and mix until the dough comes together, adding more water as needed. Work the dough until it is smooth and not sticky. Wrap in plastic and let it rest in the refrigerator for 30 minutes while you prepare the taste appareil, or filling.

To make the filling: Put about three-quarters of the onions in a steamer for 1 hour or until completely tender; you can also wrap them in foil and roast them at 350°F (175°C) for the same time, or until tender. Puree them in a blender until they're completely smooth.

With the other onions, halve each one lengthwise. Take one half and put it on your cutting board. Make a slice through the middle just to the core so that it stays together and your slices are short. Slice the onion as thinly as possible, starting at the top and moving down to the core. Repeat with the remaining onions. This can be done on a mandoline as well. Put the sliced onions into a bowl, sprinkle with 1 teaspoon salt, and toss to distribute the salt.

Preheat your oven to 325°F (175°C).

When the dough has rested, roll it out and line an 11- or 12-inch (28 or 30.5 cm) tart pan with it. Poke holes in the bottom with a fork. Fill the tart with beans on parchment or foil, or use pie weights to hold the dough down, and blind bake it for 20 minutes.

Sauté the bacon in a saucepan over medium heat until cooked, lightly colored but not crispy. Remove the pan from the heat and allow the bacon pieces to cool in the pan.

Raise oven temperature to 375°F (190°C).

Beat the eggs in a mixing bowl. Whisk in the cream, milk, onion puree, sliced onion, 1 tablespoon salt, the parsley, and the pepper and nutmeg to taste.

Pour the onion mixture into the tart shell. Sprinkle the grated cheese over the top. Sprinkle the bacon evenly over the top (feel free to drizzle any rendered bacon fat over the tart as well) and bake the tart for about 40 minutes, until just set (it should jiggle but not appear liquidy). Allow it to cool for 15 minutes before serving warm, or allow it to cool completely to serve at room temperature. This will keep well wrapped in the fridge for several days.

BEIGNETS AUX POMMES

Serves 6

Apples, battered, deep-fried, and dusted with cinnamon sugar, were a staple of my childhood. We usually had them with a bean soup or split pea soup, and they would be perfect here with the beer soup (page 45)—the sweet with savory married beautifully. You could also serve them as a dessert or a sweet with coffee, dusting them with cinnamon sugar or powdered sugar, or pairing them with a compote or marmalade. These alone made us look forward to the fall days when the weather turned cold. We used an apple corer so that we had perfect discs, but you can slice and core the apple as you wish.

1½ cups (220 g) all-purpose flour
2 eggs, separated
2 tablespoons oil, preferably grapeseed
½ teaspoon salt, plus more for whipping the egg whites
1 tablespoon sugar

7 ounces (200 ml) beer
6 medium apples
½ cup (100 g) sugar
3 to 4 tablespoons (50 ml) eau de vie (optional)
Oil of your choice for deep-frying

FOR THE CINNAMON-SUGAR MIXTURE
½ cup (100 g) sugar
1 teaspoon ground cinnamon (preferably Saigon)

To make the batter, put the flour in a bowl. Add the egg yolks, oil, ½ teaspoon of the salt, and the sugar. While mixing add the beer in three batches. Make sure the batter is fully combined, without lumps. Let it rest for about 25 minutes.

Meanwhile, peel the apples, core them using a corer, and slice them into discs about ¼ inch (6 mm) thick. Put the apples in a bowl, drizzle the sugar on them so that they become softer, and add in the eau de vie, if using.

Whip the reserved egg whites with a pinch of salt to soft peaks. Fold them into the batter.

Bring a pot of oil to 350°F (175°C).

Dip the apple slices in the batter, one at a time, and put them in the hot oil. Cook for 1 minute, then flip them and cook until they are golden brown, 2 to 3 minutes in all. Remove them to a paper towel–lined plate.

Combine the sugar and cinnamon in a small bowl, sprinkle this over the cooked beignets, and serve immediately.

BONE MARROW QUENELLES

Makes 20 to 30 dumplings

We would make these to serve with soup, most commonly with a pot-au-feu bouillon, poaching them directly in the liquid. But if you have any good chicken or beef broth, these dumplings turn it into a meal. They're half bone marrow, half starch (flour and breadcrumbs) and egg, and so are very rich and very delicate. In my house growing up, we had a hand-cranked shredder and used to turn our two- or three-day-old bread into very fine breadcrumbs, called *chapelure*. Nothing went to waste. You can use a food processor and do the same!

5 ounces (150 g) beef bone marrow, at room temperature

¾ cup (70 g) chapelure (very fine breadcrumbs made from days-old bread in a food processor)

2 tablespoons semolina

1 tablespoon all-purpose flour, plus more as needed

2 eggs

½ teaspoon freshly grated nutmeg

Salt and freshly ground black pepper

2 tablespoons chopped parsley

White Chicken Stock (page 251) or beef stock, for poaching, about 1 quart/liter (depending on size of your pot)

Broth or soup, for serving

Mash the bone marrow with a fork until it's soft as butter, making sure to take out any bone fragments (it's best if you pass it through a tamis or sieve). In a mixing bowl, combine the marrow with the breadcrumbs, flours, eggs, nutmeg, about ½ teaspoon salt, ¼ teaspoon pepper, and parsley and mix until everything is uniformly dispersed. Form the mixture into balls the size of a bing cherry, rolling them in your hands with a bit of flour.

Poach a few in barely simmering chicken or beef stock for about 10 minutes. Taste them and evaluate for texture and seasoning. If they aren't holding together, add a couple more tablespoons of flour, as needed.

Poach the remaining dumplings. Serve them with broth or soup.

DAMPFNUDEL EN COCOTTE

(Steamed Buns)

Makes about 18 to 20 buns

You can make these fluffy, comforting steamed buns to accompany the savory part of the meal or serve them sweet for dessert. My father loved them sweet. I remember I made these for him at his request a year before he died of cancer, when I was fifteen. So I like to serve them his way, with poached plums, using the poaching liquid to finish the steaming (see page 115).

When serving savory ones, omit the sugar (and if you wish, poach them in stock rather than water). Whether savory or sweet, the method is the same. The dough requires three resting periods, so plan ahead. First the dough is mixed and allowed to rise. Second eggs and butter are mixed into the dough. (Why aren't they mixed in all together? I don't know. It's just how my mother always did it. Perhaps one time she forgot to add the eggs and butter, added them midway through, and then liked the result better!) The dough rises again, and then the buns are formed and allowed to rise one last time. They are browned in butter in a Dutch oven and then liquid is added, the pot is covered tightly, and they steam (not unlike pot stickers). If you open the lid before they're cooked, they can deflate and are no good to eat. These are all about the texture.

2 teaspoons (6 g) active dry yeast
  or 9 teaspoons (25 g) fresh yeast
  (preferably SAF)
1½ to 2 cups (360 to 450 ml) warm milk
4 cups (500 g) all-purpose flour,
  plus more for dusting
¼ cup (60 g) sugar
1 teaspoon salt
2 eggs, beaten
4 tablespoons (60 g) butter, at room
  temperature

TO COOK THE BUNS

4 tablespoons (60 g) butter
2 tablespoons sugar (optional, for sweet
  version)
1 cup (240 ml) prune poaching liquid, if
  making them sweet and serving with
  cooked prunes (see page 115), or
  warm sweetened water

Combine the yeast and milk in a small bowl and whisk to incorporate the yeast.

Put the flour in a large bowl and add the sugar, salt, and the milk-yeast mixture. Work it all together until you have an elastic dough (you can use a standing mixer fitted with a dough hook). Cover the bowl with a towel and let the dough double in volume, about 1 hour.

Add the eggs and butter and work it for 5 to 6 minutes, or use a standing mixer with the dough hook to mix them in. Cover the bowl with a towel and let it double in volume, 45 to 60 minutes. Punch down the dough, then roll it out to a thickness of 1 inch (2.5 cm). With a biscuit cutter or a 3- to 4-inch (7.5 to 10 cm) glass, cut the buns. Reroll the remaining dough and cut more biscuits. Put them on a flour-dusted board or baking tray, cover with a towel, and let them rise for 30 minutes.

In a large Dutch oven, heat the butter over medium-high heat and add in the sugar, if using. Place some of the buns in the pot, giving them plenty of room (don't squeeze them in), working in

batches if not all will fit. Sauté until the bottoms have browned. Add the liquid, immediately cover the pan, and lower the heat to medium. Cook them at medium heat for 7 minutes. Resist the urge to check on them, but if using sugar be careful not to burn the caramel (use your sense of smell).

Repeat for the remaining buns. Eat them while warm.

FLEISCHSCHNACKA

(Meat-Stuffed Pasta Rolls)

Serves 8

Another excellent way to use leftover meat is to make this stuffed pasta. The stuffing is similar to the one used in the stuffed potatoes (page 64), but this one uses a good amount of fresh pork shoulder, rather than bacon, and includes no bread, so it's a more meaty, dense stuffing. And it's very easy, once the pasta is made. Just roll out the dough to the size of a piece of letter paper, spread about a half inch of the stuffing over it, roll it up, then slice it. The pasta will take the shape of coiled discs, thus the name, which means "meat" (*fleisch*) "snails." *Fleischschnacka* served with a green salad is a traditional meal in Alsace. But sometimes my mother would serve it with roast duck. As with the stuffed potatoes, extra stuffing can be saved and made into meatballs or sautéed as patties. The pasta dough is very rich with yolks, and I recommend you make it, but I suppose you could buy lasagna noodles as a substitute, cooking and cooling them before using.

FOR THE PASTA DOUGH

4¼ cups (525 g) "000" flour

2 teaspoons fine salt

¾ cup plus 2 tablespoons (200 g) egg yolks (from 11 or 12 eggs)

1 egg

1 tablespoon grapeseed or other vegetable oil

1 tablespoon apple cider vinegar

FOR THE STUFFING

Butter, as needed for sweating the onion and garlic

2 small onions, chopped

2 shallots, chopped

Salt, as needed

2 cloves garlic, smashed and chopped

1 pound (450 g) cooked beef (preferably leftover from making Pot-au-Feu, page 53, but it can be any form of beef)

14 ounces (400 g) boneless pork shoulder

2 medium eggs

3 tablespoons chopped parsley

3 tablespoons chopped chives

2 tablespoons salt

30 grinds pepper

20 gratings nutmeg

TO FINISH

2 to 3 tablespoons butter, or as needed

2 to 3 tablespoons grapeseed oil, or as needed

1 to 2 quarts/liters beef stock or White Chicken Stock (page 251)

Make the pasta dough: In a standing mixer fitted with a dough hook, combine the flour and salt. Combine the egg yolks, whole egg, oil, and vinegar in a bowl and mix or whisk them until they are evenly combined. Turn the mixer on to low speed. Slowly add the wet ingredients to the flour and mix until you have a smooth elastic dough. Remove the dough to a work surface, finish kneading it by hand, then divide it into three equal portions. Form them into discs and wrap them in plastic. Let them rest at room temperature for 45 to 60 minutes or as many as 24 hours in the refrigerator.

Make the stuffing: In a medium sauté pan over medium heat, melt the butter, then add the onion and shallot, along with a pinch of salt. When the onion is tender, add the garlic and cook for a minute or so more. Remove the onions and garlic to a plate to cool.

Grind the cooked beef and the raw pork shoulder meat together in a meat grinder through a small or medium die. (It's possible to use a food processor if you pulse the mixture, careful not to let it become overly pureed; but the texture and bite are better if you use a grinder.) When the onion is cool, add it to the meat along with the remaining ingredients. Mix well by hand until all ingredients are uniformly distributed.

To finish: Roll the pasta dough pieces into three rectangular pieces, about ⅛ inch (2 to 3 mm) thick. Put each piece of rolled-out dough between clean kitchen towels or plastic wrap. Spread the stuffing evenly over the top of each sheet of pasta, about ½ inch (1.25 cm) thick. With the long side of the dough sheet facing you, begin to roll the shorter end of the pasta to make a cylinder. Slice the cylinder into ¾-inch (2 cm) slices.

Melt the butter with the oil in a large skillet. Sauté the fleischschnacka on each side until nicely browned. Add enough stock just to cover and simmer for about 15 minutes, until the pasta is tender. If you need to cook these in batches, they can be reheated or held submerged in more warm stock.

ON SPAETZLE

Spaetzle is a quickly made pasta of flour and egg from my homeland, Alsace, which is also made throughout eastern France, Germany, Switzerland, and Austria. My mother used to make spaetzle at least once a week, often with rabbit or a beef stew. But if we had some leftover sauerkraut, she'd add it to a pan of spaetzle and mix it all together as its own dish.

Mine are especially fluffy because I soften the dough with a fat, sour cream, and egg yolks, which also enriches the dough (you could also use Greek yogurt). They're boiled, cooled, then sautéed in butter so that they puff up and brown a little and have some crunchy spots.

You can buy a spaetzle "maker," or press the batter through the holes of a colander, but I think the ages-old way, and the way my mother taught me, remains the best way to make spaetzle—spread the dough into a thin sheet on a small wooden charcuterie or cheese board (about half the size of a sheet of letter-size paper), and then with an offset spatula, using quick strokes, scrape just enough of the dough off the board into the water to create thin, long noodles. When I was a young chef, we competed to see who could make the thinnest spaetzle, the thinner the better.

It's important that your cooking water is aggressively seasoned with salt. You want to poach the spaetzle at a gentle simmer, so don't allow the water to come to a hard boil, or they'll puff too much in the water; you want them to puff, like Parisienne gnocchi, when they're being sautéed.

This is a base recipe. You can add anything you like to it to vary the spaetzle. You can mix in mushroom powder or chive oil, or a handful of chopped fresh, soft herbs to the dough. Alter the flour to half buckwheat or chestnut flour (see page 202), and they will be a little softer and darker and have a nutty flavor.

These are great with sauerkraut—you can sauté both in the same pan as my mother did—or you could do the same with caramelized onion. Sometimes we take the cooked and shocked spaetzle and put them on a sizzle platter or baking sheet, drizzle them with heavy cream, add grated Comté, with a little vinegar for seasoning, and brown them under a broiler. And you don't even have to make spaetzle—you can drop the batter off a spoon into the water to form dumplings. Of course, sautéed in butter these make a great side dish for pork, chicken, or fish. Leftovers with a salad makes a great lunch.

Spaetzle, or "sparrow," is one of the preparations that truly represents my homeland, the economical, farmhouse cooking I grew up with in Alsace. The following is our standard, all-purpose recipe.

SPAETZLE

Serves 6

When I make spaetzle at home, I usually pair it with a chicken or rabbit fricassee. You could even serve them with beef stew. Think of them as you do egg noodles, only better.

4 cups (500 g) flour, sifted

2 tablespoons salt

20 grinds fresh black pepper

¼ teaspoon (about 40 gratings) fresh nutmeg

4 whole eggs

2 egg yolks

½ cup (125 g) sour cream

½ cup (125 ml) cold water

Butter, for sautéing

Neutral oil, such as grapeseed oil, if refrigerating the spaetzle before sautéing

Put the flour in a large bowl of a standing mixer fitted with the paddle attachment. (This can also be mixed by hand, using a stiff spatula or wooden spoon.) Add the salt, pepper, and nutmeg. In a second bowl combine the whole eggs, yolks, sour cream, and cold water and whisk until everything is incorporated. Add the egg mixture to the mixing bowl and paddle on high until you have a stiff, sticky dough, 1 to 2 minutes. (It will take a good 5 minutes by hand.)

These can be poached as illustrated on the opposite page. For an alternate method, press the batter through the holes of a perforated steamer pan or colander directly into boiling water.

Cook the spaetzle in batches, and when they float, they're done and can be removed to an ice bath. Drain them and dry them (there shouldn't be too much water going into the sauté pan with them). Put them in a towel-lined bowl until you're ready to sauté.

Either reheat in butter immediately or rinse the noodles a second time and toss them with a little neutral oil such as grapeseed so they don't stick and refrigerate them for up to 2 days.

Sauté them in a frying pan with the butter to give them a little color, and when they start to puff a bit they are ready to be enjoyed.

POTATO GALETTE

Serves 8

These are so delicious we made them every other week in Alsace—simple potato pancakes. My mother would serve them with split pea soup in the winter, or with sausage. They're great just as a side to a salad or served with applesauce. What makes these pancakes special is the combination of onions, shallots, and leeks, plus the chopped herb—and of course, the aggressive pepper and nutmeg seasoning.

1 pound (450 g) peeled potatoes (preferably Yukon gold or German butterball)

1 small onion

2 tablespoons finely chopped shallots

½ cup (50 g) finely chopped leek, white part only

3 tablespoons chopped parsley

Salt (start with 2 teaspoons, and taste from there)

20 grinds pepper

20 gratings nutmeg

1 or 2 eggs

2 tablespoons all-purpose flour

Grapeseed oil, for sautéing

1 cup (110 g) grated Comté cheese (optional, but excellent)

Using a medium grater, grate the potatoes. Drain them in a colander, pressing as much liquid out as possible (if you wish, collect the water, allow the starch to sink to the bottom, pour off the water, and save the starch to be added to the potatoes later). Grate the onion and add it to the potatoes along with the shallot, leeks, and parsley. Season with salt, the pepper, and nutmeg. Add 1 or 2 beaten eggs (I don't like them too eggy, but the egg will help to bind them). Add the flour (and potato starch if you saved it) and stir until everything is mixed.

In a large sauté pan, heat ¼ inch (6 mm) of oil over medium high, and when the oil's hot, add the potato mixture in about ⅓ cup (55 g) portions, spreading the potato out with the back of a spoon so that the pancakes are thin and cook as quickly as possible. When one side is nicely golden brown, flip them over. Remove them to a paper towel–lined plate and continue cooking in batches. Taste for seasoning, salting as necessary. You can also make one large pancake the size of your pan and flip it over using a spatula, or by transferring it to another pan, however you feel comfortable doing it. Serve warm.

VEAL LIVER DUMPLINGS

Serves 8

This was a favorite of my grandad's, and a staple of Alsace, very much reflecting the rustic style of the region. Often one of the farms near ours would have more calf's liver than they needed and would give extra to us. And this is what we'd make. These light but rich dumplings are served in virtually every wine salon, or *winstub*, which is the traditional Alsatian bistro, like the *bouchons* of Lyon.

The dumplings can be served with an onion sauce or a horseradish sauce (page 94). They're also fabulous with sauerkraut, or as a component in a choucroute garnie. If you serve them on their own, along with a green salad or the pot-au-feu crudités, for example, it's worth sautéing them in a pan, as there is no sauce. If you are pairing them with horseradish, you can skip that last step.

4 tablespoons (50 g) butter, plus more for sautéing the dumplings, if desired

½ teaspoon garlic paste (1 medium clove garlic)

1 cup (125 g) chopped onion

½ cup (65 g) chopped shallots

10 ounces (300 g) veal liver, peeled if necessary, cut into pieces for grinding

4½ ounces (125 g) nicely smoked bacon, cut into lardons

5 slices (3½ ounces/100 g) dry bread, soaked in milk then squeezed out

2 medium eggs

½ cup (50 g) chopped parsley

½ cup (60 g) all-purpose flour

2⅔ tablespoons (30 g) semolina

About 4 teaspoons salt, plus more for the cooking water

¼ teaspoon pepper, or to taste

½ teaspoon nutmeg, or to taste

3 tablespoons chopped parsley, to garnish

Melt the butter in a pan over medium heat and add the garlic paste, onion, and shallot. Cook them gently until tender, without giving them color. Transfer the vegetables to a plate or a bowl and refrigerate to chill them.

Pass half the liver and bacon through the fine die of a meat grinder. (Alternatively, you can use a food processor, if you don't have a meat grinder, if you're careful only to pulse the meat and not over-puree it; it helps if the liver is very cold, so put it in the freezer for 20 minutes before processing it.) Add the chilled onion mixture and soaked bread to the grinder along with the remaining liver and bacon. (If using a food processor, add this after you've partially pureed the liver, and pulse until everything is uniformly combined.)

Stir the eggs, parsley, flour, and semolina into the ground liver mixture. Season to your taste with the salt, pepper, and nutmeg. Let it sit in the fridge for at least 30 minutes or up to a day.

Bring a large pot of water to a boil and season it well with salt.

When the water boils, reduce the heat to a simmer. Using two soup spoons, make quenelles with the liver mixture and poach them for 10 to 15 minutes, until they float.

Serve immediately, or you can sauté them in butter for a more complex flavor (though I prefer them not to be caramelized).

My Mother's Horseradish Sauce (page 94)

Veal Liver Dumplings (opposite)

MY MOTHER'S HORSERADISH SAUCE

**Makes about 2 cups
(480 ml)**

Horseradish grows wild all over Alsace, and in the fall we would go out picking it. My grandfather would sit listening to his 1950s radio, grating fifteen or twenty roots, crying the whole time from the fumes. He would sprinkle a little lemon juice or vinegar over the gratings to keep the horseradish very white.

This is one of my favorite sauces, my mother's recipe, an easy, all-purpose, piquant, creamy sauce for dumplings, for liver quenelles (see Veal Liver Dumplings, page 92), for fish, or for beef tongue. It goes perfectly with beef, so we serve it along with the meats from pot-au-feu. The long-cooked meats benefit from the contrast of the rich, spicy sauce, which has a touch of sweetness from the sugar. It should be a heavy nappé consistency (you should be able to draw a line through the sauce on the back of a spatula). If it's too loose, thicken it with a bit of slurry (a tablespoon of cornstarch mixed with a tablespoon of water added to the hot liquid). It can be served hot or cold.

1 tablespoon butter

2 tablespoons all-purpose flour

1 cup (60 g) finely grated horseradish,
    or more to taste

1 tablespoon sugar

Salt

20 grinds pepper

1½ cups (360 ml) White Chicken Stock
    (page 251)

½ cup (125 ml) crème fraîche

2 tablespoons sour cream

Several gratings nutmeg

Lemon juice

In a saucepan, melt the butter over medium heat. Whisk in the flour and cook it gently for 2 minutes or so, without giving it color. Next, add the horseradish, sugar, salt, and pepper. Cook a little more, then add the chicken stock, crème fraiche, and sour cream and bring to a boil. Reduce the heat and let it simmer for at least 10 to 15 minutes. Finish it at the end with a couple of gratings of nutmeg. Taste for seasoning and finish with some lemon juice, to wake it up. Store covered in the fridge for up to 3 days.

SCHMALTZ KNEPFLE

(Schmaltz Dumplings)

Makes enough for 8 servings

This is an old Jewish recipe, all about using leftovers—these schmaltz dumplings (matzo flour would work well for these) use day-old bread, which is cut in medium to small dice and toasted, so it has some crunch, and then folded into the dough. The first time I did this, adding bread to spaetzle dough, my cooks thought I was crazy. But this is the style of cooking—poor country cooking. Nothing is wasted and the results are delicious.

As with the spaetzle, you only want to poach them, not cook them at a rolling boil—this way they will puff slightly when they're sautéed in butter or schmaltz. And, like spaetzle, these can be done two days ahead and refrigerated. I love how, also like spaetzle, each one is a different shape, a subtle reminder that they're homemade.

These dumplings are enriched with schmaltz, rendered chicken fat flavored with onion. If you make your own schmaltz, these are a real treat. And then you sauté them in schmaltz to finish them—so delicious. But you can make these with a neutral-flavored oil. Any such fat will soften their texture. The more fat you use, the softer the dumpling will be. It should be an elastic but stiff dough. I really work this dough to give it a good elasticity.

You can do anything you want with them. They make a great side dish for veal breast, chicken, rabbit, fish, or pork and a mustard sauce. I like to add a garnish on top—such as chopped parsley, roasted onions, or caramelized sauerkraut. Or just throw sauerkraut in with them as they're browning. They're often mixed with lentils and some jus, and just served like that. They're fabulous with a poached egg. Or drizzle them with cream, top with compote, season with a few drops of vinegar, and gratiné under a broiler.

10 ounces (300 ml) schmaltz or a neutral oil, such as grapeseed oil, plus more if refrigerating the dumplings before serving

6 eggs

4 cups (500 g) all-purpose flour

½ teaspoon salt, plus more as needed

¼ teaspoon pepper

½ teaspoon freshly grated nutmeg

1½ cups (400 g) croutons (see Note)

Combine the schmaltz or oil and eggs in a bowl and whisk until they're uniformly mixed.

Combine the flour, salt, pepper, and nutmeg in a large mixing bowl. Add the egg mixture and stir with a rubber spatula until incorporated. Add ½ cup (120 ml) of water, stirring it in, and keep adding more water, up to another ½ cup (120 ml), until you have an elastic dough. It should take 5 to 10 minutes of vigorous stirring with the spatula. Taste some of the dough and adjust the seasoning as necessary. Stir in the croutons and mix until they are uniformly dispersed.

Bring a tall pot of water to a boil, add a good handful of salt (it should taste well-seasoned), then reduce to a simmer. Drop the dumplings from a spoon (they should be the size and shape of a quail egg) into the water. Remove them to an ice bath when they rise to the surface. Drain them and pat dry and either use immediately or toss them with some oil and refrigerate for up to 2 days before reheating.

Note: To make your own croutons, cut the bread into ⅓-inch (8 mm) dice (you'll need about 1½ cups) and sauté them in butter over medium heat until they're crisp. Cool completely on a rack or paper towel.

BREADS, DESSERTS, AND DRINKS

ALSATIAN BRAIDED PAIN AU PAVOT

Makes one 1¾-pound (800 g) loaf or if divided, makes two 400 g loaves

This braided, challah-like bread, called *berches* in Germany, which we would make once or twice a week at home, is an expression of the happy coexistence of the Jewish and Catholic cultures that dominated the region. Unlike challah, this contains dairy, but if you're avoiding dairy, the milk in the recipe can easily be replaced with water. It's a very versatile dough that can be savory or sweet, topped with sesame or poppy seeds. It can be eaten for breakfast or served with dinner. If you have time, mix the yeast and one-fourth of the flour and milk for at least 15 minutes and as long as several hours before mixing the dough to create a levain for more flavor.

4 cups (500 g) all-purpose flour

¾ cup plus 2 tablespoons (200 ml) warm milk or water

20 grams fresh yeast or 2 teaspoons dry yeast

1 egg, beaten

6 tablespoons (90 ml) grapeseed oil or melted butter

2 to 3 tablespoons (30 to 45 g) sugar (or less if you want it less sweet)

½ tablespoon salt

Egg wash (2 egg yolks mixed with 2 tablespoons heavy cream or milk)

Sesame or poppy seeds, as needed for garnish

In the bowl of a standing mixer fitted with a dough hook, combine 2 tablespoons of the flour, 2 tablespoons warm milk, and the yeast. Stir to dissolve the yeast and let rest for 15 minutes. Add three-quarters of the remaining flour, the egg, oil, sugar, and salt, and mix on medium speed until the dough comes together, adding the rest of the flour as needed. Continue to mix until the dough is elastic and no longer sticks to the bowl.

Cover the mixing bowl and allow it to rise, 45 minutes to 1 hour (it should almost double in size, and look neither stiff nor overly inflated; if you press a finger into the dough, the dough should give some resistance but maintain the indentation).

Turn the dough onto a cutting board and punch it down. Cut the dough into three equal pieces. Roll each into cylinders about 2 feet (60 cm) long. Pinch the ends of the three pieces together, and fold them under the bread to hold them. Braid the bread by crossing the left most cylinder over the center cylinder. Fold the right most cylinder over the left, and continue braiding until done. Place on a baking sheet covered with a towel to proof for 30 to 40 minutes, depending on the ambient temperature of your kitchen.

Preheat your oven to 400°F (205°C).

When the dough has risen for 30 minutes, brush the dough with the egg wash. Sprinkle the dough with poppy seeds and bake for about 30 minutes, until cooked through.

KOUGELHOPF

Serves 6 to 8

Kougelhopf is an Alsatian staple, our Bundt cake, gently sweet and with a delicate crumb. We eat it on Sunday mornings with coffee and with a glass of wine in the afternoon. It's usually sweet but can be savory, made with escargot or bacon. My mother made sweet kougelhopf and we'd slather our pieces with her marmalades and preserves, which she still makes—plum, quince, apple jelly, raspberry, strawberry, black cherry, and pear. She used to make 160 kilos of these confitures and clear gelées. She'll only make 10 kilos today. They're delicious, and are a great accompaniment to this cake. Try this with your favorite local jam. It's important that all ingredients are at room temperature, unless otherwise noted.

6½ ounces (200 ml) warm milk

9 teaspoons (25 g) fresh yeast

3¾ cups (475 g) all-purpose flour

½ cup (65 g) raisins, preferably golden but any kind will do

3 to 4 tablespoons (50 ml) kirsch (optional)

1 teaspoon salt

⅓ cup (75 g) granulated sugar

2 medium eggs

¾ cup (180 g) butter, plus more for the mold

Whole almonds, as needed (optional)

Confectioners' sugar, for finishing

An hour or so before you begin, make a levain by combining half the milk with the yeast and enough flour to make a batter (generous ¾ cup/100 g or so). (While this step is not strictly necessary, making a levain elevates the flavor.)

In a small dish, combine the raisins and kirsch.

In the bowl of a standing mixer fitted with a dough hook, combine the remaining scant 2¼ cups (325 g) flour, the salt, granulated sugar, eggs, and the remaining milk. Mix this dough for 10 to 15 minutes on low. Add the butter and the levain (it should have doubled in volume). Mix the dough on medium high for another 5 minutes, or until the dough no longer sticks to the bowl and is soft and pliable. Cover the bowl with a towel and let it rest for about an hour, until it has doubled in size. Poke it with your finger; the indent should remain, not spring back, but nor should the dough feel flabby and overly inflated.

Using a stiff rubber spatula, puncture the dough and stir in the kirsch-soaked raisins.

Butter your kougelhopf mold or Bundt mold, preferably a fluted one, 10½ inches (26 cm) in diameter. If it's fluted, as a traditional Alsatian mold is, put one almond in each indentation, if using. If you don't have a fluted mold, just place the almonds, if using, around the perimeter of the mold. Add the dough to the mold. Cover it with a towel and allow it to rise for 45 to 60 minutes.

Preheat your oven to 375°F (190°C).

Bake for 50 minutes to 1 hour, until a cake tester comes out clean. If the kougelhopf starts to get too dark during the baking, cover it with a piece of parchment paper and reduce the oven temperature to 350°F (175°C).

When its cooked, remove the cake from the oven, and turn it over on a cookie rack, wait 3 to 4 minutes, then remove the mold. Let it cool completely, then sprinkle with confectioners' sugar.

GSUNDHEITSKUECHE

(Good Health Cake)

Serves 8

This is a cake that every farmer would always have on hand for visitors who might stop by. Easy to make, it holds up to a week if stored well, in an airtight container (not wrapped in plastic). It's essentially flavored solely by eggs, butter, vanilla, and sometimes a splash of schnapps. It's like a lighter pound cake with a nice crust. This is delicious for breakfast or as a snack with afternoon tea or coffee. This was a recipe from my mother. I used to make it by hand to learn how to bake from scratch, but a much easier and more efficient way to make it is to use a standing mixer.

1 stick plus 1 tablespoon (130 g) very soft butter, plus more for the loaf mold

1¼ cups (165 g) all-purpose flour, sifted, plus more for the loaf mold

1½ teaspoons baking powder

1 teaspoon salt

3½ ounces (105 g) confectioners' sugar, plus more (optional) for dusting

3 eggs, separated

1 tablespoon schnapps or kirschwasser brandy, or zest of 1 lemon

2 tablespoons honey

1 tablespoon vanilla sugar or ½ teaspoon vanilla extract

5 tablespoons (75 ml) warm milk (warm it for 20 to 30 seconds in the microwave)

Glaçage (see Caprice au Kirsch, page 124; optional)

Preheat your oven to 360°F (180°C).

Butter and flour a standard loaf cake mold (8½ by 4½ by 2½ inches/22 by 10 by 6 cm).

Sift all the dry ingredients together: the flour, baking powder, and salt. Mix together well and set aside.

In the bowl of a standing mixer fitted with a whisk attachment, add, in the following order, the butter, confectioners' sugar, yolks, schnapps, honey, and vanilla sugar. Start mixing slowly until everything is well integrated, then increase to the highest speed and whip until the yolks are pale and fluffy (about 8 minutes). Reduce the spead to low, and whisk in the warm milk. Once it's incorporated, increase the speed to high for 6 minutes. Reduce the speed to low one more time, and add the dry ingredients. Mix until well incorporated, about 1 minute.

Meanwhile, in another mixing bowl, whip the egg whites to soft peaks.

Take the first mixing bowl off the stand and scrape everything down with a rubber spatula. Slowly fold in the egg whites.

Pour the batter into the mold and bake for 10 minutes. Take a knife, dip it in oil or butter to grease it, open the oven, and quickly make a shallow lengthwise cut in the center of the cake to ensure that the crust breaks. Immediately close the oven and continue baking for 30 to 32 more minutes, or until a paring knife inserted in the middle comes out clean.

Upon removing it from the oven, let it rest about 7 minutes on a rack. Then turn the cake out of the mold and let it cool completely on the rack. Before serving, finish with the glaçage or confectioners' sugar, if using.

TRADITIONAL RED WINE CAKE

Serves 8 to 10

While this is a simple cake, which we eat with coffee or tea and sometimes for dessert, the flavor combination of red wine and chocolate can't be beat. This cake is another example of the delicious simplicity of Alsatian cuisine. You can make the cake in a standing mixer with a whisk attachment, but I like doing it the way my mother did it, by hand.

1 cup (2 sticks/230 g) very soft butter, plus extra for buttering the pan

Scant 2 cups (250 g) all-purpose flour

1 tablespoon unsweetened cocoa powder (not Dutch process)

4 teaspoons (15 g) baking powder

½ teaspoon ground nutmeg

1 teaspoon salt

3 ounces (90 g) 66% or 70% dark chocolate, grated against the largest holes of a box grater, or cut into small pieces with a large-serrated knife

250 grams (about 1 cup) granulated sugar

1 tablespoon vanilla sugar or 1 teaspoon vanilla extract

3 tempered eggs

1¼ cup (315 ml) red wine (something full-bodied, such as a Cabernet Sauvignon)

TO FINISH THE CAKE

2 cups (200 g) sifted confectioners' sugar

3 tablespoons unsweetened cocoa powder

Preheat your oven to 350°F (175°C).

Butter and flour a standard 9½-inch (24 cm) bundt pan or round spring-form pan.

In a bowl, add the flour, cocoa powder, baking powder, nutmeg, and salt, and mix well. Sift the mixture and then add in the grated chocolate. Mix well and set aside.

In the bowl of a standing mixer fitted with a whisk attachment, mix the very soft butter with the granulated sugar and vanilla sugar or extract on high until it's thoroughly combined, pale, and almost frothy, and the sugar is mostly dissolved, about 8 minutes.

When this mixture is uniformly combined, add the eggs one at a time, whipping the mixture until each egg is fully incorporated. Beat on high for 5 more minutes.

Remove the mixing bowl and, using a rubber spatula, fold in one-third of the wine, followed by one-third of the combined dry ingredients. Repeat two more times until all ingredients are incorporated.

Pour the batter into the pan. Bake for 45 to 50 minutes. To check for doneness, stick a toothpick or paring knife into the center of the cake; if it comes out dry, the cake is done.

Let the cake cool for 7 to 8 minutes on a cookie rack before removing from the pan.

When the cake is completely cool, combine the confectioners' sugar with the cocoa powder and 3 tablespoons water or red wine, and stir until combined and smooth. Add more water as needed to get to a honey-like consistency. Put a platter below the rack to catch any drippings, and slowly drizzle the icing over the cake. Let the cake rest for 30 minutes to 1 hour, then serve it along with some whipped cream or the vanilla crème from the Île Flotante (page 120), or, even better, the White Wine Mousse (page 119). This cake tastes even better the next day: Store overnight at room temperature under an upside-down salad bowl.

BETTELMANN

(Beggar's Cake with Cherries)

Serves 8 to 10

We never throw anything away, and this is a good example, as it's a cake made from old bread. It's a simple cake baked in a casserole dish and makes a great dessert. For the very old-school beggar's cake, you wouldn't even pit the cherries, but I recommend taking that extra step for a more enjoyable eating experience. You can make this cake even more elegant by adding chopped chocolate to the mixture and then spooning the anglaise sauce from the Île Flotante recipe (page 120) over it to serve. It can be eaten warm or at room temperature.

2 cups (500 ml) milk

10 or 12 slices (250 g) dry white bread
   (it can be 3 days old)

3 tablespoons kirsch

⅔ cup (120 g) granulated sugar

1 tablespoon vanilla sugar or ¼ teaspoon
   vanilla extract

1 teaspoon ground cinnamon
   (preferably Saigon)

4 eggs, separated

1 cup (125 g) almond flour

1 pound (450 g) black cherries, pitted,
   or blackberries

Pinch salt

Butter for greasing the casserole,
   plus 2 tablespoons for dotting the
   top of the cake

Chapelure (very fine breadcrumbs), as
   needed for dusting the baking dish

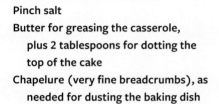

Preheat your oven to 400°F (205°C).

In a saucepan, bring the milk to a boil. Pour it over the bread and when the bread has soaked it up and the milk has cooled, break the bread apart. Pass the bread through a food mill into a mixing bowl. Add the kirsch, granulated sugar, vanilla sugar, and cinnamon. Mix very well and then stir in the egg yolks, almond flour, and cherries. Mix well again.

In a mixing bowl, combine the egg whites and salt. Beat the whites until they form soft peaks. Fold the whites into the bread mixture with a spatula.

Butter a 13 by 8½ by 3-inch (33 by 22 by 8 cm) casserole dish, and dust it with the chapelure, reserving some breadcrumbs for the top of the cake.

Pour the cake mixture into the prepared casserole and finish the top with a couple pieces of butter and some chapelure.

Bake for 1 hour or until a knife inserted into the cake comes out dry. Cool in the casserole on a cooling rack.

PAIN D'ÉPICES ALSACIEN

Makes two 8½-inch (21 cm) loaf cakes

This is a traditional holiday bread, in the same family as American gingerbread, but much more complex given that it uses both wheat and rye flour, is loaded with spices, and is rich with honey, sugar, and butter. Like many heavily spiced foods, this spiced bread should rest for 36 hours in an airtight container before being served so that the flavors can develop.

2¾ cups (350 g) all-purpose flour, sifted

1⅓ cups (205 g) rye flour, sifted

2½ teaspoons baking powder

7 teaspoons ground cinnamon (preferably Saigon)

2½ teaspoons ground ginger

2 teaspoons ground star anise

1 teaspoon ground cloves

1 teaspoon ground cardamom

1 teaspoon freshly grated nutmeg

2 teaspoons salt

¾ cup plus 2 tablespoons (200 g) butter, plus 2 tablespoons for the molds

2 cups (500 ml) good honey

¾ cup plus 2 tablespoons (200 g) packed brown sugar

4 eggs, beaten

Preheat your oven to 350°F (175°C).

Mix the flours and baking powder together in the bowl of a standing mixer fitted with a paddle. Add the cinnamon, ginger, star anise, cloves, cardamom, nutmeg, and salt.

Combine the butter and honey in a saucepan over medium heat until the butter has melted and combined with the honey and is warm but not hot. Add the brown sugar and eggs and stir to combine. Pour this mixture into the flour and spices with the mixer on medium. Mix until the ingredients are well combined.

Butter two 8½ by 4½ by 2½-inch (22 by 10 by 6 cm) loaf molds. Pour the batter in the molds and bake for 30 minutes, then reduce the oven temperature to 300°F (150°C) and bake for another 20 minutes, or until a paring knife inserted in the middle comes out clean. Remove from the oven and turn the cakes out of the molds onto a cooling rack. When cool, store the cakes, covered, at room temperature for at least 36 hours before serving.

APPLE TART À L'ALSACIENNE

Makes one 11-inch (28 cm) tart

An Alsatian tart is distinguished from other French tarts in that the fruit is baked with a custard. My mom would bake three tarts at a time in our wood-burning oven while she was also making dozens of cookies. And when I was apprenticing for my uncle, I'd make twenty of these a day!

We make tarts using all kinds of fruit: prune, plum, pitted cherries, apricots, and peaches, and the tarts are all made the same way, no matter the fruit, though for very moist fruits such as plums and peaches we usually line the bottom of the tart crust with very fine breadcrumbs, *chapelure* in French, to absorb excess moisture. And you can vary the crust as well. Sometimes we use a yeasted dough. Sometimes, if we're making Kougelhopf (page 103) as well, we make a little extra dough and use that to make a crust.

Here the tart is apple—I prefer Honeycrisps because of their sweetness and how their texture holds up to the baking—and the fruit slices ring the tart pan, creating an attractive rosette. When you pour the custard into the tart pan with the fruit, it will only partially fill the pan, leaving a quarter of the apple slices exposed, so that their edges get nicely browned while baking. Some people sprinkle sugar on top or glaze it with apricot preserves to make it shiny, but I like it just as it is.

2½ pounds (1 kg) crisp sweet apples (5 or 6 medium apples)

1 recipe Basic Tart Dough (recipe follows), blind-baked in an 11-inch (28 cm) tart pan (reserve some of the dough before rolling it out for patching any holes in the baked shell)

1¼ cups (300 ml) half-and-half

3 eggs

Scant ½ cup (80 g) granulated sugar

1 tablespoon vanilla sugar or ¼ teaspoon vanilla extract

½ teaspoon ground cinnamon (preferably roasted Saigon cinnamon)

Preheat your oven to 400°F (205°C).

Peel the apples, cut them into quarters lengthwise, and cut out the core. Cut each quarter into 4 or 5 thin wedges. Starting from the outside rim, put the apple slices, thick edge up, all along the perimeters slightly overlapping them. Continue in this way until you have filled the tart shell. It should look like a rosette when done. Bake for 20 to 25 minutes, until the apples are partially cooked and slightly browned.

To make the custard, put the half-and-half in a pan over high heat and bring to a simmer, then remove from the heat. In a separate bowl, whisk the eggs, then whisk in the granulated sugar, vanilla sugar, and cinnamon. Slowly add the hot half-and-half to the eggs, whisking continuously. Using hot half-and-half begins the cooking so the tart needs to spend less time in the oven.

When the apples are tender, reduce the oven temperature to 325°F (165°C). If you notice any cracks in the shell, patch them with a little reserved dough. Pour the custard into the tart shell with the apples. Bake for an another 15 to 20 minutes, until the custard is set.

Let the custard rest for about 10 minutes, then remove the tart from the mold, and let it cool completely on a wire rack.

BASIC TART DOUGH

This is a basic dough enriched with egg and a little milk. It is a perfect dough for most tarts, including the Apple Tart à l'Alsacienne. When you are just making the dough for one tart, as we are here, it's easiest to mix the dough by hand, but you can also use a mixer with a dough hook attachment. For a spiced tart dough, add a teaspoon each of cloves and nutmeg. This recipe also includes instructions for how to blind-bake tart or pie crusts, as we often bake the crust of tarts and pies before we fill them and cook the tart or pie itself to ensure a crisp and delicious crust. But it must be weighted down or it can buckle and bulge in the center.

Makes enough dough to line a 10- to 12-inch (25 to 30 cm) tart pan

3 cups (375 g) all-purpose flour, sifted, plus more as needed

¼ cup (50 g) plus about 3½ tablespoons sugar

1 tablespoon vanilla sugar or ¼ teaspoon vanilla extract

Pinch salt

⅔ cup (150 g) cold butter, diced, plus more for the tart mold

1 egg

7 tablespoons (100 ml) milk

In the bowl of a standing mixer fitted with a dough hook attachment, combine the flour, sugar, vanilla sugar (if using extract, add it later with the milk), and the salt. With the machine running on medium speed, add the butter and mix until you have a mealy mixture.

Beat the egg and add to it the milk, mixing it well, then gradually add it little by little to the flour, continuing to mix until the dough forms a ball. Wrap the dough in plastic and let it rest for at least an hour before using it, or up to several hours at room temperature or 24 hours refrigerated.

When ready to use, butter a 10- to 12-inch (25 to 30 cm) tart pan. Pinch off a small ball of dough to use to patch potential holes in the baked shell. Roll the rest of the dough out on a floured surface to about ⅛ inch (3 mm) thick. Lift the dough into the buttered tart mold, making sure you press it down into the corners, so that when it's cooking, the sides don't collapse. Prick the bottom of the tart many times with a fork.

To blind bake the crust, preheat your oven to 325°F (163°C). Line your tart shell with parchment paper (or aluminum foil) and fill the shell with inexpensive dried legumes, such as chickpeas. Bake the crust for 20 minutes, then remove the parchment and legumes (save the legumes in a plastic zip-top bag labeled "for blind baking" as they can be used over and over). Bake the dough for another 15 minutes, or until it is pleasantly golden brown.

Allow the blind-baked shell to cool before filling it.

TARTE AU FROMAGE BLANC

(Alsatian Cheesecake)

Serves 8 to 10

I love the cheesecake in New York, dense and delicious and full of calories. Everybody in Alsace makes this tart au fromage, which is very much like an American cheesecake, but so much airier! This cake is so light that it's almost fluffy and it includes a tart crust. It uses the fresh cheese of the region, fromage blanc, worth seeking out for this preparation. Again, as with the Bibeleskaes (page 34), you can use a high-quality ricotta pureed with a little milk, cream, or quark cheese, but fromage blanc is best.

I use a 9½-inch (24 cm) pan that's 2 inches (5 cm) deep. You can use a cake pan lined with parchment or a springform pan of that size as well.

1 recipe Basic Tart Dough (page 110), prepared only through the mixing and resting steps

Scant ¼ cup (25 g) all-purpose flour, plus more for rolling out the dough

About 1½ cups (325 g) fromage blanc (see headnote)

About ½ cup (125 g) granulated sugar (keep 1 tablespoon back for the egg whites later)

1 tablespoon vanilla sugar or 1 teaspoon vanilla extract

4 eggs, separated

⅓ cup (50 g) cornstarch

Scant 1½ cups (350 ml) heavy cream

Zest of ½ lemon

Confectioners' sugar, for dusting

Preheat your oven to 325°F (165°C).

Roll out the tart dough on a floured surface to a thickness of about ⅛ inch (3 mm), and line a 9½-inch (24 cm) cake pan or springform pan with it. Blind bake it (see page 111). When it's done, remove it and raise the oven temperature to 375°F (190°C).

Mix the cheese with the granulated sugar, vanilla sugar, and egg yolks, and whisk to thoroughly combine.

Whisk the cornstarch and flour into the cream. Add the lemon zest and whisk very well again. Whisk this mixture into the cheese mixture.

Combine the reserved granulated sugar and egg whites in a mixing bowl (the sugar prevents the whites from becoming grainy) and beat them until they form soft peaks. Gently fold them into the cheese mixture using a rubber spatula, trying to avoid popping bubbles in the meringue as much as possible (this is the critical step for an excellent texture). Pour the cheese batter into the tart pan and bake for 40 to 45 minutes. It should be jiggly, but not liquid, when you lightly shake the pan, and the top will be deeply browned and show lovely bright cracks.

Allow the tart to cool completely (it will deflate a bit) before dusting with confectioners' sugar and serving.

MY GRANDFATHER'S CINNAMON-PRUNE PIE

Serves 8

This is a simple tart, filled with a custard heavily seasoned with cinnamon and topped with prunes. People shy away from prunes in America, but I love them. When I was growing up my grandfather Michel, who lived with us on the farm, made dried prunes himself, and we always had some sort of fruit at the end of a meal. I have such great memories of using prunes. In this pie, we would stew them to plump them up and use the flavorful stewing liquid instead of milk to steam buns (page 84). This is classic Alsace. And I like to use Saigon cinnamon—the most fragrant and elegant variety. Frankly the custard and prunes are what this is all about, but I like to add a layer of whipped cream for more fun and nuts for crunch. And the crust is also spiced.

FOR THE STEWED PRUNES

1½ cups (250 g) pitted prunes
2 tablespoons sugar
1 to 2 tablespoons prune eau de vie

FOR THE TART SHELL

3 cups (375 g) all-purpose flour, sifted
2 sticks plus 2 tablespoons (250 g)
    butter, small diced and chilled
2 teaspoons sugar
1 teaspoon salt
2 teaspoons freshly grated nutmeg
1½ teaspoons ground cloves
1 egg yolk
6 tablespoons (90 ml) milk

FOR THE CUSTARD

1½ cups (350 g) heavy cream or
    half-and-half
2 eggs
2 egg yolks
4 tablespoons (50 g) sugar
1 tablespoon ground cinnamon
    (preferably Saigon)

TO GARNISH

½ cup (120 ml) whipped cream
    (optional)
Toasted chopped walnuts (optional)

Prepare the prunes: In a saucepan over high heat, combine the sugar with a generous ⅔ cup (150 ml) of water and bring to a boil. Remove from the heat and pour it over the prunes. Let the prunes sit at least 3 hours or overnight. Strain the prunes, then chop them to create a marmalade-like paste. Stir in the eau de vie.

Make the tart shell: Combine the flour and butter and mix them by hand, pinching the butter, until the butter-flour has a mealy texture. Add the sugar, salt, nutmeg, and cloves. Mix to distribute the seasonings. Add the yolk and mix by hand until the dough just comes together. Don't overwork it. Let it rest for 10 to 20 minutes. Meanwhile, preheat your oven to 340°F (170°C).

Roll the dough out to fit a 9½-inch (24 cm) pie pan. Put it in the pie pan, shaping it to the mold. Fill the shell with dried beans or pie weights and blind bake it (see page 111) for 20 to 25 minutes. Remove the beans or pie weights. If the bottom of the crust is still pale and soft, poke the bottom of the pastry with a fork and bake for another 10 minutes until the bottom of the crust is cooked. Leave the oven on, but lower it to 325°F (165°C).

Make the custard: In a saucepan over high heat, bring the cream to a boil, then set aside. Combine the eggs, yolks, sugar, and cinnamon in a large bowl, and whisk to combine uniformly. While whisking constantly, pour one-third of the hot cream into the yolks and continue whisking to temper them. At that point, whisk in the rest of the hot cream.

To complete the tart: Pour the custard into the baked tart shell and bake for 12 to 15 minutes. Allow the custard to cool and set up. Spread the prunes evenly across the top of the tart. If you wish, you can top the prunes with a layer of whipped cream and a sprinkling of toasted chopped walnuts.

LAMB BISCUIT

Serves 6 to 8

This is a lovely, delicate cake, slightly sweet and seasoned with vanilla, that we make in Alsace, typically in charming lamb-shaped cake molds, at Easter. The molds are made in Soufflenheim, the pottery capital of Alsace, where my mother is from. If you go to Alsace (page 134), this village is a must-visit for any cooking enthusiast. You see them in all the stores at that time of year. They're fun, festive cakes. I used to make these to give as gifts when I was chef at the Ritz in Manhattan. I brought a hundred lamb-shaped molds back from Alsace, although I have seen similar molds for sale in the U.S., and this can be made in a traditional cake mold, angel food cake pan, or springform pan. It's a light cake not unlike an angel food cake. This recipe will fill a standard 8½-inch (22 cm) loaf pan, or a 9-inch (23 cm) round cake pan, if you don't have a lamb mold.

FOR THE MOLD
4 tablespoons (50 g) butter, softened
⅓ cup (50 g) all-purpose flour, sifted

FOR THE CAKE
6 eggs, separated
2 whole eggs
½ cup (135 g) plus 2 tablespoons
    granulated sugar
1 tablespoon vanilla sugar or
    1 tablespoon granulated sugar
    plus ¼ teaspoon vanilla extract
1 cup (125 g) all-purpose flour, sifted
½ cup (65 g) cornstarch
1 pinch salt
Confectioners' sugar, as needed for
    dusting the finished cake

Preheat your oven to 350°F (175°C).

Butter your cake mold, then dust with the flour.

For the cake, combine the yolks and 2 whole eggs in a bowl with ½ cup (135 g) of the granulated sugar and the vanilla sugar, and whip them until the mixture is thick and creamy.

Sift the flour and cornstarch together.

In a separate mixing bowl, combine the whites and the salt. Whip them until they reach soft peaks.

Fold the whites mixture gently into the yolks until everything is uniformly mixed. Last, fold in the flour-cornstarch mixture.

Pour the batter into your mold or molds and bake for about 40 minutes. Turn off the oven, open the oven door, and leave the cake in the oven for about 8 minutes. As this is a cake without baking powder, the abrupt change in temperature, if it's removed immediately, causes the cake to collapse. The slow cooling within the oven will avoid this, and the surface of the cake will hold itself together and stay light and fluffy. While the cake is still warm, take it out of the mold and cool it on a rack. When it has cooled completely, sprinkle with confectioners' sugar.

ZIMETSCHNITTE

(Alsatian French Toast or Pain Perdu)

Serves 6 to 8

This, the Alsatian version of French toast, is how we would use day-old bread, or even better three-day-old bread. Ours is the simplest version I know. The bread is not soaked—instead, it's just dipped in milk to soften it. Next it's dipped in the egg batter and sautéed in butter until it's beautifully browned, and then you finish it with a sprinkling of cinnamon sugar. It's delicious as is, but feel free to serve with ice cream or a compote.

I use roasted Saigon cinnamon, which I believe is the very best. It's not true cinnamon but rather comes from a related tree native to Vietnam and is richer in volatile oils than true cinnamon. You can find it at Whole Foods and other high-end grocery stores.

6 to 8 (½-inch-thick/1.25 cm) slices
   dry bread
1 cup (240 ml) warm milk
3 eggs
2 tablespoons all-purpose flour

About ⅓ cup (65 g) sugar,
   combined with 1 tablespoon
   cinnamon (preferably roasted
   Saigon cinnamon)
Butter, for sautéing

Put the bread slices in a pan and pour the warm milk over them, flip them if they aren't submerged, then remove them to a rack.

In a bowl big enough to dip the bread, whip the eggs, then whisk in the flour. Add a few tablespoons of the warm milk. Put the butter in a sauté pan over medium-high heat. Once the butter is frothing (you want the butter to brown a little by the end), take each slice of bread one by one, dip them on each side in the egg mixture, then put each into the pan. Cook until golden brown, a few minutes per side. Remove them to a plate, then sprinkle them liberally with the cinnamon-sugar.

WHITE WINE MOUSSE

Serves 6 to 8

This is a light, refreshing, creamy confection that we would serve with a slice of Kougelhopf (page 103), some lady fingers, or the prune pie (page 115). It can also be simply enjoyed with fresh mixed berries. It's basically a sabayon or crème anglaise, but if you've ever spent twenty minutes over the stove whipping yolks and sugar to a sabayon consistency, you'll love this simple technique and preparation: Whip the yolks and sugar, adding some cornstarch, then pour in boiling wine while whipping, then reheat to thicken. Simple and delicious. I love using a Muscat, but you could also use Champagne.

4 eggs, separated
½ cup (100 g) sugar
1½ tablespoons cornstarch or 3 tablespoons all-purpose flour, sifted

2 cups (500 ml) Alsatian Muscat
Fresh strawberries, raspberries, blueberries, or blackberries, for serving (optional)

Combine the egg yolks, sugar, and cornstarch and whip them until the mixture is pale and very fluffy, about 5 minutes.

Bring the wine to a simmer over high heat. Add a quarter of the wine to the egg yolk mixture while whipping it. Over medium-high heat, add the egg-wine mixture to the hot wine. Bring the mixture to a simmer, whisking, so that it thickens. Remove from the heat and allow the mixture to cool.

Whip the egg whites to soft peaks. Gently fold them into the egg yolk mixture until they are completely incorporated.

Serve in cups or ramekins, with berries, if using.

ÎLE FLOTANTE ET CRÈME VANILLE

Serves 6

This is a simple, elegant dessert common throughout France, really just eggs and sugar. It begins with a vanilla sauce, a *crème anglaise*, which is then topped by meringues. You can vary this as you wish—I like to add kirsch or chopped chocolate to the meringue, or make a caramel sauce to pour over the meringues along with a sprinkling of toasted almonds. This is one of the recipes I did for the Best Apprentice of France competition. The organization chose this simple dessert because the previous two recipes were extremely complex and time-consuming, and this one demonstrates a mastery of a simple technique. See page 331 for how we prepare it at the restaurant.

FOR THE VANILLA CREAM
1 vanilla bean, split in half
2 cups (500 ml) milk
5 egg yolks
½ cup (100 g) sugar

FOR THE MERINGUES
5 egg whites
Pinch salt
¾ cup (150 g) sugar

TO GARNISH (OPTIONAL)
Caramel sauce
Toasted sliced almonds
Berries
Chopped or flaked chocolate

Make the vanilla cream: In a saucepan, scrape the seeds from the vanilla bean into the milk. Add the pod to the milk as well, bring the mixture to a boil, and then remove from the heat.

Combine the yolks and sugar in a bowl, whisking until it becomes frothy and the color becomes pale yellow. Whisk about ½ cup (120 ml) hot milk into the yolks, then pour this mixture back into the milk. Return the pan to medium-low heat, whisking and stirring until the sauce thickens. When you can draw a line through the sauce on a wooden spoon, it's done. Immediately pour the sauce into a cold bowl, discarding the vanilla pod.

Make the meringue: In a large bowl, beat the egg whites with the salt until they become frothy, then add half of the sugar. Continue whisking until you have soft peaks. Add the remaining sugar and continue whisking until you have stiff peaks and the sugar is dissolved.

Bring a pot of water to a simmer. Make large quenelles or drop large spoonfuls of the meringue into the water. They'll float. Cook for 15 to 20 seconds, then flip them to cook the other side for another 15 to 20 seconds. They are done when a toothpick or paring knife is inserted and comes out dry. (Don't wander away; they cook fast.) Remove them to a plate lined with paper towels. Carefully dry each meringue off on a paper towel, and then once dried, they are ready to top the vanilla cream.

To serve, ladle the vanilla cream into six bowls. Divide the meringues evenly among the bowls. Garnish with your preferred toppings.

MY MOTHER'S HOLIDAY COOKIES

Every holiday season my mother baked cookies. And not just to fill a dozen tins for friends and relatives. She baked hundreds of kilos. She baked seven days a week, usually starting at five A.M. and sometimes working until three in the morning. And her cookies tasted so good, everyone in the village placed their holiday cookie order with her. People would come to her before going to the local bakery.

And this is why cookies are so important to me. My mother still bakes cookies, but only several kilos now that she's getting up in years. But here are some of my favorites from her.

They fall into two general categories—butter-based cookies and specialty cookies that add extra elements to them, such as special fillings or coatings.

If you measure by weight, these ingredients can be halved or doubled depending on your needs. A general rule is that a cookie weighs about 10 grams (⅓ ounce). So if you add the weight of your ingredients, you can divide by 10 to estimate your total cookie count.

Store all cookies in an airtight container for up to 2 weeks.

TRIED-AND-TRUE BUTTER COOKIES

I love these for the childhood memories they evoke, with the simple smell of butter and sugar. I love opening a tin of them and taking in the aroma. These are also so easy to make. I find that they're best when they've aged a couple days in an airtight container.

Makes about 60 cookies

3 cups (375 g) all-purpose flour
3 teaspoons (12 g) baking powder
⅔ cup (150 g) granulated sugar
4 egg yolks
2 tablespoons milk
2 teaspoons vanilla sugar or ¼ teaspoon
   vanilla extract
10 tablespoons (150 g) melted butter

Mix the flour, baking powder, and granulated sugar together in a mixing bowl. Add the yolks, milk, vanilla sugar, and melted butter. Mix well until you have a smooth dough. Flatten it out so that it's easier to roll out, wrap in plastic, and refrigerate overnight.

Preheat your oven to 350°F (175°C).

Roll the dough out to about ¼ inch thick and use a variety of your favorite cookie cutters to make the cookies. Bake on a parchment-lined sheet pan for 8 to 10 minutes, until cooked through, turning the sheet pan halfway through the baking.

Using a spatula, carefully move to a rack to cool.

NUSLI

This is another butter-style cookie that I like to pipe from a bag using a large star tip, making a walnut-sized dollop, then swooshing the tip down and toward me, creating a scallop-like shape. My mother's recipe calls for potato starch, which I recommend if it's available. In Alsace, that was the common starch as corn wasn't a traditional Alsatian crop. I like to finish these by dipping half of each cookie in chocolate (use a double boiler to melt your chocolate). You can eat them right away but I think they're best a couple of days after baking and coating.

Makes 50 to 60 cookies

1 cup (2 sticks/240 g) butter
1¼ cups (150 g) confectioners' sugar
2 eggs
¼ teaspoon vanilla extract
2¾ cups (325 g) all-purpose flour, sifted
⅓ cup (50 g) potato starch or cornstarch
8 ounces (240 g) dark chocolate, gently
   melted in a double boiler

Preheat your oven to 350°F (175°C).

Mix all the ingredients except the chocolate together to make the dough. It should be soft enough to pipe as described above. Pipe them onto a parchment-lined sheet pan and bake for 8 to 10 minutes, until they're cooked through, turning the sheet pan halfway through the baking time. Allow them to cool completely.

To finish them, dip the thinner edge of the cookies in the chocolate and lay them on a cooling rack set over a sheet of parchment or paper towel to catch any drips.

SPRITZ

This is a drier, sweeter, crispier version of the butter cookie that also uses a nut flour for additional flavor. A traditional spritz cookie is extruded through some shape of die. We used an old-fashioned hand-cranked meat grinder to create long rectangular cookies. But you can also use a cookie press to make various shapes or they can be rolled and cut like regular butter cookies.

Makes about 80 cookies

recipe continues

1¼ cups (300 g) butter

1¼ cups (250 g) granulated sugar

1 tablespoon vanilla sugar or ¼ teaspoon
vanilla extract

1 egg, beaten

4 cups (500 g) all-purpose flour

1 scant cup (100 g) hazelnut flour or
almond flour

Preheat your oven to 375°F (190°C).

Combine all of the ingredients until you have a nicely formed dough. Pass the dough through a meat grinder fitted with a special tip to make cookies, through a cookie press, or shape into a log and slice the cookies.

Bake for 8 to 10 minutes, rotating the sheet pan 180 degrees halfway through the baking time.

VANILLA CROISSANT

This is a dough that my mother always shaped into crescents, rolling them into cylinders about 4 inches (10 cm) long and ½ to ¾ inch (about 2 cm) thick, tapering each end, and resting them on a parchment-lined tray in the curved shape of a croissant. This dough is flavored with vanilla beans and almond flour.

Makes 40 to 50 cookies

7 tablespoons (100 g) butter, at room
temperature

⅓ cup (75 g) granulated sugar

Vanilla seeds scraped from 1 vanilla pod
(put the pod in sugar to make vanilla
sugar, called for below)

1 pinch salt

1 egg yolk

¾ cup (100 g) all-purpose flour

⅓ cup (50 g) potato starch or cornstarch

⅔ cup (75 g) almond flour

Vanilla sugar, for finishing

Combine the butter, sugar, vanilla, salt, and egg yolk in a mixing bowl. Work them together with a whisk until the mixture is light and airy (as with creaming sugar). Stir in the flour, starch, and almond flour until all the ingredients are uniformly combined. Wrap the dough in plastic and let it rest in the refrigerator for at least 1 hour or up to a day.

Preheat your oven to 350°F (175°C).

Form little croissant-shaped cookies as described above. Bake them on a parchment-lined sheet pan for 10 to 12 minutes, rotating the sheet pan 180 degrees halfway through the baking time.

Let them cool on a cookie rack and then cover them with some vanilla sugar.

CAPRICE AU KIRSCH

This is a very special cookie, a round butter cookie with kirsch on top, and sandwiching a vanilla confection that is coated in a glaçage, a glaze made of confectioners' sugar.

Makes 25 to 30 cookies

FOR THE COOKIE DOUGH

1¾ cups (200 g) all-purpose flour

2 teaspoons baking powder

1 tablespoon vanilla sugar or ¼ teaspoon
vanilla extract

1 egg, beaten

⅔ cup (150 g) butter, at room
temperature

¾ cup (80 g) hazelnut flour

FOR THE FILLING

7 tablespoons (100 g) butter, at room
temperature

¾ cup (100 g) confectioners' sugar

1 tablespoon vanilla sugar or ¼ teaspoon
vanilla extract

1 egg yolk

1½ tablespoons (30 g) hazelnut flour

3 tablespoons kirsch eau de vie

FOR THE GLAÇAGE

1½ cups (200 g) confectioners' sugar

½ egg white

2 tablespoons kirsch eau de vie

Chopped pistachio, as needed to sprinkle
on top

For the cookie dough, mix all of the ingredients together into a smooth dough, wrap in plastic, and refrigerate overnight.

Preheat your oven to 350°F (175°C).

Roll the dough out to a thickness of about ⅛ inch (3 mm). Cut the dough into 1½- to 2-inch (4 to 5 cm) ovals. Re-roll the trim and continue to cut more cookies. You should have between 50 and 60 cookies. Bake them on a parchment-lined sheet pan for 8 to 10 minutes, rotating the sheet pan 180 degrees halfway through the baking time. Allow them to cool.

Make the filling by combining all of the ingredients in a bowl and mixing until everything is well combined.

Make the glaçage by mixing all of the ingredients together until everything is well combined.

Complete the cookies by spreading a dollop, a teaspoon or so, of the filling on half the ovals, and topping them with the other half. Using a pastry brush, coat the top of each cookie with the glaçage. Sprinkle the chopped pistachios onto the glaçage.

SABLÉ A LA CONFITURE

This is a very festive cookie, another sandwich-style cookie filled with a brightly colored jam, with three little circles cut out of the top so that the jam shows through.

Makes about 40 cookies

2 cups (250 g) all-purpose flour
½ cup (1 stick/120 g) butter, at room temperature
¼ cup (70 g) granulated sugar
2 eggs, beaten
1 tablespoon vanilla sugar or ¼ teaspoon vanilla extract
8 tablespoons (120 ml) raspberry or strawberry jam
Confectioners' sugar, for dusting

Combine the flour, butter, granulated sugar, eggs, and vanilla sugar in a mixing bowl and bring the dough together with a spatula. It will have the consistency of tart crust. Wrap the dough in plastic and let it rest for an hour or so.

Preheat your oven to 350°F (175°C).

Roll the dough out to about ⅛ inch (2 to 3 mm) thick. Cut them in 1½- to 2-inch (4 to 5 cm) rounds. Re-roll the trim and continue to cut more cookies. You should have around 80 rounds for 40 finished cookies. Using a pastry tip or small cutter, make three little round holes in the center of half of the rounds. Bake them on a parchment-lined sheet pan for 8 to 10 minutes, rotating the sheet pan 180 degrees halfway through the baking time. Allow them to cool.

Spread about a teaspoon of your jam on the full rounds. Top them with the rounds in which you've cut holes. Dust with confectioners' sugar.

CINNAMON STARS

These are delicious cinnamon-flavored cookies. The dough is like a sablé, very delicate, and results in a delicately crunchy cookie. I like to paint the top with a sweet glaçage.

Makes about 50 cookies

1¾ cups (200 g) all-purpose flour
⅔ cup (150 g) butter, at room temperature
½ cup (125 g) granulated sugar
¾ cup (100 g) almond flour
1 teaspoon ground cinnamon (preferably Saigon)
Glaçage (page 124) or an icing made with 8 tablespoons (65 g) confectioners' sugar mixed with 1 tablespoon water

Combine the all-purpose flour, butter, granulated sugar, almond flour, and cinnamon in a mixing bowl and bring it all together by hand, as you would a pastry dough. Wrap it in plastic and refrigerate for at least an hour and as long as one day.

Preheat your oven to 350°F (175°C).

Roll the dough out to about ¼ inch (6 mm) thick. Cut into stars. Place them on a parchment-lined sheet pan and bake for 8 to 10 minutes, rotating the sheet pan 180 degrees halfway through the baking time.

Let them cool and then, if you wish, finish them with glaçage, omitting the alcohol, or icing.

DUCHESSE

These are the poor man's macaron, an egg white batter cookie that sandwiches a chocolate filling, much easier than the finicky French macaron and just as delicious.

Makes 45 to 50 cookies

FOR THE COOKIE BATTER
5 egg whites
1 cup (200 g) sugar
1¾ cups (200 g) hazelnut flour
½ cup plus 1 tablespoon (70 g) all-purpose flour
6 tablespoons (90 g) butter, melted

FOR THE FILLING
¾ cup (1½ sticks/180 g) butter
6 ounces (180 g) milk chocolate
1¾ cups (175 g) confectioners' sugar
5 egg yolks

Preheat your oven to 350°F (175°C).

To make the cookie batter, beat the egg whites. When frothy, add a third of the sugar. Whip to soft peaks, adding the remaining sugar as you do. Fold in the hazelnut flour and all-purpose flour, then the melted butter. Using two spoons, transfer tablespoon-sized dollops onto a Silpat-lined sheet pan. Bake for 8 to 10 minutes, turning the sheet pan once in the middle of cooking. Remove the cookies to a rack to cool completely.

To make the filling, melt the butter with the chocolate in a double burner, then add the confectioners' sugar. Mix very well with a rubber spatula, then whisk in the yolks.

To finish the cookie, spread a teaspoon or two of the filling on the bottom of one cookie. Press the bottom of another cookie onto the filling so that you have a macaron-like cookie.

BEERAWECKA

(Alsatian Fruitcake)

Makes three 1-pound (500-g) loaves

This is the Alsatian version of a fruitcake, though it's much more bread-like, loaded with delicious dried fruits and nuts, richly seasoned with spices, and finished with citrus and eau de vie. It's particularly popular during the holidays, eaten for breakfast with coffee or as a snack. It actually keeps for up to 6 weeks in a cool room or refrigerator (temper for 30 minutes before serving) in a closed container or wrapped in plastic wrap. (I use the same fruits for this cake in a chutney I serve with foie gras at my restaurant: see page 224.) I recommend waiting at least one week before starting to enjoy this dense cake. During that time of maturation, the flavor gets better and better, the spices evolve in complexity, and the candied fruit keeps everything moist. Also, if you are making the effort to bake this cake, you should go ahead and make three, to give to friends or keep, especially since it will keep so well.

FOR THE MARINATED DRIED FRUITS

2 cups (400 g) dried pears
½ cup (100 g) dried prunes
¾ cup (150 g) dried figs
¾ cup (150 g) dried apricots
¾ cup (150 g) dried dates
1 cup (150 g) dried raisins
5 ounces (150 ml) plum eau de vie
  or kirsch
1 tablespoon (8 g) ground cinnamon
  (preferably Saigon)
1 tablespoon (8 g) green anise powder
1 teaspoon (3 g) ground ginger
¾ teaspoon (2 g) ground cloves
½ teaspoon (1 g) ground nutmeg
½ teaspoon (1 g) ground cardamom

FOR THE DOUGH

2 tablespoons (17 g) fresh yeast or
  2 teaspoons (6 g) active dry yeast
¾ cup (180 ml) warm milk
4¾ cups (600 g) all-purpose flour
2 large eggs
2 tablespoons (30 g) sugar
7 tablespoons (85 g) butter, at room
  temperature
Egg wash (1 egg yolk mixed with
  2 tablespoons heavy cream or milk)

FOR THE NUT-FRUIT MIXTURE

¾ cup (100 g) almonds, coarsely chopped
¾ cup (100 g) walnuts, coarsely chopped
¾ cup (100 g) hazelnuts, coarsely
  chopped
3½ ounces (100 g) candied orange peels,
  diced (you can purchase online and at
  select supermarkets and spice stores)
3½ ounces (100 g) candied lemon
  peels, diced

To prepare the marinated dried fruits, soak the dried pears in warm water for about 15 minutes. Drain them and cut them in strips. Cut the prunes, figs, apricots, and dates into small pieces, making sure to take all the pits out. Put all the cut dried fruits and the whole raisins in a mixing bowl, then add the eau de vie, cinnamon, anise, ginger, cloves, nutmeg, and cardamom. Mix well, cover, and then let the fruits rest overnight in a cool place (but not in the refrigerator).

Preheat your oven to 350°F (175°C).

To make the dough, dissolve the yeast in the warm milk (90°F/30°C or so) in the bowl of a standing mixer fitted with a dough hook (you can also mix this dough by hand, which is what my mother did). Add the flour and mix on medium speed. As the dough begins to come together, add the egg, sugar, and butter. Continue mixing until you have a smooth dough, about 10 minutes.

While the dough is mixing, in a bowl, combine the chopped almonds, walnuts, and hazelnuts. Mix well, and then add the diced orange and lemon peels. Combine well and set aside.

Turn the mixer speed to low and add the marinated dried fruits and the nut-fruit mixture. Continue to mix until all the ingredients are uniformly distributed.

Divide the dough into three equal pieces. Shape them into ovals. Put them on a sheet pan lined with parchment or a Silpat. Brush them with the egg wash and bake for 45 minutes. Cool them on a rack and store in a loose container or wrapped in foil for up to 1 month.

Gluehwein

GLUEHWEIN
(Alsatian Mulled Wine)

Makes a little more than 1 quart/liter

This is a traditional sweet, spiced wine we drink during the holidays. It's popular to have while strolling the outdoor holiday markets. The cooking reduces the alcohol to some degree (and it's diluted by the water and sugar), so it's not as strong as the uncooked wine. Enjoy it while it's hot with pain d'épices (page 109), cookies, or just on its own in cold weather.

1 quart/liter dry white Alsatian wine, such as Riesling, Pinot Gris, or Gewurztraminer

1 cup (200 g) sugar

¾ cup (180 ml) water

1 stick cinnamon

2 pieces star anise

2 cloves

20 gratings nutmeg

Zest of ½ lemon

Zest of ½ orange

Lemon or orange slices, for garnishing each glass

Combine all the ingredients in a pot and slowly bring the wine to a simmer, and continue to simmer for about 5 minutes. Strain the wine into a clean pot. Serve hot, garnishing the glasses with lemon or orange slices.

GREEN WALNUT LIQUEUR

Makes about 3½ quarts/liters

This is a very typical spiced wine of Alsace, made each year in the spring, no later than the end of June, when the walnuts on the trees are still green. All farmers or households with walnuts on their property would make this pleasantly bitter digestif, not unlike a fernet branca. Green walnuts are available online, typically beginning in May.

24 green walnuts, harvested just before the end of June

½ stick cinnamon

5 cloves

2 quarts/liters red wine

1 quart/liter eau de vie

2 pounds (1 kg) granulated sugar

Wash the walnuts and cut them into quarters. Put them in a container large enough to hold all the ingredients. Add the cinnamon stick and cloves. Add the wine and eau de vie. Add the sugar. Close the container tightly and let it mature for at least 5 weeks, stirring once a week or so.

Strain the liquid (discarding the solids) and pour into bottles. The liqueur will keep indefinitely.

ON ALSATIAN WINES

Home to one hundred miles of forested mountains and fairy-tale villages, Alsace is also one of the great wine-making regions of France.

Wine was part of my upbringing. Our family didn't go to a wine store to buy wine. We would visit wine-makers to taste their wines and buy directly from them, as well as see the nearby medieval castles. I, like most kids in Alsace, and in France, was introduced to wine at around age ten. When there was a big family dinner, I'd be given a little sip. I didn't really understand what I was tasting, but I started to become interested.

My uncle gave me a 1976 Château de Pommard when I was thirteen or so. With its Dom Pérignon–style bottle and classical label, it made me curious about red Burgundies and the region where they came from. When a friend of my mother's from the Bordeaux region learned of my interest in wine, she gave me three bottles of Château Siran Margaux. So even then, I had started aging wine in our root cellar.

By the time I'd been working in my uncle Michel's kitchen for a few years, at age fifteen or sixteen, he hosted a Christmas dinner. For the celebration he brought out a 1959 Pommard, a Pinot Noir from the Hospices de Beaune estate, not far from us in Burgundy. This bottle of wine would have been about twenty-five years old at the time. I took a sip and my head exploded. I thought, "So this is what a wine can be." This epiphany started my lifelong journey, exploring the wines of the world, discussing wines with other chefs, and grilling sommeliers with question after question. This moment also reinforced the importance of cellaring wine, the economics of buying young wines that would later become expensive, and so I began collecting wine in earnest.

But my region is quite distinct from Bordeaux and Burgundy, distinct even from the German wines made on the other side of the Rhine river. The famous German Rieslings and Gewurztraminers tend to be quite sweet, whereas the Alsatian wines made from those same grape varietals are considerably drier.

Alsatian wines are always sold by the name of the grape. There are seven main grapes that grow in the region. The following is a basic primer on these grapes and how I like to pair Alsatian wines with food.

RIESLING

Riesling is considered the prince of the dry wines in Alsace. There are multiple Grand Crus, a classification that identifies the finest still white wines of the region, which are really amazing. A few of my favorites are Schoenenbourg Grand Cru and Rosacker Grand Cru, where Clos Sainte Hune from Domaine Trimbach is made, a wine that many consider to be the best dry Riesling in the world. Good Alsatian Rieslings are characterized by an acidity and minerality that goes especially well with fish and lobster dishes.

Pairing suggestions:

Black Bass Tartare with Macadamia Nuts, Cilantro Gelée, and Puffed Barley (page 172)

Rabbit Terrine with Gewurztraminer, Hyssop, and Fines Herbes Coulis (page 175)

Smoked Sturgeon and Sauerkraut Tart with Riesling Mousseline and Caviar (page 200)

Traditional Baeckeoffe (page 61)

Traditional Presskopf d'Alsace (Cured Headcheese) (page 42)

Tripe au Riesling and Curry (page 70)

Uncle Michel's Choucroute Garnie (page 59)

Veal Liver Dumplings (page 92)

Wild Mushrooms and Louisiana Crayfish Cooked "en Baeckeoffe" (page 227)

GEWURZTRAMINER

Although it is most famous for being sweet, because of the amazing late harvest wines (*vendange tardive*) and wines made with grapes affected by noble rot (*sélection de grains nobles*), Gewurztraminer is also a one-of-a-kind wine when it's dry. With aromatics that are both fruity (with notes of grapefruit, lychee, and pineapple) and floral-spicy (rose, ginger, and smoke), it works very well with lightly spicy dishes and particularly with Asian cuisine.

Pairing suggestions (sweet versions with the desserts, dry with the savory dishes):

Apple Tart a l'Alsacienne (page 110)

Beerawecka (page 126)

Cheeses such as Munster, Maroilles, and Époisses

Chocolate Île Flotante with Sicilian Pistachios and Hazelnuts (page 331)

Dampfnudel en Cocotte (Steamed Buns) (page 84)

Cellar of the Sisters of the Divine Providence in Ribeauvillé. This is typical of the size of the casks in Alsace, with a Riesling cask in the front. This charity is involved in the well-being and education of children.

Foie gras terrine (page 181 or 184)

My Grandfather's Cinnamon-Prune Pie (page 115)

Sautéed Foie Gras with Beerawecka Fruit Chutney and Beer Reduction (page 224)

Tarte au Fromage Blanc (Alsatian Cheesecake) (page 112)

PINOT BLANC

Nice and dry, and easy to enjoy, Pinot Blanc is probably the best standard table wine in the region for consistency and quality.

Pairing suggestions:

Duck and Foie Gras Ravioli in Mushroom Fumet with Shiitake Caps and Chervil (page 208)

Free-Range Chicken Duo with Fresh Goat Cheese and Fines Herbs Emulsion (page 294)

My Onion Tart (page 81)

Potato Galette (page 91)

Rabbit Terrine with Gewurztraminer, Hyssop, and Fines Herbes Coulis (page 161)

Stuffed Veal Breast (page 66)

Veal Liver Dumplings (page 92)

PINOT GRIS

Dry Alsatian Pinot Gris are full bodied and citrusy. However, Pinot Gris is probably the most famous grape of the region because of its ability to make sweet wines that age effortlessly for decades due to high acidity and richness. Look for *vendanges tardive* and *sélection de grains nobles* wines that are aged fifteen to twenty years. These can easily compete with great Sauternes.

Pairing suggestions (for dry Pinot Gris, unless specified):

Braised Rabbit Leg "Paupiette" with Rosemary-Garlic Stuffing, Wild Mushrooms, and Chervil Sauce (page 323)

Fleischschnaka (Meat-Stuffed Pasta Rolls) (page 87)

Foie gras terrine (pair with *vendange tardive* or *sélection de grains nobles*) (page 181 or 184)

Île Flotante et Crème Vanille (pair with *vendange tardive* or *sélection de grains nobles*) (page 120)

Roasted Maine Lobster in a Folly of Herbs with Green Asparagus and Fingerling Potatoes (page 278)

PINOT NOIR

This is the only red varietal that is allowed by law in Alsace and the least common one as well, even as the grape has been becoming more famous in the region. Today the best Alsatian Pinot Noirs can rival the great red Burgundies. Look for the Pinot Noirs from the Furstentum Grand Cru made by Domaine Paul Blank.

Pairing suggestions:
Bettelmann (Beggar's Cake with Cherries) (page 108)
Braised Rabbit Leg "Paupiette" with Rosemary-Garlic Stuffing, Wild Mushrooms, and Chervil Sauce (page 323)
Charcuterie
Lamb Rack Cooked in a Haystack with Sweet Potato, Onion Marmalade, Chickpeas, and Merguez (page 314)
Lardo-Poached Maine Lobster with Fennel Puree, Caramelized Fennel, and Sauce Américaine "Au Poivre Vert" (page 276)
Potato Galette (page 91)
Squab and Foie Gras "Croustillant" with Roasted Salsify and Caramelized Ginger Jus (page 297)
Traditional Presskopf d'Alsace (Cured Headcheese) (page 42)
Venison (page 306 or 318)

MUSCAT

This is a fruity, easygoing wine, typically served as an aperitif or with a sweet Kougelhopf (page 103). It is also a great match with asparagus dishes, especially white asparagus.

Pairing suggestions:
Apple Tart a l'Alsacienne (page 110)
Kougelhopf (page 103)
Oeufs à la Neige (page 243)
White Asparagus with Smoked Salmon, Sorrel, and Trout Caviar (page 171)
White Wine Mousse (page 119)

SYLVANER

This lesser-known grape makes a fresh and delicate wine. But it's a tricky grape to work with and needs to come from a great *origine* and a talented winemaker to bring it to its full potential. Zotzenberg is the only Grand Cru vineyard, and this terroir in the commune of Mittelbergheim is shared by a handful of winemakers. Look for Domaine Boeckel, Domaine Albert Seltz, Lucas et Andre Rieffel, and Domaine Armand Gilg.

Pairing suggestions:
Apple Cider and Cumin Pickled Rainbow Trout (page 50)
Charcuterie
My Onion Tart (page 81)
Potato salad with knackwurst, or other similar savory sausage
Raw bar
Traditional Presskopf d'Alsace (Cured Headcheese) (page 42)
Uncle Michel's Choucroute Garnie (page 59)

IF YOU GO TO ALSACE . . .

Here are three of my favorite towns, all of which I recommend visiting, along with a few recommended places to eat and nearby vineyards, although there are too many to mention here. Colmar is the largest of the towns and makes for a good base, and the other towns are a twenty-five-minute car ride away.

COLMAR is a charming little city in the heart of the wine region. You will find some of the most beautiful half-timber Tudor houses in the old town, as well as a network of canals, earning the area the name "little Venice," which is especially beautiful to visit in the late spring when all the flowers and trees are in bloom. The Unterlinden Museum has an impressive collection of medieval paintings, while the Bartholdi Museum features the work of Colmar-born sculptor Frédéric Auguste Bartholdi, who designed the Statue of Liberty. Domaine Schoffit is a winery in town, and many smaller wine towns are nearby—such as Bergheim, which is home to Domaine Marcel Deiss, Domaine Spielmann, and Gustave Lorentz.

Recommended restaurants:
JY's 3, Allee du Champs de Mars, Colmar
Bord'eau 17 rue de la Poissonerie, Colmar (in the petite Venise)
Bord'eau Guesthouse, 2 Quai de la Poissonerie, Colmar (rooms right on the water in the petite Venise)
Caveau Morakoph (Winstub), 7, Rue des Trois-Epis, 7 kilometers from Colmar in Niedermorschwihr (If you go, visit Patisserie Maison Ferber, 18, Rue des Trois-Epis, famous for its confiture.)
Auberge de L'ill, 2, Rue de Collonges-au-Mt-d'Or in the nearby town of Illhaeusern
Winstub Brenner, 1 Rue Turenne, Colmar

Place des trois églises (the plaza of the three churches), in the town of Riquewihr

RIQUEWIHR is lined with cobblestone streets and still encircled by medieval walls. It is one of the most unique towns in Alsace because it suffered no damage during the world wars, offering a glimpse of what Alsace looked like hundreds of years ago. The Dolder Tower, built in 1291, is central to the town's identity and includes a museum featuring old weapons. And there is also a fourteenth-century prison, la Tour des Voleurs, well worth a visit. Hilly vineyards surround the town, which you can tour via a little tourist train.

Recommended restaurant:
La Table du Gourmet, 5, Rue de la 1ere Armee

KAYSERSBERG is magical during the month of December, when the Christmas market is going on. People come from all over Europe to see it. The village is nestled in the mountains and famed for its wines. And it was the birthplace of Nobel laureate Dr. Albert Schweitzer, whose house is a museum today.

Recommended restaurants:
Le Chambard, 9-13, Rue General-de-Gaulle
Winstub du Chambard, 9-13, Rue General-de-Gaulle
Flamme & Co, 4, Ave. General-de-Gaulle
Winery: Domaine Weinbach, 25, Route des Vins

RECOMMENDED GRAND CRU WINES, TOWN BY TOWN:

There are so many wonderful wineries that are sharing the same Grand Cru appellations that it is not possible to fit them all into this book. The examples listed below are just suggestions.

Ammerschwihr
Kaefferkopf Grand Cru
Wineck-Schlossberg Grand Cru

Bennwihr
Marckrain Grand Cru

Hunawihr
Rosacker Grand Cru

Kientzheim
Furstentum Grand Cru
Praelatenberg Grand Cru
Schlossberg Grand Cru

Mittelbergheim
Zotzenberg Grand Cru

Mittelwihr
Mandelberg Grand Cru

Ribeauvillé
Geisberg Grand Cru
Kirchberg de Ribeauvillé Grand Cru
Osterberg Grand Cru

Riquewihr
Schoenenbourg Grand Cru
Sporen Grand Cru

Sigolsheim
Mambourg Grand Cru

Zellenberg
Froehn Grand Cru

RECIPES FROM RESTAURANT GABRIEL KREUTHER

T HE FOLLOWING RECIPES ARE FROM MY LIFE AS a professional chef in America. They are the food I feature at Restaurant Gabriel Kreuther, but the inception of many of the dishes goes all the way back to my days as a sous chef at the restaurant Jean-Georges. All of it is informed by my Alsatian heritage, both in my mother's farmhouse kitchen and apprenticing for my uncle in his restaurant. In addition, there have been a number of chefs who have most influenced my approach to fine dining.

As we all stand on the shoulders of those who came before us, I want to acknowledge those chefs who have been most instrumental in leading us to where we are today.

Auguste Escoffier, of course, remains the preeminent chef for, among other things, having borrowed a page from the military and setting up a hierarchy in order to streamline the organization of his kitchens, a practice that is still used today throughout the world, and having documented all the cooking of his era. He left behind him an impressive body of work that created the foundation for our entire profession.

Paul Bocuse follows Escoffier. He brought chefs out of the kitchen and paved the way for our work to be recognized, not left behind the curtain. He was the first one who understood the power of his own image, and that press and marketing were valuable tools.

Michel Guérard, one of the founders of Nouvelle Cuisine, transformed classical French cuisine in the 1970s by creating lighter versions without diminishing taste and satisfaction, which he describes in his book *Cuisine Minceur*.

Joël Robuchon showed what perfectionism in execution and a razor focus on taste and harmony could achieve in cuisine. Pierre Gagnaire, with

little high-end training, took chances and created his own unique style of cooking and unique plating, a model followed by many.

The 1980s and '90s saw the rise of more tasting menus, partly as a result of Japanese omakase menus and their influence on Nouvelle Cuisine, and in part because food tourism became more popular, forcing popular high-end restaurants to serve the whole menu to people wanting to taste everything.

Ferran Adrià was able to revolutionize the way we think in the kitchen. He proved that if you know the fundamentals of traditional cooking well, you can innovate in a meaningful way, developing a new cooking style often emulated and rarely matched.

And finally, in my personal pantheon of chefs, there is my former boss, Jean-Georges Vongerichten. While opening restaurants for his own mentor, Louis Outhier, in Asia and throughout the world, he brought Asian ingredients into the French kitchen.

These are my picks for the most influential chefs. And each of them would have their own list. And if I carried on I'd have to mention all the cooks and chefs I worked beside on my way to where I am now. The culinary arts are a collective

Previous spread: The custom-made classic green glazed tiles covering the wall in the background were selected to evoke the famous Kachelofens stoves found in the Stube, the warmest room of the Alsatian home. Above: Part of the RGK dining room. On the right is hand-painted wallpaper inspired by a turn-of-the-century antique fabric we found encasing a jewelry box in a farmers' market in Colmar. We commissioned our architect Glen Coben's firm to adapt the fabric to this wallpaper. On the left is an abstract oil painting, Séries des Jardins de Flore, Le Printemps 2015, *by Flore Sigrist, a young Alsatian artist.*

achievement. We only advance by sharing knowledge, of ingredients, techniques, recipes.

The recipes in this section are a contribution to this shared knowledge. The chapters follow a traditional menu format, beginning with canapés and our version of cocktails in the form of jellies, or pâte de fruit, then cold and hot appetizers followed by soups and so on, with an occasional dive into a technique we use often, our method for purees or our stocks, which we've taken great care to perfect.

Always remember when you read these recipes and, I hope, try some of them yourself, that cooking isn't difficult. It's a matter of basic technique and the quality of ingredients. I'm a great advocate of technique and have worked to describe it clearly in these recipes. Cooking is a craft, one that chefs and home cooks alike continually improve on each time they pick up a knife, knead a dough, or put a sauté pan over a flame.

Happy cooking!

CANAPÉS

PRETZEL GRISSINI

Serves 10 to 20

Our executive pastry chef, Marc Aumont, was tired of doing breadsticks, which can get awfully boring day after day. So he created these delightful, delicate, crunchy pretzel *grissini* with sesame seeds. They are so, so good, and they make you smile when a glass full of them is set on the table. And they couldn't be easier as you simply cut them using a pasta cutter and spray them with a 5 percent lye solution (you'll need a spray bottle for this), which gives you that distinctive pretzel flavor.

It's one of the many ways I try to connect Alsatian tradition with fine dining in Manhattan. You'll see this desire in recipes throughout the book. Here it is the pretzel, as pretzels and beer are a common snack or start of a meal. At the restaurant it is these elegant pretzel filaments and a fine sparkling wine.

4 cups (500 g) pastry flour, plus more
    for dusting
1 tablespoon sugar
2 tablespoons salt
4 teaspoons (10 g) fresh yeast or
    1½ teaspoons (5 g) active dry yeast
⅔ cup (150 g) butter
1 ounce (30 g) food-grade lye
Sesame seeds (a good handful),
    for finishing
Fleur de sel, for finishing

Preheat your oven to 325°F (165°C).

Place the flour, sugar, salt, and yeast in the bowl of a standing mixer fitted with a dough hook. Turn the machine on to medium speed and add the butter. Mix until the dough is mealy—the butter will help prevent gluten formation and keep the breadsticks tender.

Slowly stream in ¾ cup (185 ml) of water while mixing, and continue to mix until the dough has come together. Don't overmix.

Set up your pasta machine with the spaghetti blades.

Roll your dough out to about ¼ inch (6 mm) thick and about 15 inches (38 cm) long. Cut rectangles about 4 to 5 inches wide by 15 inches (10 to 12 cm by 38 cm). Dust them thoroughly with flour and pass them through the pasta cutter. Lay the "spaghetti" on a sheet pan (they should be about as long as the sheet pan).

To shape the grissini, take two strands and make little loops and other shapes on a Silpat-lined sheet pan. Combine the lye and 2 cups (500 ml) of water in a spray bottle (be careful; the lye will burn you if it comes in contact with your skin). Mist the grissini liberally, sprinkle them with sesame seeds and fleur de sel, and bake for 10 to 12 minutes, until nicely browned and crispy. Store in an airtight container for up to a week.

BEER AND GRUYÈRE CROQUETTES

Makes 40 croquettes

These are a lovely hors d'oeuvres, crunchy outside, creamy and savory inside. And beer, which is so important in Alsatian cooking, is a major component here. The bitterness of the beer, which is reduced to a syrup, is perfectly balanced by the caramelized onion. The key here is to allow as much moisture from the potato as possible to escape after cooking, so cut the potatoes in half lengthwise as soon as they're out of the oven and allow them to cool. The fine "double-zero" flour is preferable, but all-purpose will work as well. At the restaurant, we like to garnish them with julienned roasted red pepper and Harissa aioli, the North African spicy pepper sauce mixed with aioli (which also makes a fine dipping sauce if served as a passed hors d'oeuvre). These can be made ahead and frozen for up to a month before cooking.

8½ ounces (250 g) Yukon gold potatoes
8½ ounces (250 g) russet potatoes
Salt and freshly ground black pepper
Freshly grated nutmeg
1 cup (120 g) grated Gruyère or
    Comté cheese
3 ounces (90 g) caramelized onions
    (deglazed with beer and chopped;
    see Note)
6 bottles dark beer, reduced to a syrup
    consistency (about 2.5 ounces/
    75 g)
1 teaspoon grapeseed oil
2 teaspoons butter, softened
1 egg
11 tablespoons (90 g) "00" flour
    or all-purpose flour, sifted
6½ tablespoons (60 g) cornstarch
1 cup (90 g) panko breadcrumbs
    (pulse in a food processor until fine)
Vegetable oil, for deep-frying

Preheat your oven to 425°F (220°C).

Bake the potatoes on a bed of rock salt until tender, 45 minutes to 1 hour depending on their size. Halve them immediately to let the steam out, cool slightly, peel, and pass through a food mill or ricer. Transfer the potatoes to a food processor, add salt, pepper, and nutmeg to taste, and pulse. Then add the cheese, the caramelized onions with the reduced beer, the oil, butter, and egg and pulse just until fully incorporated. Add the flour and cornstarch and pulse just until incorporated. Transfer to a bowl and let rest for 30 minutes.

Roll the potato mixture into forty 1-ounce (28 g) portions in your desired shape—I like the croquettes to be about the size of a ping-pong ball—and coat them in the panko.

Preheat the vegetable oil to 350°F to 375°F (175°C to 190°C). Fry the croquettes until golden brown and season with salt. These are best served immediately.

Note: To caramelize the onions, coat the bottom of a pan with any oil; heat the pan over medium-high heat until the pan is shimmering. Add ⅔ cup (180 g) thinly sliced onion and stir to coat with the oil. Spread the onions out evenly over the pan and let cook, stirring occasionally until they are brown. Add ½ cup (120 ml) beer to the pan, stirring and scraping up any browned pieces stuck to the bottom of the pan. Reduce the beer until no liquid remains.

ADVICE TO A YOUNG CHEF

Mentors were fundamental to my development as a chef, as they are to any chef. We learn by watching and doing. But critically we learn by watching how an older chef acts, his or her comportment, attitude toward challenges, and behavior toward colleagues. This work is hard, brutally so in some cases, many, many hours on your feet, sometimes doing the same task for hours, followed by the heady intense hours of service. Mentors are critical, and so I strive in all my kitchens to encourage mentorship of younger cooks by older chefs. It's good for the young cook and good for the kitchen generally.

If you are thinking about becoming a chef because you want to have your own television show or compete on *Top Chef*, stop now. The rise of food television and the prominence of a few chefs who have become bona fide celebrities, I believe, has given many young people the wrong idea about the profession, what it takes to get there, and what it means to be a chef. Being a chef is to be in service to those you are feeding, not to feed yourself.

If you are young and love hard work, love food, love cooking for other people, and are willing to devote a good five to seven years of your life to training, then I would recommend you consider the apprenticeship model as opposed to culinary school. Some people truly thrive after culinary school—many of today's chef-restaurateurs came out of the Culinary Institute of America, Johnson & Wales, and other leading schools. But I've seen so many young chefs come out of culinary school shouldering huge student loan debts and only remain in restaurants for one or two years. For that reason, I consider culinary school to be a risky expense, unless you've already spent one to two years in professional kitchens.

I liken becoming a professional chef to an athlete's training for the Olympics. It requires every bit as much devotion. You won't have time for much of a social life. You'll be working when all your friends aren't, nights and holidays. You won't be spending Mother's Day with your mother and you'll be cooking for other lovers on Valentine's Day.

But if a twelve-hour workday is exhilarating to you and you truly love to cook for and serve others, then, maybe, the chef's life is for you.

It was for me—I never had a doubt. The kitchen has always been my favorite place to be.

I always recommend that aspiring chefs find the best possible kitchen they can to work in, a kitchen that does everything from scratch. If you work in a kitchen where stock is made by scooping chicken stock base into water and pork chops arrive individually cryo-vaced, it's not a place to learn. That kind of kitchen is not bad, per se, but you won't learn what you need to know in a kitchen.

Take something as simple as whipped cream. I have asked more than one young cook to make me whipped cream, but the only way they know how to do it is with an ISI canister. They do not know how to make it just using a whisk. Or they have come from an upscale hotel restaurant that has eggs Benedict on its menu and the hollandaise is made from a powdered mix.

You don't have to work in a Michelin three-star restaurant. But you do have to work in a kitchen that will teach you the culinary fundamentals, techniques, discipline, and a kitchen that values mentoring. And stay there for at least a year, or better, two years.

You must first learn how to clean. That's the first thing I had to learn when I became an apprentice. You must learn how to source the right quality products and you must remember that each time you have great proteins in your hands, there was a loss of life to give you that, and you must have respect for that life. You must learn how to treat products—how to receive them, break them down as necessary, store them, and not to waste them. Research tells us that as much as 40 percent of food that is sold in the U.S. is wasted, and so it's even more important that you learn how to use amazing products to their fullest extent. Being a chef is only partly about cooking the food.

And you must be organized. If you are not organized, you simply won't have enough time to complete your work. When we have a new young cook, we always make sure they have a list of the day's work. If you have a good list, you can get twice as much done. Organization comes first, food second.

When I interview a prospective young chef, I like to know why they want to do this work, what in their history has led them here. And of course, I like to know

All chefs convene pre-service to discuss the night, issues any of us may be having, address any questions. Each day a different chef will share information with the group on a new topic they've been assigned to study. And we recite the restaurant's mission: Genuine passion and a relentless pursuit of excellence drive us to create an authentic and memorable experience.

what they love to cook and eat and why. I ask them what restaurants they've been to in the last couple weeks. They may say Mexican or Italian, and that's fine. But if I ask them, what fine-dining restaurants they've been to recently—they are applying to be a chef at a fine-dining restaurant after all—and they say, "I would love to go to Per Se, but I don't have the money," well, that tells me something. If they say, "I saved up for six months to go to Per Se," that tells me something else.

My parents didn't have the money to go to nice restaurants. I had to save my money.

If I am interested in hiring a young chef—if they have a good résumé and references, they appear to be passionate about the work, curious about food, and are a good human being generally—they must spend one or two services in my kitchen so that we can see how they work.

Are they organized? Do they have a list? Do they work clean? Are they curious? And most importantly, how do they work with others? Do they arrive early and stay late? Are they helpful to the other chefs? A kitchen is a team.

And when you work in our kitchen, you become a part of that team and it is our job to teach and mentor you. We aim to teach young chefs about quality ingredients, what to look for and to respect the integrity of the products; to be responsible and use the ingredients to their fullest extent to minimize waste; to learn how to work closely with small producers, farmers, fishermen, and foragers; to support sustainable and reasonable farming practices; to be active in pushing food giants to adhere to treating all livestock humanely; and generally to be an active participant in, and proponent of, a sustainable, humane food system.

And if I find the right chef, and he or she stays beyond two, four, five, or six years, then I am very lucky. My core team has been with me for more than a decade. To watch a young chef who starts out on the amuse-bouche station or garde-manger and work his or her way up to a sous chef position, that's one of the most gratifying things I experience as a chef.

SALMON ROE BEGGAR'S PURSES
WITH GOLD LEAF

**Makes 20 to 25
(5-inch/13 cm)
crêpes**

Stuffed crêpes are terrific canapés to serve at parties, but they can also be part of the garnish for a more elaborate dish. Here the filling is smoked sour cream with salmon roe and chives (with the enticing gold leaf for visual effect), but you could fill the crêpes with any of the purees (see pages 324–327) with additional garnishes.

There are two ways of doing these crêpes, depending on the nonstick pans you have. We have very large ones and so we make one very large crêpe from which we can cut three or four crêpes with a ring cutter. But if you have a small pan, you'll need to make one at a time. In either case, the trick is to get your pan to the right temperature, swirl the batter in the pan to coat the bottom, and pour the rest out, or the crêpe will be too thick.

The smoked sour cream is optional. We use a smoke gun, a hotel pan, and plastic wrap to smoke ours. If you have the capacity to smoke at low temperatures, I recommend it.

FOR THE CRÊPES

3 eggs
1 cup plus 3 tablespoons (285 ml) milk
1 cup (125 g) all-purpose flour, sifted
½ teaspoon salt
1 teaspoon grapeseed or other neutral
   oil, plus more for cooking

Combine the eggs and milk and whisk together. Pour one-quarter of the egg-milk mixture over the flour and salt and whisk well. It will be thick, and it's important at this stage to make sure there are no lumps. When the batter is smooth, add the rest of the egg mixture gradually while mixing. Whisk in the oil. Pass the batter through a fine-mesh sieve and let it rest for 1 hour at room temperature.

In a nonstick pan with a little oil, cook 2 to 3 tablespoons of the batter, or enough to make a roughly 5-inch (13 cm) crêpe. Or, for perfectly uniform crêpes, pour the batter into a 4½-inch (11 cm) ring cutter. Repeat with the remaining batter, adding more oil if needed. If you are

making a pan-sized crêpe, scoop batter into a ladle and coat the bottom of the pan with a thin layer, swirling the batter once and pouring what doesn't stick to the bottom back into the bowl. Cook only on one side. When the top of the crêpe has congealed, remove it to a plate or a baking tray as you cook the rest. Allow each crêpe to cool before stacking them so they don't stick to one another.

FOR THE FILLING

6 tablespoons (90 g) salmon roe
6 tablespoons (30 g) Marcona almonds,
   toasted and coarsely chopped
3 tablespoons chopped chives
½ cup (120 ml) smoked sour cream
   (or plain sour cream, if smoking is
   not possible)
Salt and freshly ground black pepper
30 chives, blanched and shocked in
   ice water (in the event that a few
   break while tying)

TO GARNISH

Gold leaves (optional)
20 to 25 slices of lime (about 3 limes)

In a mixing bowl, combine the salmon roe, almonds, and chopped chives, then add about half the smoked sour cream and season with a little salt and pepper. Lay the crêpes out shiny side up (this is the stickier side and will help hold the crêpes together). Using a piping bag, make a little mound of smoked sour cream in the center of each crêpe. Top with a loose teaspoon of the filling with the almonds and roe. Pinch the edges of each crêpe together and tie with a blanched chive.

Using tweezers, garnish with flakes of gold leaf, if desired. Rub each purse 4 to 5 times on the lime slices, then set each purse on its respective slice to serve. Do not eat the slice of lime; it is for seasoning only.

SMOKED SALMON AND COMTÉ GOUGÈRES

Makes about 30 gougères

Gougères, sometimes called cheese puffs, are common throughout France. They make great hors d'oeuvres and are one of the easiest to make in the restaurant. We freeze them so they can be baked from frozen anytime you need them. They can be eaten plain, but I like to fill them, as here with a mixture of smoked salmon and cheese.

FOR THE GOUGÈRES

2 tablespoons milk powder
2 teaspoons salt
1 teaspoon sugar
7 tablespoons (105 g) butter
1¼ cups (150 g) all-purpose flour, sifted
2½ ounces (75 g) Béchamel (recipe follows)
2½ ounces (75 g) Comté cheese, shredded (about 11 tablespoons)
4 eggs

Make the gougères: Combine the milk powder, 1 cup (250 ml) of water, the salt, sugar, and butter in a saucepan over high heat and bring to a boil. When the butter has melted, lower the heat to medium-low and add the flour, stirring constantly. The flour will gelatinize and create a loose dough/batter that pulls away from the sides of the pan. Continue to stir for 10 minutes, to ensure the flour is completely cooked. Remove from the heat.

Warm the béchamel and stir in the cheese until combined. Stir this mixture into the batter. Let the batter sit for a few minutes to cool off, then add the eggs one by one, stirring until each egg is incorporated before adding the next.

Put the batter into a piping bag and chill for 30 minutes or so. Pipe the gougères onto a Silpat-lined sheet pan (they should be about 30 grams, about

1 heaping tablespoon, each, about the size of a golf ball). Freeze and store in an airtight container until ready to bake, up to 4 weeks.

To cook, preheat your oven to 375°F (190°C). Put your gougères on a Silpat-lined sheet pan and bake for 7 minutes, then reduce the oven temperature to 325°F (165°C) and bake for another 25 minutes, or until golden and cooked through.

FOR THE SMOKED SALMON FILLING

8 ounces (225 g) smoked salmon
6 tablespoons (90 ml) sour cream, plus more as needed for garnish
2 ounces (60 g) Cheddar
1 ounce (30 g) blue cheese
1 clove garlic, minced
1 teaspoon Dijon mustard
Tabasco
Salt and freshly ground black pepper
5 tablespoons (80 g) red tobiko (flying fish roe), for garnish
2½ tablespoons minced chives, for garnish

Prepare the filling: In a food processor, combine the salmon, sour cream, Cheddar, blue cheese, garlic, mustard, and Tabasco and season with salt and pepper. Pulse until they're uniformly combined. Taste and adjust seasoning as necessary.

To finish the gougères, pipe the salmon filling into each cooked gougère, from the bottom. Dip the top of each gougère in sour cream and garnish with tobiko (about ½ teaspoon per gougère) and chives (about ¼ teaspoon), or as you wish.

BÉCHAMEL

Make about ½ cup (120 ml)

1 tablespoon butter
1½ tablespoons all-purpose flour
½ cup (125 ml) cold milk
2 teaspoons Dijon mustard
⅛ teaspoon cayenne pepper

Melt the butter in a saucepan over medium heat, then add the flour. Stir for several minutes, until the roux becomes golden and the flour smells cooked. Whisk in the milk and bring to a simmer. Add the Dijon and cayenne. Continue to cook for another 2 to 3 minutes to ensure the flour is cooked. It should be the consistency of pastry cream.

SAVORY KOUGELHOPF
AND CHIVE SOUR CREAM

Serves 6

Kougelhopf is a traditional bread of Alsace, usually made sweet and served in the morning or after-noon with coffee or tea, a once-a-week preparation—which is why I wanted to serve it in my Man-hattan restaurant. To make it elegant while giving my clientele a taste of my native land, I bake small savory loaves and serve them as a kind of bread course with a creamy herbed spread. At the restau-rant we slice the kougelhopf and hold it together with raffia. Before serving, we warm it in the oven for 4 minutes, and the raffia is released by the waiter in the dining room. At home, if desired, for fun, you can have one of your dinner guests release it. You can use six small 4¾-inch (12 cm) individual kougelhopf molds or one large kougelhopf or Bundt pan, 10½ inches (26 cm) in diameter.

FOR THE KOUGELHOPF
1¾ cups (210 g) all-purpose flour, sifted
1⅔ cups (195 g) pastry flour
1½ teaspoons sugar
1 tablespoon salt
3 teaspoons (8 g) fresh yeast or
  1 teaspoon (3 g) active dry yeast
2 eggs
¾ cup plus 2 tablespoons (210 ml) milk
4 tablespoons (60 g) butter, plus more
  for buttering the mold or molds

Put the flours, sugar, salt, and yeast in the bowl of a standing mixer fitted with a dough hook and turn the mixer to medium low to combine. Then, with the mixer still running, add the eggs one at a time. Scrape down the bowl as necessary. Add the milk, and continue to mix. Turn the speed to medium. When a solid dough forms, add the butter a little bit at a time, continuing to scrape down the sides. When the dough pulls away from the sides, it's done. Pull on it—there should be some resistance.

Put on a floured tray or sheet pan lined with parchment, cover with plastic wrap, and refrigerate overnight.

The next day, 2 hours before you're ready to bake, remove the dough from the refrigerator and shape immediately. If making individual kougelhopfs, use a paring knife to cut the dough into six equal square pieces. Scale out each one (4½ ounces/125 g per piece) to double-check that they are equal in size. If not, just pull some dough from one portion and add it to the piece that needs a little more. Brush the insides of the molds or mold with melted butter.

To shape individual portions, fold each corner into the center and punch it down hard with the heel of your hand until you have a tight circular piece. Roll it into a tight boule. Repeat with the other pieces. If using a single mold, make a single boule.

Use your elbow to press a hole in the middle of each boule so that it looks like a bagel and will fit in the mini Bundt pan, or large Bundt pan if you're making a single Kougelhopf. Place each piece in a mold and let rest for 1 to 2 hours, until about doubled in size.

Preheat your oven to 325°F (163°C).

When the dough has risen, bake for 30 minutes, or until cooked through.

FOR THE CHIVE SOUR CREAM
1½ tablespoons yogurt powder
1¾ cups (420 ml) sour cream
Tabasco, to taste
Salt (about 1 teaspoon)
Pepper
⅓ to ½ cup (75 to 125 ml) Chive Oil
  (page 233)

Combine everything except the chive oil in a mixing bowl, then slowly whisk in the oil, making sure the cream doesn't break. Check the seasoning and adjust as necessary.

PÂTE DE FRUITS

Traditionally, *pâte de fruits* are fruit purees gelled with pectin, coated in sugar, and served as a type of soft fruit confection, or jelly, on the *mignardise* tray (the bite-sized treats that come at the very end of the meal). But we tend to serve them in the beginning of the meal as an early cocktail course. This part of the menu was conceived by chef de cuisine Joe Anthony, about three years ago. When the influx of gelling powders like agar and gellan—technically called hydrocolloids, but just think of them as thickeners—appeared with the Modernist Cuisine movement, he thought we should see how we could put them to use. Currently under the direction of sous chef William Cesark, the following recipes are primarily his creations, incorporating all of our input toward perfecting them.

These are just plain fun to make and to serve. They're unusual, flavorful, lightly alcoholic (the Jell-O shot taken to the furthest extremes of elegance), and always put a smile on the diner's face.

For the gels themselves, the method is almost always the same. The powders are added to some of the liquid components of the pâte de fruits, simmered, then cooled slightly and combined with the remaining ingredients (it's best not to cook fruit juices and alcohol to keep the flavors fresh). They are then strained and allowed to set. The amounts of the gelling powders vary depending on the firmness you want and the thickness of what you are gelling (a puree requires less thickener). And some fruit purees—cherry, kiwi, pineapple, and mango—have enzymes that will prevent a puree from gelling, so they must first be cooked. But once you understand the basic principles and method, then, as Will puts it, "You can play." We often combine them, creating layers of different flavored gels by allowing one liquid to set, then pouring a different liquid on top.

We've designed all of these recipes to fit into a one-eighth sheet pan, which measures 9 by 6 inches (23 by 15 cm), the easiest way to make them. At the restaurant we like to set them in silicone candy molds. We use what's called a nonstick silicone "pomponette" mold with 24 domes about 1⅓ inches (34 mm) wide, because they are more elegant than cubes. (Both the sheet pan and the mold are available online at JBPrince.com.)

We use the following four thickeners: Agar, derived from seaweed and activated by heat, provides the backbone of the gel. Gellan gum is basically a sugar created by bacterial fermentation. Pectin is a sugar found in fruit often used to thicken jellies and jams and the thermoreversable pectin we use can be heated and then will solidify again as it cools. Gelatin is an animal-based gelling agent. We use silver gelatin sheets (see the Note on page 172). Each sheet weighs 2.5 grams, or about 6 grams bloomed. Three sheets are equal to one envelope or ¼ ounce of granulated gelatin. These four gelling agents are what determine the final texture of the pâte de fruit, which should be smooth and tender. And we've worked hard to get the balances right so that all the pâte de fruits have a very elegant texture.

All these ingredients can be found at online specialty food shops such as the Modernist Pantry and Gourmet Food World.

Because the weights for these ingredients are so critical, we only recommend weighing ingredients for these recipes to achieve good results. Because we will assume you are weighing with a digital scale, and digital scales weigh grams, we will only be using metric weights in the following recipes. (If you don't have a scale, I highly recommend you buy one; they're an invaluable tool in the kitchen, especially for baking.) For those who may not have a scale but still want to play, guesstimate using the following measurements: 1 teaspoon of gellan equals 4.7 grams; 1 teaspoon of agar equals 3 grams; 1 teaspoon of pectin equals 2.2 grams. A one-eighth sheet pan will yield fifty-four 1-inch (2.5 cm) cubes. Some of the recipes yield slightly more than one full sheet pan; leftovers will gel and set in whatever mold or cup you might have.

To cut or portion gels that are molded, carefully turn out the sheet pan onto a board and remove the plastic wrap. Fill a bain-marie insert or bowl with hot water. Dip a knife or cutter into the water, dry it, and make a cut. Dip the knife or cutter each time you do so.

Many of these recipes include simple syrup, 1 part water to 1 part sugar, because we always have it on hand. If you don't, simply add half the weight of the simple syrup as water and half as sugar; the liquids all need to be simmered regardless of how the sugar is added.

Finally, gels freeze well. They'll keep for a week well wrapped. This is especially convenient when using the candy molds. To serve them, we pop them out of their molds and allow them to thaw in the fridge for 30 minutes before serving.

THE LAST WORD PÂTE DE FRUIT

Makes fifty-four 1-inch (2.5 cm) cubes

A gelled version of the Prohibition-era Chartreuse cocktail, this is the most basic of the *pâte de fruits* because it's simply one mixture poured into a small sheet pan. The fennel fronds and dill not only give it floral notes, but also serve as a kind of interior garnish for this green-hued gel. We simply cut these into cubes and serve. This is a great all-purpose method and recipe.

6 grams salt

3 grams agar

3 grams gellan gum

2 grams thermoreversible pectin

140 grams simple syrup (70 grams sugar dissolved in 70 milliliters of water)

430 milliliters apple juice

6 sheets silver gelatin, soaked in ice water until softened

40 milliliters gin, plus a few drops to refresh

100 milliliters Chartreuse

70 milliliters lime juice (4 to 5 limes), plus a few drops to refresh

20 milliliters yuzu juice

¼ teaspoon rose water

2 tablespoons chopped fennel fronds and dill, plus more fennel fronds for garnish

In a small saucepan, combine the salt, agar, gellan gum, pectin, simple syrup, and about one-fourth of the apple juice and whisk or blend with a hand blender to distribute the powders. Put the pan over high heat, just until it comes to a boil, then reduce the heat and gently boil for 2 minutes to activate the agar (we always set a timer).

Remove it from the heat, squeeze the water out of the gelatin, and add it to the pot. Stir to melt the gelatin. If necessary, put the pan over low heat to help it melt. Pour this into a bowl set in an ice bath and stir with a rubber spatula to cool it slightly warmer than body temperature, so you do not cook out or lose the flavor from the citrus and alcohol. You want it warm, not hot (it will start to set if it gets too cold, in which case you should reheat it to melt it down again). Once it is down to a warmer temperature add the remaining liquids (gin, Chartreuse, lime juice, yuzu juice, rose water, and remaining

apple juice) to the bowl. Pass it through a fine-mesh sieve and stir in the fennel fronds and dill. Taste and add a few drops of lime and gin to refresh the flavors.

Line a one-eighth sheet pan, 9 by 6 inches (23 cm by 15 cm), with plastic wrap. Pour in the liquid. Once filled and there are small air bubbles on top, you can remove them by using a small kitchen torch and going over the top quickly with the flame, if you have one. Let the pâte de fruit sit on the counter until it is slightly set (about 30 minutes). Once it's slightly set place it on a flat surface in the fridge for at least 12 hours to fully set before slicing.

To serve, turn it out onto a cutting board. Hold your knife in a bain-marie of hot water or under running hot water, dry it, and make your first cut, rewarming frequently for the cleanest cuts possible. Garnish with fennel fronds.

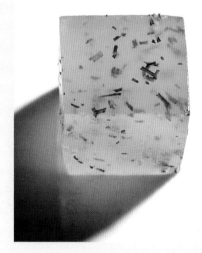

AMER-BIERE PÂTE DE FRUIT

Makes about 54   Picon is a brand of Amer and is a French aperitif, slightly bitter and with an orange flavor. You can buy it, but we prefer to make our own. It's often added to beer in Alsace to create a more flavorful and complex drink, thus this *pâte de fruit*. We make a separate froth, gelled, so that it looks just like a miniature beer. The gel can be made ahead, but the foam is best made the day you intend to serve it.

FOR THE BEER GEL

6 grams salt

4 grams agar

3 grams gellan gum

2 grams thermoreversible pectin (see page 154 for more information)

100 grams simple syrup (50 grams sugar dissolved in 50 milliliters water)

670 milliliters Meteor Beer (or any IPA you wish)

7 sheets silver gelatin, soaked in ice water until softened

40 milliliters homemade Amer Picon (recipe follows)

80 milliliters lemon juice (about 1½ lemons)

50 grams mandarin orange puree, reduced over medium heat to 25 grams (half of the volume)

Make the beer gel: In a small saucepan, combine the salt, agar, gellan, pectin, simple syrup, and 100 milliliters of the beer and whisk or blend with a hand blender to distribute the powders. Put the pan over high heat, just until it comes to a boil, then reduce the heat and gently boil it for 2 minutes to activate the agar (we always set a timer).

Remove it from the heat, squeeze the water out of the gelatin, and add it to the pot. Stir to melt the gelatin. If necessary, put the pan over low heat to help it melt. Pour this into a bowl set in an ice bath and stir with a rubber spatula to cool it slightly warmer then body temperature (100°F/38°C), so you do not cook out or lose the flavor from the citrus and alcohol (it will start to set if it gets too cold, in which case you should reheat to melt the gelatin). When the liquid is warm, add the Amer Picon, lemon juice, mandarin puree, and remaining beer and strain through a fine-mesh sieve. Taste and add a few drops of fresh lemon juice or beer to enhance the flavor, if needed.

Line a one-eighth sheet pan (9 by 6 inches/23 by 15 cm) with plastic wrap and pour in the liquid. Once filled and there are small air bubbles on top, you can remove them by gently using a small kitchen torch and going over the top quickly with the flame, if you have one. Let the pâte de fruit sit on the counter until it is slightly set (about 30 minutes). Once it's slightly set, place it on a flat surface in the fridge for at least 12 hours to fully set before slicing. Make the beer head only after the gel is firmly set.

FOR THE ORANGE "BEER HEAD" CLOUD

450 grams orange juice, reduced to 250 grams (simmer over medium-high heat for about 15 minutes)

1 tablespoon salt

2 tablespoons sugar

5 sheets silver gelatin, soaked in ice water until softened

35 grams yuzu juice

To make the orange beer head: After the beer gel has set, bring the reduced orange juice to a simmer, then remove it from the heat, and add the salt, sugar, and gelatin, squeezed of excess water. Stir to melt the gelatin and strain through a chinois or sieve.

Pour it into a bowl set in an ice bath and stir with a rubber spatula to cool it to around body temperature, warm but not hot. Stir in the yuzu juice. Transfer it to the bowl of a standing mixer fitted with a whisk. Whisk on high until it has quadrupled in volume, 30 to 40 minutes.

Spread the foam quickly, as it will start to set, over the set beer gel with an off-set spatula, smoothing it off so it is even.

Chill until the foam is set, about 2 hours.

Remove the gel from the pan and cut, using a 1-inch (2.5 cm) round cutter, dipped in warm water.

FOR THE GARNISH

Julienned candied ginger, a few pieces per serving (recipe follows)

1 tablespoon grains of paradise (see page 181 and Note)

Note: Toast the grains of paradise in a pan over low heat for about 7 minutes. Move them around to prevent them from burning, and cool. Once cool, blend to a powder using a spice grinder or coffee grinder.

Garnish with the candied ginger and a pinch of grains of paradise.

Amer-Biere Pâte de Fruit

Muscat and Strawberry Pâte de Fruit

Gewurztraminer and Mango Pâte de Fruit

The Last Word Pâte de Fruit

AMER PICON LIQUEUR

Makes 360 milliliters

320 milliliters Averna
30 milliliters coffee liqueur
12 grams Angostura bitters
2 grams orange bitters

Combine the ingredients and stir to mix.

You will have extra liqueur that can be saved in your bar indefinitely, and here is a traditional Alsatian aperitif in which to enjoy it. Pour 1½ ounces of this liqueur into a beer glass, then add a cold IPA beer on top. Make sure it has a head on it.

CANDIED GINGER

Makes about 40 1-inch/2.5 cm rounds

40 grams sugar
40 grams water
20 grams ginger, julienned

Dissolve the sugar in the water in a small saucepot. Add the julienned ginger and simmer until tender, 4 to 5 minutes.

GEWURZTRAMINER AND MANGO PÂTE DE FRUIT

Makes about 54

This is a two-toned *pâte de fruit* made with a thick layer of a wine gel on the bottom and a thin layer of a fruit puree gel on top, which is then garnished with a lime gel. We chill these in round silicone candy molds, but you could also use a one-eighth sheet pan to make the layers. The lime gel recipe included here makes 800 grams, twice what you will need for this, but you have to make that much in order for it to blend. Reserve and use the extra for garnish on fish crudo or raviolis.

FOR THE GEWURZTRAMINER GEL

600 grams Gewurztraminer, divided separately into 300 ml uncooked and 300 ml reduced down to 150 milliliters

260 milliliters simple syrup

7 grams salt

4 grams agar

3 grams gellan gum

2 grams thermoreversible pectin (see page 154 for more information)

6 sheets silver gelatin, soaked in ice water until bloomed, softened

8 milliliters elderflower liqueur

82 milliliters lime juice

To make the Gewurztraminer gel, combine the 150 grams of reduced Gewurztraminer, simple syrup, salt, agar, gellan, and pectin in a small pan, whisking to mix the powders. Put the pan over high heat, just until it comes to a boil, then reduce the heat and gently boil for 2 minutes to activate the agar (we always set a timer).

Remove it from the heat, squeeze the water out of the gelatin, and add it to the pot. Stir to melt the gelatin. If necessary, put the pan over low heat to help it melt. Pour this into a bowl set in an ice bath and stir with a rubber spatula to cool it slightly warmer then body temperature (100°F/38°C), so you do not cook out or lose the flavor from the citrus and alcohol (it will start to set if it gets too cold, in which case you should reheat to melt the gelatin). Mix in the elderflower liqueur, lime juice, and remaining uncooked Gewurztraminer. Strain.

Line a one-eighth sheet pan (9 by 6 inches/23 by 15 cm) with plastic wrap and pour in the liquid, leaving it about four-fifths full. Allow it to set at room temperature before adding the mango gel.

FOR THE MANGO GEL

245 grams mango puree

262 grams passion fruit puree

2 grams agar

1.5 grams gellan gum

1 gram thermoreversible pectin (see page 154 for more information)

4 grams salt

4 sheets silver gelatin sheets, soaked in ice water until bloomed, softened

10 milliliters lime juice, plus more as needed

Lime gel (recipe follows)

To make the mango gel, combine the mango puree, passion fruit puree, agar, gellan, pectin, and salt in a small pan, whisking to mix in the powders. Put the pan over high heat, just until it comes to a boil, then reduce the heat and gently boil for 2 minutes to activate the agar (we always set a timer).

Remove it from the heat, squeeze the water out of the gelatin, and add it to the pot. Stir to melt the gelatin. If necessary, put the pan over low heat to help it melt. Pour this into a bowl set in an ice bath and stir with a rubber spatula to cool it to around body temperature, warm but not hot (it will start to set if it gets too cold, in which case you should reheat to melt the gelatin).

Cool slightly, seasoning with the lime juice. Strain.

Once the Gewurztraminer is set in the molds at room temperature, pour the mango on top and let it sit at room temperature for 30 minutes, then place in the fridge for 12 hours to firmly set it.

Remove the gel from the pan to a cutting board, mango side up. Hold your knife in a bain-marie of hot water or under running hot water, dry it, and make your first cut, rewarming each time for the cleanest cuts possible. Cut into 1-inch (2.5 cm) cubes or as desired and garnish with dots of lime gel.

FOR THE LIME GEL

300 grams water

70 grams sugar

14 grams agar

400 grams lime juice (from 20 to 25 limes, depending on the quality and size)

Salt and freshly ground black pepper

Combine the water, sugar, and agar in a small pan, whisking to mix in the powders, over high heat, and bring to a boil, then reduce heat and gently boil for 2 minutes. Remove from the heat. Add the lime juice and let it set for 2 hours in the fridge. Once set, break into small pieces and blend on high in a high-speed blender until smooth, then pass through a chinois or fine-mesh sieve. It should be a smooth, thick gel that can be piped from a squeeze bottle or pastry bag and hold its shape.

MUSCAT AND STRAWBERRY PÂTE DE FRUIT

Makes about 54

This combines the sweet floral notes of Muscat (along with elderflower liqueur) with the sweet-tart flavor of strawberry, enhanced with yuzu. As with the mango pâte de fruit, this has a thin layer of fruit gel on the bottom.

FOR THE STRAWBERRY GEL

2 grams agar

1.5 grams gellan gum

1 gram thermoreversible pectin
(see page 154 for more information)

4 grams salt

138 milliliters simple syrup

262 grams strawberry puree

5 sheets silver gelatin, soaked in ice
water until softened

100 milliliters yuzu juice

To make the strawberry gel, combine the agar, gellan, pectin, salt, simple syrup, and 100 grams of the strawberry puree in a small pot, and blend using a hand blender or whisk to distribute the powders. Put the pan over high heat, just until it comes to a boil, then reduce the heat and gently boil for 2 minutes to activate the agar (we always set a timer).

Remove it from the heat. Squeeze the water out of the gelatin, and add it to the pot. Stir to melt the gelatin. If necessary, put the pan over low heat to help it melt. Pour this into a bowl set in an ice bath and stir with a rubber spatula to cool it to around body temperature, warm but not hot (it will start to set if it gets too cold, in which case you should reheat to melt the gelatin). Add the remaining strawberry puree and the yuzu juice, then strain.

Line a one-eighth pan, 9 by 6 inches (23 cm by 15 cm), with plastic wrap. Pour enough strawberry gel to fill about one-fifth of the pan. Let the pâte de fruit sit at room temperature until it is slightly set (about 30 minutes) before adding the next layer.

FOR THE MUSCAT GEL

4 grams agar

3 grams gellan gum

2 grams thermoreversible pectin
(see page 154 for more information)

7 grams salt

90 milliliters simple syrup

650 milliliters Muscat

6 sheets silver gelatin, soaked in
ice water until bloomed, softened

6 milliliters elderflower liqueur

50 milliliters lime juice

To make the Muscat gel, combine the agar, gellan, pectin, salt, simple syrup, and 125 milliliters of the Muscat in a small pot, and whisk to distribute the powders. Put the pan over high heat, just until it comes to a boil, then reduce the heat and gently boil for 2 minutes to activate the agar (we always set a timer).

Remove it from the heat, squeeze the water out of the gelatin, and add it to the pot. Stir to melt the gelatin. If necessary, put the pan over low heat to help it melt. Pour this into a bowl set in an ice bath and stir with a rubber spatula to cool it to around body temperature, warm but

not hot (it will start to set if it gets too cold, in which case you should reheat to melt the gelatin). Allow to cool slightly and add the remaining 525 milliliters Muscat, the elderflower liqueur, and the lime juice.

Pour onto the set strawberry gel, let it sit at room temperature for about 30 minutes, then place in the fridge on a flat surface for 12 hours to fully set.

Remove the gel from the pan to a cutting board, strawberry side down. Hold your knife in a bain-marie of hot water or under running hot water, dry it, and make your first cut, rewarming each time for the cleanest cuts possible. Cut into 1-inch (2.5 cm) cubes or as desired.

COLD APPETIZERS

TARTARE OF YELLOWFIN
TUNA AND DIVER SCALLOPS
with Caviar

162

RAW DIVER SCALLOPS
with Jalapeño Coulis, Black Radish,
and Grated Pecans

165

SCALLOP CEVICHE
with Tahitian Vanilla Beans and
Toasted Buckwheat Seeds

166

FENNEL PANNA COTTA
with Cockles, Orange Emulsion,
and Caviar

168

WHITE ASPARAGUS
with Smoked Salmon, Sorrel, and
Trout Caviar

171

BLACK BASS TARTARE
with Macadamia Nuts, Cilantro
Gelée, and Puffed Barley

172

RABBIT TERRINE
with Gewurztraminer, Hyssop,
and Fines Herbes Coulis

175

QUAIL AND FOIE GRAS
PRALINE
with Black Truffle Gelée and Fines
Herbes Salad

177

*ON THE FOIE GRAS
TERRINE*

180

FOIE GRAS TERRINE
with Cantaloupe, Duck Prosciutto,
and Preserved Porcini

181

FOIE GRAS TERRINE AND
TOASTED PISTACHIO PRALINE
with Fennel Pollen Waffle
and Smoked Date Jam

184

HAMACHI, BLACK
PÉRIGORD TRUFFLE, AND
FOIE GRAS MILLE-FEUILLE
with Grapes, Celeriac, and Truffle
Vinaigrette

188

ALASKAN KING CRAB
"CANNELLONI"
with Sea Urchin Coulis

190

BRAISED TRUMPET
ROYALE SALAD
with Bouchot Mussels and Harissa
Vinaigrette

193

KUMAMOTO OYSTERS
"EN PANNEQUET"
with Smoked Salmon Sauce

194

*CLASSICAL CUISINE
VERSUS MODERNIST
CUISINE*

197

TARTARE OF YELLOWFIN TUNA AND DIVER SCALLOPS

WITH CAVIAR

Serves 6

The first time I made this was as sous chef at Jean-Georges. Some VIPs arrived and I had to come up with a special dish fast. Tuna and scallops—chopped as tartare and garnished with caviar—was both easy to make on the fly and also felt luxurious. I seasoned the fish with oil first to coat it evenly, and then added flavor in layers—chives, pepper, and some lemon juice. This dish really highlights the quality of the products. When I opened Atelier at the Ritz, I put it on the menu, and by popular demand, it became a signature dish of mine. When I was selected as one of the 10 Best New Chefs by *Food & Wine* magazine, I decided to make it for the gala dinner at their annual food festival in Aspen.

5 tablespoons (75 ml) balsamic vinegar

1 tablespoon sugar

3 tablespoons (45 ml) Chive Oil (page 233)

1 Persian cucumber, cut into paper-thin slices

2 teaspoons grapeseed oil

Salt and freshly ground black pepper

9 ounces (250 g) sushi-grade yellowfin tuna, cut into ¼-inch (6 mm) cubes

9 ounces (250 g) sushi-grade diver scallops, cut into ¼-inch (6 mm) cubes

1½ teaspoons hazelnut oil

1½ teaspoons extra-virgin olive oil

3 ounces (85 g) Osetra caviar

2 tablespoons finely chopped chives

½ lemon

Baby red-veined sorrel or baby sunflower, for garnish

To make the tartare, bring the vinegar and sugar to a boil in a small saucepan. Boil, stirring, until syrupy and reduced by half, about 2 minutes. Set aside to cool completely, then transfer to a squeeze bottle. At the same time, transfer the chive oil into its own small squeeze bottle.

Divide the cucumber slices among six chilled serving plates, shingling them in two adjoining lines. Rub the slices with ½ teaspoon of the grapeseed oil, then sprinkle with salt and pepper. Cover and chill until ready to serve.

Combine the tuna and scallops in a bowl set over a large bowl of ice. Mix gently just until dispersed. Add the hazelnut and olive oils and the remaining 1½ teaspoons grapeseed oil. Gently mix just until evenly coated, then add the caviar, chives, and a pinch each of salt and pepper and gently stir to evenly mix. Squeeze the juice from the lemon over the mix and turn once more gently.

Divide the tartare among the rows of chilled cucumbers, spooning it in a line. Spike the tartare with the sprouts. Squeeze a line of balsamic vinegar and chive oil on the plate alongside each line of tartare. Serve immediately.

RAW DIVER SCALLOPS
WITH JALAPEÑO COULIS, BLACK RADISH, AND GRATED PECANS

Serves 6

Combining hazelnut oil with pecans gives a quintessential American nutty boldness without overwhelming the delicate scallops. This dish is American in that it uses excellent local products, while also featuring a common ingredient from my homeland, the black radish, which has a very fragrant, distinctive aroma (though you could substitute daikon radish or even white radish for it). Salty fingers, a succulent that grow in salt marshes, are a cousin of the better-known sea beans, but they are saltier and juicier. I like using them in this recipe as they are a nice counterbalance to the candy-like sweetness of the raw scallops with their natural, crunchy texture and juicy brine.

FOR THE JALAPEÑO COULIS
9 ounces (250 g) jalapeños
½ cup (125 ml) grapeseed oil
Salt
¼ cup (60 ml) hazelnut oil
¼ cup (60 ml) simple syrup (30 g sugar
    dissolved in 30 milliliters water)
2 tablespoons (30 g) lemon juice

To make the coulis, trim off the stems from the jalapeños, then halve the peppers lengthwise. Wearing gloves, pick out the seeds and ribs and discard. Cut the halves into ¼-inch (6 mm) slices crosswise.

Heat the grapeseed oil in a medium saucepan over medium heat. Add the sliced jalapeños, season with salt, and cook, stirring often, until slightly softened, about 3 minutes. Add 7 tablespoons (100 ml) of water, bring to a boil, and cover. Boil until the water evaporates, about 6 minutes.

Transfer the jalapeños to a quart-sized deli container, along with the hazelnut oil, simple syrup, and lemon juice. Puree with an immersion blender until smooth, adding a scant tablespoon or more water if needed to blend well. Press the mixture through a fine-mesh sieve.

FOR THE SCALLOPS
12 sushi-grade diver scallops (U-12)
Grapeseed oil
Salt and freshly ground white pepper
8 ounces (226 g) black radish, scrubbed
    and trimmed
Hazelnut oil
6 salty fingers or sea beans, cut into
    ⅛-inch pieces
1 lemon
6 pecans
Aleppo pepper
Tiny edible flowers

To make the scallops, remove and discard the tough muscles from the scallops, then cut each scallop into four even, thin slices. Arrange the slices on a cold tray, rub with just enough grapeseed oil to make the tops shine, then sprinkle with salt and pepper.

Cut the radish in quarters and very thinly slice crosswise. Season with a little salt, hazelnut oil, and grapeseed oil and toss to lightly coat.

Arrange the scallops on six cold plates, dividing evenly and slightly overlapping them in a fan or flower shape. Twist each black radish slice into a cornet and spike into the scallops. Scatter the salty fingers on top. Zest the lemon directly on top of all the scallops, then use the same Microplane to zest the pecans on top. Sprinkle with Aleppo, garnish with the flowers, pour three tablespoons of jalapeño coulis all around, and serve immediately.

SCALLOP CEVICHE
WITH TAHITIAN VANILLA BEANS AND TOASTED BUCKWHEAT SEEDS

Serves 6

This ceviche is about texture—the delicate scallops contrast with the crunch of the buckwheat, which gives the shellfish some backbone. I usually do this with Nantucket bay scallops in season because they have more bite and are even sweeter than diver scallops. Vanilla is great with scallops (lobster, too, for that matter), as it highlights the natural sweetness of fresh seafood.

The final garnish here, what gives the dish some crunch, is rye crisps, simple good rye bread, very thinly sliced, and dehydrated in a very low oven.

⅓ cup (55 g) buckwheat groats
½ small fennel bulb, plus fronds
    for garnish
1 pound (455 g) sushi-grade bay or
    diver scallops
4 tablespoons (60 ml) grapeseed oil
½ Tahitian vanilla bean
1 lime
1½ tablespoons (6 g) finely chopped
    scallions
Juice of 2 lemons
Salt and freshly ground white pepper
Thin slices of rye bread toasted
    until crisp

Place the buckwheat in a small skillet over medium heat. Toast, shaking the pan occasionally, until browned and popping, about 3 minutes. Remove from the heat and cool completely. Transfer to a parchment-lined cutting board and press the bottom of a clean heavy pan against them to crack into bits.

Take the half fennel bulb and cut out the core, then thinly slice crosswise on a mandoline. Keep in ice water to crisp and curl.

If using bay scallops, halve them through their equators against their fibers. If using diver scallops, remove and discard tough muscles, then cut each from top to bottom with their fibers into four slices. Put in a bowl set over a larger bowl of ice and chill.

Pour the oil into a medium bowl. Split the vanilla bean lengthwise in half, then scrape out the seeds and pulp with the knife and place them in the oil. Grate the zest of half the lime directly into the bowl. Whisk well.

Pour the vanilla dressing over the chilled sliced scallops still set over ice and mix to evenly coat. Add the scallions and crushed buckwheat seeds and mix, then fold in the lemon juice. Season to taste with salt and pepper. Return to the refrigerator to chill for 10 to 15 minutes.

When ready to serve, drain the fennel well. Divide the ceviche among six chilled serving plates and top with fennel slices and fronds. Serve with rye bread crisps.

FENNEL PANNA COTTA
WITH COCKLES, ORANGE EMULSION, AND CAVIAR

Serves 6

When I was young I didn't like the anise flavor of fennel, but over time it grew on me and I began to admire its subtle taste. This dish, which is from my days at the Modern, puts this flavor on show in a panna cotta with cockles, caviar, and an orange emulsion made from reduced orange juice, seasoned with some of the cockles' cooking liquid. The orange, fennel, and brininess of the caviar and cockles make for a lovely pairing.

FOR THE FENNEL PANNA COTTA

1 tablespoon butter
4½ ounces (125 g) fennel, very thinly sliced
1 pinch fennel seeds
⅓ cup (75 ml) cold water
Salt and freshly ground white pepper
½ cup (125 ml) heavy cream
2 sheets silver gelatin, soaked in ice water until softened

Lightly coat six 2-ounce (60 ml) aluminum ramekins with nonstick cooking spray and set them on a half sheet pan.

Melt the butter in a large saucepan over medium heat and add the fennel and fennel seeds. Stir, then add the water. It should barely cover the solids. Add 2 pinches of salt and 2 to 3 grinds of white pepper, stir well, and bring to a boil. Reduce the heat to a simmer, cover partially, and cook just until the fennel is soft and wilted, about 10 minutes. Remove from the heat and add the cream, then stir well and return to medium heat. Adjust the heat to maintain a steady simmer for 5 minutes. Remove from the heat and add the gelatin leaves, squeezing out excess water. Stir until they melt.

Transfer to a blender and puree until very smooth. Season to taste with salt and pepper, then strain through a fine-mesh sieve. Divide among the ramekins and refrigerate uncovered until cold and set. Cover completely with plastic wrap and keep refrigerated until ready to serve.

FOR THE COCKLES

1 pound (455 g) cockles
1 tablespoon extra-virgin olive oil
1 ounce (25 g) shallot (1 medium), cut into ⅛-inch (3 mm) slices
1 sprig thyme
½ cup (125 ml) dry white wine

Tap the hinged side of each cockle to make sure it closes. That means it's alive. If it doesn't close, discard it. Purge the cockles of sand and grit by placing in a small bowl and running cold water over them for 20 minutes.

Heat the oil in a medium saucepan over medium-high heat. Add the shallot and cook, stirring, until softened (but don't let it take on color), about 3 minutes. Add the cockles, raise the heat to high, and stir and shake the pan to coat the cockles with the oil and shallots. Add the thyme and wine, cover, and cook, stirring occasionally, until the cockles open, about 4 minutes.

Using a slotted spoon or spider, transfer the cockles to a sheet pan to cool; reserve the cooking liquid. When the cockles are cool enough to handle, remove the cockles from their shells; discard the shells. Transfer the cockles to an airtight container and refrigerate immediately.

Pour the reserved cooking liquid and the liquid accumulated on the pan with the cockles through a fine-mesh sieve into a small saucepan. Bring to a boil over medium heat, then boil until reduced by half. Pour slowly through a fine-mesh sieve into a bowl, leaving behind the last of the liquid with its sediment. Set the bowl over a larger bowl of ice and water to cool quickly. You need about 3 tablespoons (45 ml) for the emulsion.

When the cockles are cold, remove their stomachs, which have a lot of sand. Cut a small slit in one end of a cockle belly, then press the belly flat against the cutting board with your finger to squeeze it out through the slit. Transfer the cleaned cockle to a bowl set over a bowl of ice and repeat with the remaining cockles. Add just enough cockle juice to keep them moistened.

FOR THE ORANGE EMULSION

¾ cup (180 ml) fresh orange juice

3 tablespoons (45 ml) reduced cockle
   juice (from above)

1 tablespoon extra-virgin olive oil

4 teaspoons grapeseed oil

1 tablespoon lemon juice

Salt and freshly ground white pepper

Bring the orange juice to a boil in a medium saucepan. Continue boiling until reduced by half. Pour into a metal bowl set over a larger bowl of ice and water. Whisk until room temperature, then whisk in the cockle juice and both oils to emulsify. Whisk in the lemon juice, then season to taste with salt and pepper.

FOR THE GARNISH

2 ounces (60 g) Osetra caviar

Celery leaves, fennel fronds, or
   chervil leaves

Dip the base of a panna cotta ramekin in warm water for 5 to 7 seconds to loosen the panna cotta. Quickly and carefully invert it onto the center of a shallow bowl, then lift off the mold. Spoon the orange emulsion around it and top with the cockles. Garnish with the Osetra caviar and the celery leaves. Repeat for the remaining servings.

WHITE ASPARAGUS
WITH SMOKED SALMON, SORREL, AND TROUT CAVIAR

Serves 6

I grew up in a part of the world that loves white asparagus. Every spring we'd buy and eat as much as we could while they lasted. Everyone was served a pound—that was the typical portion size. We kids would go around to the farmers knowing they couldn't sell broken ones and we'd buy them cheap—which meant more tips, the best part. My mother used to prepare it in many ways, with vinaigrettes, hollandaise sauce, bearnaise sauce. And we'd keep the cooking liquid and use it as the base for soup. The spears were always cooked simply, with minimal water, a pinch of salt, a little sugar, and maybe some herbs.

I learned from my mother that white asparagus freezes beautifully, so when it's in season, I buy a lot, peel it, and freeze it so that we can have it all year round. It cooks from frozen in 5 minutes in boiling water.

When I was at Atelier in the Ritz, I wanted to bring this special vegetable to life for New Yorkers. White asparagus goes beautifully with salmon but I didn't just want to serve them simply with sliced salmon. So I wondered if we could make a sauce out of the salmon—it sounded a little crazy, but when we all tasted it, smoked salmon with shallots, half-and-half, and vermouth, it was delicious—and another example of entwining Alsace and New York fine dining.

FOR THE SAUCE

2 shallots, chopped
1 tablespoon olive oil
⅔ cup (160 ml) dry vermouth
7 ounces (200 g) smoked salmon, roughly chopped
2 cups (500 ml) half-and-half
1 tablespoon tomato paste
Slurry (2 tablespoons cornstarch mixed with 2 tablespoons water)
1 teaspoon sherry vinegar, or to taste
Salt and freshly ground black pepper

In a saucepan over medium-high heat, sweat the shallots in the olive oil until they're tender. Add the vermouth and reduce it by half, then add in the chopped smoked salmon and cook it for a minute or two, just until it starts breaking apart. Add the half-and-half and tomato paste and bring it to a simmer. Turn the heat to low and continue to cook for 8 to 10 minutes. Puree it all in a blender and pass it through a fine-mesh sieve into a saucepan, pressing on the solids to get all the liquid out.

Reheat it gently and add enough of the cornstarch slurry to give it a nappé consistency (you should be able to draw a line through the sauce on the back of a spatula). Add the vinegar. Pour it into a bowl set in ice to chill it quickly.

When the sauce has cooled, taste and season accordingly with salt and pepper. Be spare with the salt, as the salmon has been cured with salt.

TO FINISH

12 large white asparagus, peeled and woody ends removed
9 ounces (250 g) sushi-quality salmon, cut into six ⅛-inch crosscut slices
Grapeseed oil, as needed
Fleur de sel
Cracked black pepper
Chopped chives
2½ ounces (75 g) trout or salmon caviar
Red vein sorrel leaves
12 borage flowers

Place the asparagus in a steamer and cook until tender, 7 to 10 minutes. Remove to an ice bath and chill. Remove them to a paper towel–lined plate. These can be refrigerated for a day.

Spoon a generous helping of the sauce onto each of six plates. Top it with two stalks of asparagus. On a separate plate, rub the salmon with oil and season with fleur de sel, pepper, and chives. With a spatula, place a salmon fillet between the two asparagus stalks on each plate. Garnish the asparagus with the caviar, red sorrel, and borage flowers.

Note: Large white asparagus freeze well when fresh. Peel them and lay them on a sheet pan lined with parchment paper and freeze them. Once frozen, place them carefully in multiple zip-top plastic bags (a dozen asparagus per bag at the most), then store them in an airtight plastic container with a lid in the freezer. They can be kept for up to 6 months. To cook them, bring salted water to a boil, add the frozen asparagus, and cook until tender, 5 to 10 minutes.

BLACK BASS TARTARE
WITH MACADAMIA NUTS, CILANTRO GELÉE, AND PUFFED BARLEY

Serves 6 to 8

This is a dish to prepare with pristine fresh fish, preferably black bass or salmon. What distinguishes it is the garnish—crunchy puffed barley and macadamia nuts, Aleppo or Espelette pepper, and plenty of citrus—all of which enhance and showcase the freshness of the fish. It's important to coat the diced fish first with grapeseed oil, which remains fluid even at refrigerated temperatures. The oil prevents the salt from curing the fish. We want the seasoning, but we don't want it to cook the fish.

The cilantro gelée is a fabulous acidic, aromatic seasoning that finishes the dish. It's lovely with this fish or any fish. It would also make a great mignonette sauce for oysters.

1½ pounds (700 g) black bass fillet or
    salmon, cut into ¼-inch (6 mm) dice
3 tablespoons grapeseed oil
3 tablespoons chopped macadamia nuts
5 tablespoons chopped chives
2 tablespoons chopped celery leaves
1 teaspoon Aleppo or Espelette pepper
6 tablespoons (106 g) finely chopped
    fennel
3 tablespoons brunoised (very finely
    diced) red bell pepper
1 tablespoon salt
30 grinds pepper
1 tablespoon extra-virgin olive oil
3 tablespoons (45 g) Cilantro Gelée
    (recipe follows)
1 tablespoon lime zest
1½ teaspoons lemon zest
1 teaspoon lemon juice
2 teaspoons lime juice

In a bowl set in ice, combine the fish and grapeseed oil. Mix well. Add the macadamia nuts, chives, celery leaves, Aleppo or Espelette, fennel, and bell pepper, and mix to combine. Add the salt, pepper, olive oil, and cilantro gelée. Add the citrus zest and juices. Mix well. Taste and adjust the seasoning as desired.

FOR THE GARNISH
Puffed Barley (recipe follows)
Micro herbs and flowers
Cilantro Gelée (recipe follows)
Fennel fronds
Olive oil
Granny Smith apple, cut into thin slices

Divide into six or eight portions on plates as desired (in a ring mold, if you wish). Garnish with the barley, micro herbs, cilantro gelée, and fennel fronds, a drizzle of olive oil, and slices of apple. Serve immediately.

CILANTRO GELÉE

3½ tablespoons (50 ml) Champagne
    vinegar
½ habanero chile pepper, seeded
½ teaspoon salt
10 black peppercorns
5 cilantro sprigs, chopped
3 ounces (85 g) pineapple, chopped
1 clove garlic, halved, germ removed,
    smashed
6 sheets (15 g) silver gelatin, soaked in
    ice water until softened (see Note)

Note: There are five different grades of gelatin, defined by weight. In our kitchen, we always use silver, so everybody knows the weight and strength of a sheet. Any "color" can be used, as long as the final weight is achieved.

Platinum = 1.75 g
Gold = 2 g
Silver = 2.5 g
Bronze = 3.5 g
Titanium = 5 g

Combine a scant 2 cups (450 ml) of water with the vinegar, chile, salt, and peppercorns in a pan and bring to a boil. Let the liquid cool and pour over the chopped cilantro, pineapple, and smashed garlic. Let marinate for at least 24 hours in the refrigerator.

Strain the pineapple liquid into a saucepan. Add the gelatin, squeezed of excess water, and reheat until the gelatin has dissolved completely. Refrigerate.

When ready to use, stir or dice the gelée.

PUFFED BARLEY

You can buy puffed barley, but the barley you puff yourself is best. It's simple to do—cook it, dehydrate it, and then fry it.

1¼ cup (250 g) pearl barley
Salt
Grapeseed oil, for frying

Cook the barley in 2 quarts/liters of water until tender, about 30 minutes. Season with salt. Spread it out on a Silpat-lined sheet pan and bake at 150°F (175°C) for 2½ hours.

Fry in 375°F (190°C) oil until it puffs and floats to the surface. Remove it to plate or tray lined with paper towels. While it's best used immediately, any leftovers can be stored for a week in an airtight container.

RABBIT TERRINE
WITH GEWURZTRAMINER, HYSSOP, AND FINES HERBES COULIS

Serves 6

I grew up with rabbits cooked in many ways. It was common on our table. While this dish employs the farm-cooking techniques that made up my childhood, I've refined the presentation for a Michelin star–worthy preparation. Again, I use basic techniques to make use of the whole animal and, with a little imagination and a bright herb sauce, transform the dish. Served this way it's a study of the rabbit—a rabbit terrine, with an herb coulis, cured loin, and a rabbit liver puree sandwiched between small potato chips. On the other hand, it's simple charcuterie.

The hyssop is a prominent flavor in this dish. Common in Alsace, hyssop is a shrub we use like an herb. It's in the mint family and is my favorite herb. I looked for it at the Union Square Greenmarket, but no one had it. Out for a walk not far from where we live in Chelsea, in the Hudson River Park at West Fifty-Fifth Street, I saw it growing and picked it. It has a minty flavor, but there's really nothing quite like it (and it seems to have many medicinal benefits as well). If you can't find it, replace it in this recipe with two star anise pods and twelve mint leaves.

FOR THE RABBIT TERRINE

1 whole rabbit (with heart, liver, and kidneys—we get ours from the wonderful purveyor D'Artagnan)
1 small bunch chervil
1 small bunch parsley
½ bunch (about 2 ounces/55 g) hyssop (if unavailable, 2 star anise pods and 12 mint leaves)
2 bay leaves
2 cloves garlic, smashed
1 (750-ml) bottle Gewurztraminer (reserve ½ cup/120 ml for the loin marinade)
3 cups (700 ml) White Chicken Stock (page 251), or more if needed (rabbit needs to be covered)
1 tablespoon (8 g) salt, plus more to taste
30 grinds pepper, plus more to taste
6 sheets silver gelatin, soaked in water until softened (see Note on page 172)
6 poached quail eggs, to garnish (optional)

Preheat your oven to 350°F (175°C).

Break down the rabbit into pieces, reserving one loin, separating the legs from the carcass, then halving the carcass, so that it fits efficiently in a pan or Dutch oven. Reserve the kidneys, heart, and liver.

Make a bed of the chervil, parsley, hyssop, bay leaves, and garlic in the bottom of a small pan or Dutch oven. Lay the rabbit pieces on top. Add the wine, reserving ½ cup (120 ml) for the loin marinade, and the stock. The rabbit should be completely covered in liquid. Season with the salt and pepper.

Cook the rabbit in a water bath: Put the pan or Dutch oven, covered, in a roasting pan and fill the roasting pan with hot water until it comes halfway up the sides of the pan or Dutch oven, and cook in the oven for 2 to 2½ hours, until the rabbit is fork tender. Allow it to cool to room temperature in the cooking liquid. Pick all the meat from the bones. Strain the cuisson, or cooking liquid, and reduce it to 3 cups (750 ml), simmering on the stovetop over medium heat.

Make a gelée of the cuisson by adding the gelatin sheets, squeezed of excess liquid. Season it with salt and pepper to taste.

Put about ¼ cup (40 g) of the meat in 4-ounce (120 ml) ramekins, if you prefer to serve unmolded, or serving bowls. Ladle about 3½ tablespoons (50 ml) of the cooking liquid over the rabbit portions. Give the rabbit in each ramekin or bowl a couple pokes with a spoon to make sure the liquid is thoroughly mixed in. Refrigerate until completely chilled.

FOR THE RABBIT LOIN MARINADE

1 teaspoon allspice
1 tablespoon (18 g) juniper berries
1 teaspoon black peppercorns
1 star anise
2 cloves
½ cup (125 ml) orange juice
1 cup (250 ml) Gewurztraminer
1 bay leaf
3 sprigs thyme
1 sprig rosemary
Reserved rabbit loin

recipe continues

Toast the allspice, juniper berries, peppercorns, star anise, and cloves for the marinade over medium-high heat until fragrant, about 2 minutes. Combine the orange juice and wine with the toasted spices. Then add the bay leaf, thyme, and rosemary. Coat the reserved rabbit loin with the liquid and then marinate, refrigerated and covered, overnight.

FOR THE LOIN CURE

½ cup (65 g) salt
½ cup (100 g) sugar

Combine the salt and sugar. Remove the loin from the marinade and pat it dry. Cover it in the cure for 30 minutes. Remove the loin from the cure, rinse, and dry. The loin is good to go at this point, but if you have a smoker, it is excellent smoked for 10 minutes or so.

FOR THE FINES HERBES COULIS

2 eggs, at room temperature
3 cups (100 g) loosely packed Italian parsley leaves
1½ cups (45 g) chervil leaves
⅓ cup tarragon leaves
¼ teaspoon cayenne pepper, or to taste
Salt
3 to 4 dashes Tabasco
¾ cup (180 ml) grapeseed oil

Bring a pot of water to a boil for the eggs. Submerge the eggs and cook for 4 minutes, then remove them to an ice bath. Peel them.

In a blender, combine the eggs with the parsley, chervil, tarragon, ½ cup (125 ml) of water, the cayenne, salt, and Tabasco. Blend until the herbs are pureed. With the blender running on high, pour in the oil in a steady stream. Taste and adjust the seasoning as needed. Pass through a fine-mesh strainer into a bowl. Set in ice.

FOR THE POTATO CHIPS

3 or 4 Yukon gold potatoes (about 1 inch/ 2.5 cm in diameter), thinly sliced for chips (This should yield 40 thin slices; you'll use only 24. This is because when they bake in the oven, about 30 percent break or tear and are not good enough to be used.)
Simple syrup (2 ounces/60 grams sugar dissolved in ¼ cup/60 milliliters water)

Preheat your oven to 150°F (65°C) or to its lowest setting.

Dip the potato slices in the syrup for 2 minutes. Drain the excess, lay them on a Silpat, and place another Silpat on top. Bake for 45 minutes, or until crisp.

FOR THE RABBIT LIVER PÂTÉ

Reserved liver, kidneys, and heart of the rabbit
3½ ounces (100 g) chicken liver (about 2 livers)
1 teaspoon grapeseed oil, plus more for sautéing
2 tablespoons plus 1 teaspoon Cognac
⅛ teaspoon Quatre Épices (recipe follows)
¼ teaspoon ground juniper berries
Salt and freshly ground black pepper
1 tablespoon minced parsley

Sauté the livers, kidneys, and heart in the oil until the liver is medium-rare, 1 to 2 minutes. Add 2 tablespoons of the Cognac, flame it, and sauté until the Cognac has cooked off (to flame a sauce hold a match or a lighter to it; if you have a gas stove, you can also tilt the pan so the sauce comes close enough to the flame that the flame will ignite the fumes). Chop the meat into a paste. In a mixing bowl, combine the paste with the remaining 1 teaspoon of Cognac, the quatre épices, ground juniper berries, and salt and pepper to taste. Stir in the parsley and 1 teaspoon of grapeseed oil.

To finish the dish: Unmold the rabbit terrines, if using ramekins. Spoon the fines herbes coulis generously over the top of the terrines. Spread some pâté on a potato chip, cover with a second chip, then repeat to make a triple-decker pâté-and-potato-chip sandwich. Serve each portion of terrine, with one potato chip sandwich, a ½-inch-thick (1.25 cm) slice of cured loin, and a poached quail egg, if using.

QUATRE ÉPICES

This is a classical French spice mixture, common in pâtés. I also use it in the stuffed rolled pasta on page 302.

Makes about 2 tablespoons (28 grams)

2 tablespoons (16 g) black peppercorns
1 teaspoon (3 g) whole cloves
2 teaspoons (6 g) ground ginger
1 teaspoon (3 g) ground nutmeg

In a dry sauté pan over medium high heat, toast the peppercorns and cloves until they become fragrant, about 1 minute. Allow them to cool, then grind them in a spice grinder. Combine this mixture with the ginger and nutmeg, stir to combine, and store in an airtight container for up to a month.

QUAIL AND FOIE GRAS PRALINE
WITH BLACK TRUFFLE GELÉE AND FINES HERBES SALAD

Serves 12

When I made the move to the Ritz, my biggest challenge was to break away from Jean-Georges Vongerichten's cooking. Finding your own personality can be a problem for chefs, and much depends on who you worked for, as well as your personal taste. A painter or writer, before a blank slate, must find his or her own voice. It is the same with chefs. I had to learn to translate who I am to my cooking, and I discovered that sometimes one dish can really bring your identity into focus.

This was one such dish for me. Quail and foie gras are common in Alsace. In addition, the preparation makes use of trimmings to create a whole new dish, so that nothing goes to waste. I learned this from my uncle—how to use everything. Drawing on influences from my past, I was able to create something new. And while this dish takes some work and uses expensive ingredients, it's certainly one of the most delicious recipes in this book.

You can buy truffle juice in specialty gourmet stores or online. As a commercial kitchen, we buy it in pint-sized cans, but you can find it in cans as small as 2 ounces (60 ml). An important note: There are many truffle products on the market, and there is only one way to guarantee you get the legitimate product for the money it is worth: by double-checking its scientific name on the label. For the black truffle you should see: *Tuber melanosporum*. For the white truffle, the Latin name is *Tuber magnatum pico*. Also, be aware that truffle juice and truffle oil are different products. Stay away from truffle oil—it's mostly fake essences, which give you an artificial flavor.

FOR THE QUAIL FOIE BALLS
6 quail (3½ to 4 ounces/105 to 120 g each)
1 pound (450 g) foie gras
1 egg
2 tablespoons port wine
1 tablespoon Cognac
2 tablespoons foie gras cure (page 184)
Salt
12 large Bibb lettuce leaves

To debone the quail, separate the boneless thighs from the drumsticks, then cut the skin ends from the thighs. Be sure to look out for bone and cartilage bits and skin on the thighs and scrape them off and save them. Use your fingers to feel for bones and cartilage between the breast halves and cut each breast in half and remove the bones, along with the skin. Then, cut the boneless skinless breast halves in thirds lengthwise, then in quarters crosswise for a ½-inch (1.25 cm) dice. Do the same with the thigh meat. You should end up with 10¼ ounces

(290 g) of diced quail meat and 12 drumsticks. Reserve the drumsticks until you are ready to make the confit.

Put the foie gras on a clean sheet of plastic wrap. Separate the two lobes, then push on them slowly with your thumbs, moving from the centers outward to find the veins. Use a spatula or spoon to push the foie gras open, then pull walnut-sized bits of foie away from the veins. It's more efficient to pull the foie away from the veins rather than pull the veins out. There will be a little foie left on the veins. If the veins aren't too bloody, you can pass them through a tamis to get any foie off of them.

Transfer the deveined foie pieces to a large bowl, along with the egg, port, Cognac, foie gras cure, and diced quail. Using gloved hands, toss until evenly coated. Press a piece of parchment paper directly on the surface of the mixture to prevent oxidation and refrigerate. Let it marinate for about 15 minutes.

Bring a large, wide saucepot of salted water to a boil. Fill a large bowl with ice and water. Add the lettuce to the boiling water and cook just until wilted, 15 to 30 seconds. Immediately lift out the lettuce and dunk into the ice water, then drain well and pat very dry between paper towels. Reserve the leaves. Keep the water boiling.

Lay a large sheet of plastic wrap on your work surface. Place about 2 heaping tablespoons (65 to 70 g) of the quail foie mixture in the center. Gather the plastic wrap around the mixture to squeeze and shape tightly into a ball, twisting the top of the plastic wrap to secure the ball. Wrap the plastic-wrapped ball in foil, shiny side in to deflect heat. Repeat with the remaining ingredients.

Drop the balls into the reserved boiling water. Cook for 20 minutes, stirring the balls occasionally, then turn off the

recipe continues

heat and let them rest in the hot water for 5 minutes. Fill a large bowl with ice and water. Transfer the balls to the ice water. Refrigerate for at least 3 hours or overnight. The ice water will shock the fat to the outsides of the balls. Remove the chilled balls from the ice water bath and refrigerate, still wrapped, for 24 to 48 hours to let the flavors really mix and mingle.

Unwrap a ball, place in the center of a blanched lettuce leaf, and wrap the lettuce neatly around it. Repeat with the remaining balls. Store in the refrigerator until ready to serve.

FOR THE QUAIL LEG CONFIT
12 quail drumsticks (from above)
1 tablespoon extra-virgin olive oil
1 teaspoon port wine
1 teaspoon Cognac
Grapeseed oil, for confiting

Toss the drumsticks with the olive oil, port, and Cognac in a large bowl. Let sit for 5 minutes to absorb the flavors, then transfer everything to a large saucepan and add enough grapeseed oil to cover.

Heat the oil to 160°F to 170°F (70°C to 75°C). Confit until the meat is tender, 10 to 15 minutes. Allow the drumsticks to cool and refrigerate until chilled, at least 2 hours (they will keep for months if submerged in fat). To serve, return the oil to confiting temperature and when the legs are warm, drain well and serve.

FOR THE BLACK TRUFFLE GELÉE
½ cup plus 1 tablespoon (145 ml) black truffle juice
2 sheets silver gelatin, soaked in ice water until softened
5 grinds white pepper

Heat the truffle juice in a small saucepan over medium-low heat until warm. Drain the gelatin and add to the juice, then stir until it dissolves. Whisk in the white pepper, then bring to a simmer. Remove from the heat and pour into a shallow 9- by 13-inch (23 by 33 cm) baking pan. Refrigerate until set and firm, at least 4 hours.

When ready to serve, chop and crush with a fork.

FOR THE PROSCIUTTO CHIPS
6 paper-thin slices prosciutto

Preheat your oven to 150°F (175°C), convection if you have it.

Place the prosciutto on a parchment paper–lined sheet pan in a single layer. Cover with another sheet of parchment and with another sheet pan to weigh them down.

Bake until dry and crisp, about 1 hour. Cool completely. The chips can be stored for up to a week in an airtight container.

TO GARNISH
12 white button mushrooms, peeled and cut into ¼-inch (5 mm) dice
1 medium (2½-ounce/60 g) black truffle, *Tuber melanosporum* (optional), cut into ¼-inch (5 mm) dice
Microgreens
12 teardrop tomatoes, halved

Put a lettuce-wrapped ball on a serving plate. Warm half the crushed truffle gelée in a small saucepan over low heat until melted, then remove from the heat and add the remaining half to keep it liquid but ready to set. Spoon some of the mixture over the cold ball so that the gelée sets onto the ball. If needed, refrigerate to set the gelée. Arrange the diced mushrooms and truffle over the gelée to stick in a pattern. Repeat with the remaining balls, gelée, mushrooms, and truffle.

Arrange the confit quail legs, greens, and tomatoes all around, then top with the prosciutto crisps. Serve immediately.

ON THE FOIE GRAS TERRINE

A foie gras terrine is one of my favorite things to eat. I not only come from a region where foie gras terrines were an important tradition, but also my maternal grandfather, Joseph Stutter, raised geese and ducks for foie gras; that was his trade. And my father, Léon Kreuther, worked for one of the biggest distributors in the country.

As it was traditionally considered a delicacy, in my family, and in most families in Alsace, we ate foie gras only two times a year, during the Christmas holidays and at Easter. My mother always put a truffle in the center, and I loved this truffle so much when I was a kid I'd go around to all the adults and ask them for their truffle. Sometimes they'd even give it to me. At the restaurant, I'll serve it adorned with melon, duck prosciutto, and preserved porcini (page 181) or with toasted pistachio praline, fennel pollen waffle, and smoked date jam (page 184). But at home ours were always very simply prepared—in a terrine mold, with salt and pepper, and a little wine or Cognac. And we'd serve it with brioche or some grilled farm bread, along with some wine jelly, white wine, or Madeira, or sometimes some of the jelly left over from cooking pot-au-feu (page 53), seasoned with Madeira. The terrine itself is very much who I am.

The following three recipes show ways that I serve it at the restaurant, but you could use my basic method to make a fabulous but simple terrine like we used to enjoy at home in Alsace that would be delicious just with grilled country bread and a cold glass of Gewurztraminer. I urge you to give this method a try—it's really just warmed in the oven, just enough to stir it to distribute the seasoning and give it a nice, smooth texture with chunks of foie throughout. To make this basic, but still exquisite terrine, follow either of the first two foie gras terrine recipes through to the second to last step—cooling it in an ice bath while stirring—then simply transfer it into any mold of your choice lined with plastic wrap, pressing it down and smoothing it over, and then cover the top tightly with plastic wrap and refrigerate for two days before using/serving. Each terrine has subtle and differing seasonings and different alcohols—choose the mixture that will suit your tastes. It's really the method that's key to these preparations.

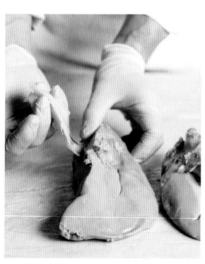  

A foie gras has two lobes. Each must be carefully deveined. Don't worry too much about hurting the foie gras itself when you do, as it will be flattened into a hotel pan. We first put down a layer of seasoning on the bottom of the pan, put the foie in, and spread it out so that it has an even thickness. We then season the top and stipple it deeply so that the wine we add to finish it with touches as much foie as possible. We then cover the pan with foil, chill it for an hour in the fridge, then put it in a 250°F (121°C) oven just for a few minutes, till it reaches about 120°F (48°C), just as it begins to render. Then you can shape or mold it as you wish (save the rendered fat to season other food!).

FOIE GRAS TERRINE
WITH CANTALOUPE, DUCK PROSCIUTTO, AND PRESERVED PORCINI

Serves 8

This is a different way of creating texture and flavor with foie gras—shaping it in the form of a small dome that's filled inside with mushrooms, duck prosciutto, and almonds, and spiking the outsides with shards of broken peppery tuile. The tuile is seasoned with grains of paradise, a West African spice related to cardamom that has a pungent, black-pepper-like flavor with hints of citrus. You want to balance the sweetness of the melon and the foie, counterbalance it with spice and salty prosciutto and almonds, so that the flavors explode in the mouth. It's better to crush the peppercorns by hand to get different textures and have less powder. The cracked peppers give flavor and texture without too much heat and the personality of each seasoning stays distinct. We cook and preserve our porcini in oil, but store-bought porcinis, preserved in olive oil, are good as well. I really love the foie technique itself because the gentle cooking of just warming the foie through allows you to limit how much fat it releases.

FOR THE FOIE GRAS

2 teaspoons kosher salt, plus more
   for seasoning
1 pinch pink salt
½ teaspoon sugar
⅛ teaspoon cayenne pepper
20 grindings white pepper
2 gratings nutmeg
1 grating cinnamon stick
1 grade-A foie gras (1 pound/500 g), at
   room temperature for 1½ to 2 hours
½ tablespoon Cognac
1½ tablespoons Sauternes

To make the salt cure for the foie gras, in a small bowl, combine the kosher salt, pink salt, sugar, cayenne, white pepper, nutmeg, and cinnamon and set aside.

Put the foie gras on a clean sheet of plastic wrap. Separate the two lobes, then push on them slowly with your thumbs, moving from the centers outward to find the veins. Use a spatula or spoon to push the foie gras open, then pull walnut-sized bits of foie away from the veins. It's more efficient to pull the foie away from the veins rather than pull the veins out. There will be a little foie left on the veins. If the veins aren't too bloody, you can pass them through a fine-mesh sieve to get any remaining foie off of them.

Lightly sprinkle the salt cure over a pan large enough to hold the foie gras. Place a 1-inch-thick layer of foie gras bits over the cure, lightly sprinkle with more cure, and repeat the layering. When all the foie and cure is used, flatten the mixture into the pan, then drizzle with the Cognac and Sauternes, coating it completely. Use your index finger to poke holes throughout to help the alcohol evenly distribute.

Cover the pan tightly with foil so no light or oxidation gets to the foie, then refrigerate for 45 minutes to 1 hour.

Preheat your oven to 250°F (121°C).

Uncover the pan, pour off excess liquid, and put it in the oven just long enough to warm it up, 3 to 5 minutes. Stay in front of it and don't get distracted; you'll see that it will start to slowly render fat that is very yellow. Depending on the quality of the liver, you will lose about 10 to 15 percent of the fat, and you don't want to lose more. Check with a thermometer that it has reached 120°F to 130°F (48°C to 50°C), then spoon out most of the fat on top, removing as much as you can without taking any of the meat. You can reserve this fat for another use. (I like to drizzle it on seared foie or cook quail in it. It's also great to use for frying simple hash browns.)

Transfer the foie and the fat remaining in the pan to a bowl and set over a larger bowl of ice and water. Stir gently to re-emulsify the mixture. Season to taste with salt at this point. There should be some chunks of foie still so stir gently with a spatula when seasoning.

Transfer 2½ tablespoons (35 g) of the mixture to a 2¾-inch-diameter dome mold lined with plastic wrap. Use an offset spatula to spread an even layer of foie around the inside of the mold leaving a thumb-sized divot that will hold the garnish. Cover the foie with plastic wrap and press firmly directly against the surface, then put another dome mold on top to press in firmly. Repeat with the remaining foie. Refrigerate for 1 to 2 days.

FOR THE CANTALOUPE SAUCE

12¾ ounces (360 g) from roughly
   ½ cantaloupe, peeled, seeded, and
   cut into large dice
1 teaspoon salt, plus more to taste
2 dashes Tabasco sauce
1 tablespoon white balsamic vinegar
4 tablespoons (60 ml) grapeseed oil

recipe continues

Place the cantaloupe in a large saucepan, set over medium heat, and add 1 tablespoon water. Cover and cook, stirring occasionally, until very soft and the liquid has come out of the melon and the melon is a darker shade of orange, about 5 minutes. Puree until smooth using an immersion blender. Set the saucepan with the puree over a bowl of ice and water and stir until cool to preserve the melon's color and flavor. You should have a scant 1 cup (225 ml) of puree.

When cool, add the salt, Tabasco, and vinegar. Buzz with the immersion blender to mix. With the blender running, add the oil in a steady stream to emulsify. Add 1 tablespoon water and buzz until smooth. Season to taste with salt. Refrigerate until ready to use, up to 2 days.

FOR THE PEPPER TUILE CRUST

2 teaspoons pink peppercorns
1 teaspoon black peppercorns
1 teaspoon white peppercorns
1 teaspoon Sichuan peppercorns
2 teaspoons grains of paradise
1½ tablespoons (33 g) glucose
3 tablespoons (65 g) honey
3 tablespoons (35 g) granulated sugar
6 tablespoons (85 g) butter, very soft
2 tablespoons (30 ml) milk
½ teaspoon (1½ g) NH pectin
    (thermoreversible pectin; see page
    154 for more information)
3 tablespoons panko breadcrumbs
    (pulse in a food processor until finely
    ground)

Put all the peppercorns and grains of paradise on a half sheet pan and press firmly with a heavy saucepan to crack them.

Transfer to a dry skillet and set over medium heat. Toast, swirling the pan often, until the spices are fragrant. Toasting with heat allows the essential oils of the spices to come out and bring out flavor.

Add enough water to cover the spices and bring to a simmer. Drain through a fine-mesh sieve, then return to the skillet. Cover with cold water and bring to a simmer again. Drain and repeat one more time. Blanching the spices three times gets rid of excess powder.

Whisk the glucose, honey, granulated sugar, butter, milk, pectin, panko, and blanched pepper mixture in a large bowl by hand until very smooth. Refrigerate in an airtight container for a day or two to make the mixture easier to spread and for the flavors to mature and harmonize.

Preheat your oven to 350°F (175°C), on the convection setting with a low fan if you have it. If using a conventional oven, preheat it to 375°F (190°C).

Using a tuile stencil set (available in specialty cooking supply stores, such as JB Prince, or online), place the stencil onto a half sheet pan lined with a Silpat, and spread about 1 heaping teaspoon of the pepper crust mixture evenly in the mold. Repeat to fill the pan, spacing the tuile 2 inches (5 cm) apart. Bake until dark brown and bubbly, 10 to 12 minutes. Cool completely on the pan. Repeat with the remaining batter.

FOR FILLING THE FOIE GRAS DOME AND GARNISH

2 ounces (60 g) finely diced porcini
    conserva
2 ounces (60 g) finely diced duck pro-
    sciutto (set aside 1 ounce/30 g
    to garnish)
4 ounces (120 g) finely diced toasted
    almonds (set aside 2 ounces/60 g
    to garnish)
16 pinches celery leaves, minced
    (set aside 8 pinches to garnish)
2 teaspoons plus a few drops grape-
    seed oil
Salt and freshly ground black pepper

Mix the porcini, prosciutto, almonds, celery leaves, and 2 teaspoons oil together in a medium bowl. Season to taste with salt and pepper.

To assemble, unwrap the plastic wrap from the top of the foie mold. Spoon in one-eighth of the filling and spread evenly, pressing it into the foie. Carefully flip the mold onto the serving plate, then remove the mold and plastic wrap. Spoon the cantaloupe sauce all around, then garnish the outside of the dome with the reserved prosciutto, almonds, and celery leaves (we use tweezers for this). Break the pepper crust into pieces and spike it into the foie. Finish with a few drops of grapeseed oil in the cantaloupe sauce. Repeat with the remaining ingredients and serve immediately.

FOIE GRAS TERRINE AND TOASTED PISTACHIO PRALINE
WITH FENNEL POLLEN WAFFLE AND SMOKED DATE JAM

Serves 10

I created this recipe on a cooking trip in Japan and added tart orange to counter the sweet dates and Strega, an Italian herbal liqueur, considered a digestif. Its distinctive yellow color comes from saffron. The alcohol content is comparable to most spirits, but it has a sweetness and viscosity typical of liqueurs. Among its approximately seventy herbal ingredients are mint and fennel, giving it a complex flavor with minty and coniferous notes.

This waffle recipe was given to me by a colleague in Europe, and I promised to never reveal the recipe, but now I'm putting it in a book—the old custom of hiding recipes from colleagues is obsolete! The waffles are made with a yeasted batter, flavored with fennel pollen, which gives it an anise flavor. If you have leftovers, they freeze beautifully. You can serve these as dessert or for breakfast. And, of course, like toasted brioche, they go beautifully with foie gras.

This is the same technique we use in the previous terrine recipe (page 181), with slightly different seasonings. This recipe includes Saigon, or Vietnamese, cinnamon, the most fragrant and elegant variety on the market. Pink salt is used to maintain an appealing color and also to preserve it. And the dominant seasonings are Alsatian favorites, cinnamon and nutmeg, along with a hit of cayenne.

FOR THE FOIE GRAS

1½ teaspoons kosher salt, plus more to taste

1½ teaspoons pink salt

1 teaspoon sugar

¼ teaspoon cayenne pepper

½ teaspoon freshly ground white pepper

3 gratings nutmeg

1 grating toasted Saigon cinnamon stick

1 grade-A foie gras (1 pound/500 g), at room temperature for 1½ to 2 hours

2 tablespoons Sauternes or white port

1 tablespoon brandy or Armagnac

To make a cure for the foie gras, in a small bowl, combine the kosher salt, pink salt, sugar, cayenne, white pepper, nutmeg, and cinnamon and set aside.

Put the foie gras on a clean sheet of plastic wrap. Separate the two lobes, then push on them slowly with your thumbs, moving from the centers outward to find the veins. Use a spatula or spoon to push the foie gras open, then pull walnut-sized bits of foie away from the veins. It's more efficient to pull the foie away from the veins rather than pull the veins out. There will be a little foie left on the veins. If the veins aren't too bloody, you can pass them through a fine-mesh sieve to get any foie off of them.

Lightly sprinkle the salt cure over a standard glass or ceramic casserole dish large enough to hold the foie gras. Place a 1-inch-thick (2.5 cm) layer of foie gras bits over the cure, lightly sprinkle with more cure, and repeat the layering. When all the foie and cure is used, flatten the mixture flat into the pan, then drizzle with the Sauternes and brandy, coating it completely. Use your index finger to poke holes throughout to help the alcohol evenly distribute.

Cover the pan tightly with foil so no light or oxidation gets to the foie, then refrigerate for 45 minutes to 1 hour.

Preheat your oven to 250°F (121°C).

Uncover the pan, pour off excess liquid, then put it in the oven just long enough to warm it up and melt 10 to 15 percent of the fat (120°F to 130°F/48°C to 50°C), 3 to 5 minutes. Spoon out most of the fat on top, removing as much as you can without taking any of the meat. You could reserve this fat for another use. (I like to drizzle it on seared foie or cook quail in it.)

Transfer the foie and the fat remaining in the pan to a bowl and set over a larger bowl of ice and water. Stir gently to re-emulsify the mixture. Season to taste with salt at this point. There should be some chunks of foie remaining, so stir gently with a spatula when seasoning.

Transfer the mixture to a 2 by 3 by 5½-inch (5 by 7.5 by 14 cm) loaf pan mold. Tap the foie in the mold to settle into an even layer, then press plastic wrap directly on its surface. Refrigerate for 1 to 2 days.

recipe continues

FOR THE ROASTED PISTACHIOS

Makes 1½ cups

1 pound (450 g) unsalted shelled pistachios

Preheat your oven to 350°F (175°C).

Spread the nuts on a sheet pan and roast for 7 to 10 minutes, until heated through and fragrant.

Cool completely, then pulse in a food processor until small chunks are formed. Shake in a medium-mesh sieve to get rid of pistachio dust. Reserve the tiny chunks in the sieve.

FOR THE DATE JAM

Makes 3 cups

2 pounds (1 kg) pitted Medjool dates
4 tablespoons (60 ml) sherry vinegar
1 teaspoon cayenne pepper
2 teaspoons salt
Freshly ground white pepper

Preheat your oven to 140°F (60°C). Put 7 ounces (200 g) of the dates on a parchment paper–lined half sheet pan. Put in the oven to dehydrate overnight, about 8 hours. Cool completely.

Prepare a smoker or smoking gun with applewood chips. Heavily smoke the regular and dried dates until they're smoked to saturation.

Transfer the smoked dates to a pot and add enough water to just cover them. Bring to a boil over high heat, then reduce the heat to a simmer and cook until the dates are very mushy and falling apart and the liquid is pasty and thick. You don't want to reduce all of the liquid, but you also don't want a loose puree.

Transfer the dates to a blender and puree until smooth. Add the sherry vinegar, cayenne, salt, and white pepper to taste.

Start blending on low speed, then gradually raise the speed. Scrape the bowl occasionally and stir the mixture with a spatula without hitting the blade.

Pass the date mixture through a fine-mesh sieve and cool to room temperature. Transfer ½ cup (120 ml) to a piping bag, seal the open top, and refrigerate until ready to use. The remaining jam can be stored in the refrigerator for up to 4 weeks.

Note: This date jam is delicious with hard cheeses such as Cheddar, Gruyère, Comté, Emmenthal, or Parmigiano-Reggiano.

FOR THE STREGA GEL

½ bottle (375 ml) Strega
¼ teaspoon salt
1¾ sheets silver gelatin, soaked in ice water until softened (see Note on page 172)
1 tablespoon plus 1 teaspoon lemon juice

Pour the Strega into a deep saucepan. Very carefully light on fire and let the alcohol burn off.

Sprinkle the salt over the hot Strega. Add the gelatin, squeezed of excess water, to the Strega and whisk until dissolved. Transfer to a bowl set over a larger bowl of ice and water. Whisk until cool. Season with the lemon juice.

Transfer to a half hotel pan or other container and refrigerate until set, at least 1 hour. When ready to serve, push the gel through a potato ricer directly into a piping bag. Seal the open end and refrigerate. It can be refrigerated for up to 2 days.

FOR THE FENNEL POLLEN WAFFLES

Makes about 12

3 cups (700 ml) milk
3½ ounces (100 g) sugar
3 ounces (90 g) fresh yeast
4 cups (500 g) all-purpose flour
2 tablespoons fennel pollen
1 tablespoon salt
8 large eggs, separated, at room temperature
1¾ cups (3½ sticks/390 g) butter, melted

Warm the milk and sugar in a saucepan over medium heat, stirring occasionally, until just warm to the touch, 120°F to 140°F (50°C to 60°C). Remove from the heat, add the yeast, and whisk until dissolved. Let sit until foamy, 5 to 10 minutes.

Meanwhile, whisk the flour, fennel pollen, and salt in a medium bowl. When the yeast is foamy, whisk in the egg yolks one at a time. While whisking, drizzle in the butter and continue to whisk until incorporated. Gradually add the flour mixture and whisk until there are no lumps. Don't overwork the flour. Transfer to a large bowl.

In another clean bowl, whip the egg whites until medium-stiff peaks form. Fold the whites into the yolks in thirds. Rotate the bowl while mixing very gently from the center to the edge. Cover and refrigerate until bubbly and cratered on top, at least 40 minutes. The most important part now is to let the batter rest so the flour absorbs the liquids. If you refrigerate the dough overnight, you have to fold down the batter because the yeast will be too airy.

Heat a waffle iron to medium-high. Coat lightly with nonstick cooking spray, then spoon into the iron. For a 5-inch (12 cm) square waffle iron, you need about ¾ cup (115 g) of batter per waffle. Transfer to a

wire rack to cool until ready to use. These can be made in advance, then wrapped individually while still hot and immediately frozen. They can then be heated for 10 minutes in a 350°F (175°C) oven, until crisp and heated through.

ASSEMBLING THE FOIE GRAS TERRINE

1 small fennel bulb, quartered, cored, then sliced paper thin, plus blossoms and fronds
3 tablespoons Orange Puree (page 326)
Small mint leaves
Food-grade Egyptian star flowers or pansies
Yellow celery leaves

Place the fennel bulb slices in a bowl of ice and water to crisp.

Preheat your oven to 350°F (175°C).

Trim any oxidized brown parts off the foie gras. Break into 2-tablespoon (35 g) chunks, then use gloved hands to roll into 2-inch-diameter (5 cm) balls. Roll the balls in the roasted pistachios to coat, pressing the nuts in to completely crust the balls.

Trim the waffle edges and cut each into 2 vertical slices. Put the waffles in the oven on a rack set in a half sheet pan to crisp, 2 to 3 minutes.

Pipe the Strega gel in the center of a plate in a 2-inch (5 cm) circle, then pipe three ½-inch (1.5 cm) dots of orange puree around it. Put the foie ball in the center of the gel. Drain the fennel on paper towels, then curl 3 pieces around the ball. Place 4 torn mint leaves around the ball. Put a waffle on the plate and pipe the date puree and Strega gel in alternate cavities. Sprinkle the fennel blossoms and fronds over the cavities. Alternate the star flowers and celery leaves around the plate. Repeat with the remaining components. Serve immediately.

HAMACHI, BLACK PÉRIGORD TRUFFLE, AND FOIE GRAS MILLE-FEUILLE
WITH GRAPES, CELERIAC, AND TRUFFLE VINAIGRETTE

Serves 12 You could do this with tuna or king salmon if hamachi isn't available. It changes the flavor, but there's still harmony. Whatever fish you use, it needs to be the best. You can buy a foie gras terrine or pâté or a foie mousse or make your own. Every layer needs to be seasoned properly for the explosion of flavor and harmony of taste. It's an expensive dish, but it is impressive and perfect for a dinner party (so this recipe makes twelve servings). It's well worth the investment of time and money.

FOR THE MILLE-FEUILLE

12¾ ounces (360 g) foie gras terrine
    (store-bought or see page 180)
2¾ ounces (75 g) black truffle
1 pound (455 g) cleaned hamachi fillet
Grapeseed oil
Salt and freshly ground white pepper

Leave the foie gras terrine out at room temperature to temper. When it's soft enough to spread, wear gloves and smash it by hand until smooth and pasty, then pass it though a tamis (or mesh strainer) into a bowl to make sure there are no veins. If you don't have a tamis, pick out the veins if there are any, then puree in a food processor and transfer to a bowl.

Peel the truffle and reserve the peels for the vinaigrette. Cut the truffle into very thin (1.5 mm) slices.

Line a 5 by 6 by 1-inch (12 by 16 by 2.5 cm) mold with plastic wrap. Cut the hamachi into ⅛-inch (2 to 3 mm) slices and arrange them in a single layer in the prepared pan with no gaps between the slices. You'll need about 10 slices. Cut a hamachi slice into bits to fill in any remaining gaps like puzzle pieces. Drizzle a tiny bit of oil over the fish and spread all over the fish, then sprinkle lightly with salt and pepper.

Using a silicone spatula, fold the foie gras until it's smooth and the consistency of butter. Dollop a little less than half of the foie gras (5¼ ounces/150 g) over the fish, then very gently and slowly spread it with an offset spatula into a thin, even layer. Try to not displace the fish slices.

Keep rotating the pan as you spread to give a very flat and smooth layer about ⅛ inch/3 mm) thick. Top with an even layer of truffle slices (1 ounce/28 g), breaking slices as needed to fill in any gaps. Dollop a bit of the foie gras over the truffle slices and spread like a thin film to secure them. Repeat the layering, finishing with a final layer of hamachi.

Press plastic wrap directly against the top, then wrap the whole pan in plastic wrap. Top with another pan of the same size, then weight it down with a 3-pound (1.4 kg) weight for the layers of fish, foie, and truffle to interlock. Refrigerate for at least 2 hours and up to 48 hours.

FOR THE TRUFFLE VINAIGRETTE

4 tablespoons (60 g) black truffle juice
    (see page 177, Quail and Foie Gras
    Praline, for sourcing and information)
5 teaspoons (25 g) sherry vinegar
¾ teaspoon salt
Freshly ground white pepper
1½ tablespoons (34 g) glucose
4 teaspoons hazelnut oil
Truffle peelings (from above), chopped

Bring the truffle juice to a simmer in a small saucepan over medium heat. Simmer until reduced by half, then transfer to a bowl. Whisk in the vinegar, salt, and a few grindings of white pepper. Whisk in the glucose until syrupy and smooth, then whisk in the oil until emulsified. Stir in the chopped truffle peelings. These are best used immediately.

TO ASSEMBLE

36 Parisienne-sized (⅜-inch/1 cm)
    celery root balls, blanched
Fleur de sel and cracked black pepper
¼ teaspoon lemon juice
12 large seedless red grapes, each cut
    into 3 coins
Tiny celery or chervil leaves, for garnish
2 teaspoons heavy cream

Toss the celery root balls in the truffle vinaigrette and let stand while preparing the terrine.

Uncover the terrine and unmold onto a cutting board. Trim the edges to smooth any rough edges (and snack on them). Cut the terrine crosswise into thirds, then cut each third into quarters crosswise. Cut each piece in half. You should have 24 rectangles. Arrange 2 rectangles on each serving plate top to bottom to form one large rectangle (2 by 3 inches/5 by 7.5 cm) and sprinkle with fleur de sel and cracked black pepper.

Stir the lemon juice into the celery root balls. Arrange 3 grape coins on each plate, then top each coin with a celery root ball and garnish with the celery leaves. Drizzle the vinaigrette all around. Dot the plate with the heavy cream to break up the plate.

ALASKAN KING CRAB "CANNELLONI"
WITH SEA URCHIN COULIS

Serves 6

I love serving king crab. When I had a dish on the menu calling for only large chunks of it, we would have a lot of extra crab in small pieces or shredded. It was still delicious crab, but what would be an elegant way of serving it? I live in New York, where Italian cuisine is a strong presence, so I thought to enclose the crab in a dough like a cannelloni. I found the traditional pasta dough too chewy for this delicate dish, so I use a hot water dough, and I roll it very thin through a pasta machine. (The dough will make more than you'll need, but it's hard to make less in a food processor. Leftover dough can be rolled and frozen and used for pasta or raviolis.) And creating an uni sauce gives this an almost Asian feel; this is true melting pot cuisine.

FOR THE CANNELLONI DOUGH

4 cups (500 g) all-purpose flour
1 teaspoon salt
1 cup (240 ml) boiling water
1 teaspoon white vinegar
Grapeseed oil, for brushing the pasta

Put the flour and salt in a food processor. With the machine running, add the boiling water and vinegar and run until the dough is mealy, a few seconds, and can be worked by hand to turn it into a smooth dough. Knead the dough until it can be shaped into a disc. Wrap it in plastic and refrigerate it for 20 minutes or so.

Roll the dough through a pasta roller many times on the widest setting, folding it in thirds each time until it is smooth and elastic. Roll it out in successively narrower settings until the second-to-last or last setting. It should be thin and translucent.

Cut the dough into twelve 4½-inch (12 cm) squares.

In a large pot of boiling, salted water, cook the pasta, about a minute or so, then remove to an ice bath.

Lay them out on a sheet of oiled parchment paper, brushing them gently with oil to prevent them from sticking.

FOR THE SEA URCHIN COULIS

3 tablespoons vermouth
¼ teaspoon cayenne pepper
1 teaspoon salt
6 ounces (180 g) sea urchin roe
3 tablespoons grapeseed oil
½ tablespoon lemon juice

Put the vermouth in a pot, bring to a simmer, and reduce it by one-third, then add ½ cup (120 ml) of water. Add the cayenne and salt. Remove the pan from the heat and add the sea urchin roe, stirring to cook it slightly. Transfer the mixture to a blender and blend until the coulis is frothy. Blend in the grapeseed oil. Strain it into a bowl set in ice to chill it. Add the lemon juice.

FOR THE CRAB MIXTURE

10 ounces (300 g) king crabmeat, roughly chopped
3 tablespoons grapeseed oil
Lemon juice
Salt and freshly ground black pepper
⅛ teaspoon cayenne or Aleppo pepper

Mix the crabmeat with the grapeseed oil to coat, then season with lemon juice. Taste and season with salt, black pepper, and cayenne to taste.

TO GARNISH (OPTIONAL)

1 piece of nori seaweed, ⅔ inch (1.6 cm) in length, julienned
2 ounces (60 g) Osetra caviar
Chopped chives
Seasonal baby herbs and flowers
Aleppo pepper

Place about 3 teaspoons (20 g) of crab filling along one edge of a pasta square. Roll the dough around the crab so that you have a full cylinder of crab, just until the pasta comes together (it should stick to itself). Trim excess pasta. Repeat with the remaining pasta squares.

Froth the coulis with a hand blender, and divide the coulis among six plates. Place one cannelloni on top of each plate. Garnish as desired and serve immediately.

BRAISED TRUMPET ROYALE SALAD
WITH BOUCHOT MUSSELS AND HARISSA VINAIGRETTE

Serves 6

This dish is a song to the wonderful, meaty Trumpet Royale mushroom and to using mussels in an unusual way. The mushrooms have a great texture, both delicate and chewy, and serve as a bed for a mussel salad. Bouchot mussels are small, intensely flavored, and sweet.

FOR THE BOUCHOT MUSSELS

4½ pounds (2 kg) Bouchot mussels
Pinch salt
3 tablespoons grapeseed oil, plus more
　for sautéeing
1 small yellow onion, sliced
½ fennel bulb, thinly sliced
2 cloves garlic, smashed
2 sprigs thyme
2 bay leaves
1 cup (250 ml) dry white wine

Soak the mussels in cold water with a good pinch of salt to purge them. Remove any large beards from the mussels, and discard any broken ones or ones that don't close.

In a large pot over medium-high heat, add the oil and sweat the onion, fennel, and garlic until translucent. Turn the heat to high and add the mussels, thyme, and bay leaves and stir. Add the white wine and cover the pot immediately. Shake the pot after about 45 seconds. After another 30 seconds or so, stir the mussels to make sure they all cook. Continue to cook them for another minute after they open (you want them slightly overcooked so that they cut nicely but not so much that they shrink and dry out). Transfer them to a sheet pan to cool. Strain the stock and reserve for another use. When they're cool enough to handle, remove them from the shell (discard any mussels that don't open). Cut each mussel in half.

FOR THE TRUMPET ROYALE MUSHROOMS

6 large Trumpet Royale mushrooms
3 tablespoons grapeseed oil
Salt and freshly ground black pepper
8 sprigs thyme
2 bay leaves
2 cups (450 ml) White Chicken Stock
　(page 251)

Preheat your oven to 350°F (175°C).

Sear the mushrooms in grapeseed oil in an ovenproof sauté pan over high heat until they're golden brown, then season them with salt and pepper. Add the thyme, the bay leaves, and chicken stock, allow the stock to come to a simmer, then cover the pan and put it in the oven for 20 minutes, or until the mushrooms are tender. Cut into planks, about ⅛ inch (3 mm) thick, reserving any trim.

FOR THE HARISSA VINAIGRETTE

2 tablespoons almond oil
3 tablespoons grapeseed oil
2 tablespoons lemon juice, plus more
　to taste
4 tablespoons Harissa Oil (page 233)

Combine the almond oil, grapeseed oil, lemon juice, and harissa oil. Whisk well, and season to taste with more lemon juice as needed.

TO GARNISH

1½ tablespoons minced chives
Food-safe flowers
4 tablespoons (25 g) lightly toasted
　almond slices
1 ripe Asian pear, peeled and cut in 1-inch
　(2.5 cm) cubes, tossed lightly with
　grapeseed oil
6 slices Ibérico ham or prosciutto

To assemble the dish, warm the sliced mushrooms (in a microwave or oven or on the stove).

In a bowl, mix the mussels with any mushroom trim and enough harissa vinaigrette to coat them. Add 1 tablespoon of minced chives and stir them in.

Line each plate with the warmed sliced mushroom to form a square or rectangle. Top the mushrooms with the mussels. Garnish with more minced chives, food-safe flowers, toasted almonds, and a final drizzle of harissa oil. Wrap a piece of ham around each cube of pear and spear with a fork, serving the fork on the side of the plate.

KUMAMOTO OYSTERS "EN PANNEQUET"
WITH SMOKED SALMON SAUCE

Makes 4 full
servings or 12
tasting servings

This used to be a favorite dish for many when I was at the Modern and is an easy way to eat oysters. There's no shucking or slurping them from their shells here. I thought it'd be elegant to make a sauce with a salmon color to contrast with the oysters.

If you can't find Kumamoto oysters, choose another plump, sweet one, such as Kusshi, which has a nice pop. Irish smoked salmon is ideal for the sauce.

A special note on one of the garnishes: Borage is a medicinal plant with lovely edible blue flowers that taste just like oysters, so we often use them as a garnish with oyster dishes. We get ours from Farmer Jones Farm at the Chef's Garden in Huron, Ohio, which is a great organic source for specialty flowers and baby vegetables, herbs, and microgreens, direct from the farm.

FOR THE APPLE CIDER VINEGAR GELÉE

1 tablespoon chopped shallot

6 ounces (180 ml) apple cider vinegar

1½ teaspoons balsamic vinegar

1 tablespoon sugar

4 sheets silver gelatin, soaked in ice water until softened (see Note on page 172)

Combine the shallot, both vinegars, and sugar in a small saucepan. Heat to 160°F (71°C), then remove from the heat. Lift the gelatin sheets out of the cold water, squeeze dry, and stir into the vinegar mixture until they dissolve.

Pour the mixture into a small, shallow-rimmed pan. Refrigerate uncovered overnight to set. When solid, unmold and chop.

FOR THE CHAMPAGNE GELÉE

1 cup (250 ml) Champagne

4 sheets silver gelatin, soaked in ice water until softened

Heat the Champagne in a small saucepan to 160°F (71°C), then remove from the heat. Lift the gelatin sheets out of the cold water, squeeze dry, and stir into the Champagne until they dissolve.

Pour the mixture into a small, shallow rimmed pan. Refrigerate uncovered overnight to set. When solid, unmold and chop.

FOR THE SMOKED SALMON SAUCE

1 tablespoon extra-virgin olive oil

5 tablespoons (40 g) chopped shallot

Salt

1¾ cups (420 ml) extra-dry vermouth

6 ounces (180 g) smoked salmon, chopped

1 tablespoon tomato paste

2 cups (500 ml) half-and-half

Freshly ground black pepper

2 teaspoons lemon juice

Heat the oil in a large saucepan over medium heat. Add the shallot and a pinch of salt and cook, stirring, until the shallot is tender without taking on any color, 1 to 2 minutes. Add the vermouth, bring to a boil, then cook until reduced by half to burn off the alcohol, about 3 minutes.

Add the smoked salmon and tomato paste and cook, stirring, until the salmon disintegrates, about 2 minutes. Add the half-and-half and a small pinch each of salt and pepper and bring to a simmer. Don't over-salt, because the salmon is salty. Simmer, stirring occasionally, until reduced and thickened, about 8 minutes.

Transfer the mixture to a blender and puree until very smooth and the color deepens, 1 to 2 minutes. Strain through a fine-mesh sieve into a bowl set over a larger bowl filled with ice and water. Whisk the mixture until cold. Season to taste with salt and pepper.

Right before using, blend in the lemon juice with an immersion blender.

recipe continues

FOR THE SALAD

Scant 2 tablespoons grapeseed oil, plus more for serving

7 ounces (195 g) white parts of leeks, halved lengthwise, then washed and chopped

Salt

12 outer, green Bibb lettuce leaves, blanched and pressed dry between paper towels (see page 177)

12 shucked Kumamoto oysters

3 tablespoons (50 g) salmon roe, for serving

6 white button mushroom caps, peeled and cut into batons

1 lemon wedge

Pepper

12 borage flowers, for serving

Heat the oil in a medium saucepan over medium heat. Add the leeks and a pinch of salt and cook, stirring, until tender but without any color, 3 to 4 minutes. Transfer to an airtight container and refrigerate until cold.

Lay the lettuce leaves down, shiny sides out, and press down on the ribs to flatten. If the leaves are small, you may want to use up to 1½ or 2 together. Cut out thick white ribs at the bottoms, or any brown parts. Spread 1 teaspoon of the leeks in the center, then cover evenly with 1 teaspoon Champagne gelée and lay an oyster on top. Finish with ¾ teaspoon vinegar gelée piped onto a spoon and flattened onto the oyster as if rolling down a carpet. That way you get an even taste of the gelée with each bite because it's not in a mound. Fold in the long sides of the lettuce leaves and pinch them together to close gently. Press down on the ends of the leaves, then fold them in over the center. Flip the lettuce packet over seam side down. Plump and pinch it into a neat packet. Chill until ready to serve. Repeat with the remaining ingredients.

To plate, spoon about 3½ tablespoons (40 g) smoked salmon sauce onto a plate. Rub a little grapeseed oil over a lettuce bundle to make it shine, then arrange over the sauce. Top with salmon roe. Place the mushrooms in a bowl and squeeze the lemon wedge over. Drizzle with grapeseed oil, sprinkle with salt and pepper, and toss to lightly coat. For each plate, arrange one-sixth of the mushroom batons on the plate like a Jenga tower. Garnish with borage.

CLASSICAL CUISINE VERSUS MODERNIST CUISINE

There is no new school without the old school. The debate about which one is better—traditional braise versus sous vide, sabayon by whisk or sabayon by iSi gun—has almost no significance because it is more about good cooking and amazing flavors and textures. Great food is timeless.

Modernist cuisine is built on the foundation of classical cuisine, and we can look at it as a natural evolution in the art of doing things in an increasingly precise way, with greater control over textures and flavors. For successful results, there are a few key tenets: an understanding that there needs to be a balance between old methods and newer ones; that a dish should be recognizable; that the integrity of a product and its unique textures are respected; and that the cook understands where the line is before his or her dish is deemed gimmicky.

It is very important to learn the tried-and-true basics of the so-called old school. It is a huge help to the young cook and he or she will discover how empowering it can be. The chef must maintain the integrity of the product, learn how to properly season, how to create compelling flavor profiles with layers and textures, while learning how to use ingredients to their fullest extent. When you have a solid grasp of the culinary fundamentals, the sky is the limit. Too often I see young chefs with not enough experience wanting to use all the newest techniques without understanding their roles. The result is food that the diner can't identify with. There's no connection. The diner is lost and puzzled as he or she gazes down at the dish. That feeling is then exacerbated when the taste and textures are not pleasurable because of the overuse of this or that technique or powder.

Often the textures are too similar to one another because of the overuse of sous vide cooking; flavors become flat and monochromatic in order to achieve a striking appearance. It's so beautiful looking that you expect perfection, but then once it's in your mouth, it feels like a deception. It makes me sad to see a young cook, not knowing that there is another way, rely on an iSi canister of whipped cream instead of simply pouring some fresh heavy cream into a bowl and using a whisk. The same goes for a regular hollandaise sauce. These are not just "old school" techniques—they're Cooking 101, and you have to know them to be a versatile cook and chef. And if you don't know the fundamentals, then no modern tool can make you a better cook. It astonishes me how many of the young generation has no idea how a proper mayonnaise is made.

Extreme molecular cooking, driven by the rise of overextended tasting menus, has proven over time to be best exhibited in small bites. In such settings, they can be interesting, surprising, and intriguing. However, when chefs scale up to a full-course dish, they can easily become boring and unsatisfying.

As you'll see, my dishes are all rooted in fundamental technique, have a variety of textures, with very little reliance on sous vide or the chemicals popularized by modernist cuisine. But on the other hand, I also will create a dish of beans and truffles and make it more elegant using an iSi gun to finish the dish with an airy puree, or find the perfect textures for the pâte de fruits using the agar and gellan gum popularized by Ferran Adrià.

Bottom line: Learning how to balance both approaches and mastering flavor combinations and profiles are huge assets in pursuing the next level of one's culinary career.

HOT APPETIZERS

SMOKED STURGEON
AND SAUERKRAUT TART
with Riesling Mousseline
and Caviar

200

BUCKWHEAT SPAETZLE
with Tuna Paillard and
Seared Foie Gras

202

POTATO GATEAU
with Hickory Smoked Bacon,
Onions, and Comté

205

DUCK AND
FOIE GRAS RAVIOLI
in Mushroom Fumet with
Shiitake Caps and Chervil

208

SWEETBREAD RAVIOLI
with Mustard Jus and Vin Jaune

210

SMOKED EEL CARBONARA
with Squid Ink Cavatelli
and Toasted Pumpkin Seeds

212

TEMPRANILLO RISOTTO
with Crispy Duck
and Fried Oregano

214

TARBAIS BEANS AND
BLACK PÉRIGORD TRUFFLE
in a Mason Jar with
Sunchoke Espuma

217

POACHED FARM EGG
with Pimento Nage, Millet,
and Roasted Chestnuts

218

ROASTED KING CRAB LEGS
with Jalapeño-Hazelnut Vinaigrette
and Black Trumpet and
Grapefruit Crumble

220

RIESLING-BRAISED
SCALLOPS
with Uni Espuma,
Tapioca Crisp, Kumamoto
Oyster, and Caviar

222

SAUTÉED FOIE GRAS
with Beerawecka Fruit Chutney
and Beer Reduction

224

WILD MUSHROOMS
AND LOUISIANA CRAYFISH
Cooked "en Baeckeoffe"

227

SAUTÉED SULLIVAN
COUNTY FOIE GRAS
with Basil Nage and Nutmeg

230

SMOKED STURGEON AND SAUERKRAUT TART
WITH RIESLING MOUSSELINE AND CAVIAR

Serves 6

My fine-dining colleagues said I'd never be able to put sauerkraut on a fine-dining menu. But it's part of my heritage, my Alsatian DNA. When I first served this dish at the Modern nearly a decade ago, I wasn't sure how it would be received. It quickly became a best-seller and remains immensely popular to this day. At the Restaurant Gabriel Kreuther, we serve the tartlets under a cloche, which we fill with applewood smoke from a smoking gun. If you like, you can do the same. Its sea-saltiness balances sauerkraut's deep tartness, as does the richness of a white wine sabayon.

Also, it's not *just* about the sauerkraut; another key element is the fish we use, which is rarely served in the U.S. We know from choucroute (page 59) that smoked meats go perfectly with sauerkraut, so that's how we treat the fish. Years ago, I'd never have been able to get away with this dish in a Michelin-starred restaurant in Alsace—I'd have been reprimanded! But now, in New York, it's one of my signature dishes.

FOR THE TARTLET SHELLS

1 package (1 pound/450 g) phyllo dough, thawed if frozen

9 tablespoons (125 g) clarified butter (see Note)

Note: To make the clarified butter, melt it in a 1-quart/liter saucepan over low heat, without stirring, 10 to 15 minutes, until melted and the solids separate from the fat. Remove from the heat; let stand 5 minutes. Skim off the foam. Slowly pour off the clear yellow liquid, leaving behind the residue of milk solids that has settled to the bottom of the pan.

Preheat your oven to 350°F (175°C).

Place a sheet of phyllo dough on your work surface. Brush with clarified butter and stack another sheet on top. Repeat to form a stack of three sheets with butter on each sheet. Make two more stacks in the same way.

Using a 5-inch (12 cm) ring mold as a guide, cut six rounds out of the phyllo stacks. Center a round over a 3-inch-round (7.5 cm) tartlet mold and press into the bottom and up the sides. Press another tartlet mold over the phyllo stack. Repeat with the remaining phyllo rounds.

Bake the tartlet shells until golden brown and crisp, 8 to 10 minutes. (Leave the oven on.) Carefully remove the top tartlet molds, then remove the shells from the bottom mold. Invert the shells onto a wire rack to let excess butter drip off and cool completely.

FOR THE MOUSSELINE

1 cup (250 ml) Riesling or other dry white wine

½ shallot, chopped

12 black peppercorns, cracked

4 large egg yolks, at room temperature

7 tablespoons (100 g) clarified butter (see Note), very warm

4 tablespoons (60 ml) grapeseed or other neutral-flavored oil

Salt

Cayenne pepper

Juice of ½ lemon

Combine the wine, shallot, and peppercorns in a small saucepan. Bring to a boil, then simmer until reduced by half. Strain through a fine-mesh sieve.

Whisk the egg yolks in a heatproof bowl, then whisk in the hot strained wine. Set the bowl over a saucepan of simmering water and continue whisking until very frothy. While whisking, add the butter, then the oil in a slow, steady stream. Season to taste with salt and cayenne, then whisk in the lemon juice. Turn off the heat and keep warm over a 130°F to 140°F (55°C to 60°C) water bath.

TO ASSEMBLE

7 ounces (210 g) hot-smoked sturgeon fillets, smoked trout, smoked scallops, or hot-smoked king salmon, skin removed if necessary

½ pound (220 g) sauerkraut (page 60), heated and drained well

1 ounce (30 g) white sturgeon caviar

Chopped chives and edible flowers, for garnish

Raise the oven temperature to 450°F (230°C).

Cut the sturgeon into ⅛-inch-thick (3 mm) slices. The slices should be able to fit in the tartlet shells without overhang. If necessary, trim the slices to the right length.

Put the tartlet shells on a half sheet pan. Divide the sauerkraut among the tartlet shells, pressing gently into an even layer. Arrange the smoked sturgeon slices in a single layer on top, putting about 3 slices on each. Bake until heated through, 1 to 1½ minutes.

Strain the mousseline through a fine-mesh sieve. If you have a siphon, fill it with the mousseline, then charge the canister with two charges of N2O. Shake the canister and pipe a dollop of mousseline on top of each tart. Alternatively, whisk the mousseline until very foamy and spoon on top of the tarts.

Spoon a quenelle of caviar on top of each tart and then garnish with the chives and edible flowers. Serve immediately.

BUCKWHEAT SPAETZLE
WITH TUNA PAILLARD AND SEARED FOIE GRAS

Serves 6

In this elegant appetizer, each bite is a different experience, moving from hot caramelized foie gras to chilled tuna to warm spaetzle. Layering different temperatures keeps the eating experience exciting. So does a mix of peppercorns along with the sweet-and-sour gastrique sauce. While all the parts make for a delicious whole, some can be served alone too. The tuna can be a light chilled crudo starter and the spaetzle a versatile side dish. Here, I added buckwheat flour to give the noodles a complex earthy nuttiness. See page 88 for more on spaetzle.

FOR THE GASTRIQUE
1 tablespoon (13 g) sugar
1½ tablespoons (22 ml) Banyuls vinegar
½ cup (125 ml) red wine
2 tablespoons (16 g) minced shallots
½ teaspoon (3 g) cracked black
　　peppercorns
¼ teaspoon (1.5 g) cracked Szechuan
　　peppercorns
½ cup (125 ml) Chicken Jus (page 252)
1 tablespoon butter, at room
　　temperature

To make the gastrique, cook the sugar in a saucepan over medium-high heat without stirring until dark amber. Add the vinegar and stir, scraping up hardened bits. Repeat with the red wine. Bring to a boil, then add the shallots and both cracked peppers.

Reduce the heat to maintain a simmer and cook until reduced by half, 7 to 10 minutes. Add the jus, bring to a boil, then simmer for 5 minutes longer. Strain through a fine-mesh sieve into another saucepan, stir in the butter until incorporated, and keep hot over low heat.

FOR THE SPAETZLE
2½ tablespoons (35 g) butter
Buckwheat Spaetzle (recipe follows)
3 tablespoons (26 g) chopped shallots
3 scallions, chopped
3 tablespoons plus 1 teaspoon (50 ml)
　　sherry vinegar
2 tablespoons (30 ml) lower-sodium
　　soy sauce
2 tablespoons (30 ml) gastrique (from
　　above)
¼ cup (60 ml) heavy cream, whipped to
　　soft peaks
Salt and freshly ground black pepper

Melt the butter in a large skillet over medium-high heat. When the butter starts to foam, add the spaetzle, gently separating the pieces and stirring continuously. Add the shallots and scallions and continue stirring until the spaetzle are heated through.

Reduce the heat to medium-low and add the vinegar, soy sauce, and gastrique, reserving the rest for finishing the dish before serving. Stir for 1 minute, then fold in the cream and season to taste with salt and pepper. Keep warm over low heat.

FOR THE TUNA
10 ounces (300 g) highest-quality
　　yellowfin tuna, cut into 6 even slices
2 tablespoons plus 2 teaspoons (40 ml)
　　hazelnut oil
Freshly ground black pepper
3 tablespoons snipped chives

Put the tuna slices between sheets of plastic wrap in a single layer. Pound gently into very thin slices. Remove the top sheet of plastic wrap.

Brush the oil on the tuna, then grind pepper directly on top. Sprinkle with the chives.

recipe continues

FOR THE BUCKWHEAT SPAETZLE

1¾ cups (220 g) all-purpose flour
½ cup (60 g) buckwheat flour
1 teaspoon salt, plus more as needed
Pinch of freshly ground white pepper
¼ nutmeg, grated
6 tablespoons (90 ml) milk
3 large eggs
Grapeseed oil, as needed

Sift both flours with the salt, pepper, and nutmeg into the bowl of a standing mixer. Fit with the paddle attachment and mix on low. With the machine running, add the milk in a steady stream, then the eggs, one at a time. Beat until incorporated, then scrape the bowl. Beat on high speed until the batter is very sticky. Let rest for 30 minutes.

Bring a large pot of salted water to a boil. Fill a large bowl with ice and water. Working in batches if necessary, press the spaetzle batter through a perforated metal steamer basket or a colander with large holes directly into the boiling water. When the strands of dough begin to float, transfer them to the ice water bath with a slotted spoon.

Drain the spaetzle well. Toss with just enough oil to coat and prevent the strands from sticking. Use immediately or refrigerate for up to 3 days.

FOR THE FOIE GRAS

6 slices foie gras (each 1⅓ ounces/40 g), pounded lightly to flatten
Salt and freshly ground black pepper
2 tablespoons all-purpose flour, sifted
Grapeseed or other neutral-flavored oil, as needed
5½ tablespoons (80 ml) Banyuls vinegar
6 tablespoons (1 tablespoon per serving) gastrique (page 202)
Baby greens, for garnish

Season the foie gras slices with salt and pepper. Dredge both sides of each slice in the flour, then shake off excess.

Heat a large skillet over medium-high heat and coat with a thin slick of oil. The foie gras will release grease as it cooks as well. Working in batches if necessary to avoid crowding the pieces, add the foie gras to the hot oil in a single layer. Sear, turning once, until you get a nice dark char on each side. Turn off the heat and add the vinegar. The vinegar will sputter rapidly. As soon as it stops, transfer the foie gras to the serving dishes, placing the slices on top of the tuna.

To serve the dish, divide the spaetzle among six warm, shallow bowls. Top with the seasoned tuna, then the foie gras. Using a spoon, drizzle the hot gastrique all over. Garnish with the greens.

POTATO GATEAU
WITH HICKORY SMOKED BACON, ONIONS, AND COMTÉ

Serves 6

These are another way to use the potato. Here, as the container for a tart of bacon and cheese—use a high-quality bacon, such as Benton's. Potato is sliced very thin, partially cooked in clarified butter, then used to line small tartlette pans, cut so that the slices can be folded over the top. The potato is very versatile. You could prepare larger slices the same way, fill them with a stuffing, seal them with a second slice, then fry it for a potato ravioli.

While the filling is very easy to make, these are meant to be very elegant tarts and take some time to prepare if you want them to be beautiful. The goal is to line the tarts so that you have a striking pinwheel effect when you turn the tarts out. Use six non-fluted tartlette molds (4½ inches/11 cm in diameter).

recipe continues

1 bunch scallions, thinly sliced

Grapeseed oil

Salt

4 ounces (120 g) pearl onions, peeled and thinly sliced

6 ounces (180 g) bacon, small diced, lightly cooked to render the fat but without coloring the bacon*

4 ounces (120 g) grated Comté cheese (1¼ cups)

5 medium large Yukon gold potatoes, peeled

2 cups (500 ml) clarified butter (see page 201)

⅔ cup (80 g) raspberries

7 tablespoons (105 ml) Champagne vinegar

2 tablespoons honey

2 tablespoons pumpkin seed oil

* Note: An artisanal smoked Virginia ham is a great substitute for the bacon.

First make the filling by sautéing the scallions in grapeseed oil, seasoning them with salt. Separately sauté the pearl onions in oil until tender, seasoning them with salt. Remove from the heat. When the pearl onions have cooled, mix them with the bacon, then add the cheese and mix until the cheese is uniformly distributed.

Cut the potatoes into planks about 3½ inches (9 cm) long and about ¾ inch (2 cm) thick. Round off the ends of each plank for an elegant appearance. Slice the potato on a mandoline so that you have translucently thin slices of potato, 3½ by ¾ inches (9 by 2 cm). Lay them out on a kitchen towel and with another towel blot them dry. You'll also need to cut six thin rounds of potato for the center of the tartlette pan.

Heat the clarified butter to about 200°F (93°C). Blanch the strips of potato until they are tender and just pliable enough to bend without tearing, a few minutes or so. Lay them on a rack over a sheet pan. Blanch the six rounds as well. When the potatoes are cool, put one potato round in the center of each tartlette pan. Working one by one, lay the strips of potatoes in a pan by placing one tip in the center of the round and half of the potato hanging over the edge of the tartlette pan. Overlap the next strip in the same manner so that all the strips extend like spokes of a wheel from the center out. Repeat with the remaining tartlette pans and potato strips. This should create a pinwheel effect when they are removed from the pans.

Preheat your oven to 350°F (175°C).

Spread a layer of sautéed scallion on the potatoes in the bottom of each tartelette pan, then fill them with the onion-cheese filling (if you have leftover potato you can add it to the filling).

Put a large, flat sauté pan over medium-high heat. Place the tartlette pans into the sauté pan and add a little oil, to help conduct the heat. Cook for 5 to 7 minutes, until the edges of the tartelette pans are bubbling. Transfer the sauté pan to the oven and bake for 12 minutes, then increase the heat to 375°F (190°C) for another 3 minutes, so that the bottom is crisp and the filling is hot.

While they are cooking, make the sauce by blending the raspberries with the Champagne vinegar. Strain into a saucepan and bring just to a simmer. Remove from the heat and stir in the honey. When the sauce is cool, stir in the pumpkin seed oil (it should be served broken, or not emulsified).

When the potato tarts are finished baking, you can turn them out into a sauté pan and cook for a few minutes over medium-high heat to make the tops (now the bottoms) crispy, or simply turn them out onto a plate. Serve the tarts along with a spoonful of the vinaigrette.

DUCK AND FOIE GRAS RAVIOLI
IN MUSHROOM FUMET WITH SHIITAKE CAPS AND CHERVIL

Serves 6

This rich ravioli, filled with chicken breast and duck and foie gras, also contains salty, dense duck prosciutto, which gives a pleasing chewiness to the pasta. You can make this prosciutto at home (pack a duck breast in salt for 24 hours in the refrigerator, then rinse the salt off and set on a rack or hang to dry at room temperature for 7 days) or buy it from a purveyor; we use D'Artagnan. The broth uses well-cooked mushrooms for its base—white button mushrooms are an underrated ingredient. Here they make a fabulous broth with wine and some stock (and a little soy sauce for seasoning).

FOR THE RAVIOLI DOUGH

2½ cups (300 g) all-purpose flour
1 egg
5 egg yolks
2 teaspoons salt
1 tablespoon apple-cider vinegar

In the bowl of a standing mixer fitted with a dough hook, combine the flour, egg, yolks, and salt, and mix until a dough forms (if it's too dense, add a little water). Add the vinegar at the end of mixing (this prevents the dough from discoloring). Turn the dough out onto your work surface, form it into a disc, cover it with a towel, and let it rest for an hour or so.

FOR THE STUFFING

2 ounces (60 g) duck breast, small diced
8 ounces (240 g) chicken breast,
    small diced
5 ounces (150 g) foie gras,
    medium diced
4 ounces (120 g) duck prosciutto,
    small diced
About 2 teaspoons salt, or to taste
30 grinds pepper, or to taste
1 egg, beaten
Egg wash (2 egg yolks mixed with
    2 tablespoons heavy cream or milk)

Combine the duck breast, chicken breast, foie gras, and duck prosciutto in a mixing bowl and stir well to distribute all the ingredients. Add the salt and pepper, and

stir. Stir in the egg so that you have moist stuffing. Refrigerate until ready to use, up to two days.

FOR THE MUSHROOM FUMET

4 tablespoons (120 ml) olive oil
1 pound (455 g) white button mush-
    rooms, sliced
Salt
4 shallots, chopped
4 cloves garlic, smashed and roughly
    chopped
¼ cup (60 ml) white wine
3½ cups (875 ml) White Chicken Stock
    (page 251)
¼ teaspoon soy sauce
A few drops sherry vinegar
3 tablespoons butter, to finish the fumet
    before serving

Heat the olive oil in a large saucepan over medium-high heat. When it's melted, add the mushrooms and cook them until they're nicely caramelized, 10 minutes or so, salting them as you do. Add the shallot and garlic and continue to cook for a few more minutes. Add the white wine and chicken stock and simmer gently for about 30 minutes, until the stock is reduced by about half. Strain the stock through a fine-mesh sieve into a saucepan, pressing on the mushrooms to get as much liquid as possible from them (you'll need about 1½ cups/375 ml for six portions). Season with the soy sauce and vinegar. Before serving, bring the sauce back up to heat and whisk in the butter.

TO GARNISH (OPTIONAL)

30 small shiitake mushroom caps,
    sautéed in olive oil until nicely colored
Fresh parsley

To complete the dish, roll out the pasta through the widest setting on your roller, folding it in thirds each time and running it through again. Roll the pasta through successively smaller settings on your pasta roller until it's very thin (typically the penultimate setting; it should be thin and delicate but also easy to work with).

Lay the rolled pasta on your work surface. Cut out discs with a 3-inch (7.5 cm) ring cutter. You'll need 60 discs. Put 10 grams, a tablespoon or so, of the stuffing into the center of the discs. Brush one half the perimeter of the pasta with egg wash. Make triangular shaped ravioli by pinching one half of the ravioli together, then fold the opposite end up toward the sealed half, pressing all edges together to seal the raviolis.

Bring a large pot of well-salted water to a boil. Add the raviolis and cook them for 3 to 4 minutes, until done. Strain and place ten raviolis in each of six bowls.

Finish the dish by spooning the warm fumet over the raviolis. Garnish with the shiitakes and parsley, if using, and serve immediately.

SWEETBREAD RAVIOLI
WITH MUSTARD JUS AND VIN JAUNE

Serves 6

These are warm, comforting raviolis, served in a jus seasoned with mustard and vin jaune. It's important to chop the blanched and peeled sweetbreads by hand so that they have a great texture. Vin jaune is an oxidized, sherry-like wine made in the Jura region, in eastern France, near Alsace, from Savagnin grapes. It's very high in acid and is what we would use in Alsace, but it can be expensive here so it's fine to use a less expensive option, such as Tio Pepe, a Spanish sherry that's similar in flavor.

This ravioli dough differs from the previous dough in that it uses more egg and, importantly, semolina flour. When you use semolina, you can cook the pasta longer without making it soggy, which is handy here, as the farce, or, as we say, the stuffing, requires longer cooking.

FOR THE RAVIOLI DOUGH

1½ cups (190 g) all-purpose flour
1 cup (180 g) "000" semolina
2 teaspoons (10 g) salt
2 eggs
4 egg yolks
1 tablespoon olive oil

In a standing mixer fitted with a dough hook, combine the flour, semolina, and salt. In a mixing bowl, beat the eggs and egg yolks together and then slowly add them to the flour mixture, followed by the oil, with the mixer on medium speed until the dough comes together. Shape the dough into a disc, wrap it in plastic, and let it rest in the refrigerator for about 8 hours or overnight.

FOR THE RAVIOLI STUFFING

2 tablespoons olive oil
⅓ cup (50 g) minced shallot
Salt
2½ ounces (75 g) white button mushrooms, roughly chopped
2 tablespoons butter
9 ounces (270 g) blanched, peeled, and chopped sweetbreads
1½ ounces (45 g) zucchini peel, chopped
⅓ cup (50 g) dry golden raisins, chopped
1½ cups (45 g) parsley leaves, blanched, shocked, and chopped
Pepper
2 ounces (60 g) ricotta cheese
Egg wash (2 egg yolks mixed with 2 tablespoons heavy cream or milk)
¼ cup (25 g) grated Parmesan cheese
30 gratings nutmeg

Put the olive oil in a large saucepan over medium-high heat, then add the shallot. Add a teaspoon or so of salt. When the shallot is translucent, add the mushrooms and cook them until the moisture they release has cooked off. Add the butter, then the sweetbreads and cook until heated through, a minute or two. Add the zucchini peel, raisins, and parsley. Season with salt and pepper, tasting until you feel the stuffing is well-seasoned. Remove them to a plate to cool, then stir in the ricotta until it's uniformly mixed.

FOR THE JUS

1 cup (250 ml) White Chicken Stock (page 251)
½ cup (125 ml) dry white wine
2 tablespoons Dijon mustard
Salt and freshly ground black pepper
1 tablespoon butter
6 tablespoons (90 ml) vin jaune or Tio Pepe, to finish the sauce
2 tablespoons whipped cream

In a saucepan over medium-high heat, combine the chicken stock and white wine, bring to a simmer, and reduce by half. Whisk in the Dijon mustard, season with salt and pepper, then whisk in the butter. Adjust seasoning to taste.

When you're ready to serve, bring it up to a simmer, and add the vin jaune. Remove the jus from the heat and whisk in the whipped cream (you can give it some froth by doing this with a hand blender, if you wish).

TO GARNISH (OPTIONAL)

2 tablespoons julienned button mushrooms (cut into matchsticks)
2 tablespoons julienned zucchini peel
6 Champagne grapes, cut into wedges
Microgreens
⅓ cup (30 g) grated Parmesan
Nutmeg

To complete the dish, roll out the pasta through the widest setting, folding it in thirds each time and running it through again. Roll the pasta through successively smaller settings on your pasta roller until it's very thin (typically the penultimate setting; it should be thin and delicate but also easy to work with).

Lay the rolled pasta on your work surface. Cut out discs with a 3-inch (7.5 cm) ring cutter. You'll need 42 to 48 discs. Put 10 grams, a tablespoon or so, of the stuffing into the center of the discs. Brush one half of the perimeter of the pasta with egg wash and fold it together to seal the pasta in semicircular raviolis.

Bring a large pot of well-salted water to a boil. Add the pasta and cook it for 3 to 4 minutes or until done. Strain and place seven or eight raviolis in each of six bowls. Spoon the jus over the raviolis. Season with the Parmesan and nutmeg. Garnish as desired and serve immediately.

SMOKED EEL CARBONARA
WITH SQUID INK CAVATELLI AND TOASTED PUMPKIN SEEDS

Serves 6 to 8

This dish came about, as many dishes do, because we had an abundance of an ingredient to make use of—in this instance, smoked eel. Chef de Cuisine Joe Anthony played around with it and came up with a number of dishes. This was the best. Any smoked fish will work. Bluefish would be interesting. We buy our eel cooked and smoked so it's easy to remove the skin and spine from the meat, reserving the spine to fortify the sauce. Also, we've paired this pasta in a cavatelli shape with squid ink, which can be left out if you prefer. The key here though is the smoke on the eel, which mimics the bacon in a traditional carbonara.

FOR THE PASTA DOUGH

2¾ cups (350 g) all-purpose flour
2 cups (360 g) "000" semolina
1 teaspoon salt
1 egg
6 egg yolks
2 tablespoons olive oil
1 tablespoon squid ink (optional)
1 tablespoon apple cider vinegar

Combine all the ingredients in the bowl of a standing mixer and mix on medium speed until the dough is smooth and no longer sticks to the side of the bowl. Knead it by hand until it feels velvety smooth. Shape it into a disc, wrap in plastic, and refrigerate for a few hours or overnight.

To shape the cavatelli, cut the dough into four or five pieces. Roll the dough pieces into ¼-inch-thick (6 mm) ropes. Cut the rope into 1-inch (2.5 cm) lengths. Using the tips of your index and middle fingers, firmly press down on each piece and then pull the dough toward you so that it lengthens a bit and forms a curl. Repeat with the remaining pieces. Refrigerate for up to a day or freeze for up to 3 weeks.

FOR THE CARBONARA SAUCE

2 small shallots, thinly sliced
3 tablespoons grapeseed oil
12 ounces (360 g) smoked eel, from 1½
    to 2 eels, skinned, spine removed and
    reserved, meat saved for serving
3½ cups (875 ml) heavy cream
2 cups (250 ml) White Chicken Stock
    (page 251)
2 bay leaves
1 teaspoon black peppercorns
1 teaspoon fish sauce
2 teaspoons bonito flakes

In a skillet over medium-high heat, sweat the shallots in the grapeseed oil until translucent, add the spine, and cook it for a minute or so. Add the cream, chicken stock, bay leaves, peppercorns, and fish sauce. Simmer for 30 minutes, partially covered to allow for some evaporation and to keep it from boiling too hard. Remove from the heat and stir in the bonito flakes. Allow to steep for 10 minutes. Strain through a fine-mesh sieve. Reserve the sauce and the meat separately and keep warm. Discard the spine.

FOR THE PUMPKIN SEED CRUMBLE

½ cup (65 g) pumpkin seeds
½ cup (40 g) panko breadcrumbs
Salt
2 tablespoons (30 g) clarified butter
    (see page 201), melted

Preheat your oven to 325°F (160°C).

In a food processor, pulse the pumpkin seeds and panko separately to a coarse grind. Mix with a pinch of salt and the clarified butter. Spread the mixture on a Silpat and bake, mixing every 4 minutes until golden brown, about 20 minutes. Cool and store in an airtight container for up to 3 days.

FOR THE EGG YOLK "CONFIT"

2 cups (500 ml) grapeseed oil
6 to 8 egg yolks

Heat the oil in a saucepan to 145°F (63°C) when you're ready to prepare the carbonara (you should have enough). Gently warm the egg yolks in the oil for 5 to 6 minutes, then remove the pan from the heat until ready to serve the yolks.

TO FINISH THE DISH

2 tablespoons minced shallots
1 teaspoon minced garlic
1 tablespoon grapeseed oil
3 tablespoons (45 g) cold butter
3 tablespoons Tio Pepe, or to taste
Lemon juice or sherry vinegar
1 cup Microplaned Parmigiano-Reggiano
6 scallions, greens only, finely sliced on
    the bias
Micro herbs (optional)
Freshly ground black pepper
Fleur de sel

To finish the dish, boil the pasta in well-salted water until tender but still with some bite, 4 to 5 minutes.

As you do, sauté the shallots and garlic in the oil in a large sauté pan until tender. Add the carbonara sauce and the eel meat. Add the cooked pasta and toss. Add the butter, Tio Pepe, and lemon juice or sherry vinegar. Add the Parmigiano-Reggiano and half the scallions. Taste and adjust the seasoning. Divide into six to eight bowls. Sprinkle each with the pumpkin seed crumble. Garnish with the remaining scallions, micro herbs, if using, and top with an egg yolk confit. Garnish the yolk with pepper and fleur de sel.

TEMPRANILLO RISOTTO
WITH CRISPY DUCK AND FRIED OREGANO

Serves 6

This is a very rich and satisfying risotto made with the full-bodied wine Tempranillo, from Spain. Why this red? I love the sound of it! Tempranillo. But any relatively inexpensive full-bodied wine will work well. The duck and skin are ground and sautéed until the bits of skin are crunchy and the duck is chewy. It's got great bite. You'll need to grind this meat; you can't chop it in a food processor. If you don't have a grinder, chop it by hand (freeze the skin for easier chopping) or ask your butcher to do it for you. We always make our risottos ahead, chill them, and finish them at service—a handy technique if you are serving this for guests.

FOR THE RISOTTO BASE

⅔ cup (80 g) finely chopped onion
2 tablespoons (18 g) finely chopped
    shallot
7 tablespoons (105 ml) olive oil
½ cup (120 g) butter
9 ounces (270 g) Arborio rice
2 cups (480 ml) dry white wine
6 cups (1.5 liters) White Chicken Stock
    (page 251)
1 tablespoon salt
Pepper

In a large sauté pan over medium heat, cook the chopped onions and shallots in the olive oil and ¼ cup (60 g) of the butter until translucent, then add the rice and stir to coat it well. Add the white wine and cook until has completely evaporated. Then add a third of the stock and simmer, stirring constantly with a wooden spoon or spatula, adding another third when the first cooks off. Add the remaining stock, season it with the salt and pepper, and reduce until the risotto is creamy but still a little crunchy. The whole process of reducing the wine and stock should take about 12 minutes. Stir in the remaining butter. Pour the par-cooked risotto on a sheet pan lined with parchment paper, and chill it until ready to complete the dish.

FOR THE DUCK

3 tablespoons grapeseed oil
2 duck magret duck breasts, ground
    through a medium die

Put the oil in a large sauté pan over medium heat and cook the duck until the skin is crispy and the meat is almost chewy, 20 minutes or so. Remove to a sheet pan lined with parchment, fat and all, until ready to use. You can make this a day ahead and refrigerate it, then rewarm it.

TO FINISH THE RISOTTO

1 (750-ml) bottle Tempranillo red wine
    or other full-bodied red wine
1 tablespoon olive oil
2 cups (150 g) finely julienned radicchio
1 cup (250 ml) White Chicken Stock
    (page 251), or as needed
6 tablespoons (40 g) grated Pecorino
    Romano
Salt and freshly ground black pepper
Freshly grated nutmeg
2 tablespoons (30 g) butter
4 leaves fresh mint, cut into chiffonade
Fried oregano leaves (see Notes)
3 tablespoons preserved lemon peel,
    small diced (home-cured or store-
    bought; see Notes)

Notes: To fry the oregano leaves, heat oil to 375°F (190°C) degrees in a very small saucepan or frying pan over high heat. Test that the oil is hot enough by dropping in an oregano leaf: if it sizzles, goes crisp straightaway, and turns a brighter shade of green, the oil is ready. If the oil is too hot, the oregano will go dark green. Put them all in and, when fried, remove to a paper towel and season with a little salt.

To home-cure lemons, pack them in salt for 3 weeks or longer. Remove from the salt, rinse, and use only the peel. As long as the lemons are submerged in salt, they'll keep indefinitely.

In a saucepan over high heat, reduce the wine to 1 cup (250 ml).

In a skillet over medium-high heat, add the olive oil and sauté the radicchio until it is wilted. Add the parcooked risotto and half the chicken stock and cook until the rice begins to absorb the liquid. Add the duck and stir. Add half the reduced wine, stir it in, then add the remaining chicken stock and reduced wine, continuing to stir constantly. When the rice is tender but toothsome, add the Pecorino, and season with salt, pepper, and nutmeg. Finish by stirring in the butter.

Divide among six plates, and garnish with the mint, oregano, and preserved lemon peel.

TARBAIS BEANS AND BLACK PÉRIGORD TRUFFLE
IN A MASON JAR WITH SUNCHOKE ESPUMA

Serves 6

Here I combine the cheapest of ingredients, dried beans, with the most expensive, foie gras and truffle (though you may forgo the foie gras, if you wish). These white runner beans from Tarbais are best known for being used to make cassoulet. This style of bean is available at Ranch Gordo. Large white kidney beans can be substituted. I serve this in a small mason jar at the table, rather than an elegant serving dish. It grounds you, this casual service piece, encourages you to relax and enjoy your meal and your company. Also, I like that the diner can unseal the jar, redolent with black truffle, and inhale the aroma. We finish it with sunchoke espuma, in effect a sunchoke coulis shot from an iSi gun at the table. This is perfect to make for guests as it can be prepared a day or two in advance, refrigerated, then reheated in a water bath for 30 minutes to serve. I love the drama of this dish.

1 cup (227 g) Tarbais beans, soaked in water overnight

Sachet d'épices (carrot, celery, onion or leek, thyme, and bay leaf, tied together in cheesecloth)

2 tablespoons (30 g) butter

1 shallot, finely chopped

1 clove garlic, finely chopped

4 tablespoons (60 ml) Madeira

Salt and freshly ground black pepper

2 ounces (60 g) foie gras terrine, optional (store-bought or see page 180)

1 black truffle, *Tuber melanosporum* (about 3¼ ounces/90 g), peeled with peels reserved

Fleur de sel

Crispy puffed wheat (can be purchased at any supermarket)

FOR THE ESPUMA

1 medium Yukon gold potato (7 ounces /210 grams or so), peeled

7 ounces (210 g) sunchokes

2 cups (500 ml) White Chicken Stock (page 251)

1 cup (250 ml) heavy cream

Salt and freshly ground black pepper

Put the beans and their soaking water in a pan with the sachet and simmer them gently until they're tender, about 1½ hours. Strain, but reserve the cooking liquid. Discard the sachet. When they're cool enough to handle, pop them out of their skins (discard the skins).

In a small saucepan over medium heat, melt the butter. Add the shallot and cook until it is translucent, then add the garlic and cook for another 30 seconds or so. Add the Tarbais beans, stir, then add 2 tablespoons of the Madeira. Mix well and season to taste with salt and pepper.

Divide the bean mixture among six 7-ounce (200 ml) mason jars. Add a small slice of foie gras terrine, if using (about ½ ounce/15 g per jar). Slice your truffle into ¼-inch (6 mm) slices and lay them in the jars. Top with some fleur de sel. Add 1 teaspoon of Madeira to each jar, seal, and refrigerate until ready to cook. These can be refrigerated for up to 3 days.

For the espuma, or foam, peel the potatoes and sunchokes and cut them into small pieces. Cook them in the chicken stock until soft, 5 to 10 minutes, then add the cream and simmer for 5 more minutes. Blend the mixture in a blender. Pass it through a sieve. Season it with salt and pepper. It should be as thin as a coulis, not thick like a puree, so that it will foam when shot from an iSi container. Fill the iSi gun, fitted with two charges. Reserve in a bain-marie of warm water until ready to serve. You will likely have more of this than you need, but it can be refrigerated and used with other dishes.

Forty-five minutes before you want to serve the beans, remove them from the refrigerator. Prepare a water bath on the stovetop—a pot big enough to contain all six jars lined with a kitchen towel and filled with water. Place the jars in the water, and make sure they are completely covered so that they seal completely. Weigh them down with a pan as they may want to float to the surface. Bring the water temperature up to about 190°F (90°C). Set a timer for 30 minutes, then remove the jars.

To serve, open the jars and then fill each with plenty of sunchoke espuma. Sprinkle crispy puffed wheat on top.

POACHED FARM EGG
WITH PIMENTO NAGE, MILLET, AND ROASTED CHESTNUTS

Serves 6

This dish is all about the sauce, a pimento nage, or broth, which is delicious with so many things—lobster, scallops, chicken, or here, a simple poached egg and an ancient, and in my view, underappreciated grain, millet, which is healthful, flavorful, and has a great bite. It keeps well, so use the extra as a sauce for any mild main course. This uses pimentos but is great even with roasted red bell pepper. I also love the chestnuts. You can buy them peeled and cooked or braise your own in chicken stock just until tender. Cooking eggs in plastic wrap ensures a perfect poached egg every time and has an interesting advantage: Herbs and flavored oil can be added to the wrap to give the egg a unique flavor. In addition, there is no loss of egg white, as there is in traditionally poached eggs, and it gives the egg volume and a three-dimensional presentation. (For the traditional way of poaching eggs, see page 247.)

FOR THE PIMENTO NAGE

⅔ cup (150 g) butter
⅓ cup (45 g) sliced shallots
Salt
3 ounces (90 g) prosciutto, diced
3 ounces (90 g) Spanish chorizo, diced
1 teaspoon black peppercorns, cracked
    beneath a heavy skillet
2 pimentos, or cherry peppers, roughly
    chopped (these are large red heart-
    shaped chili peppers that measure
    3 to 4 inches/7.5 to 10 cm long and
    2 to 3 inches/5 to 7.5 cm wide, canned
    and sold in better grocery stores
    or online)
¼ jalapeño, seeds removed
1 cup (250 ml) dry Riesling
4 cups (960 ml) White Chicken Stock
    (page 251), gently simmered until
    reduced to 2 cups
¼ cup (60 ml) Banyuls vinegar, gently
    simmered until reduced by half

In a saucepan, brown the butter over medium-high heat, then add the shallots and 1 teaspoon of salt, or to taste. Add the prosciutto, chorizo, and cracked pepper. Cook for a minute or so, until the meat is lightly colored. Add the chopped pimento and jalapeño, wine, stock, and vinegar and bring to a simmer. Cover with a parchment lid (for more on this method, see page 59), reduce the heat to low, and cook for 30 minutes. Strain through a fine-mesh sieve, reduce by one-third, and cool until ready to use.

FOR THE MILLET

½ small onion (60 g), minced
2 tablespoons (30 g) butter
Salt
1 cup (200 g) millet
1½ cups (375 ml) White Chicken Stock
    (page 251), plus more for reheating

Preheat your oven to 400°F (205°C).

Sweat the onion in the butter in a saucepan until translucent but without color, adding 2 teaspoons salt or to taste. Add the millet and cook it in the dry pan to toast it, 3 to 4 minutes. Bring the stock to a boil in a separate pan. Pour the boiling chicken stock over the millet, cover it with a parchment lid (see page 59), and put it in the oven for 15 minutes. It will still have a slight crunch to it.

When you're ready to serve it, add more chicken stock to reheat it and finish cooking it until tender, 4 to 5 minutes.

FOR THE CHESTNUTS

18 peeled and cooked chestnuts
1 cup (250 ml) White Chicken Stock
    (page 251) or duck stock

Simmer the chestnuts in a sauté pan filled with the stock until the stock is reduced to a glaze, 15 to 20 minutes.

FOR THE POACHED EGGS

3 tablespoons olive oil, duck fat, or butter
6 eggs
Chopped chives
Fleur de sel
Coarsely ground pepper
Food-safe flowers, for garnish (optional)

Brush 1½ teaspoons oil, fat, or butter on one side of a piece of plastic wrap large enough to fit inside a ramekin with plenty of overhang. Insert the plastic wrap inside a mold (or a small cup). Repeat 6 times.

Carefully break 1 egg into each plastic-wrapped mold. Tie off the plastic wrap with a piece of string. A loose mold will form a smoother egg; a tighter wrap will give a patterned appearance to the cooked egg.

Drop (or hang) the plastic wrap into barely simmering water and cook 6 to 8 minutes, until the top white is set and the yolk is still runny.

Remove the eggs from the pot and carefully cut the plastic wrap from each egg. Serve immediately or chill in an ice bath and reheat as noted below.

Place about ½ cup (120 g) of the hot millet in the center of each of six wide bowls. Reheat your eggs in hot tap water for a few minutes if you poached them in advance. Place them in the center of the millet. Garnish with chives, fleur del sel, pepper, and flowers, if using. Place three chestnuts on each plate. Whisk or mix the pimento nage until it's frothy and spoon it generously around the millet.

ROASTED KING CRAB LEGS
WITH JALAPEÑO-HAZELNUT VINAIGRETTE AND BLACK TRUMPET AND GRAPEFRUIT CRUMBLE

Serves 6

This is a fun dish of opposites—sweet, tender crab with savory, chewy mushrooms, the hot crumble and the cold crab, and the real star, besides the crab itself, the jalapeño vinaigrette, which is a beautiful green and deeply flavored with the jalapeño and hazelnut oil. Black trumpet mushrooms should always be blanched in water to which a generous handful of sugar has been added (in the same way you would salt water for pasta) to counteract the residual bitterness they often have. The crumble is straightforward—you could add cinnamon and sugar to it to make it a dessert topping. You'll need ring molds that are about 3 inches (7.5 cm) tall and 1½ to 2 inches (4 to 5 cm) in diameter.

3 king crab legs

Shell the crab legs: Cut the shells with kitchen shears or scissors to keep the meat intact. Three crab legs gives you six nice little "logs" of meat, as each leg has separate pieces of meat on each side of the joint. Shred any extra meat by hand and reserve. If you don't use it all, cover with plastic and refrigerate for later use.

FOR THE JALAPEÑO-HAZELNUT VINAIGRETTE

10 jalapeños, seeds and ribs removed, thinly sliced
2 tablespoons extra-virgin olive oil
Salt
1 tablespoon simple syrup (1 tablespoon/ 15 g sugar dissolved in 1 tablespoon/ 15 ml water)
3½ tablespoons (50 ml) lemon juice, plus more as needed
2 tablespoons hazelnut oil
5 tablespoons (75 ml) grapeseed oil

First make your vinaigrette by gently cooking the sliced jalapeños in a saucepan with the oil, just until tender, then adding ½ cup (120 ml) of water. When the liquid is hot, add a teaspoon or two of salt and cook until the water has cooked off.

Puree the peppers in a blender until they're thoroughly smooth. Pass them through a chinois into a bowl set in ice.

Stir until the puree has cooled. In a clean mixing bowl, weigh out 3½ ounces (100 g, or about 7 tablespoons) of the puree (extra can be refrigerated and used elsewhere as desired). Whisk in the simple syrup and lemon juice. Whisk in the oils. Taste and adjust the seasoning with more salt or lemon juice. Refrigerate until ready to serve.

FOR THE BLACK TRUMPET AND GRAPEFRUIT CRUMBLE

½ cup (60 g) almond flour
¾ cup (95 g) all-purpose flour
4 tablespoons (60 g) melted butter, plus more for sautéing
2 tablespoons grapeseed oil
1 shallot, minced
5 ounces (150 g) black trumpet mushrooms, washed and blanched in sweet water
¾ cup (180 ml or so) White Chicken Stock (page 251)
Salt
2 tablespoons chopped chives
1 grapefruit, peeled and segmented
1 tablespoon brunoised (very finely diced) jalapeño
Chervil
Food-safe flowers, for garnish (optional)

Preheat your oven to 350°F (175°C).

Combine the almond flour, all-purpose flour, and melted butter in a bowl and mix until you have a uniform crumble mixture. Refrigerate it.

In a saucepan over medium-high heat, add the grapeseed oil and some butter for sautéing, and sweat the shallots until tender, then add the black trumpet mushrooms. Add a little chicken stock to moisten the mushrooms and distribute the heat. Add salt, a teaspoon or so. When the mushrooms are heated through, add the chives, stir them in, and remove the pan from the heat.

Cut the grapefruit sections in thirds or quarters, depending on how big they are (you'll need a single layer to fit inside the mold).

Fill each rectangular or round mold two-thirds full with the trumpet mushrooms, topped by a layer of grapefruit, topped by the crumble (you'll likely have crumble left over).

Bake until golden brown, about 15 minutes.

Unmold the crumbles onto serving plates. Divide the vinaigrette among the plates, making a pool beside the crumbles, and put one crab meat "log" and about 2 tablespoons (65 to 75 g) of shredded crab in the center of the vinaigrette. Garnish with the brunoised jalapeño, chervil, and flowers, if using, and serve immediately.

RIESLING-BRAISED SCALLOPS

WITH UNI ESPUMA, TAPIOCA CRISP, KUMAMOTO OYSTER, AND CAVIAR

Serves 6

This is one of our more elaborate caviar dishes, but what I like most about it is the Riesling-braised scallops. Cooking scallops rare is relatively new. Before new American cuisine, scallops tended to be cooked to death. That's what I do here, braising them in wine for a good 25 to 30 minutes, but I think you'll like the results, as they take on a completely different texture and flavor than sautéed scallops, very rich, almost creamy.

But then we go further, making a sea urchin foam, and a tapioca tuile, and add an oyster to the dish along with the caviar—a celebration of the sea.

FOR THE BRAISED SCALLOPS

6 tablespoons (90 g) butter
5 ounces (150 g) minced shallot
Salt
1¾ pounds (800 g) scallops, cut into
    ½-inch (1.25 cm) dice
¾ cup (180 ml) dry Riesling
Zest of 2 lemons
4 tablespoons parsley leaves, cut into
    a chiffonade
Pepper
4 tablespoons (60 ml) dry vermouth

In a wide skillet over medium heat, add the butter and shallots and sweat the shallots until tender but not browned, seasoning with a four-finger pinch of salt or to taste. Add the scallops and cook for 25 to 30 minutes, stirring frequently. The scallops will release a lot of liquid which must cook off. Add the dry Riesling and continue to cook, stirring, until all the liquid is gone and the scallops are lightly caramelized. Remove from the heat and cool. Just before serving, add the lemon zest, parsley, more salt if needed, pepper, and vermouth.

FOR THE UNI ESPUMA

1¼ cups (300 ml) water or dashi
1½ teaspoons salt
½ teaspoon (1 g) cayenne pepper,
    plus more as needed
8 ounces (227 g) uni (sea urchin)
5 tablespoons (75 ml) grapeseed oil
1 tablespoon yuzu juice
½ teaspoon lemon juice
2 teaspoons dry vermouth
½ teaspoon (2 g) gellan gum (see Note)
1½ sheets silver gelatin, soaked in ice
    water until softened
½ teaspoon (1 g) xanthan gum

Note: Gellan gum is a food additive typically used to bind, stabilize, or texturize processed foods. It's similar to other gelling agents, including guar gum, carrageenan, agar agar, and xanthan gum. Gellan gum also works as a plant-based alternative to gelatin, which is derived from animal skin, cartilage, or bone. We are using all three to get to a perfect balance of texture for the espuma. These can be found at online specialty stores like the Modernist Pantry.

Put the water or dashi, salt, and cayenne in a pan and bring it to a boil, then add the uni. Allow the water to return to a boil and simmer for 10 seconds, then transfer to a high speed blender. Blend on high speed for 1 minute, until smooth, then turn the speed to low and stream in the grapeseed oil. Strain the mixture through a fine-mesh sieve into a bowl set in ice and stir to cool. Add the yuzu juice, lemon juice, and dry vermouth.

When ready to load the iSi gun, put 1½ cups (350 ml) of the coulis along with the gellan into a pan over high heat and bring to a boil, then simmer for 1 minute. Add the rest of the coulis and bring to a simmer, then remove from the heat and add the gelatin and xanthan gum, stirring until the gelatin is dissolved. Taste and adjust the seasoning (you may want more cayenne). Add the uni sauce to a 1-quart/liter-size iSi gun and put in two charges.

FOR THE TAPIOCA CRISP

3 cups (700 ml) water
½ cup tapioca pearls
1 teaspoon squid ink (optional)
Vegetable or grapeseed oil for
    deep-frying

Preheat your oven to 175°F (80°C).

Pour the water into a saucepan, and add in the tapioca pearls. Bring to a simmer and boil for about 20 minutes or until the pearls are translucent. Drain, and rinse the tapioca pearls under cold water. Transfer them to a bowl and stir with a spoon. If you are using the squid ink, add it and stir until it's uniformly mixed.

Spread the tapioca onto a sheet pan lined with parchment paper or a Silpat mat, and dry it in the oven for 4 hours or until it is completely dry. Let it cool. Break the tapioca into pieces sized to your liking (fitting your fryer).

Heat your frying oil in a deep-fryer to 375°F (190°C) and fry the pieces for 3 to 4 seconds. Remove to a tray lined with paper towel. Season to taste with salt and pepper or other spices. These crisps can be used in many different ways, such as for canapés.

TO COMPLETE THE DISH

1 teaspoon ground coffee
Fried tapioca crisp (from above)
Lemon gel (see page 230)
12 Kumamoto oysters, shucked
2 ounces (60 g) Osetra caviar
Micro herbs
Food-safe flowers

Reheat the scallops and divide them evenly into six bowls (preferably narrow deep ones). Shoot the espuma in the iSi gun over the scallops. Sprinkle each with coffee. Garnish each tapioca crisp with lemon gel, oysters, and caviar. Finish with herbs and flowers.

SAUTÉED FOIE GRAS
WITH BEERAWECKA FRUIT CHUTNEY AND BEER REDUCTION

Serves 6

Beerawecka (page 126) is an Alsatian brioche-style spiced bread with dried apple, pear, and walnuts—the autumnal flavors that inspired the creation of this chutney. The beer reduction, thick like a balsamic reduction, has a lot of bitterness, which is nice with the dried fruit. Cranberries make this more American. I like the tartness of the cranberries, which I discovered here. I like cranberry relish with a cheese plate and have happy memories of the first time I ate it with Patricia and her family for a Thanksgiving dinner in New Hampshire. Serve any leftover chutney with cheese.

FOR THE BEERAWECKA FRUIT CHUTNEY

4 tablespoons (60 g) butter
1 ounce (30 g) shallots, very finely chopped
Salt
8 ounces (225 g) Bartlett pear (1 large), peeled, cored, and cut into ½-inch (1.25 cm) dice
2 ounces (60 g) dried Black Mission figs, stemmed and cut into ¼-inch (6 mm) dice
½ cup (60 g) dried Turkish apricots, cut into ¼-inch (6 mm) dice
½ cup (70 g) dried cranberries
½ cup (60 g) dried blueberries
8 ounces (227 g) Granny Smith apple (1 large), peeled, cored, and cut into ½-inch (1.25 cm) dice
⅓ cup (90 ml) dark beer
1 whole star anise
½ cinnamon stick
Freshly ground black pepper
1 teaspoon cayenne pepper
1 tablespoon Pain d'Épices Powder (recipe follows) or ground gingerbread cookies
1 tablespoon white wine vinegar

Put 1 tablespoon butter in each of two large saucepans and melt over medium heat. Add the shallots to one, season with salt, and stir well. Add the pear to the other, season with salt, and toss to coat. Cook both, stirring occasionally, until golden, about 2 minutes. Scrape the pear onto a plate or pan and refrigerate. Add the figs, apricots, cranberries, and blueberries to the shallots.

Melt the remaining 2 tablespoons (30 g) butter in a skillet over medium heat, and then add the apple and a pinch of salt. Cook, stirring occasionally, until golden, about 2 minutes. Scrape onto a plate or pan and refrigerate.

Into the pot with the dried fruit, add the beer, star anise, and cinnamon stick. Bring to a boil over high heat, stirring occasionally, then reduce the heat to simmer, stirring often, until the fruit totally soaks up the beer, about 2 minutes. Season with salt, pepper, and the cayenne. The fruit should be saturated, but there should still be liquid in the pan just below the line of solids. Stir in the pain d'épices, then the vinegar. Let sit for 30 minutes to maximize the absorption of the liquid. When ready to serve, fold in the apple and pear so they stay crunchy. Serve the chutney at room temperature or warm but not hot. Leftover chutney can be easily stored in a glass container, as you would with a marmalade, and can be enjoyed with a cheese plate.

FOR THE BEER REDUCTION

1 (12-ounce/360 ml) bottle dark beer
⅓ cup (50 ml) glucose syrup
Salt and freshly ground black pepper
Pinch cayenne pepper
Pinch Pain d'Épices Powder (recipe follows)
1 teaspoon white wine vinegar

Combine the beer and glucose syrup in a deep pot and bring to a boil over high heat. Adjust the heat to maintain a simmer, then simmer until reduced by three-quarters, skimming any foam that rises to the surface, about 7 minutes. Season with salt, pepper, and cayenne. Cool completely, then stir in the pain d'épices.

When ready to serve, stir in the vinegar.

FOR THE FOIE GRAS

1 grade-A foie gras
Kosher salt and freshly ground black pepper
Fleur de sel
Pain d'Épices Powder (recipe follows)

Let the foie gras stand at room temperature for 30 minutes to temper, then cut into six ¾-inch-thick (2 cm) slices; remove any large veins. (You won't be able to cut the foie gras cold; it will break into large and small chunks.)

Preheat your oven to 300°F (150°C).

Heat a small skillet over medium heat until very hot. The foie takes color quickly, so the pan needs to be very hot first. As it pan-roasts, the fat will render and sear the foie nicely. Season both sides of a slice of foie gras with kosher salt and black pepper, then drop it in the hot skillet cut side down. The foie will start to bubble and melt right away. Tilt

recipe continues

the skillet so the fat can run under the foie. Adjust the heat to maintain a steady sizzle. When the side that is touching the pan is a dark golden brown, about 3 minutes, flip carefully. Cook the other side until browned, about 3 minutes. Transfer to the oven and bake until the foie is firm, about 3 minutes. When you squeeze it, it should feel like a water balloon. Transfer to a plate, reserving the fat in the skillet, and sprinkle the foie with fleur de sel, pain d'épices powder, and black pepper. Repeat with the remaining foie slices.

TO FINISH

Pain d'Épices Powder (recipe follows)
1 cup yellow frisée
18 to 24 baby red-veined sorrel leaves (3 to 4 per serving)
2 tablespoons grapeseed oil
1 tablespoon fresh lemon juice
Salt and freshly ground black pepper
6 Candied Pecans (recipe follows)
6 Pain d'Épices Chips (recipe follows)

Make a quenelle of about 2 large tablespoons (32 g) of chutney and center on the plate. Sprinkle pain d'épices powder all over the plate and arrange a slice of the foie next to the chutney.

Toss the frisée and sorrel with oil to lightly coat and lemon juice to flavor. Season to taste with salt and pepper. Arrange next to the foie gras slice.

Put two candied pecans on the plate, then drizzle the reduction all over, along with the reserved foie fat. Spike the foie with a pain d'épices chip. Repeat with the remaining ingredients. Serve immediately.

PAIN D'ÉPICES CHIPS AND POWDER

1 small loaf pain d'épices (page 109) or other dense dried fruit and nut bread, very thinly sliced

Preheat your oven to 200°F (93°C).

Put the bread slices on a sheet pan in a single layer. Bake for about 45 minutes, until very dry and crisp.

Cool completely in the pan on a rack. Reserve three-quarters of the slices as chips.

Pulse the remaining one-quarter in a spice grinder until finely ground to create a powder. Both the chips and the powder can be held in an airtight container for up to 3 days.

CANDIED PECANS

½ egg white
4 ounces (120 g) pecans
⅓ cup (70 g) sugar
¼ teaspoon cayenne pepper
Salt

Preheat your oven to 300°F (150°C).

Line a sheet pan with parchment paper.

Beat the egg white with a fork in a bowl until foamy on top. In another bowl, combine the pecans with just enough of the beaten egg white to lightly coat. Spread the sugar in an even layer on a rimmed plate. Spread the coated pecans on top and toss to evenly coat with the sugar.

Lift the sugared pecans out of any excess sugar and transfer to the prepared sheet pan, spreading in a single layer.

Bake, stirring once halfway through, until the egg white coating is dried out but not too dark, about 15 minutes. Season with cayenne and a pinch of salt. Cool completely and store in an airtight container for up to 3 days.

The leftover candied pecans can be easily enjoyed on their own or with a nice cheese plate, just like the chutney.

WILD MUSHROOMS AND LOUISIANA CRAYFISH
COOKED "EN BAECKEOFFE"

Serves 4

This is inspired, of course, by the traditional Alsatian *baeckeoffe* (page 61). I feel grounded in fine dining with dishes like this, using country cuisine as the inspiration for a more formal plate. I can do it with frog legs, shrimp, crab, or even just mushrooms. Here I'm using crayfish, so common in Alsace, and mushrooms, finished with a simple elegant chive sauce.

You can choose different mixes of mushrooms for different tastes and textures, about 1½ pounds (680 g) total. I like buttons, chanterelles, morels, and hen of the woods when they're in season. These were my father's favorites. I also love blue foot mushrooms, which smell like fallen wet leaves, like the forest. Their texture doesn't alter when cooked.

You can make this either family-style, using one large cocotte, or in individual portions. In either case, everything needs to be cold going into the baking dish. The cold assembled cocotte can be refrigerated, up to one day.

The pastry, which bakes in the oven around the edge of the cocotte, has a double purpose of sealing the juices in the cocotte and being the bread to eat alongside the stew.

FOR THE MUSHROOMS
- 2 tablespoons (30 g) unsalted butter
- 2 tablespoons extra-virgin olive oil
- 4 ounces (120 g) porcini mushrooms, feet peeled, caps brushed clean (3 cups)
- 4 ounces (120 g) blue foot mushrooms, cleaned well, trimmed, and quartered lengthwise (2½ cups)
- 4 ounces (120 g) hen of the woods mushrooms, cleaned well, trimmed, and broken up
- 6 ounces (160 g) chanterelle mushrooms, cleaned well, trimmed, stems peeled, then cut into 1-inch or ½-inch (2.5 or 1.25 cm) pieces (3 cups)
- 2 tablespoons (20 g) finely chopped shallot
- 2 ounces (60 g) leek, white part only, halved lengthwise and cut into 1/16-inch slices (1 cup)
- Salt and freshly ground black pepper

Melt half of the butter (1 tablespoon) in the olive oil in a Dutch oven over medium heat. When the butter is foamy and pale yellow, add the porcinis, stir well, and raise the heat to medium-high. You want the juices to render and for the mushrooms to sear a bit. When the porcinis are browned in spots, after 1 minute, add the blue foots and hen of the woods and stir well for 1 minute. Add ½ tablespoon butter and stir to melt. Add the chanterelles and stir well for 1 minute, then add the remaining ½ tablespoon butter and stir to melt.

Add the shallots and leeks and season with salt and pepper. Stir well for 2 minutes, then remove from the heat. The leeks should be barely wilted because they'll continue to cook in the oven. Transfer to a parchment paper–lined sheet pan and spread in a single layer. Refrigerate to chill.

FOR THE CHIVE CREAM
- 1 cup (250 ml) half-and-half
- Salt
- 1 cup (45 g) snipped chives

Bring the half-and-half and a pinch of salt to a boil in a small saucepan over medium heat. Add the chives and return to a boil. Remove from the heat and immediately transfer to a blender. Puree until very smooth.

Pass the sauce through a chinois into a bowl set over a large bowl filled with ice and water. Whisk the sauce to cool completely. This will keep for 2 to 3 days refrigerated.

recipe continues

TO FINISH

24 Louisiana crayfish or 16/20-count shrimp, shelled and deveined

Kosher salt and freshly ground black pepper

3 tablespoons (40 g) butter

2 cloves garlic, very thinly sliced

½ bunch chervil

5 ounces (150 g) chilled puff pastry

1 large egg beaten with 1 tablespoon water

1 tablespoon poppy seeds

Fleur de sel and cracked black pepper

Preheat your oven to 375°F (190°C).

Spread the chilled mushrooms in one large cocotte or divide among four small ones. Season the crayfish with salt and pepper, then arrange them on top of the cold mushrooms in a single layer. Put ½ teaspoon butter on top of each crayfish, then put 1 garlic slice over each nub of butter. Scatter the chervil on top. Close the cocotte lid.

Cut the puff pastry into 1-inch (2.5 cm) strips, then squeeze the strips together and roll like a snake to form a ½-inch (1.25 cm) diameter rope. Brush the edges of the cocotte where the lid and base meet with the egg wash, then press the rope over the egg, wrapping it around the cocotte. Trim any excess dough to allow the two ends of the rope to meet. Then press the rope flat to seal the gap between the lid and base. Brush the pastry with egg wash, then sprinkle with the poppy seeds, fleur de sel, and cracked black pepper.

Bake until the pastry is golden brown, 20 minutes for smaller cocottes and 25 minutes for a large one.

Reheat the chive cream in a small saucepan and whisk well.

Pry the pastry off the cocotte, then remove the cocotte lid. Drizzle the chive sauce all over the stew and serve immediately with the pastry.

SAUTÉED SULLIVAN COUNTY FOIE GRAS
WITH BASIL NAGE AND NUTMEG

Serves 8

Foie gras is a great luxury, misunderstood by many, including the New York City council, which approved a ban on its sale beginning in 2022. But I grew up on a farm, and in a country, where foie gras was a part of life, so I will keep serving it and in turn helping the farmers of LaBelle farms, in New York's Sullivan County, make a living from the land and their humanely cared for animals. While we often think of foie gras as a fall and winter dish, especially around the holidays, for its luxury and richness, here is a spring interpretation, with a bright green basil nage, strawberries (pickled), and spring onions to go with sautéed slabs of duck liver.

1 grade-A foie gras, cut into eight ¾-inch (2 cm) slices

FOR THE PICKLED STRAWBERRIES
½ cup (125 ml) Champagne vinegar
1 thyme sprig
1 tablespoon sugar
8 ounces (225 g) little strawberries, frozen

Combine all the ingredients except the strawberries with 1¼ cups (300 ml) of water in a saucepan and bring to a boil. Pour the mixture over the frozen strawberries. Let the liquid cool, then store in the fridge for up to 3 weeks.

FOR THE BASIL NAGE
1 cup (250 ml) half-and-half
1 teaspoon salt
⅔ cup (20 g) basil
¼ cup lightly packed baby spinach
2 tablespoons (30 g) butter, plus 1 tablespoon for finishing

Bring the half-and-half to a boil with the salt, then add the spinach and basil. Boil for 30 seconds and transfer to a blender. Blend on high until the mixture is smooth, then add the butter, blending until it's incorporated. Strain through a chinois into a bowl set in ice to cool it as quickly as possible.

FOR THE LEMON GEL
4 teaspoons sugar
2 teaspoons (3.5 g) agar powder
Pinch salt
A few grindings pepper
7 tablespoons (115 ml) lemon juice

Combine 5 tablespoons (75 ml) of water with the sugar, agar, a pinch of salt, and a few grinds of pepper in a saucepan. Bring it to a boil over high heat, then reduce the heat and simmer the mixture for 2 minutes. Remove from the heat and stir in the lemon juice. Let it set, then break it apart or dice it and blend on high until it's smooth. Pass through a fine-mesh sieve and put it in a squeeze bottle.

TO GARNISH
8 spring onions, trimmed to leave an inch of green, thickly sliced, sweated in butter and water until tender, seasoned with salt and freshly ground black pepper
Fleur de sel and cracked black pepper
Freshly grated nutmeg
Lemon supremes from 1 lemon (peeled and segmented wedges, flesh only)
Food-safe flowers, for decorating

To finish the dish, set a large sauté pan over medium-high heat and let it get hot. Season the foie gras with salt and pepper. When the pan is hot, add the foie gras and cook for 2 to 2½ minutes per side. They should be nicely caramelized on the outside and medium rare inside.

Make a bed with one onion per plate. Drizzle the plate with the lemon gel. Set a piece of foie gras on each onion. Reheat the basil nage, adding a tablespoon of butter and frothing it with an immersion blender. Spoon some of the nage onto each plate. Garnish the foie gras with fleur de sel, black pepper, and lots of grated nutmeg, finishing them with the lemon supremes and flowers. Place three to five of the pickled strawberries around the foie gras and serve immediately.

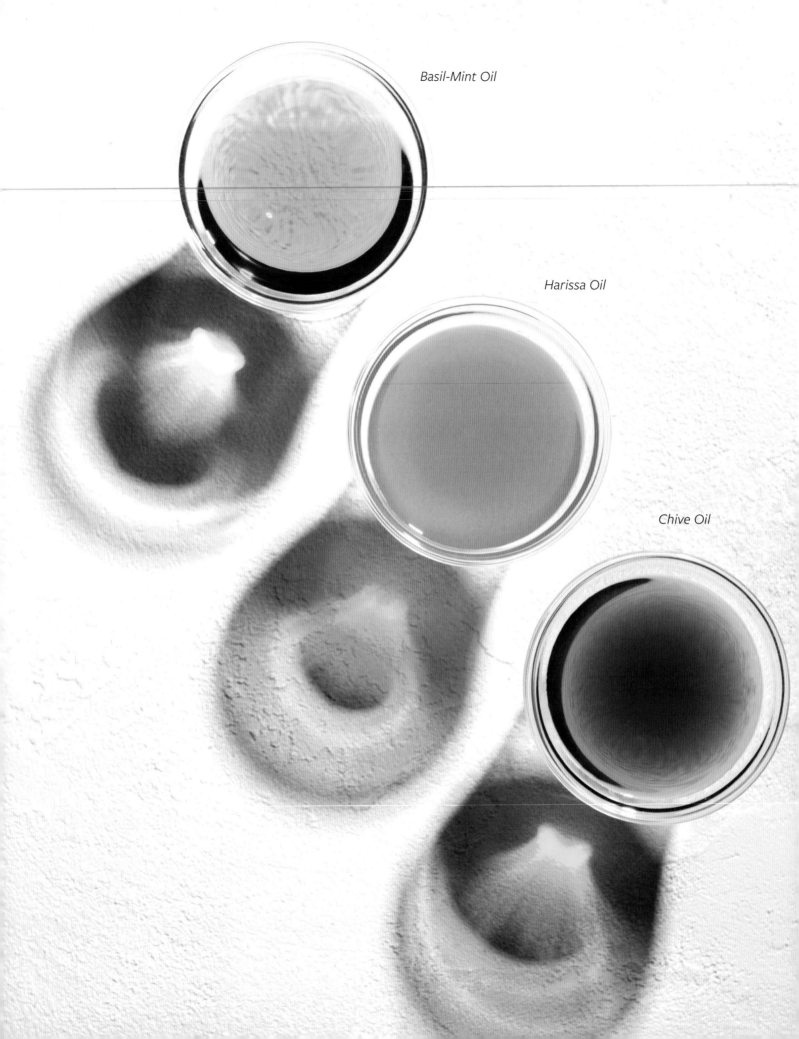

Basil-Mint Oil

Harissa Oil

Chive Oil

OILS

I love to use oils because they can bring another layer of flavor and complexity to a dish. Yes, they also add a dramatic visual element, which I like, too, but I never garnish a dish with an infused oil unless it enhances the flavors. Our oils are almost always made from scraps, a way to use as much of the food as possible. When making chive oil, we use the chives that aren't beautiful enough to serve but are still full of flavor. We make a lobster oil from the carcass of the lobster. It's another way to avoid wasting anything.

When making oils, we almost always use a neutral oil. My preference is grapeseed oil, because it doesn't congeal when refrigerated. One of the most important fundamental techniques of making infused oils is to carefully monitor the heat. If the oil gets too hot, it can destroy the flavor. I like to heat the oils to between 165°F and 170°F (74°C and 79°C), no higher. Finally, after straining through a coffee filter or layers of cheesecloth, store the oil in small containers in the refrigerator for up to two weeks. Infused oils can also be frozen for up to two months. This allows you to make a larger batch, store in small quantities, then refrigerate to thaw them slowly as needed.

BASIL-MINT OIL

Makes about ½ cup (120 ml)

⅔ cup (15 g) basil leaves
¼ cup (6 g) mint leaves
½ cup (120 ml) grapeseed oil
Pinch salt

Combine the ingredients in a blender and blend thoroughly. Put the mixture into a saucepan and bring it to about 175°F (80°C) to set the color. Strain it through a coffee filter. Refrigerate for up to 2 weeks.

HARISSA OIL

Makes about ½ cup (120 ml)

3 tablespoons harissa paste
¾ cup (180 ml) vegetable or grape-
    seed oil

In a small pan over medium heat, whisk together the harissa paste, oil, and 3 tablespoons water. Bring the liquids to 170°F (80°C) to set the color, then remove from the heat and let sit for 15 minutes. Repeat this two more times. Pass the mixture through a coffee filter. Refrigerate for up to 2 weeks.

Note: We add water here to prevent the harissa from turning brown. When the water boils, that is your indicator that the oil is hot enough to proceed with the rest of the recipe. Oil alone gets too hot too quickly and burns out the natural color of the harissa. We do not add water to the herb oils, because there is natural moisture in the herbs.

CHIVE OIL

Makes about 1¼ cups (300 ml)

1½ cups (360 ml) grapeseed oil
5 cups (150 g) roughly chopped chives

Pour a small amount of the oil in the bottom of a blender, then add the chives. Blend, then add the oil once the chives are chopped. Once thoroughly blended, put the oil in a saucepan and simmer over medium-low heat to a temperature of 170°F (80°C), until a bright green color sets. Immediately strain through a coffee filter or two layers of cheesecloth into a bowl set in ice. Put the oil in a plastic squeeze bottle or covered container and refrigerate for up to a week.

SOUPS

ROASTED BUTTON
MUSHROOM SOUP
with Toasted Chorizo-Potato
Raviolis

236

PEASANT FLOUR SOUP
with Frog Legs and Scallions

238

FENNEL-COCKLE VELOUTÉ
with Blue Shrimp Tartare

240

CHILLED BACALAO SOUP
with Celery Leaves, Potato
Pancakes, and Hyssop "Oeufs à la
Neige"

242

FENNEL AND ALMOND
GAZPACHO
with Smoked Salmon Dominos and
Salmon Roe

244

CHILLED WHITE
ASPARAGUS SOUP
with Poached Egg and Morels

247

CHILLED CUCUMBER AND
MINT SOUP
with Alaskan King Crab

248

ROASTED BUTTON MUSHROOM SOUP
WITH TOASTED CHORIZO-POTATO RAVIOLIS

Serves 12 (makes 3 quarts/liters soup and 36 ravioli)

A long time ago, I used to cook for my uncle Philippe, my mother's younger brother, who was a butcher by trade, and his close friends, because he was so eager to learn how to cook. During the holidays, they would pony up the money to buy the ingredients and he and I would cook together six-course meals for the eight of us for a week. That way I learned a lot of butchering techniques from him, and he learned cooking techniques from me, particularly how to refine stocks and jus from scratch. That was how I tried out a lot of things, including this soup.

With this flavorful preparation, which uses humble button mushrooms, you can be tricked into thinking you are eating a more elegant mushroom like porcini. I used to do this dish at the Modern. It sold like crazy. Everyone loved it. You can serve each component alone too, the ravioli as canapés, the soup as soup.

FOR THE MUSHROOM SOUP

1½ quarts/liters White Chicken Stock (page 251)
3 sprigs thyme
3 sprigs parsley
¾ cup (1½ sticks/180 g) butter
5 pounds (2.3 kg) white button mushrooms, sliced
3 ounces (90 g) sliced shallots (from about 3 medium shallots)
2 cloves garlic, peeled and smashed
Salt

Heat the chicken stock with 4 cups (960 ml) of water in a stockpot until boiling. Add the thyme and parsley and return to a boil, then reduce the heat to keep steaming.

In a very large, wide heavy pan, melt half the butter over medium-high heat until it's past foamy and almost browned. Add 1½ pounds (680 g) of the mushrooms, stir well, and spread in a single layer. Let sit without moving so their water comes out and they can get some color. After you hear the water coming out of the mushrooms, about 3 minutes, add half the shallots. Stir well for 1 minute, then add 1 smashed garlic clove and toss. Cook, stirring occasionally, for about 5 minutes, then transfer to another pan. Repeat with the remaining butter, another 1½ pounds (680 g) mushrooms, and the remaining

shallots and garlic in the same pan, then scrape the first batch of mushrooms into the second. Continue cooking, stirring occasionally, until the mushrooms are very dark brown and smell smoky, about 5 minutes longer. Cook it well because this is the initial step to get a nice flavor, but be careful not to burn it or it can become bitter.

Scrape all the mushrooms into the steaming stock. Pour 4 cups (960 ml) water into the mushroom pan and stir and scrape up all the browned bits, then pour into the stock. Bring the mixture to a boil, then cover, reduce the heat to a simmer and cook for 10 minutes. Season to taste with salt, then cover and simmer for 20 minutes longer. Remove from the heat and pass through a fine-mesh sieve, pressing with a ladle or a large spoon to extract all the juices from the mushrooms, and then discard the mushrooms.

Pour the strained soup into a clean saucepan and bring to a boil. Add the remaining 2 pounds (940 g) mushrooms and return to a boil. Cook just until the mushrooms are cooked through, about 2 minutes. Season to taste with salt, then remove from the heat.

Blend in batches until very smooth, passing each batch through a fine-mesh sieve. Season to taste with salt.

FOR THE TOASTED CHORIZO-POTATO RAVIOLIS

1 large baking potato (15½ ounces/440 g)
Grapeseed oil
8 ounces (225 g) Spanish cured spicy chorizo, quartered lengthwise, then sliced
1 tablespoon butter
1 medium shallot, finely chopped
Salt
7 ounces (210 g) scallions, very thinly sliced
2 large egg yolks

Preheat your oven to 325°F (160°C). Line three sheet pans with Silpat mats or parchment paper.

Peel the potato, then use a mandoline to cut at least 36 paper-thin slices lengthwise. Brush the prepared pans with oil to lightly coat, then arrange the potato slices on the pans in a single layer nearly touching. Brush the slices with oil to lightly coat.

Bake until tender and pliable but not brown, 4 to 5 minutes. They should be more translucent and a pale yellow color. Cool on the pans on wire racks.

To make the filling, put the chorizo through a meat grinder or pulse in a food processor until very finely ground with some small bits.

Melt the butter in a large skillet over medium-high heat, then add the shallot. Stir well, season with salt, and stir for 30 seconds more. Add the scallions, stir gently, and season with salt. Cook, stirring often, until bright green and tender, about 3 minutes. Add the ground chorizo and stir gently to evenly mix together for 1 minute. Transfer to a very large bowl to cool. Cover and refrigerate until chilled so that the filling will hold together.

Beat the egg yolks in a bowl, then lightly brush a thin sheen on the rim of 1 potato slice. Spoon a scant teaspoon of filling in the center of the potato slice, then fold the potato slice in half to form a half-moon ravioli, pressing the edges to seal. Repeat with the remaining potato slices, yolks, and filling.

Coat a large nonstick skillet with grapeseed oil and heat over medium-high heat. When hot, add three raviolis. Cook, turning once, until evenly browned, 1 to 2 minutes per side. Drain on paper towels, season with a little salt, and keep warm. Repeat with the remaining raviolis, reheating the oil between each batch and replenishing the oil as needed.

TO SERVE
2 tablespoons soy sauce
Salt and freshly ground black pepper

Heat the mushroom soup until steaming hot. Whisk in the soy sauce, then season to taste with salt and pepper.

Divide the soup among twelve soup plates. Serve each plate with three ravioli.

PEASANT FLOUR SOUP
WITH FROG LEGS AND SCALLIONS

Serves 8

This is a soup my mother used to do (page 47), but here I make it more complex to serve in my restaurant. It's very traditional, and sometimes it has semolina or the water from cooking vegetables. I used to go into the forest with my father and my brothers early in the morning or late at night with a flashlight to look for frogs and put them in buckets with ice to bring home to my mother. The small white ones were best. Today we get them from Peerless Fish in Brooklyn. A good substitute here would be bay scallops or ruby red shrimp from Maine.

FOR THE SOUP

7 tablespoons (105 g) butter
¾ cup (100 g) all-purpose flour
Extra-virgin olive oil
1 pound (455 g) white button mushrooms, cut into ¼-inch (6 mm) slices
5 ounces (150 g) yellow onions, chopped
5 ounces (150 g) smoked ham, cut into ½-inch (1.25 cm) dice
3 ounces (90 g) applewood-smoked slab bacon, cut into ½-inch (1.25 cm) dice
6 cups (1.5 liters) cold White Chicken Stock (page 251)
4 cups (1 liter) cold water
3 sprigs thyme
½ bay leaf
Salt and freshly ground black pepper

Preheat your oven to 400°F (205°C).

Melt the butter in a large saucepot over medium heat. Add the flour all at once and whisk continuously to mellow the raw flavor of the flour, so the soup won't end up with a mealy taste. Transfer the saucepot to the oven and continue cooking, whisking every 10 minutes, until the mixture is the color of peanut butter, about 20 minutes total. It should look shiny and smell like roasted hazelnuts.

Meanwhile, fill a large skillet with olive oil to a depth of ⅛ inch (3 mm) and heat over medium high. When hot, add the mushrooms, raise the heat to high, and cook, tossing occasionally, until very brown, about 6 minutes. Add more oil to coat the bottom of the skillet, then add the onions. Cook, stirring occasionally, until the onions take on some color, about 3 minutes. Add the ham and bacon and cook, stirring often, until lightly browned, about 2 minutes. Turn off the heat and carefully add a little of the stock to deglaze the pan.

Transfer the roux from the oven to the stovetop. (Remember that the pot is hot, so cover the handle with a dry kitchen towel.) Whisk over low heat until there are no lumps. The mixture should be liquid and the scent should be of toasted flour. Continue whisking until the mixture is as brown as caramel, about 5 minutes.

While whisking the roux rapidly, add the remaining cold stock in a slow, steady stream. Whisk continuously and rapidly to prevent any lumps from forming. Continue whisking while adding the cold water. Raise the heat to medium and keep whisking until the mixture comes to a boil.

Add the thyme and bay leaf, then season with a little salt and pepper. Add the mushroom mixture and stir well. Pulse with an immersion blender to explode the flavors of the elements without actually blending the soup until smooth. Strain through a fine-mesh sieve and press on the solids to extract as much liquid as possible. When ready to serve, puree with an immersion blender again until frothy on top.

FOR THE FROG LEGS

24 frog legs (1½ pounds/700 g)
½ cup (125 ml) crème fraîche
Grapeseed oil
Salt and freshly ground black pepper
2 tablespoons (30 g) butter
8 scallions, white and pale green parts halved lengthwise then thinly sliced crosswise (¾ cup), greens thinly sliced and reserved for plating

Toss the frog legs with the crème fraîche in a large bowl to lightly and evenly coat. Coat a large skillet with oil and heat over high heat. When hot, add half of the frog legs in a single layer. Cook, tossing occasionally, until golden brown, about 1 minute. Season with salt and pepper, then add half the butter and scallions. Toss until evenly coated and sizzling, about 1 minute. The scallions should be bright in color and tender. Drain in a colander, then on paper towels. Season with salt. Repeat with the remaining ingredients.

TO SERVE

1 cup (45 g) radish sprouts
½ cup salty fingers, or substitute sea beans (see page 165)
½ cup (120 ml) whipped cream

For each serving, center a ring mold in a soup plate. Press 2 tablespoons sprouts into the ring mold, then arrange 3 frog legs on top. Sprinkle with 1 tablespoon each scallion greens and salty fingers. Buzz the whipped cream into the soup with an immersion blender, then pour 1 cup (240 ml) soup around the center and serve immediately.

FENNEL-COCKLE VELOUTÉ
WITH BLUE SHRIMP TARTARE

Serves 6

This soup is a play on hot and cold and was on our opening menu, but the velouté was made from clams instead of cockles—an equally good option. We make use of what we have and what's best. We pour the velouté tableside over a disc of rouille, which is a traditional condiment for a bouillabaisse or seafood stew, on which a cylinder of toast holds the tartare. I love the bite of blue shrimp, but if you have access to Santa Barbara prawns, those are fabulous too. Just like the soup, though, the toast can be filled with anything you wish—a crab salad garnished with julienned radish or diced cucumber, for instance. No matter what your ingredients, this is a very elegant preparation.

FOR THE FENNEL-COCKLE VELOUTÉ

2 pounds (900 g) cockles

⅔ cup (150 g) butter

2 fennel bulbs, brown exterior pieces discarded, thinly sliced

1 onion, thinly sliced

2 cups (500 ml) Riesling

2 cups (500 ml) Chardonnay

2 small bay leaves

8 sprigs thyme

½ teaspoon (3 g) black peppercorns, cracked

1 teaspoon fennel seeds

2 cups (500 ml) White Chicken Stock (page 251)

4 cups (1 liter) heavy cream

Salt and white pepper

¼ cup (60 ml) dry vermouth, or as needed for finishing

Lemon juice

Rinse the cockles in cold water for 1 hour, changing the water several times.

In a large saucepan over medium heat, melt the butter and add the fennel and onion. Cook gently for 30 minutes or so without browning them. Add the Riesling and Chardonnay, bring to a simmer, and reduce by half.

Place the cockles in a large sachet with the bay leaves, thyme, cracked black peppercorns, and fennel seeds and secure it with butcher's twine. Add the sachet to a saucepan along with the chicken stock and heavy cream. Bring the liquid to a low simmer, partially cover the pan with a lid, and cook for 1½ hours or so, stirring occasionally. Remove the sachet and squeeze out as much liquid as you can; reserve the liquid.

Blend the soup base in a high-speed blender and pass it through a fine-mesh sieve. In a saucepan, combine the blended soup base with the reserved liquid from the cockle sachet–infused stock and cream. Bring to a light boil for 1 to 2 minutes. Season with salt, pepper, vermouth, and lemon juice. Chill thoroughly.

FOR THE ROUILLE

4½ ounces (135 g) baked, peeled Yukon gold potato

4½ ounces (135 g) jarred piquillo pepper or roasted red peppers

3 tablespoons Dijon mustard

2 cloves garlic, cooked in a microwave on high for 45 seconds

Sherry vinegar

Salt and freshly ground black pepper

Combine the potato, piquillo pepper, mustard, and garlic in a food processor. Puree. Season with the vinegar and salt and pepper to taste. We fill very shallow 2-inch (5 cm) disc molds and freeze them. But however you wish to shape them is fine—for instance, you can spread a layer on parchment and use a ring cutter after the rouille has been frozen. This will make more than you need but it keeps well frozen, for up to a month.

FOR THE BLUE SHRIMP TARTARE

1 pound (455 g) blue shrimp, cleaned, small diced

3 tablespoons grapeseed oil

2 tablespoons brunoised (very finely diced) fennel

2 tablespoon brunoised (very finely diced) celery

2 teaspoons brunoised (very finely diced) shallot

1 tablespoon brunoised (very finely diced) red bell pepper

Salt

Juice and zest of 1 lemon

3 tablespoons chopped chives

12 tarragon leaves, roughly chopped

In a bowl set in ice, combine the shrimp and oil and toss until the shrimp is evenly coated. Add the fennel, celery, shallot, and red pepper, tossing well and finishing with the salt, lemon juice, lemon zest, and finally the chopped chives and tarragon leaves.

FOR THE WATERCRESS GRANITA

1 cup (250 ml) watercress juice (from about 3 bunches, or 1 pound/450 g, watercress)
1 teaspoon citric acid

Mix the juice and citric acid until the acid is dissolved. Pour it into a container and freeze (the frozen juice will be scraped with a fork to serve).

FOR THE BREAD TUILE

10 to 12 slices seven-grain bread, thinly sliced (about ⅛ inch/3 mm)
3 tablespoons (45 g) warm clarified butter (see page 201)

Preheat your oven to 325°F (165°C). Cut strips of bread 5 to 6 inches (12 to 15 cm) long and 2 inches (5 cm) wide. Brush them with the butter until they are flexible enough to wrap around a 2-inch (5 cm) ring mold. Bake until completely dry (about 15 minutes), cool, and remove from the ring molds. We are using up to 12 slices of bread, due to breakage during the baking or handling process.

TO GARNISH (OPTIONAL)

Caviar
Tobiko (flying fish roe)
Sea urchin roe
Decorative flowers (make sure they're food-safe)
Hyssop

To finish the dish, place a frozen disc of rouille in each bowl. Place a tuile on top and fill the tuile with the shrimp. Garnish the shrimp as desired. When ready to serve, pour the soup into the bowl around the tuile. Finish with the granita, scraping it with a fork, into the texture of Italian ice.

CHILLED BACALAO SOUP
WITH CELERY LEAVES, POTATO PANCAKES, AND HYSSOP "OEUFS À LA NEIGE"

Serves 6

I ate a lot of cod when I was growing up, both fresh (*cabillaud*) and salted (*morue* in French but more commonly referred to as bacalao). We would make brandades, cooked in milk or cream, or sometimes treat the cod like a schnitzel. Here I wanted to use salt cod to make a light, refreshing, cold, creamy soup. Part of the fish needs to be blended thoroughly, so a high-speed blender is required here. One of my favorite parts of this is the garnish for the soup, *oeufs à la neige*, poached meringues, which are typically served as part of dessert (see page 120), but here I make a savory version with garlic and that beguiling mint-like herb, hyssop. I find it growing wild in Manhattan. If you don't have access to hyssop, you can approximate it here by substituting 3 tablespoons each of chopped fresh sage and mint.

The pancakes are like an excellent blini. I like to serve them on the side of the soup.

FOR THE SOUP

1 pound (455 g) salt cod (bacalao), soaked in water for 24 hours, refreshing the water 3 or 4 times
½ bunch parsley
2 bay leaves
5 sprigs thyme
1 star anise
20 celery leaves
1 cup plus 6 tablespoons (300 g) fromage blanc
1¼ cups (300 ml) sour cream
2 teaspoons grapeseed oil
7 tablespoons (100 ml) heavy cream
Salt (sparingly, as the cod is salty)
Cayenne pepper (about ¼ teaspoon)
Ornamental food-safe flowers, celery leaves, microgreens, basil chiffonade, or Basil-Mint Oil (page 233), as desired, for garnish

Poach the cod gently in water along with the parsley, bay leaves, thyme sprigs, star anise, and celery leaves for 12 to 15 minutes, just until the fish is tender and flakey. Strain and save 1 cup (240 ml) of cooking liquid.

Put a little less than half (about 250 g) of the cod in a high-speed blender, reserving the rest for garnish, adding enough of the reserved cooking liquid so that the fish blends easily. Blend until very smooth, then pass the fish through a fine-mesh sieve. Add the fromage blanc, sour cream, grapeseed oil, and heavy cream to the fish and blend until everything is well integrated. Pass the mixture through a tamis to a bowl set in ice and chill completely. You can add a few ice cubes to the soup directly to help chill it. Season with salt and cayenne pepper and reserve in the fridge until ready to serve.

FOR THE POTATO PANCAKES

3 ounces (90 g) cooked Yukon gold potato (from 1 large potato, roasted and peeled)
2 tablespoons milk
¼ cup (30 g) all-purpose flour
¼ cup (30 g) buckwheat flour
1 egg, beaten
1 tablespoon (8 g) fresh yeast or 1 teaspoon (3 g) active dry yeast
Grapeseed oil, for sautéing
1 tablespoon butter

Pass the cooked potato through a tamis. Add the milk to the potato puree, then the flours and the beaten egg. Mix the yeast with a tablespoon of warm water to dissolve it and stir it into the potato. Let it rise for about 2 hours at room temperature.

In a nonstick frying pan over medium heat, add enough oil to coat the bottom of the pan, along with the butter. Drop tablespoons of the batter into the pan to make small potato pancakes, about 1½ inches (4 cm) in diameter, and cook the pancakes until golden brown on each side. Repeat with the remaining batter. You should have enough to make about 30 pancakes. Keep warm until ready to serve.

FOR THE OEUFS À LA NEIGE

3 egg whites
1 teaspoon salt
1 medium clove garlic, smashed and chopped into a paste (about ¼ teaspoon)
2½ tablespoons (30 g) sugar
15 gratings nutmeg
2 tablespoons chopped hyssop or 3 tablespoons each of chopped sage and mint, if not available
Pepper
1 to 2 tablespoons red tobiko (flying fish roe)

Beat the egg white with the salt and garlic puree until frothy, then add half of the sugar. Continue to whisk the eggs vigorously. When the egg whites have formed a meringue, add the remaining sugar, the nutmeg, and hyssop. When the eggs whites have reached medium stiff peaks, scoop large spoonfuls into simmering water. You should have enough to make 12 to 18, depending on the size. Cook them until they're heated through, 15 to 20 seconds per side, and remove to a paper towel–lined tray. Allow them to cool. Finish them with some freshly ground pepper and the tobiko.

To serve, divide the soup among six bowls. Add the reserved bacalao to the center of the bowls. Add two or three oeufs à la neige to each bowl and finish the plate with some microgreens, edible flowers, celery leaves, basil chiffonade, or basil-mint oil. Serve the warm pancakes on the side.

FENNEL AND ALMOND GAZPACHO
WITH SMOKED SALMON DOMINOS AND SALMON ROE

Serves 6

I love fennel, and that's what this soup is all about. This gazpacho was a beloved dish during one of the cooking demonstrations I did at De Gustibus. It's extremely elegant—especially with the salmon and salmon roe garnish—but is very easy to prepare.

FOR THE GAZPACHO

2 tablespoons almond oil or olive oil

1 small onion, chopped

3 fennel bulbs (1 pound/500 g), outer layer discarded, chopped (reserve the fronds for garnish)

2¼ cups (560 ml) half-and-half

3 ounces (90 g) Marcona almonds

1 star anise

1 teaspoon fennel seeds

1 to 2 teaspoons sherry vinegar

Tabasco (optional, but recommended)

Salt and freshly ground black pepper

To make the gazpacho, in a saucepan over medium-high heat, add the almond oil. Add the onion and fennel and sweat until they are soft but without color, 5 to 7 minutes. Add the half-and-half, then add enough water just to cover the onion and fennel. Simmer for 20 minutes. Add the almonds and simmer for 10 more minutes. Add the star anise and fennel seeds, then cover and remove from the heat. Let it steep for about 15 minutes covered with a lid. Remove the star anise and puree the mixture in a high-speed blender, pass through a fine-mesh sieve, and cool over ice. Once cooled, add the sherry vinegar, Tabasco, if using, and salt and pepper to taste.

FOR THE SMOKED SALMON DOMINOS

6 ounces (180 g) smoked salmon, sliced into 18 (3 per serving) (⅓-ounce/10 g) rectangles the size of dominos

2 ounces (60 g) salmon roe

Reserved fennel fronds or bronze fennel fronds

Microgreens and edible flowers, for garnish

3 tablespoons extra-virgin olive oil or almond oil, for garnish

To serve, arrange 3 pieces of salmon in each soup bowl. Divide the salmon roe atop the salmon. Garnish with the fennel fronds, edible flowers, and microgreens. Pour some gazpacho around the salmon and drizzle the olive oil into the soup. Serve the bowls with the rest of the gazpacho on the side in a soup tureen or a nice pitcher to be poured into the bowls at the table.

CHILLED WHITE ASPARAGUS SOUP
WITH POACHED EGG AND MORELS

Serves 6

This is a way to use byproducts—the stems and peels of white asparagus, which are so expensive. If you can't find fresh morels, you can use dried ones and cover them with cold water until soft, about 15 minutes. Lift them out with your hands, which will help you make sure any sand is left behind. Repeat five to six times to make sure there's no grit or sand left, and never pour out the water while the morels are in the bowl or the sand will stick to the morels.

Make this in April or May, when white asparagus is in season and there are so many edible flowers you can use as garnish. It's nice to enjoy cold when the weather starts to warm, but you can serve it warm too.

FOR THE SOUP

1 pound (455 g) white asparagus
Salt
2 tablespoons (30 g) butter
3 ounces (60 g) leek, white part only, thinly sliced (⅔ cup)
1 small clove garlic, smashed and minced
5 ounces (150 g) Yukon gold potato, peeled and thinly sliced
½ cup (125 ml) half-and-half
Freshly ground white pepper

Trim and peel the asparagus and put the trimmings and peels in a large saucepan. Cover with 2 quarts/liters cold water and add a pinch of salt. Bring to a boil over high heat, then boil for 30 minutes to extract the flavor. Strain through a fine-mesh sieve and keep warm.

Cut the tips off the asparagus and reserve for garnish. Cut the stalks into 1-inch (2.5 cm) pieces.

Melt the butter in a large saucepan over medium heat. Add the leek and a pinch of salt. Cook, stirring, for 2 minutes. Add the garlic and stir for 30 seconds. Add the cut asparagus stalks, stir well, season with salt, and cook until sizzling and sweating a bit. Add 4 cups (1 liter) of the warm asparagus stock and the potatoes. Bring to a boil over high heat, stirring to mix.

Cover and keep boiling to really cook everything through, about 30 minutes. When the vegetables are very tender, puree in a blender with the half-and-half until very smooth, in batches if needed.

Immediately strain through a chinois or fine sieve, whisking to pass the soup through quickly into a metal bowl. Season to taste with salt, and the white pepper, then set over a larger bowl of ice and water to chill quickly.

FOR THE MORELS

2 tablespoons (30 g) butter
1 tablespoon finely diced shallot
Salt
1 small clove garlic, smashed and minced
3½ ounces (105 g) fresh or reconstituted dry morels, trimmed and halved lengthwise (quartered if large)
½ cup (125 ml) White Chicken Stock (page 251)
Freshly ground black pepper
1 sprig thyme
½ bay leaf

Melt the butter in a medium saucepan over medium heat. Add the shallot, season with salt, and cook, stirring, for 1 minute. Add the garlic and cook, stirring, for 30 seconds. Add the morels, stir well, then season with salt. If using fresh morels, cook, stirring occasionally, until the water cooks out, 6 to 7 minutes.

Add the stock, season with salt and pepper, and bring to a boil over high heat. Add the thyme and bay leaf, pressing them into the boiling liquid. Scrape down the sides of the pot, stir well, cover, and simmer over low heat until all the liquid has evaporated, about 30 minutes.

Double-check the seasoning and adjust as necessary, then cool to room temperature and discard the thyme and bay leaf.

FOR THE POACHED EGGS

1 teaspoon salt
2 tablespoons white vinegar
6 eggs

Fill a 12-inch (30.5 cm), high-sided skillet with water and bring to a boil, then add the salt and white vinegar. Reduce the heat to low and crack the eggs into the pan. Don't swirl the water or disturb the eggs. Cook for 4 minutes and, with a perforated spoon, lift each egg from the water. You can poach the eggs in advance, shock them in ice water, and keep them refrigerated for up to 8 hours, until ready to serve, or you can poach them à la minute.

Note: For an alternative egg-poaching method, see page 219.

TO FINISH

Divide the morels among six serving plates (about ¼ cup/25 g each). Top each mound with a poached egg. Shave the reserved asparagus tips with a mandoline, then arrange the thin slices around the mounds and eggs to form pyramids. Pour the soup all around. Season with some coarsely ground black pepper and serve immediately.

CHILLED CUCUMBER AND MINT SOUP
WITH ALASKAN KING CRAB

Serves 6

This is a light refreshing soup of cucumber and mint that's garnished with crab. If buying frozen crab, let it thaw in the fridge; don't soak it in water. Cook as quickly as possible to keep flavors fresh and be careful not to make it too minty. You can augment the soup with extra-virgin olive oil or herb oil.

FOR THE SOUP

1 small onion, chopped

1 tablespoon olive oil

2 cloves garlic, chopped

4 large cucumbers, peeled and thinly sliced (you'll need about 1½ pounds/ 700 g sliced cucumbers)

1 cup (250 ml) White Chicken Stock (page 251)

3 tablespoons heavy cream

Salt and freshly ground black pepper

8 to 10 small mint leaves, julienned

2 to 3 teaspoons sherry vinegar, or to taste

¼ teaspoon cayenne pepper, or to taste

To make the soup, in a large skillet over medium-high heat, sauté the onion in the olive oil until translucent, a minute or so. Add the garlic and cook another 30 seconds or so, then add the cucumber and sauté for a minute or so. Add the chicken stock and simmer for 5 minutes. Add the cream and salt and pepper to taste, and boil for 3 minutes. Transfer the cucumber soup to a blender, add the mint, and blend thoroughly. Strain the mixture into a bowl and set in ice to chill it. Season with the vinegar and cayenne and more salt if necessary.

FOR THE GARNISH

3 Alaskan king crab legs

1 large tomato, peeled, seeded, and diced

Salt and freshly ground black pepper

Lemon juice

Olive oil or Chive Oil (page 233; optional)

Diced tomato, apple, or cucumber (optional)

To prepare the garnish, remove the crab meat from the shell and coarsely chop. Mix with the tomato and season to taste with salt, pepper, and lemon juice.

To serve, divide the crab, about 1½ ounces (40 g) each, among six bowls (use a ring mold for an elegant appearance). Ladle the soup around the crab. Drizzle the olive or chive oil over the crab, if using. Garnish with the diced tomato, apple, or cucumber if desired. Serve immediately.

STOCKS AND JUS

Stocks and jus are not common preparations on the farm, so I learned these during my apprenticeship with Uncle Michel. And these iterations are the result of working and refining them ever since.

When I opened my restaurant in 2015, we, of course, had all of these stocks and jus, but they changed depending on various factors—who was making them, who was finishing them, what was coming into the kitchens. Jake Abbott, who worked his way up to sous chef, took it upon himself to create what is in effect a stock program, refining and streamlining our stocks and jus. This is important for a restaurant that makes hundreds of gallons of stock a week and any number of jus (concentrated stocks) and the many derivatives that those jus become. This commitment to quality and consistency came from his love of the process and the stock itself, a magical essence. He has researched, and really studied, stock making for the past ten years, comparing the way Alain Ducasse and his team makes theirs with how Heston Blumenthal and the team at the Fat Duck makes theirs, for instance, or the way the French Laundry uses stocks to make their quick stocks, like the jus here. And he's become an expert at the finer points of stocks, which is great for consistency at the restaurant, but it's knowledge that's equally applicable to any kitchen, whether you're making one liter or hundreds. They are not called the *fond de cuisine*, the foundation of cuisine, for nothing.

What Jake stresses most is care. You have to pay close attention to stocks, to wrest every bit of flavor from all this valuable trim, the bones and cartilage and meat, attending your pan and taking care to scrape down any fond on the sides of your pan (the browned protein from the meat). You can't rush a stock. You can't make veal jus on the fly, not one that's worthwhile. You have to pay attention to the time; you must skim; you must be aware of what flavors are volatile and what ingredients truly require long cooking. If you cook volatile ingredients with the long-cooking ones, you will have what Jake calls a dead stock, a stock that may have flavor and body but doesn't taste fresh and bright and light on the palate.

We use two stocks that are the basis for all our meat-based sauces, a white veal stock and a white chicken stock, white meaning that the bones are not roasted. When we want roasted flavors, we add roasted bones when making the jus. The veal bones and calf's feet are blanched for the veal stock. And not just brought to a boil then strained and rinsed, but rather cooked for an hour, then returned to the pot and rinsed with warm water first. This is important. If you wash the bones in cold water, Jake noticed, the gelatin solidified, preventing the impurities from being removed. We then rinse the bones three times with cold water. They are then cooked for twelve hours. Chicken stock, on the other hand, is cooked for only four hours. Veal and beef bones are larger and more dense and so it takes considerably more time to extract their collagen.

And for both stocks, the volatile aromatic ingredients, such as the onion, celery, carrot, and herbs, are added at the end, cooked only for an hour, just the right amount of time to pull their flavors out but not so long that you kill those flavors or disintegrate the vegetables, fragments of which will absorb the valuable stock and end up being discarded.

We use three primary jus, stock that is fortified then reduced: a veal jus, beef jus, and chicken jus. Of course, we'll use all of our bones in various ways—we make a roasted duck stock or a squab jus for dishes featuring those birds. But the following are the five principle stocks and jus that are the backbone of our meat sauces, the most versatile and essential for any cook.

For fish, we make a traditional fumet, sort of. We throw in some zest and spices to enliven a traditional stock using the bones of white fish, such as black sea bass, fluke, snapper, tilefish, but not cod, which can be fishy, nor red-meated-fatty fish. It's a light, bright, refreshing fumet.

All stocks can be frozen for up to 8 weeks. Very reduced stocks can be frozen in ice cube trays so that you can use small amounts as needed without thawing a big batch and refreezing it.

WHITE CHICKEN STOCK

Makes 4 quarts/liters

This is our most used and valuable stock. Period. (White designates that the bones are not roasted before being simmered; brown denotes that the bones have been roasted.)

3½ pounds (1½ kg) chicken backs or carcasses, cut into 2-inch (5 cm) pieces

7 ounces (210 g) chicken feet, blanched (see method in Chicken Jus, page 252)

Salt

6 ounces (180 g) onion, diced

8 ounces (240 g) celery, diced

3½ ounces (105 g) carrot, diced

Sachet d'épices (1 bunch green leek tops, 3 teaspoons white peppercorns, 2 sprigs thyme, 2 sprigs parsley, 1 small sprig rosemary, 1 bay leaf, tied together in cheesecloth)

Rinse the bones with cool water. In a large pot, combine the chicken bones and feet and add 5 quarts/liters water and a large four-finger pinch of salt. Bring it to a low simmer and cook for 3 hours. Add the onion, celery, carrot, and sachet and simmer for another hour. Remove the pot from the heat and let rest for 20 minutes. Strain through a fine-mesh sieve and cool. Refrigerate in a covered container for up to 4 days, or freeze for up to 2 months.

CHICKEN JUS

**Makes 1 pint
(480 ml)**

This is a two-part process. We first use roasted chicken bones and feet to make the jus. But then we fortify it with roasted chicken wings and vegetables. When you cook a stock or a jus this long, you're pulling out abundant gelatin, but the long cooking time deadens the flavor, so we want to add that flavor back, with a second reinforcement.

8 ounces (240 g) chicken feet

Salt

3 pounds (1.4 kg) chicken bones
(backs and other carcass pieces),
cut into 2-inch (5 cm) pieces

3½ pounds (1.6 kg) chicken wings,
cut into 2-inch (5 cm) pieces

7 tablespoons (105 ml) red wine
(in fall and winter) or white wine
(in spring or summer)

4 quarts/liters White Chicken Stock
(page 251)

4 ounces (120 g) onion

4 ounces (120 g) celery

2 ounces (60 g) carrot

Preheat your oven to 400°F (220°C).

Put the chicken feet in a saucepan and cover with cold water and a big, four-finger pinch of salt. Bring the pot to a boil, then lower the heat to a strong simmer. Skim any foam that rises to the top. Simmer for 20 minutes. Strain and return the feet to the pot. Cover them with warm water and strain. Repeat with cold water three more times.

Spread the chicken bones on a rack on a sheet pan. Do the same with the chicken wings. Roast the chicken in the oven for 25 to 30 minutes, until it's golden brown and looks delicious. Remove the chicken from the rack, keeping the wings separate from the bones. Put the sheet pans over medium heat and deglaze them with the wine and some water. (Sometimes we put parchment on the sheet pans, which catches all the juices that then caramelize on the parchment; instead of deglazing a pan, we simply put the piece of parchment directly in the stock, which dissolves the caramelized juices.) Add the deglazed wine juices to the pot and reduce to a glaze consistency. Add the roasted bones and blanched feet. Add the chicken stock. Bring the stock to a boil, then reduce the heat to a simmer, and simmer for 3 hours. The stock will reduce a little; just replace the loss with water if it goes down more than an inch or so. Strain.

Combine the strained jus and the wings in a pot for what is called the reinforcement—the browned roasted flavor, of the wings, the collagen from the skin and bones, and the flavor from the meat, along with the aromatics. Bring this to a boil, then reduce to a low simmer and cook for 1 hour. Add the onion, carrot, and celery and simmer for another hour. Strain through a chinois or a strainer lined with a towel, a clean apron (what we use at the restaurant), or three layers of cheesecloth into a saucepan. Press down on the solids to get as much liquid out as possible.

Simmer on medium-high and reduce the jus to a pint (480 ml), occasionally skimming any film that collects on the surface (no need to over-skim). As you do, scrape the fond from the side of the pan into the jus (it adds to the flavor and can burn if not removed). If you began with a very large pot, you may want use progressively smaller pots as you reduce, straining the jus through a fine-mesh sieve into a clean pot as you do. Refrigerate in a covered container for up to 4 days, or freeze for up to 2 months.

WHITE VEAL STOCK

Makes 4 quarts/ liters

White veal stock is one of the most valuable essences in the kitchen, giving a boost of serious gelatin and enhancing the flavor of whatever bones and meat you add to it.

3 pounds (1.3 kg) mixed veal bones (they should have a good balance of bone, cartilage, and meat), cut into 2-inch (5 cm) pieces

1 pound (455 g) calf's feet

1 teaspoon salt

6 ounces (180 g) onion, cut into large dice

8 ounces (240 g) celery, cut into large dice

3 ounces (90 g) carrot, cut into large dice

Sachet d'épices (1 bunch green leek tops, 1 tablespoon white peppercorns, 2 sprigs thyme, 2 sprigs parsley, 1 small sprig rosemary, 1 bay leaf, tied together in cheesecloth)

In a pot, cover the bones and calf's feet with cold water and bring it to a boil. Reduce the heat to achieve a strong simmer. Skim and discard the foam. Simmer for 1 hour. Rinse the bones with warm water once, and then rinse again three times with cool water.

Return the bones to a clean pot, then add 5 quarts/liters of water and the salt. Bring the pot to a low simmer and cook for 11 hours. Add the vegetables and the sachet and simmer for another hour. Remove from the heat and rest for 20 minutes. Strain through a fine-mesh sieve and cool. Refrigerate in a covered container for up to 4 days, or freeze for up to 2 months.

VEAL JUS

Veal jus is the base for so many of the classic sauces. Here is our version of a demi-glace, the reduced veal stock that serves as a base for a range of classical French sauces. Veal stock is considered neutral and because of this is essential—it gives extraordinary body and enhances the flavors of the other ingredients without asserting its own. So if we add it to the beef jus, it carries the beefy flavor. But with our veal jus, because it is so powerful, we use chicken stock as the base, and fortify it with chunks of veal breast, maybe the best cut of any animal for stock- and sauce-making because of its voluminous cartilage (collagen/gelatin) for body and meat for flavor. Notice that we use only onion and celery in our veal jus, no carrot, which my sous chef Jake Abbott feels makes the jus too cloyingly sweet. The blanched calf's foot is added for even more body. A good butcher should be able to get you calf's feet and also cut them into pieces for you.

1 pound (455 g) calf's foot (about a half of one), cut into a few pieces

Grapeseed oil, as needed, for sautéing the veal

6½ pounds (3 kg) veal breast, cut into 2-inch (5 cm) pieces

2 to 3 tablespoons (30 to 40 g) butter

6 ounces (180 g) onion, cut into large dice (1-pint/480-ml deli container)

8 ounces (240 g) celery, cut into large dice (1-pint/480-ml deli container)

4 quarts/liters White Chicken Stock (page 251)

Put the calf's foot pieces into a small saucepan, cover them with cold water, and bring them to a boil over high heat, then reduce the heat and simmer for 20 minutes. Strain the bones and rinse under warm water, then cold water (if washed in cold water first, the gelatin seizes, preventing impurities from being washed away). At the restaurant we'll rinse them three times in cold water.

Preheat your oven to 375°F (190°C, or 350°F/175°C if you have a convection oven).

In a large pot or Dutch oven over medium-high heat, add the grapeseed oil. When the oil is hot, add just enough of the veal breast to cover the bottom of the pan and cook to brown them. If you crowd them, they may not brown well. Cook them in batches and take your time. You want to get a nice roasted color on them, so they look good enough to eat. Remove the first batch to drain and cook the remaining veal. They will leave a fond on the bottom of the pan. This is flavor. As Jake says, you're cooking the pan as much as you are the meat and bones (see the White Chicken stock, page 251, for a particularly good example). You're cooking the fond, so be careful not to burn it, or you'll lose all that flavor.

When you've cooked the veal and removed it from the pan, dump the fat (it's overcooked at this point, but it has done its job) and add the butter, onion, and celery. Lower the heat to medium low. Cook them to bring out their sweetness. While the vegetables are sweating, their natural moisture will seep out of them and start to deglaze the pan. Once they are softened and the pan is mostly

deglazed (the stock you are about to add will finish it off), return the veal and the calf's foot to the pot. Add the chicken stock. Bring the pot to a boil. As soon as it reaches a boil put it in the oven, uncovered, for 3 hours.

Remove the pot from the oven. It will have reduced some and left fond on the sides of the pan. Take a few minutes to scrape the fond into the stock by splashing the stock onto it and scraping. This is flavor. Strain through a chinois or strainer lined with a towel, a clean apron (what we use at the restaurant), or three layers of cheesecloth into a saucepan. Press down on the solids to get as much liquid out as possible.

Simmer on medium-high and reduce the jus to a pint (480 ml), occasionally skimming any film that collects on the surface (no need to over-skim). As you do, scrape the fond from the side of the pan into the jus. If you began with a very large pot, you may want use progressively smaller pots as you reduce, straining the jus through a chinois into a clean pot as you do. Refrigerate in a covered container for up to 4 days, or freeze for up to 2 months.

BEEF JUS

**Makes 1 pint
(480 ml)**

This jus uses a technique Jake learned, and loved, from a chef who had taken it from the kitchen of Alain Ducasse. The roasted meat is simmered in chicken stock until the stock is completely cooked off, reduced to a glaze, which then coats the meat, and is cooked further until there is a very thick fond on the bottom of the pan and on the sides, so thick that if feels rough and the bottom of the pan is scarcely visible. This is then deglazed with the vegetables and a little wine. It results in a very rich and beefy jus.

Grapeseed oil, as needed, for sautéing
   the beef
6½ pounds (3 kg) beef trim, cut into
   2-inch (5 cm) pieces
2 quarts/liters White Chicken Stock
   (page 251)
3 tablespoons (45 g) butter
¾ ounce (20 g) cloves garlic
4 ounces (120 g) shallot, cut into
   large dice
3 ounces (90 g) leek, cut into large dice
7 tablespoons (105 ml) red wine
2 quarts/liters White Veal Stock
   (page 253)

In a large pot or Dutch oven over medium-high heat, add the oil. When the oil is hot, add beef in one layer. Brown the meat in batches until it looks delicious. Pour off the fat and add the chicken stock, scraping any fond from the bottom of the pan. Add the beef and bring the stock to a simmer. Cook, stirring occasionally, until the stock has almost cooked off. Begin stirring the meat more frequently now, until all the stock has cooked off. Continue cooking the beef until the pan is dry and the meat is glazed, and the glaze begins to stick to the pan on the bottom and sides. The jus and meat will begin to fry in the fat. When you have a thick roasted fond on the bottom and sides of the pan, remove the meat and discard the fat.

Add the butter to the pan over medium heat. Add the garlic, shallots, and leeks. Sweat the vegetables and use them and the butter to begin deglazing the pan. Once the deglazing has begun and some of the fond is coming off the pan, add the wine and continue to deglaze, pulling the pot off the heat and returning it as needed to deglaze it all. You want to reduce the wine by about half, or until the alcohol has cooked off.

Return the beef to the pot along with the veal stock. Bring this to a simmer, carefully scraping off anything brown stuck to the sides of the pan. All fond should be dissolved into the stock. Simmer for 2 hours.

Strain through a strainer lined with a white kitchen towel, or five or six layers of cheesecloth, into a saucepan. Press down on the solids to get as much liquid out as possible.

Simmer over medium-high heat and reduce the jus to a pint (480 ml), occasionally skimming any film that collects on the surface (no need to over-skim). As you do, scrape the caramelization from the side of the pan into the jus. It's a good idea to use progressively smaller pots as you reduce, if you can, for a slower, more controlled reduction, straining the jus through a fine-mesh sieve into a clean pot. Refrigerate in a covered container for up to 4 days, or freeze for up to 2 months.

LOBSTER STOCK

**Makes 5 cups
(1.2 liters)**

We use the heads and legs of the lobster for our stock. It's very important to cut off and discard all the feathery gills. The other critical point is to crush the bones after they've been sautéed to squeeze out as much flavor as possible. We use lobster stock as a base for a lobster bisque or a consommé. And we reduce it for sauces for lobster dishes, of course, but we can also use it to make sauces for other shellfish, for meaty fish such as snapper or halibut, or even for pasta.

10 lobster heads, cleaned and gills removed, and the legs from those lobsters, roughly chopped

½ cup (120 ml) olive oil

3 medium onions, finely chopped

1 medium carrot, finely chopped

2 celery stalks, finely chopped

1 leek (whites and light greens only), finely chopped

½ fennel bulb, finely chopped

2 small heads of garlic, split in half

¾ cup (200 g) tomato paste

1 cup (240 ml) brandy

1 (750 ml) bottle dry white wine

2 tablespoons tarragon leaves

1 small bunch thyme

½ cup (12 g) basil, chopped

2 pieces star anise

2 tablespoons black peppercorns

Preheat your oven to 450°F (230°C).

Heat a large ovenproof pot or rondeau over high heat. Add the chopped lobster and put the pot in the oven for 20 to 25 minutes. Add the onions, carrot, celery, leek, fennel, and garlic, stir to combine, and return to the oven for about 5 minutes. Add the tomato paste and return to the oven for another 5 minutes, being careful not to burn the tomato paste.

Use a mallet or something heavy to crush the lobster heads and legs to extract flavors. On the stovetop over high heat, deglaze the pot with the brandy and flame it. Add the white wine and simmer until reduced by at least half. Add 3½ quarts/liters (about 1 gallon) water and the tarragon, thyme, basil, star anise, and peppercorns. Bring to a boil, reduce to a medium simmer, and cook for 1½ hours.

Blend the stock with an immersion blender, breaking up the lobster as much as possible. Strain the stock through a colander or perforated hotel pan to remove the largest solid pieces. Then strain the stock through a chinois.

Return it to the pot and bring to a simmer over high heat, then lower the heat to medium and let it simmer until it's reduced by 75 percent, to about 5 cups (1.2 liters).

Blend the stock again with an immersion blender, and a second time in a high-speed blender, for 1 minute per batch. This will extract the flavor from the smallest particles. Pass through a fine-mesh sieve and cool down. Refrigerate until ready to use. Refrigerate in a covered container for up to 4 days or freeze for up to 2 months.

FUMET

(Fish Stock)

Makes 2 quarts/ liters

At the restaurant we prefer to use lighter white fish that is available locally for our fumet. Most often we use black sea bass. However, fluke, snapper, and smaller tilefish are acceptable and available most of the year here. Ask your fishmonger for these fish bones, or explain you need fish for stock and they should know. A general rule is to avoid red or very oily fish. We buy whole fish and break them down ourselves. You should too.

We use ginger and orange peel because they add nuance to the fumet's flavor. We choose to keep the fins and eyes, because they give the fumet gelatin (the entire head has a lot of gelatin, so we use it, but make sure to leave it whole, because if split it can cloud the fumet). Some say eyes can make a fumet bitter. We have found that quick, careful cooking prevents that.

2 pounds (1 kg) fish bones, including head and fins, gills removed, cut into pieces

2 teaspoons salt, plus more for soaking

4 tablespoons (60 g) butter

2 cloves garlic, peeled and smashed

13 ounces (390 g) leeks, whites only, thinly sliced

13 ounces (390 g) onion, thinly sliced

5 ounces (150 g) carrot, peeled, thinly sliced

4 ounces (120 g) celery, thinly sliced

1 (750-ml) bottle Coteaux du Layon, or similar sweet wine

½ ounce ginger, thinly sliced

¼ cup parsley stems

3 sprigs thyme

3 bay leaves

3 strips orange zest, taken off with a peeler

3 quarts/liters cold water

To prepare the bones, remove the gills and cut the carcass into pieces with kitchen shears or a knife. Keep the head intact. Soak the bones in ice water with a big four-finger pinch of salt, and refrigerate for at least 2 to 3 hours or, better, overnight. Strain the bones and rinse thoroughly under cold running water. Pat them dry and lay them on a rack.

In a pot appropriate for the bones you have, melt the butter over medium-low heat and sweat the garlic for 5 minutes without browning it. Add the leeks, onion, carrot, celery, and 2 teaspoons salt and sweat them all until softened, 4 to 5 minutes. Add the wine and reduce by half (the alcohol should be completely cooked off). Add the bones with the ginger, parsley stems, thyme, bay leaves, and orange zest and continue to cook for 5 minutes. Add the water and bring to a boil, then reduce to a gentle simmer and cook for 45 minutes. Skim any foam that forms at the surface. Remove from the heat and let steep for 1 hour. Strain through cheesecloth. Refrigerate in a covered container for up to 4 days, or freeze for up to 2 months.

SEAFOOD

BLUE SHRIMP
ZUCCHINI BLOSSOMS
with Cardamom Jus

260

AMERICAN RED SNAPPER
with Carrot Confit and Cumin

263

HALIBUT
with Celery Root Puree, Hen of the
Woods, and Riesling Cockle Sauce

264

ON TROUT

267

SLOW-COOKED
RAINBOW TROUT
with Seasonal Farm Vegetables
and Chicory Emulsion

269

CHORIZO-CRUSTED COD
with White Bean Puree

270

OLIVE OIL–POACHED
ORA KING SALMON
with Root Vegetable Julienne and
Horseradish Broth

273

SLOW-ROASTED
ORA KING SALMON
with Comté Cheese Crust, Braised
Beets, and Sicilian Pistachio Sauce

274

LARDO-POACHED
MAINE LOBSTER
with Fennel Puree, Caramelized
Fennel, and Sauce Américaine
"Au Poivre Vert"

276

ROASTED MAINE LOBSTER
IN A FOLLY OF HERBS
with Green Asparagus and
Fingerling Potatoes

278

GRILLED MAINE LOBSTER
with Toasted Cashew, Baby
Carrots, and Lobster-Ginger
Sabayon

281

LANGOUSTINE AND DIVER
SCALLOPS STUFFED
CABBAGE
with Red Bell Pepper, Chive, and
Caviar Coulis

284

BAKED DAURADE ROYALE
with Autumn Vegetable Julienne
and Gewurztraminer Oyster Broth

287

SLOW-COOKED SABLEFISH
with Green Onion, Green Apple,
Coconut, and Basil-Mint Oil

288

SPICED HAMACHI FILLET
with Baby Leeks and Blood
Orange–Mustard Sauce

291

BLUE SHRIMP ZUCCHINI BLOSSOMS
WITH CARDAMOM JUS

Serves 4 to 6

This is a celebration of the zucchini, made elegant and unusual with a shrimp-and-zucchini stuffing and a light cardamom broth. I believe Roger Vergé was one of the first chefs to popularize the gorgeous zucchini flower. They can be used as a wrapper for any kind of filling (halibut would make an excellent substitute for the shrimp; I prefer blue shrimp because they have such a good bite). Zucchini blossoms are often battered and fried, but I prefer sautéing them and then roasting them so that their beauty isn't hidden and their delicate flavor and texture come through.

FOR THE STUFFED ZUCCHINI BLOSSOMS

18 blue shrimp (about 1 pound/450 g), cleaned
2 teaspoons salt
Pepper
2 tablespoons dry vermouth
1 tablespoon olive oil
½ small zucchini, skin on, cut into brunoise, and lightly cooked in butter to soften them
12 zucchini blossoms, pistils carefully removed

Coarsely chop the shrimp and put them in a mixing bowl set in ice. Add the salt, pepper to taste, vermouth, olive oil, and zucchini, tossing to combine. Pipe or spoon the stuffing into the flowers, just until they're full enough that the tips enclose the stuffing completely.

FOR THE CARDAMOM JUS

½ onion (about 3 ounces/100 g), chopped
1 small leek (about 2 ounces/50 g), chopped
½ small carrot (about 2 ounces/50 g), chopped
½ rib celery (about 1 ounce/30 g), chopped
½ cup (1 stick/120 g) butter
1 cup (250 ml) dry white wine
2 cups (500 ml) White Chicken Stock (page 251)

8 green cardamom pods, crushed
Salt and freshly ground black pepper
Cayenne pepper

Combine the onions, leek, carrot, and celery and 2 tablespoons of the butter and cook until very soft but not brown. Add the wine and simmer until it's reduced by half. Add the chicken stock. Simmer to reduce by about one-third. Strain it through a fine-mesh sieve into a clean pan over medium-high heat. Add the cardamom pods and reduce the mixture by two-thirds. Whisk in the remaining 6 tablespoons (90 g) butter and season with salt, pepper, and cayenne to taste. Pass through a fine-mesh sieve. Keep warm until reheating to finish the dish.

TO FINISH

1 tablespoon butter, plus more if needed
1 tablespoon grapeseed oil
6 baby zucchinis, cut into ribbons, lightly salted
6 pattypan squash, cut into six pieces each, gently sautéed in butter until tender
2 tablespoons brunoised (very finely diced) jarred piquillo pepper, or substitute red bell pepper
Microgreens and flowers
Eggplant chips (thinly sliced eggplant, dehydrated until crisp; optional; see Note)

Note: To make the eggplant chips, in a dehydrator, place eggplant slices evenly spaced out on a dehydrator tray. Set the dehydrator to 140°F to 145°F/60°C and let the eggplant dehydrate for 4 to 6 hours (depending on the thickness or until they get crispy). Store in an airtight container or bag.

Preheat your oven to 300°F (175°C).

Heat the butter and oil in a sauté pan over medium-high heat. When the butter is foaming, add the stuffed zucchini flowers and lower the heat to medium. Cook gently on all sides for a couple minutes, basting with butter (add more butter if there's not enough to baste with). Add a couple tablespoons of water to the pan to keep the heat low and put the blossoms in the oven for 5 minutes or until the stuffing is cooked through. Remove them to a plate lined with paper towels.

Divide the zucchini flowers among bowls. Spoon hot jus around them. Garnish with zucchini ribbons, pattypan squash, piquillo pepper, microgreens and flowers, and eggplant chips, if using, and serve immediately.

AMERICAN RED SNAPPER
WITH CARROT CONFIT AND CUMIN

Serves 6

This dish is all about the carrot confit and the resulting broth, olive oil flavored with orange and cumin. It would work well with any white mild fish, but I love snapper and I cook it so that its skin is crisp. To do this I score the skin so that the fillet doesn't buckle in the pan and the skin stays flat against it. I also like to smear a little crème fraîche on the skin. Some people flour it but I like to keep the skin visible and the crème fraîche adds a layer of fat that helps cook the skin.

FOR THE CARROT CONFIT
2 pounds (1 kg) Thumbelina baby carrots, or other small carrots, peeled
3 cloves garlic, sliced
1 tablespoon (20 g) cumin seeds
Zest of 1 orange
1 quart/liter orange juice (from 10 to 12 oranges)
2 quarts/liters olive oil

Preheat your oven to 275°F (135°C).

For the carrot confit, combine the carrots, garlic, cumin, orange zest, orange juice, and olive oil, and put them in a Dutch oven or saucepan. Cook for 2½ to 3 hours, checking on them periodically to make sure they are okay. Remove the carrots to a hotel pan or baking dish. Strain the cooking liquid through a fine-mesh sieve. Use just enough of the cooking liquid to cover the carrots to reheat in the broth. Reduce the remaining broth by half. Take off the heat and set aside, while you cook the fish.

FOR THE FISH
6 red snapper fillets (4 to 5 ounces/ 120 to 150 g), skin on, scored in a crosshatch
Salt and freshly ground black pepper
2 to 3 tablespoons crème fraîche (optional)
3 tablespoons grapeseed or vegetable oil, for sautéing
3 tablespoons butter, for sautéing

Season the fillets with salt and pepper. Spread a thin film of crème fraîche on the skin, if using. In a nonstick sauté pan over medium-high heat, add equal parts butter and oil, just enough to coat the pan (about a tablespoon each). When the pan is hot, add the fillets skin-side down, working in batches if necessary. Cook until the skin is crisp, pressing down on the fillets, 2 to 3 minutes. Turn the fillets and finish cooking them, another minute or so, just until the center is warm. Repeat with the remaining fillets.

On a sizzler platter or in a sauté pan, heat up the carrots in enough broth to just cover them. When hot, remove the carrots to a plate. Cover slightly to keep warm. Reduce the broth to a sauce consistency. Add the reserved already reduced olive oil and orange juice.

TO FINISH
4 tablespoons (8 g) chopped cilantro

Divide the warm carrots among six bowls, ladle about 4 ounces (120 ml) of the reduced cooking liquid over them, top with the sautéed snapper, garnish with cilantro, and serve immediately.

HALIBUT
WITH CELERY ROOT PUREE, HEN OF THE WOODS, AND RIESLING COCKLE SAUCE

Serves 4

I used to go with my father to the woods to hunt for mushrooms. He loved foraging, and one of his favorites to find was hen of the woods. We would bring extras to my uncle's, where we'd braise them with tomatoes and garlic like a ragù, or sauté them with garlic as a simple accompaniment, as in this dish. At my uncle's place, we would make this with salmon, turbot, or trout, and different garnishes. But the Riesling sauce is such a standout in my memory that I have re-created it here. To make it, you want a drinkable, affordable wine. There's no need to use a fifty-dollar bottle of wine in this sauce.

4 tablespoons (60 g) butter
3 ounces (90 g) carrots, peeled and cut into ⅛-inch (3 mm) slices
5 ounces (150 g) onions, cut into ⅛-inch (3 mm) slices
Salt
½ bottle (325 ml) dry Riesling
2 cups (480 ml) White Chicken Stock (page 251)

Melt the butter in a large saucepot over medium heat, then add the carrots, onions, and a pinch of salt. Cook, stirring occasionally, until the carrots have a little bit of softness but no color and the onions are translucent but not brown, about 7 minutes.

Add the wine, bring to a boil over high heat, and boil hard until reduced by half, about 7 minutes. Add the chicken stock, bring to a boil, then reduce the heat to simmer until the liquid has reduced to a scant 2 cups (480 ml), about 17 minutes.

Remove from the heat, then pass through a fine-mesh sieve, pressing hard on the solids to extract all their liquid.

FOR THE COCKLE SAUCE

Grapeseed oil
2 ounces (60 g) shallot, thinly sliced
8 white peppercorns
Salt
½ cup (120 ml) dry white wine
1 pound (450 g) cockles, cleaned well
6 tablespoons (85 g) butter, cut in cubes
4 tablespoons (60 ml) Tio Pepe sherry
24 North Sea little shrimps, poached in their brine (available cooked in specialty food stores or online)
1 tablespoon salmon roe
2 teaspoons chopped chives

Coat the bottom of a small saucepan with grapeseed oil and set over high heat. Add the shallot, peppercorns, and a pinch of salt. Cook, stirring often, until the shallots are translucent but with no color, about 1 minute. Add the wine and bring to a boil. Add the cockles, cover, and shake the pan. Cook, shaking the pan occasionally, until the cockles open, 2 to 3 minutes. Immediately transfer to a plate using a slotted spoon, then immediately pluck out the cockles from their shells.

Strain the cooking liquid, along with any liquid accumulated on the cockle plate, through a fine-mesh sieve into a small saucepan. Take ⅓ cup of the liquid and reduce it to 3 tablespoons. Pull the muscles off the cockle bellies and discard. Transfer the cockle bellies to the remaining strained cooking liquid.

Combine ½ cup (120 ml) of the sauce base with the 3 tablespoons of reduced cockle liquid/juice in a small saucepan. Season to taste with salt. Heat over low heat, adding a cube or two of butter at a time, stirring well to let each addition incorporate before adding the next. When all the butter has been added and the sauce is smooth, stir in the sherry, then the cockle bellies.

Right before serving, remove from the heat and stir in the shrimp, salmon roe, and chives.

recipe continues

FOR THE SAUTÉED ASPARAGUS

8 asparagus spears
Grapeseed oil
Salt

Snap the tough woody ends from the asparagus, then trim the ends neatly. Peel the asparagus stems, starting just below the tips. Cut the asparagus into 4½-inch (11 cm) pieces.

Coat a large skillet with grapeseed oil and set over high heat. When the oil is hot, put down the asparagus in a single layer and sizzle until browned and just tender, about 2 minutes. Season with salt and remove from the heat.

FOR THE HEN OF THE WOODS

Grapeseed oil
4 ounces (120 g) hen of the woods mushrooms, cut into 8 to 12 large chunks
2 cloves garlic, smashed
2 sprigs thyme
Salt

Generously coat a large skillet with grapeseed oil and set over high heat. When the oil is hot, put down the hen of the woods in a single layer, along with the garlic and thyme. Season with salt, then cook, basting the mushrooms with the oil in the pan while swirling the pan, until browned and tender, about 2 minutes. Remove the cooked mushrooms to a paper towel–lined plate and discard the garlic and thyme.

FOR THE HALIBUT

4 halibut fillets (4 ounces/120 g each), skinned
Salt and freshly ground white pepper
½ cup (1 stick/115 g) butter
⅔ cup (180 ml) dry white wine
White Chicken Stock (page 251)
Celery Root Puree (page 326)

Season the fish all over with salt and white pepper. Melt the butter in a large sauté pan. Add the fish in a single layer, then add the wine. Add enough stock to come halfway up the sides of the fish. Gently swirl the pan so the fish move back and forth so you know it's not sticking. Cook in the hot liquid, basting continuously, until the fish is white on the bottom, about 2 minutes.

Carefully flip the fish over and continue basting and cooking until the fish is just white on the bottom, about 2 minutes. Cover and remove from the heat. The fish will finish cooking in the still-warm pan.

To finish the dish, spoon ¼ cup (80 g) celery root puree in a circle on each of the four serving plates. Put a halibut fillet in the center of each plate and coat the fish with the cockle sauce. Arrange the asparagus and hen of the woods around the fish. Serve immediately.

ON TROUT

In Alsace, we treasure trout. We catch them in the rivers and streams throughout Alsace and rush to cook them into the great specialty of our region, truite au bleu. Immediately after killing and gutting the fish, we poach it in an acidic court bouillon. The acid turns the skin blue. As a kid, I loved that magic trick of a dish—and the fresh-from-the-water sweetness of the fish.

In restaurants in France, trout swim in freshwater aquariums. Fishermen pull up to the service doors in their trucks and sell chefs whole basins filled with fish still splashing furiously. The chefs slide the lot into the aquariums where they will swim until they hit a hot pan. My favorite preparation is when the just-slain fish is roasted whole, with almonds, seasoned with only lemon juice, salt, and pepper. The platter arrives at the table, sizzling, the fish hissing steam, the butter-roasted almonds bubbling and crackling. Beautiful.

Of course, almost every restaurant in Alsace also offers the classic trout meunière—the fillets sautéed in browned butter, served with lemon and capers—or sometimes you'll find it served with morels or another wild mushroom sauce. Trout can also be smoked or pickled (page 50), served with salad, or even adorned with Asian seasonings and turned into a tartare. In Alsace, we love trout in all its forms because we care deeply about where our food comes from, and we know trout has always come from our rivers.

It's been exciting for me to see the increasing American interest in knowing the origins of ingredients and showcasing my love of trout in my restaurants. My trout comes from Ty Bartosh at Green-Walk Trout Hatchery in Bangor, Pennsylvania, a sustainable fishery that delivers trout the day it comes out of the water.

If you're buying trout from a market, look for tight flesh and a nice clean smell. Fish should never smell fishy. When they do, they're done. Ask the fishmonger how long the trout have been out of the water. If it's been 3 to 4 days, make sure you cook the fish that night. If the fish was caught that day, put the fish on a rack or perforated tray set over a pan of ice, cover with plastic wrap, and refrigerate for 36 hours. (Adjust the hours accordingly: 24 hours for day-old fish; 12 hours for 2 days out of water.) The resting time allows the flesh to relax. The bones will slide out much more easily from the raw flesh and the meat will be perfectly tender when cooked.

If the folks at the store don't know when the fish arrived, you should be shopping elsewhere!

SLOW-COOKED RAINBOW TROUT
WITH SEASONAL FARM VEGETABLES AND CHICORY EMULSION

Serves 4 or 8

This preparation is a very elegant and easy way to prepare boned fillets, perfuming the inside of the trout with tarragon, slowly baking them so they stay tender, and serving them with a vibrant chicory sauce, which really is what this dish is about.

Chicory is an herbaceous plant whose root is roasted and ground. Many who grew up during World War II associate it with times of scarcity, as it was often used as a coffee substitute. But even after coffee became readily available again, my grandfather, who lived with us, brewed chicory every morning for our family. And it does have a unique bitter, coffee-like flavor that works beautifully in a sauce. Today it is pretty widely available at health food stores and Whole Foods.

This can be served as a main course for four, or as a smaller course for eight. If it's for eight guests, each trout needs to be split in half once they are "sandwiched," before cooking, so that you achieve an attractive, clean cut.

And here's a great trout tip: If you have skin-on fillets, the skin is easily removed with a chef's torch; just run the flame back and forth across it, and it peels right off.

FOR THE CHICORY SAUCE

¾ cup plus 2 tablespoons (210 ml) White Chicken Stock (page 251)
½ ounce (15 g) chicory
10 tablespoons (150 ml) heavy cream
4 tablespoons (60 g) butter
Salt and freshly ground black pepper
Lemon juice

In a saucepan over medium-high heat, reduce the chicken stock by half; add the chicory and cream, and simmer for 3 minutes. Let it rest for 5 to 10 minutes, then strain through a fine-mesh sieve into a clean pan. Reheat to serve, and emulsify in the butter, frothing it with a hand blender if you wish, and seasoning the sauce with salt and pepper and lemon juice.

FOR THE TROUT

4 whole rainbow trout (about 10 ounces/300 g each), halved, filleted, and skinned
Salt and freshly ground black pepper
2 tablespoons soft butter
16 tarragon leaves, cut into ½-inch (1.25 cm) pieces
12 to 20 long chives, blanched and shocked
Red peppercorns, chopped
Fleur de sel

OPTIONAL GARNISHES, BLANCHED AND SHOCKED

8 baby carrots
8 pearl onions
1 cucumber (trimmed)
8 baby turnips
4 baby fennel, cut in half
8 almonds
24 snap peas

Preheat your oven to 275°F (135°C).

Season the trout with salt and pepper. Lay four pieces of trout skin side down on your work surface, and spread the soft butter on top of each. Season with salt and pepper and then place the pieces of tarragon leaves down the center of the length of each. Lay the other half of the fillets on top, skin side up. The goal is to maintain the natural shape of the trout by marrying the fillets, even though the skin has been removed. Line a sheet pan with four layers of parchment paper. This will prevent overcooking the trout and keep it moist. Tie each fillet stack widthwise with the chives to hold them in place for an elegant appearance and place on the prepared sheet pan.

Bake for 5 to 7 minutes. Let them rest a few minutes before serving them with the sauce and garnishing with the red peppercorns, fleur de sel, and your preferred blanched garnishes, if using.

CHORIZO-CRUSTED COD
WITH WHITE BEAN PUREE

Serves 6

I began cooking this at the Ritz, in 2002, where I landed after leaving Jean-Georges. It showcases my culinary heritage and my way of thinking when developing a dish.

In Alsace, we like our food relatively acidic, sharpened with vinegar, horseradish, or mustard. But acidity, like in this sherry vinegar sauce or the spicy chorizo sausage, has to be balanced by the other ingredients—the neutral bean puree, the mild fish, and the rich butter and cream. I love the way the chorizo, which acts like a seasoning coating the cod, brings the fish alive. And while the fish is impressive on its own, this dish is special because of the creamy white beans. You can use the bean technique below anytime you want whole beans or a flavorful puree.

The best way to get nice, thick cod fillets is to buy a 2-pound (850 to 950 g) side of center-cut cod, skinless, then cut the flesh into even, thick pieces. Save and use the trim for the mousseline.

FOR THE CHORIZO COD

6 thick skinless portions of cod fillets,
  cut out from the whole fillet
  (about 4½ ounces/130 g each)
Salt
¼ cup (60 ml) heavy cream
Freshly ground black pepper
8 ounces (250 g) Spanish chorizo, casing
  removed, very thinly sliced

Square off your fillets so that they are a neat, clean shape. You will need about 2¾ ounces (80 g) of cod trimmings to make the mousseline.

Puree the cod scraps and a pinch of salt in a food processor until smooth. With the machine running, slowly pour in the cream through the feed tube. Season to taste with salt and pepper. Divide the puree among the fish, spreading a thin layer on the smooth (skinned) side of each fillet.

Arrange the chorizo slices in overlapping layers on top to look like fish scales or shingles on a roof. Press them down lightly with your fingers to make them adhere to the fish. Carefully flip the fish over onto a parchment paper–lined half sheet pan. Press down on the fillets gently to ensure the chorizo adheres tightly. Cover with plastic wrap and refrigerate to set the chorizo for 45 to 60 minutes.

For a more refined finish, trim the edges of the chorizo straight along the sides of the fish while still on the parchment-lined pan.

  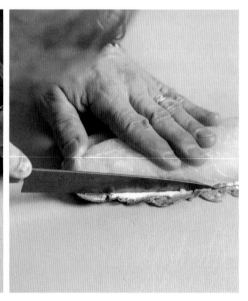

FOR THE SAUCE

1¼ cups (300 ml) White Chicken Stock
(page 251)

⅓ cup (80 g) butter, cut into small dice

7 tablespoons (100 ml) aged Xeres
(sherry) vinegar

Salt and freshly ground black pepper

Bring the stock to a boil in a small sauce-pan. Boil until reduced by two-thirds, then turn the heat to low. Add the butter a little at a time while stirring to emulsify. Repeat with the vinegar. Season to taste with salt and pepper. Keep warm.

TO FINISH THE DISH

7 tablespoons (100 ml) grapeseed
or other neutral-flavored oil

Salt and freshly ground black pepper

⅓ cup (80 ml) plus 3 tablespoons heavy
cream, whipped to soft peaks

1½ cup White Bean Puree (page 327)

½ cup cooked whole white beans

2 tablespoons extra-virgin olive oil

2 tablespoons (30 g) butter

1 small bunch chives, finely chopped

Micro basil, for garnish

Preheat your oven to 350°F (175°C).

Divide the grapeseed oil between two large nonstick ovenproof skillets over medium-high heat. Place the fish, chorizo side down, into the skillets and season with salt. Cook until the chorizo is golden brown, then carefully flip the fillets over. Remove the skillets from the heat and add 3 tablespoons water to each skillet. Be careful; the oil may splatter.

Transfer the skillets to the oven. Bake until the water evaporates and a cake tester or thin-bladed knife slides through the fish with no resistance. When you remove the tester, the metal tip should feel warm. Transfer the fish, chorizo side up, to six serving plates and reserve the cooking oil in the skillets.

While the fish cooks, blend ⅓ cup (75 ml) of the cream into the bean puree until fully incorporated. Whisk the remaining 3 tablespoons cream into the sauce until frothy. Season both to taste with salt and pepper.

Heat the olive oil and butter together in a large skillet over medium heat until the butter melts. Drain the whole beans and add them to the skillet. Cook, stirring, until heated through. Season to taste with salt and pepper, then fold in the chives.

Dollop two large spoonfuls of the bean puree next to the fish and scatter the whole beans all around. Drizzle the sauce generously around the plates and then drizzle on some of the reserved chorizo-cod cooking oil. Garnish with the basil and serve.

OLIVE OIL–POACHED ORA KING SALMON
WITH ROOT VEGETABLE JULIENNE AND HORSERADISH BROTH

Serves 6

This dish started with the horseradish, which grows wild all over Alsace. I was making a horseradish tea to use as a sauce and it was as strong as wasabi. I loved it. I served it simply with vegetables, and people loved the punch of this simple dish. Here I add cream to enrich it, serve it with the same vegetables, and because it's like wasabi, very rare, olive oil–poached salmon.

FOR THE VEGETABLES
Salt
2 leeks, white parts only, julienned
1 carrot, julienned
1 bulb fennel, thinly shaved crosswise
1 medium daikon radish, julienned

Bring salted water to a boil in a pot and blanch each vegetable separately in the water for 1 minute, and then drain and shock in an ice bath. Once they are cold, strain them and put them on a paper towel– or kitchen towel–lined tray.

FOR THE HORSERADISH BROTH
1½ cups (375 ml) heavy cream
2 teaspoons salt
Pepper to taste
Slurry (1 tablespoon cornstarch mixed with 1 tablespoon water)
1 horseradish root, peeled, finely grated (about 2 cups/200 g)

Bring ½ cup (120 ml) water and the heavy cream to a boil in a medium saucepan over high heat, seasoning with the salt and pepper to taste. Reduce the heat and add the slurry. Simmer until thickened. Add the horseradish and allow it to steep for 5 minutes or so. Pour the sauce through a fine-mesh strainer lined with a coffee filter. If not using immediately, chill in an ice bath.

FOR THE POACHED SALMON
1½ to 2 quarts/liters extra-virgin olive oil (enough to submerge the salmon in your pot)
6 pieces salmon, 3 to 4 ounces (90 to 120 g) each
2 teaspoons fleur de sel
Coarsely chopped black peppercorn, or coarsely ground from a mill

Fill a medium saucepan with the olive oil and place a small metal rack on the bottom of the saucepan or line it with two or three layers of parchment paper. Bring the oil to 160°F (71°C). Put the salmon in the oil, making sure the pieces are completely submerged. If the temperature drops, return it to 160°F (71°C). (If you would like your salmon slightly more cooked than rare, bring your oil to a temperature of 170°F/73°C.)

Cook the salmon for 10 to 12 minutes, checking doneness at the 7-minute mark.

Remove the salmon to a plate lined with paper towel and blot the oil from it. Sprinkle each piece of fish with the fleur du sel and the cracked peppercorns.

TO FINISH THE DISH
2 tablespoons olive oil
2 tablespoons Dijon mustard
Salt and freshly ground black pepper

Just before serving, reheat all the vegetables together in a pan with about 2 tablespoons water. When it's warm, add the olive oil and Dijon mustard and toss. Season with salt and pepper to taste.

In a saucepan over medium heat, warm the horseradish sauce. Do not boil, as this will cause it to taste bitter. Remove from the heat, and taste and adjust the seasoning. Use a hand blender to make it frothy.

To serve, place a mound of vegetables in the center of six bowls. Set a piece of salmon on top. Spoon the warm, frothy horseradish sauce around it.

SLOW-ROASTED ORA KING SALMON
WITH COMTÉ CHEESE CRUST, BRAISED BEETS, AND SICILIAN PISTACHIO SAUCE

Serves 6

This is all about the pistachio oil, from the maker J. Leblanc, expensive but so good. It can be bought online. The pristine quality of this oil is what makes this dish a standout. Any compromise in the quality of the oil will take away the integrity of the dish. It is served with very gently cooked, really just warmed, salmon. To cook the salmon so delicately, it's important to put four layers of parchment beneath the fish as a heat barrier. I also make a flavorful "skin" for the fish out of breadcrumbs and cheese dyed with squid ink.

FOR THE VEGETABLES
30 pieces yellow and red beets, cut with a Parisienne scoop (or a melon baller)
⅔ cup (150 g) butter
1 tablespoon salt
18 red pearl onions, soaked in warm water, peeled
¼ cup (60 ml) red wine vinegar

Simmer the beets in 2 cups (480 ml) of water along with the butter and salt until tender, 15 minutes or so.

Simmer the onions in 1 cup (240 ml) of water and the vinegar until the onions are tender, 10 to 15 minutes.

Set aside the cooked beets and onions and rewarm when ready to serve.

FOR THE COMTÉ CRUST WITH SQUID INK
¾ cup (60 g) panko breadcrumbs
4 tablespoons (50 g) butter, softened
2 ounces (60 g) grated Comté cheese (about 10 tablespoons)
2 teaspoons poppy seeds
1 teaspoon squid ink
Salt and freshly ground black pepper

Place the panko breadcrumbs into a food processor and pulse them. Add the soft butter and blend. Blend in the cheese, poppy seeds, squid ink, and salt and pepper to taste. Turn the dough out onto

parchment paper and, placing another sheet on top, roll the dough out until it's about ⅛ inch (3 mm) thick. Freeze for up to 3 days (if holding it in the freezer for more than 8 hours, rewrap the dough in plastic once it's frozen; it will keep for about a month). Remove from the freezer when ready to prepare the dish. Cut the crust to the size of the top of the salmon pieces, or just slightly smaller.

FOR THE PISTACHIO SAUCE
2 cups (500 ml) White Chicken Stock (page 251)
Salt
2 tablespoons (30 g) butter
7 tablespoons (105 ml) pistachio oil, or more as needed
Cayenne pepper to taste
Juice of 1 lemon
Pepper

In a saucepan, simmer the chicken stock with 1 teaspoon of salt until it is reduced by half. Put it in a blender and with the blender running, add the butter and then the pistachio oil until it is well emulsified. Depending on the color and fragrance of the oil, you may want to add more for a better and brighter green color. Just before serving, bring it to a simmer, then take it off the heat. Add cayenne to taste, the lemon juice, and pepper to taste, and froth it up with a whisk or stick blender.

FOR THE SALMON
6 salmon fillets (3 to 4 ounces/90 to 120 g each), skin removed
Grapeseed oil
Salt and freshly ground black pepper
6 tablespoons (90 g) salmon roe
6 borage flowers

Preheat your oven to 275°F (135°C).

Line a sheet pan with four layers of parchment paper. Rub the salmon with oil and season with salt and pepper. Place them on the parchment. Bake for about 8 minutes. Remove them from the oven and turn on your broiler.

Place one squid ink crust on each piece of salmon. Put under the broiler for 30 to 45 seconds.

To finish the dish, divide the beets and onions among six bowls and top with the pistachio sauce. Place a piece of salmon in the center of the bowl. Garnish each with 1 tablespoon of salmon roe and 1 or 2 borage flowers.

LARDO-POACHED MAINE LOBSTER
WITH FENNEL PUREE, CARAMELIZED FENNEL, AND SAUCE AMÉRICAINE "AU POIVRE VERT"

Serves 4

On lobster, I love a classical sauce Américaine, which is typically some mixture of lobster stock seasoned with tomato, wine, brandy, and cayenne, enriched with butter. But I thought I'd give it a little more kick, by treating the lobster more like a steak and creating an au poivre sauce, to which reduced lobster stock is added and enriched. I also gently poach the lobster in seasoned fat so that it's very tender. This recipe calls for long peppercorns, a lovely pepper variety available online. If you grate some and taste it, you'll notice a pleasant numbness on the tongue, more so than with regular black pepper. You can use the substitutes listed at right, but it is worth seeking out.

FOR THE SEASONED LARDO

2 pounds (900 g) highest-quality lardo

2 star anise

1 tablespoon fennel seeds

3 sprigs thyme

6 sage leaves

3 long peppercorns, smashed or broken (use Sichuan or Tellicherry peppercorns, if unavailable)

Set a water bath to 160°F (70°C). Place the ingredients in a zip-top bag, making sure to get all the air out of it, and put it in the water bath for 2 hours. Allow to cool to room temperature, then refrigerate for 1 day.

FOR THE LOBSTER

6 tablespoons (90 ml) white wine (optional)

2 tablespoons Pernod (optional)

4 live Maine lobsters (1½ pounds/675 g each), boiled in salted water for 1½ minutes and deconstructed as on page 281

Combine the wine and Pernod, if using, and fill a syringe with it. Inject each tail and claw with the mixture.

In a pot tall enough to submerge the lobster in the fat, bring the seasoned lardo to 150°F (65°C). Put a small wire rack, five layers of parchment, or an improvised rack made using aluminum foil on the bottom of the pot (the idea is to keep the lobster from touching the hot metal bottom of the pan). Add the lobster and try to maintain 150°F (65°C) as you cook it, 12 to 15 minutes. It's done when it no longer feels squishy and gives gentle resistance to the touch.

FOR THE SAUCE AU POIVRE

1 tablespoon grapeseed oil

1 ounce (30 g) finely minced shallots

1 ounce (30 g) rinsed, minced green peppercorns

4 tablespoons (60 ml) brandy

1 cup (250 ml) heavy cream

Salt and black pepper

Combine the oil, shallots, and peppercorns in a saucepan over medium heat and cook until the shallots are translucent, a minute or so. Add the brandy and flambé it, reducing it by half (to flame a sauce hold a match or a lighter to it; if you have a gas stove you can also tilt the pan so the sauce comes close enough to the flame that the flame will ignite the fumes). Add the cream, bring it to a simmer, and season with salt and pepper.

TO FINISH THE DISH

1 cup (240 ml) Lobster Stock (page 256), reduced to ¼ cup (60 ml)

Garnishes (optional):

Baby fennel, blanched, shocked, and sautéed in a pan until lightly caramelized

Baby artichokes, braised in water or stock until tender

Fennel Puree (page 325)

Baby turnips, blanched, shocked, and glazed with a little chicken stock and butter

Radishes, glazed, prepared the same way as the turnips

Asian pear, peeled and thinly sliced, raw, room temperature

Combine the green peppercorn sauce with the reduced lobster stock and bring to a simmer for 2 minutes to reheat. If you would like to mount the sauce with some butter, or thicken it with slurry, be my guest!

Spoon the hot sauce onto the plates, top with the lobster, and include garnishes of your choice. Here we used caramelized baby fennel, baby artichokes, glazed turnips and radishes, and for a little crunch and freshness, sliced Asian pear.

ROASTED MAINE LOBSTER IN A FOLLY OF HERBS
WITH GREEN ASPARAGUS AND FINGERLING POTATOES

Serves 4

My surname in German, *kräuter*, translates to "herbs." It's fitting because our family's cooking always revolved around our herb garden. We snipped fresh greens in warm weather and then dried whatever was left, including seeds, for the winter. This combination of dried and fresh herbs in a dish of lobster with asparagus and fingerling potatoes celebrates the transition from winter to spring. It's for that time of year when there's enough of a chill to crave the dried herbs in the hot Pernod sauce, but enough warmth still in the air to rain fresh leaves over the whole dish.

For the fresh herb garnish, use the best herbs you can snip from your garden or find at your market. The list below is what I like to use. Vary the proportions depending on the potency of the herbs, using more mild ones and less fragrant ones.

FOR THE HERB SAUCE

1 teaspoon cracked black pepper
1 teaspoon dried thyme
1 dried bay leaf
1 teaspoon ground star anise
1 teaspoon fennel seeds
1 teaspoon rubbed sage
1 teaspoon dried lovage
1 teaspoon salad burnet
½ teaspoon dried lemongrass
½ teaspoon dried mint
½ teaspoon dried marjoram
½ teaspoon dried oregano
½ teaspoon dried rosemary
1 cup (250 ml) White Chicken Stock
   (page 251)
1 slice ginger
8 tablespoons (120 ml) Pernod or Ricard
3 tablespoons (45 g) butter
2 tablespoons whipped cream
Salt and freshly ground black pepper

Combine all of the dried spices and herbs together in a large saucepan and crush them with your hands to blend them together. Add the chicken stock, ginger, and 3 tablespoons of the Pernod. Bring to a boil over high heat and boil for 2 minutes, then remove from the heat. Let steep for 20 minutes.

Meanwhile, bring the remaining 5 tablespoons Pernod to a boil in a small saucepan. Boil until reduced to 2 tablespoons. Stir into the herb stock.

Strain the herb stock through a fine-mesh sieve into a clean saucepan. Bring to a boil and boil until reduced by a third. Reduce the heat to low and add the butter. Mix with an immersion blender until smooth. Stir in the cream, season to taste with salt and pepper, and keep hot.

FOR THE FRESH HERB GARNISH

4 mint leaves
1 lovage leaf
6 parsley leaves
4 cilantro leaves
3 marjoram leaves
10 salad burnet leaves
2 sorrel leaves
4 tarragon leaves
8 chervil leaves
3 oregano leaves

Thinly slice all of the fresh herb leaves and mix well in an airtight container. Refrigerate until ready to use

recipe continues

FOR THE LOBSTER AND VEGETABLES

Salt

8 fingerling potatoes, scrubbed

1 bunch green asparagus, trimmed and peeled

4 live lobsters (1¼ to 1½ pounds/ 675 g each)

4 tablespoons (60 g) butter

7 tablespoons (100 ml) olive oil

Freshly ground black pepper

Preheat your oven to 425°F (220°C).

Bring a medium saucepan of salted water to a boil. Add the potatoes and boil until soft. Drain well. At the same time, bring another saucepan of salted water to a boil. Fill a large bowl with ice and water. Add the asparagus to the boiling water and cook until bright green and crisp-tender. Immediately transfer to the bowl of ice water. When cool, drain well and cut into 2-inch (5 cm) lengths.

Bring a large stockpot of salted water to a boil. Fill a large bowl with ice and water. Immerse the lobsters in the boiling water. Boil for 1½ minutes, then transfer to a cutting board. Break off the claws, holding onto them with a kitchen towel. Transfer the lobster bodies to the bowl of ice water. Return the claws to the boiling water and boil for 7 more minutes. Transfer to the bowl with the ice water. Cool for 5 minutes. Drain all of the lobster very well.

Carefully crack the claws and remove the meat, keeping the pieces whole. Clean the coagulated white protein off the claw meat and reserve the meat. Break the heads off the lobster bodies and reserve for stock. Split the tails in half lengthwise with a very sharp knife and keep the meat in the shells. Remove and discard the central veins of the tails.

Heat two large cast-iron skillets over high heat. Divide the butter and oil between the skillets. When the butter melts, place the lobster tails meat side down in the skillets. Cook for 2 minutes, then flip. Balance the claw meat on top of the tails and baste with the butter-oil in the skillets. Transfer to the oven. Roast until the lobster meat is cooked through, 4 to 5 minutes.

Carefully remove from the oven. With a fork, spike the tail meat and remove from the shells. Season all of the meat to taste with salt and pepper. Reserve the cooking butter-oil for serving.

To complete the dish, divide the potatoes among four serving bowls and smash a bit with a fork. Arrange the lobster tails and claws on top, then scatter the asparagus around the meat. Puree the hot herb sauce with an immersion blender, then spoon all around. Sprinkle the fresh herbs on top, then drizzle with some of the lobster cooking oil-butter. Serve immediately.

GRILLED MAINE LOBSTER
WITH TOASTED CASHEW, BABY CARROTS, AND LOBSTER-GINGER SABAYON

Serves 4

I lived on a farm in land-locked Alsace, so the only lobster I knew was in the cookbooks I devoured as a teenager. You could get lobster, but it was prohibitively expensive. So I wouldn't taste lobster until I was seventeen, toward the end of my time working for my uncle at his restaurant.

I love the charred flavor of grilled lobster and the way it combines with the other elements of this dish: whole baby carrots sautéed then lightly glazed and coated in a cashew crumble, seasoned with an especially flavorful curry powder called Vadouvan (we prefer the Spice House brand), and a creamy lobster-ginger sauce. Lobster can be cooked very gently if you want it to be tender. I also like the good chewy bite of lobster cooked over flames.

FOR THE LOBSTERS
4 live Maine lobsters
   (1½ pounds/675 g each)

FOR THE GRILLING
3 tablespoons grapeseed oil
Salt

To precook the lobsters, blanch them in heavily salted, boiling water for 90 seconds. Remove them from the boiling water; remove the legs and claws, plunge the bodies into an ice bath, and return the claws to the boiling water for 7 more minutes. When the lobster bodies are thoroughly chilled (at least 5 minutes in the ice bath), separate the tail from the body (reserving the carapace and head) and remove the tail meat by cracking open the shell, keeping the meat intact. Using a cake tester or toothpick, slide it through the underside of the tail and gently remove the center vein. Store the tails on ice wrapped in plastic until ready to cook.

Allow the claws to become cool enough to handle but still warm. Snap off the lower pincer, allowing the meat inside to remain connected to the main claw. Crack the claw shell once or twice with a knife, being careful not to damage the meat. Remove the claw meat from the shell, ideally removing the cartilage in the center of the claw. If it remains in the claw, remove it. Clean any white albumen adhering to the meat. Chill the claws in an ice bath.

Remove the knuckle meat from the arms and chill. Once chilled, store the knuckles and claws wrapped in plastic and on ice along with the lobster tails.

FOR THE CASHEW CRUMBLE
2 cups (160 g) panko breadcrumbs
2 tablespoons (12 g) Vadouvan curry
   powder
1 teaspoon (5 g) sugar
Salt
9 tablespoons (125 g) clarified butter
   (see page 201), melted
12 ounces (360 g) raw cashews

Preheat your oven to 275°F (135°C).

Combine the panko, curry powder, sugar, and salt in a bowl. Add the clarified butter and mix until completely and evenly mixed. Pulse the cashews in a food processor until they are coarsely chopped. Mix the cashews and panko together. Spread it on a parchment- or Silpat-lined sheet pan and toast in the oven until golden brown, 10 to 15 minutes. Cool and store in an airtight container until ready to use.

recipe continues

FOR THE BABY CARROTS

12 baby carrots (preferably of varying color, leaving about ½ inch/1.25 cm of stem on each)

2 tablespoons grapeseed oil

Salt and freshly ground black pepper

2 sprigs thyme

1 tablespoon butter

4 tablespoons (60 ml) White Chicken Stock (page 251)

1 teaspoon sherry vinegar

Clean the carrots with an abrasive sponge or peeler, making sure to clean the dirt around the stem. In a sauté pan over low heat, add the oil, then the carrots. Season them with salt and pepper. When the carrots are about half cooked (still crunchy), about 7 minutes, add the thyme and butter. Cook for another 2 minutes, then add the chicken stock and sherry vinegar and reduce it to a glaze, tossing to cover all sides of the carrots. Remove them from the pan and coat them with the cashew crumble.

FOR THE SHALLOT WINE

Generous ¾ cup (200 ml) Chardonnay

1 tablespoon Champagne vinegar

½ teaspoon black peppercorns, cracked

2 sprigs thyme

1 bay leaf

2 ounces (60 g) shallot, sliced

Combine all the ingredients in a saucepan over high heat, bring to a simmer, then reduce the heat to medium low and cook until the wine is reduced by two-thirds. Strain through a chinois. This may make more than the 3 tablespoons (45 ml) called for in the recipe.

FOR THE LOBSTER SABAYON

4 to 5 egg yolks (80 g)

4½ tablespoons (65 ml) White Chicken Stock (page 251)

¼ teaspoon cayenne pepper

1 sheet silver gelatin, soaked in ice water until softened (see Note on page 172)

½ teaspoon salt, plus more for grilling the lobster

9 tablespoons (125 g) butter

2 teaspoons lemon juice

2 cups (500 ml) Lobster Stock (page 256), reduced to 7 tablespoons (105 ml)

1 teaspoon ginger juice (grate ginger on a box grater and press the juice out of it)

Dry sherry

Tabasco

Freshly ground black pepper

Grapeseed oil

Set a water bath to 160°F (70°C). Place the yolks, 3 tablespoons (45 ml) shallot wine, the chicken stock, cayenne, gelatin (squeezed of excess water), salt, and butter in a zip-top bag, making sure to get all the air out of it, and put it in the water bath for 1 hour. Empty it into a container and blend it with a hand blender until it's smooth. Add the lemon juice, lobster stock, and ginger juice and blend again. Season to taste with the dry sherry, Tabasco, salt, and pepper. Put the sauce in an iSi gun with two charges.

To finish the dish, remove the lobsters from the refrigerator 20 minutes before cooking them. Start your grill (we prefer a small Japanese grill with Binchotan charcoal, but a charcoal grill works fine as well). Brush the lobster lightly with grapeseed oil and season lightly with salt. Grill the lobsters gently over medium heat for 7 to 10 minutes, depending on their size, turning every 90 seconds or so to ensure even cooking. Let them rest for 2 to 3 minutes before serving. We shoot the sauce from the iSi gun first onto the plate, set the lobster on top, and garnish the plate with the warm cashews and carrots.

LANGOUSTINE AND DIVER SCALLOPS STUFFED CABBAGE
WITH RED BELL PEPPER, CHIVE, AND CAVIAR COULIS

Serves 6

Stuffed cabbage is very Alsatian. It is a meal built on leftovers, usually from leftover pot-au-feu meat or choucroute garnie—cabbage wrapped around cooked pork or beef, in combination with uncooked meat, such as ground pork, that's seasoned and mixed with bread and eggs.

As should be quite clear by now, I love using cabbage in high-end dishes, and so for this preparation I decided to use the very best langoustines and diver scallops. It's an expensive dish, but it highlights great products. It's either good or it's not. There's no in between with shellfish. I used to make this dish at the Ritz and people would come back just for it.

FOR THE COULIS
3 tablespoons (45 g) butter
2 tablespoons very finely chopped shallot
Salt and freshly ground white pepper
4 tablespoons (40 g) red bell pepper, peeled and finely diced
½ cup (120 ml) Fumet (page 257) or White Chicken Stock (page 251)
3 tablespoons whipped cream
3 tablespoons snipped chives
2 ounces (60 g) Osetra caviar

Melt 1 tablespoon (15 g) of the butter in a small saucepan over medium heat, then add the shallot, a pinch of salt, and white pepper to taste. Stir fast and well for 1 minute, then add the red bell pepper and stir until the shallot is tender and translucent, about 2 minutes. Add the stock and bring to a boil slowly to preserve the pepper's color.

Adjust the heat to maintain a simmer and simmer until the pepper is tender and the sauce has reduced by one-third, about 5 minutes. Reduce the heat to stop the simmering but keep the sauce warm, then add the remaining 2 tablespoons (30 g) butter, whisking to emulsify.

Remove from the heat and season to taste with salt and white pepper. Whisk in the whipped cream and season to taste again. Just before serving, stir in the chives and caviar.

FOR THE STUFFED CABBAGE
Salt
12 large Savoy cabbage leaves, kept whole
8 langoustines, shelled and deveined, tails cut into ½-inch (1.25 cm) pieces
4 jumbo diver sea scallops, tough muscles removed, scallops cut into ¼-inch (6 mm) dice
1 tablespoon (5 g) peeled and finely diced ginger
2 tablespoons (18 g) shallots, very finely chopped
Freshly ground white pepper
Pinch cayenne
8 teaspoons butter, very soft

Bring a large pot of salted water to a boil. Dip in the cabbage leaves, one at a time, until bright green and tender, 1 to 2 minutes. Immediately transfer to a bowl of ice and water. When cold, drain well, then gently pat dry between paper towels.

Combine the langoustines, scallops, ginger, and shallots in a large bowl and stir gently to mix evenly. Sprinkle with salt, white pepper, and a tiny pinch of cayenne. Mix again. Taste and adjust the seasonings.

Put one cabbage leaf on a work surface and cut out the thick white center rib. Crisscross the two leaf halves so that they form a plus sign. Spread 1 teaspoon butter where the two leaf pieces overlap in the center, then arrange a mound of seafood filling (3 tablespoons/45 g) over the butter. Fold the leaves over the filling and tuck in around the filling to completely enclose. Put the stuffed cabbage on a clean, damp kitchen towel and squeeze gently to form into a round shape. Place on a plastic wrap–lined sheet pan. Repeat with the remaining cabbage leaves and filling.

Prepare a steamer with rapidly boiling water. Arrange the stuffed cabbages in the steamer in a single layer. Steam until a cake tester inserted in the center is very hot when you pull it out and touch it against your lip, about 10 minutes. You want the seafood to be cooked through but not dry.

To finish the dish, divide the hot coulis among six serving plates and arrange a stuffed cabbage on top. Serve immediately.

BAKED DAURADE ROYALE
WITH AUTUMN VEGETABLE JULIENNE AND GEWURZTRAMINER OYSTER BROTH

Serves 6

I love daurade royale, a slightly oily fish, for its flakiness and fattiness, so it doesn't dry out when cooked. It's the most refined of the species for its rich, succulent, meaty flavor, similar to pompano or red snapper. It's important that you buy very fresh daurade. The sauce is simple but delicious—reduced Gewurztraminer with crème fraîche and oysters—all over a bed of julienned root vegetables.

FOR THE VEGETABLES

2 cups (240 g) julienned carrots
1 cup (120 g) julienned celery
1 cup (120 g) julienned parsnip
Salt
1 cup (145 g) seeded, julienned cucumber
1 to 2 tablespoons butter
¼ teaspoon cayenne pepper

Blanch the carrot, celery, and parsnip, separately, one at a time, in salted water until tender (a minute or so), then shock in an ice bath. Mix together well, along with the cucumber. When ready to serve, heat all the vegetables in the butter and season with cayenne.

FOR THE OYSTER BROTH

1 (750 ml) bottle dry Gewurztraminer
3 shallots, sliced
1½ cups (375 ml) crème fraîche
Salt
Cayenne pepper
Juice of 1½ lemons
18 oysters, shucked, held in their juice, chopped (you'll need about 6 tablespoons of oyster meat)
2 tablespoons dry vermouth
3 tablespoons parsley chiffonade

In a saucepan over high heat, combine the wine and shallots and reduce the wine by three-quarters. Reduce the heat to medium, add the crème fraîche and reduce by about one-third in volume, to nappé consistency (you should be able to draw a line through the sauce on the back of a spatula). Season with salt, cayenne, and the lemon juice. Set aside.

When ready to serve, reheat the sauce, then add the oysters and vermouth. Stir until the oysters are heated through, about a minute. Stir in the parsley.

FOR THE FISH

3 large fillets daurade, halved (each 3 to 4 ounces/90 to 120 g)
Salt and freshly ground black pepper
Olive oil (about 2 tablespoons)
Cayenne pepper (a pinch per fillet)
¾ cup (180 g) Celery Root Puree (page 326)
1 tablespoon parsley chiffonade
12 to 18 chive flowers

Preheat your oven to 275°F (135°C).

Season the daurade with salt and pepper and drizzle with olive oil. Sprinkle with the cayenne. Cover a baking sheet with three or four layers of parchment to protect it from the direct heat of the metal. Bake for 10 minutes.

While the fish cooks, rewarm the vegetables and finish the broth.

Remove the fish from the oven and let it rest. Put a couple of tablespoons of the puree onto each plate and divide the vegetables among them. Place a fillet on the puree and spoon the broth generously over the fish.

Garnish with the fresh parsley chiffonade and chive flowers and serve immediately.

SLOW-COOKED SABLEFISH
WITH GREEN ONION, GREEN APPLE, COCONUT, AND BASIL-MINT OIL

Serves 6

I discovered sablefish from purveyors here in America who were having trouble selling it. I'd never heard of it before, but I tried it and found it to be fantastic. It's a lot like Chilean sea bass, mild, flavorful, rich, thick, and flakey. It's now become something of a luxury here. This recipe would work with any similar fish, such as the sea bass or cod or even king salmon. The apple, coconut, basil and mint are great vibrant flavors to pair with this fish.

FOR THE WILD RICE
¼ cup (50 g) chopped shallots
2 tablespoons (30 g) butter
½ cup (80 g) button mushrooms, sliced
¾ cup (150 g) wild rice, rinsed under
    cold water
3 cups (720 ml) White Chicken Stock
    (page 251)
Salt and freshly ground black pepper

Preheat your oven to 300°F (150°C).

In a medium saucepan over medium heat, sweat the shallots in the butter until translucent. Add the mushrooms and cook for 5 minutes. Add the wild rice and chicken stock and season with salt and pepper. Bring it to a simmer, cover, and put it in the oven for 1 hour to 1 hour and 15 minutes, stirring occasionally, until tender.

FOR THE GREEN ONION, APPLE, AND COCONUT SALAD
1 Granny Smith apple, cored, skin on
1¾ ounces (50 g) fresh coconut
2 green onions
2 tablespoons julienned ginger
6 basil leaves, julienned
Salt and freshly ground black pepper
3 tablespoons lemon juice (about 1
    lemon)

Cut the apple in wedges, then make paper thin slices on a mandoline. Cut the coconut and green onion on a mandoline into paper-thin slices. In a large bowl, mix the apple, coconut, green onions, ginger, and basil and season with salt and pepper. Toss it all with the lemon juice.

FOR THE SABLEFISH
2 pounds (900 g) sablefish, skin on,
    cut into 4- to 5-ounce (120 to 150 g)
    portions
Grapeseed oil
Fleur de sel
Cracked black pepper

Preheat your oven to 200°F (93°C).

Rub the fish with oil and arrange fish, skin up, on a baking sheet lined with a few layers of parchment paper. Bake until translucent, 20 to 25 minutes, depending on the thickness of the fillet. Remove the skin (if it's well cooked, the skin should come off easily). Season with fleur de sel and cracked black pepper.

FOR SERVING
Basil-Mint Oil (page 233)

Make a bed of the wild rice in the center of each plate. Set a fillet on each. Top with the apple salad and drizzle the plate with the basil-mint oil.

SPICED HAMACHI FILLET
WITH BABY LEEKS AND BLOOD ORANGE–MUSTARD SAUCE

Serves 6

Americans know hamachi mainly through sushi restaurants, where it can often be confused with yellowtail tuna, so I wanted to broaden its uses by serving it lightly cooked with an intriguing spice mixture that features licorice. (I find it amusing that some diners who happily order hamachi sushi will send the fish back, not wanting to eat the fish rare.)

I used to chew on licorice twigs as a boy—they're not powerfully flavored like the candy but rather sweet and elegant. We buy the roots and make our own powder from them. They also make excellent aromatic skewers for grilling meat. You can use licorice already in powdered form, available online. The second star of this dish is the blood orange sauce, which is very acidic to stand up to the strong flavors of this dish. As ever, the fish itself is very gently cooked, seared on the spiced side, then finished for a few minutes in the oven.

FOR THE BLOOD ORANGE–MUSTARD SAUCE

1 cup (250 ml) blood orange juice
½ cup (125 ml) Fumet (page 257)
2 teaspoons Dijon mustard
Juice of ½ lemon
1 tablespoon butter
Salt and freshly ground black pepper

In a medium saucepan over medium-high heat, reduce the orange juice by two-thirds. Add the fumet and bring the liquid back to a simmer. Add the Dijon mustard and lemon juice, then swirl or whisk in the butter. Season with salt and pepper, and let it rest for at least 15 minutes before reheating to serve.

FOR THE FISH

2 teaspoons licorice powder
½ teaspoon ground mace
½ teaspoon ground nutmeg
½ teaspoon ground cloves
½ teaspoon fennel powder
6 portions hamachi fillet (each 4 to 5 ounces/120 to 150 g)
Salt
Cayenne pepper
Grapeseed oil, for sautéing

Preheat your oven to 350°F (175°C).

Combine the licorice, mace, nutmeg, cloves, and fennel powder, and mix until well combined.

Press the flat side of the fillets into the spice powder. Season the rounded side with salt and cayenne.

In a sauté pan over medium-high heat, add the oil. When it's hot, put the fillets in the pan spice side down. Cook for 30 seconds or so—the licorice will caramelize quickly—then flip the fillets, add 3½ tablespoons (50 ml) of water or so to cool the pan, and put the pan in the oven for 3 to 4 minutes.

TO GARNISH

9 baby leeks, white and pale green parts, blanched, shocked, and halved
12 blood orange segments
6 baby fennel, blanched and shocked
2 small Japanese cucumbers, peeled and sliced

Serve in bowls with the reheated sauce and the vegetable garnishes.

MEAT

FREE-RANGE CHICKEN DUO
with Fresh Goat Cheese and Fines
Herbs Emulsion

294

SQUAB AND FOIE GRAS
"CROUSTILLANT"
with Roasted Salsify and
Caramelized Ginger Jus

297

LONG ISLAND CRESCENT
DUCK BREAST
with Black Trumpet Marmalade,
Confit Fleischschnacka, and
Banyuls Jus

301

BEEF TENDERLOIN
"À LA FICELLE"
with Roasted Beets, Bone Marrow
Crouton, and Horseradish Sauce

304

FALLOW VENISON LOIN
with Walnut Crumble,
Seasonal Vegetables, and
Sauce Salmis

306

MAPLE-BRINED BERKSHIRE
PORK TENDERLOIN
with Butternut Squash
Puree, Walnuts, and Mustard-
Curry Jus

309

BEER-BRAISED PORK BELLY
with Sauerkraut, Apple-Ginger
Salad, and Ginger Jus

312

LAMB RACK COOKED
IN A HAYSTACK
with Sweet Potato, Onion
Marmalade, Chickpeas,
and Merguez

314

VENISON LOIN, PHEASANT,
FOIE GRAS, AND BLACK
TRUFFLE PIE

318

LIGHTLY SMOKED
ROASTED BLACK ANGUS
BEEF TENDERLOIN
with Sunchoke Soufflé and
Périgourdine Sauce

320

BRAISED RABBIT LEG
"PAUPIETTE"
with Rosemary-Garlic Stuffing, Wild
Mushrooms, and Chervil Sauce

323

FREE-RANGE CHICKEN DUO
WITH FRESH GOAT CHEESE AND FINES HERBS EMULSION

Serves 4

This is an elegant and efficient way to prepare whole chickens, using all of the bird. If you have access to well-raised birds, this is an especially fine way to celebrate it. I'm going to describe how I would prepare it for four people, but there's no reason you couldn't increase the amounts as needed if you wanted to cook this for a group of six or eight, with one chicken serving two people. This dish requires planning ahead, but if you like to cook and to butcher, this is a satisfying cooking experience and finished dish, with a light cream and herb sauce. Obviously, you could simply ask your butcher to break down the bird for you; you can use a store-bought organic chicken broth; you don't have to make the garlic puree; you can just make the sauce and serve it over sautéed chicken breasts (the goat cheese makes it rich and tangy and silky)—it's all a matter of how much work you want to put into it.

Obviously it's also possible to do the whole thing start-to-finish yourself, butchering the chickens, and using the carcass and trim to make stock (the stock will both be used to cook the chicken and be reduced for the final sauce). This recipe will assume that you have a quart of good chicken stock on hand.

Serve this with a green vegetable such as spinach, a potato puree, or wild rice and a nice vegetable dish, such as cauliflower. It's both rustic and elegant at the same time.

2 chickens, ideally 3 to 3½ pounds
   (1.3 to 1.5 kg) each
Salt and freshly ground black pepper
1 quart/liter White Chicken Stock
   (page 251)

To butcher the birds, remove the leg and thigh pieces. Separate the thigh from the leg (there's a white line of fat that runs over the joint; cut through that and your knife should slip right through the joint). Remove the wing tip and wing flat from the wing, leaving the drumette, and reserve the wing pieces for stock. Remove the breast from the carcass, keeping the wing joint attached. Clean the drumette of its meat, scraping the bone clean for an elegant presentation, often called a supreme cut. Remove the skin from the drumsticks. Chop off the end of the drumstick so that the meat bunches up at the top (if you can, use strong tweezers or pliers to pull as many of the tendons out as possible, which will make this more tender to eat, and leaves the bone clean, again for an elegant appearance).

Season the breasts, drumsticks, and thighs with salt and pepper, wrap, and refrigerate.

FOR THE THIGH STUFFING
1 tablespoon minced shallot
7 ounces (210 g) mushrooms (preferably wild, but button mushrooms are
   fine too)
2 tablespoons grapeseed oil
Salt and freshly ground black pepper
1 teaspoon finely chopped ginger
Several gratings of nutmeg
1 tablespoon chopped chives
1 to 2 tablespoons sour cream

To make the stuffing, in a sauté pan over medium-high heat, cook the shallots and mushrooms in the oil until the mushrooms are tender. Remove them to a cutting board and when they're cool enough to touch, chop them coarsely. Season them with salt and pepper to taste, ginger, and nutmeg. Add the chives and chill completely for 20 minutes. Stir in the sour cream so that the mushrooms hold together. Cover and refrigerate until ready to use.

FOR THE GARLIC PUREE
10 ounces (300 g) peeled garlic
   (from about 3 heads)
Salt

To make the garlic puree, put the garlic in a pan of water and bring it to a boil, to make the garlic mild and soft. If it's very strong garlic, blanch it three times. Press the garlic through a sieve and heat it in a sauté pan with salt to taste until it has a pipeable consistency. Chill it, then put it in a piping bag, preferably with a small piping tip.

Prepare the chicken. Prepare and cook the thighs and drumsticks: Score the insides of the thigh meat. Put them between layers of plastic wrap or parchment and flatten them with a mallet or the bottom of a skillet. Lay them on squares of cheesecloth large enough to enclose the thighs and stuffing on your work surface. Divide the mushroom stuffing among them. Wrap each tightly into a ball and secure the cheesecloth with kitchen string.

recipe continues

Bring your chicken stock to a simmer, add the thighs and drumsticks, and poach them for 15 minutes. You can chill them in the stock if preparing this dish ahead, or remove them to a plate and cover with plastic until you're ready to finish the dish.

Cut a pocket down the length of the breast, starting from the fat end. Pipe the garlic puree into the pocket.

FOR THE SAUCE

2 cups (500 ml) White Chicken Stock (page 251), reduced by three-quarters, to about ½ cup (120 ml)
5 ounces (150 ml) heavy cream
7 tablespoons (105 ml) sour cream
5 ounces (150 g) goat cheese
¼ cup (60 ml) yogurt
Salt and freshly ground black pepper

To make the sauce, bring the reduced chicken stock to a simmer, then whisk in the cream, sour cream, goat cheese, and yogurt. Season with salt and pepper to taste. Set aside.

TO FINISH

3 tablespoons grapeseed oil
¾ cup (180 ml) White Chicken Stock (page 251), warm, plus ½ cup (120 ml) for rewarming the thighs and basting
3 tablespoons chopped parsley
2 tablespoons chopped chervil
1 tablespoon chopped chives

Finish the dish: Preheat your oven to 325°F (165°C).

Rewarm the drumsticks and thighs in chicken stock if needed. Remove the cheesecloth from the thighs.

Sear the stuffed chicken breasts in the oil over medium-high heat for about 2 minutes on each side. Transfer them to a casserole dish layered with four sheets of parchment paper (the paper will prevent the breasts from cooking too fast and will also keep them moist). Add the warm chicken stock, along with the thighs and drumsticks, and put it in the oven for 8 to 10 minutes, until the breasts are just cooked through. Baste the chicken midway through to keep it all moist.

Remove the chicken from the oven, and discard the parchment. (If you wish, you can add any juices into the sauce.) Bring the sauce to a simmer, then put it in a blender with the parsley, chervil, and chives and blend until the sauce is a lovely shade of green and the herbs are chopped. Pour the sauce over the chicken in the casserole and serve family-style.

SQUAB AND FOIE GRAS "CROUSTILLANT"
WITH ROASTED SALSIFY AND CARAMELIZED GINGER JUS

Serves 8

I created this dish when I was at the Ritz after William Grimes, in an otherwise favorable review, said the meat dishes on the menu were a weakness. I worked quickly to get some high-end excellent meat dishes on my menu, and this was a highlight and remains one of my, and my staff's, favorite preparations.

Squab and foie gras are a classical pairing. But how to combine them so this pairing felt new? Because New York is such a melting pot, I thought I'd turn it into a spring roll, or at least use that idea, enclosing the two in a spring roll–like wrapper. Sautéed squab breasts sandwich a generous slab of foie gras, which is wrapped in a cabbage leaf, and then in a sheet of *feuille de brick*, a kind of North African phyllo dough, to give it a crispy shell. I finish this *croustillant* with a caramel-ginger jus and seasonal garnish. (Feel free to use whatever garnish is appropriate given the season and your locale.)

The squab and foie must be thoroughly chilled after being sautéed and before being wrapped, so plan that into your cooking time.

FOR THE CARAMELIZED GINGER JUS

2 tablespoons (25 g) sugar

1 ounce (30 g) ginger, cut into thin slivers then diced

Juice of 2 lemons

6½ ounces (200 ml) Chicken Jus (page 252), heated to a simmer

Salt and freshly ground black pepper

2 tablespoons (30 g) butter

4 tablespoons (60 ml) olive oil

To make the sauce, in a heavy-bottomed saucepan over medium heat, add the sugar. As it begins to melt, tilt the pan so that the sugar coats the bottom of the pan and caramelizes evenly. When it's a nice amber brown, add the chopped ginger and cook until it's dark brown. Deglaze the pan with the lemon juice. Then add the hot jus and simmer it very gently, for 8 to 10 minutes to infuse the sauce with the ginger. Strain through a chinois into a clean pan. Reheat, seasoning it with salt and pepper, then mount the butter into it. Before serving, stir the olive oil into the sauce but don't emulsify it in.

FOR THE CROUSTILLANT

8 whole boneless squab breasts, halved, skin removed

Salt and freshly ground black pepper

6 tablespoons (90 g) butter

4 slices duck foie gras, about 2½ ounces (75 g) each (about the size of the squab breast)

12 large Savoy cabbage leaves, ribs removed

9 sheets feuille de brick (see headnote)

6 tablespoons (150 g) clarified butter, (see page 201), melted

Olive oil

Grapeseed oil, for sautéing

To make the croustillant, season the squab breasts with salt and pepper. In a large sauté pan over medium heat, melt half the butter, then sauté the breasts on both sides just to give them some color, basting with the butter as you do. Remove them to a rack to cool, then refrigerate them until chilled, 30 to 60 minutes.

Put a large sauté pan over medium-high heat. When the dry pan is hot, add the foie gras and sauté until both sides are nicely caramelized but the interior is still cool. Remove to the rack with the squab breasts and refrigerate until chilled, 30 to 60 minutes.

Melt the remaining butter in a large sauté pan over medium heat and sauté the cabbage leaves in batches, making sure that they are well coated with butter (this will help them adhere to each other). Add a few tablespoons of water to the pan as you do (you just want to tenderize them, not color them). Season with salt and pepper, then remove them to a rack or plate to cool at room temperature, 10 minutes or more.

recipe continues

Assemble the packages. Sandwich one piece of foie gras between two breasts. Wrap them in the cabbage leaves to completely enclose them, squeezing them so that they are completely compressed.

Brush the sheets of feuille de brick with the melted clarified butter. Cut four 2-inch (5 cm) strips and reserve, covered by a towel, to seal the finished croustillant.

Enclose each of the cabbage-wrapped packages in one sheet of feuille de brick, folding one end under the rectangle, and the other side over the top.

Wrap each squab block around the center with 2-inch (5 cm) strips to seal into dough-wrapped blocks.

Refrigerate until everything is thoroughly chilled, at least 2 and up to 24 hours.

When ready to cook, preheat your oven to 350°F (175°C).

Remove the blocks from the refrigerator and sauté each package over medium-high heat in the remaining clarified butter, until all sides are crisp and golden brown. Remove them to a rack set in a sheet pan and put them into the oven for 4 to 5 minutes. Allow them to rest 5 minutes (this will finish heating the foie gras through).

TO GARNISH (OPTIONAL)

8 squab legs, thigh bones removed, sautéed until the skin is crisp

8 tablespoons Cabbage Puree (page 325)

8 slices hen of the woods or maitake mushrooms, sautéed

16 baby carrots, peeled and slowly sautéed

2 medium pieces salsify, washed and slowly whole sautéed, then cut on the bias into 2-inch (5 cm) sticks

1 tablespoon pomegranate seeds

4 cippolini onions, sliced crosswise into ⅛-inch (3 mm) slices and sautéed

Micro spinach

Crystal lettuce

Salt and freshly ground black pepper as needed

Halve each block widthwise. Serve with your choice of garnishes and the caramelized ginger jus.

The "croustillant" begins with sautéed foie gras. It is then sandwiched between two seared squab breasts and wrapped in sautéed Savoy cabbage. This package is wrapped in feuille de brick, a North African pastry dough, thin like phyllo dough but sturdy enough that it won't break during the final cooking.

LONG ISLAND CRESCENT DUCK BREAST

WITH BLACK TRUMPET MARMALADE, CONFIT FLEISCHSCHNACKA, AND BANYULS JUS

Serves 6

This is an elaborate main course using three ducks, but if you love to cook and combine multiple elements, it's a great dish. It involves confiting the legs to make a stuffing for the Alsatian snail-shaped pasta *fleischschnacka* (see page 87 for the traditional preparation). The pasta is served with pan-roasted duck breast and vegetables.

I created the topping for the duck breast after watching customers avoid the skin, which can be fatty but has so much flavor. So, to keep this flavor but make it irresistible, I decided to remove the skin from the breast and deep-fry it, then grind it to a paste with black trumpet mushrooms (originally it was truffles, very luxurious), fried shallots, and herbs. We then spread this on the duck where the skin had been, as an intensely flavored component to the dish.

You could save time, of course, any number of ways—buying duck legs already confited or buying the breasts separately, for instance, and that's fine. In any case, it's important that you have crescent duck breasts or moulard magrets (the moulard is a cross between a male Muscovy duck and a female White Pekin duck), which are especially meaty and flavorful and best served medium rare and pink as a steak.

3 whole ducks, between 5 and 6 pounds (2.5 to 3 kg) each

FOR THE DUCK LEGS CONFIT
½ cup (66 g) salt
½ cup (100 g) sugar
2 bay leaves
1 tablespoon juniper berries
1 tablespoon black peppercorns
4 sprigs thyme
½ sprig rosemary
Enough duck fat (from butchering the duck and rendering) and/or lard or olive oil to cover the legs (about 3½ pounds/1.5 kg)
Butter, for sautéing the duck

Separate the legs from each of the ducks where they attach to the carcass. Remove the skin from the breast and reserve for roasting into cracklings. Reserve as much fat and other skin as you can to render for the confit. Remove the duck breasts from the carcass. Reserve the carcass and wings for stock. (Alternately, you could buy six magret breasts and six duck legs separately if you prefer not to do the butchering.)

To make the duck legs confit, combine the salt, sugar, bay leaves, juniper, peppercorns, thyme, and rosemary and mix well to create the cure. Rub the duck legs with plenty of the cure mix. Put them in a container skin side down, cover, and refrigerate overnight.

Preheat your oven to 250°F (121°C).

Wipe the cure from the duck legs and place them in a vessel that will hold them compactly, allowing you to use as little fat as possible. Cover the legs with whatever fat you're using. If you rendered your own fat and don't have enough to cover, add enough olive oil or lard so that the legs are submerged. Cover tightly with a double layer of foil and cook in the oven until tender, 2½ to 3 hours. Cool the legs in the fat.

You'll need the meat from only one or two of the duck legs for this recipe. Save the remaining legs in the fat in your refrigerator—they will keep indefinitely if stored properly and submerged in the fat. Roast or broil until heated through and the skin is crisp. Serve with roasted potatoes and a salad with any of the vinaigrettes (page 77) for a fabulous duck confit meal.

recipe continues

FOR THE CONFIT FLEISCHSCHNACKA

5 ounces (150 g) duck confit meat (from 1 or 2 duck legs), skin removed (save the skin; it will be a component for the black trumpet marmalade to crust the duck breast later)

1 fresh duck liver (about 3 ounces/80 g), chopped (chicken liver would work as well)

½ ounce country bread (about 1 slice), soaked in milk and squeezed dry

1 tablespoon chopped chives

1 tablespoon chopped parsley

1 tablespoon chopped chervil

1 teaspoon Quatre Épices Powder (page 176)

1½ teaspoons Dijon mustard

Salt (not too much; the confit is salty) and pepper

½ recipe pasta dough (page 87)

Egg wash (1 yolk beaten with 1 tablespoon cream or milk)

Combine all the ingredients except for the pasta and egg wash in a bowl and mix until uniformly combined. Taste and adjust the seasoning.

Roll out the pasta dough into thin sheets. You'll need two 5- by 4-inch (12 by 10 cm) rectangles. Cook the pasta sheets in salted boiling water for about 2 minutes. Drain but don't shock them in ice water. When they are cool enough to handle, spread a ¼-inch (6 mm) layer of the stuffing over the sheets of pasta, leaving ¼ inch along one of the 5-inch (12 cm) lengths clean. Brush this strip of pasta with the egg wash. Roll each piece of pasta into a cylinder ending at the egg-washed end, sealing. Wrap each cylinder in plastic, tightening each at both ends, and freeze for up to 1 week. (Freezing facilitates even cutting without changing their shape; so remember to remove them from the freezer about 45 minutes before you want to do the actually cutting so that they aren't completely solid.)

Cut the semi-frozen cylinders of pasta into ½-inch-thick (1.25 cm) discs and reserve until needed.

FOR THE PICKLED RED PEARL ONIONS

18 red pearl onion, peeled and halved

1 tablespoon allspice berries

2 tablespoons honey

½ cup (125 ml) rice wine vinegar

1 bay leaf

Put the onions in a pot, cover with water, bring to a boil, then strain and put into a container.

In a small saucepan over medium heat, toast the allspice, about a minute or so, until it's fragrant, then add the honey and cook until it caramelizes, a couple of minutes. Add the vinegar and bay leaf with ⅓ cup (75 ml) of water. Bring it to a boil and pour the boiling liquid over the onions. Store in the refrigerator overnight before using (these will keep for several weeks, refrigerated).

FOR THE CARAMELIZED APPLES

3 tablespoons sugar

1 apple, peeled and cut into 6 wedges, core removed

Put the sugar in a sauté pan over medium heat. Cook until you have an amber caramel. Add the apple and cook, stirring to coat the wedges with the caramel as they cook. Cook them until they are tender but still have some bite, about 10 minutes. These can be stored in the refrigerator for up to 3 days.

FOR THE TURNIPS

18 baby turnips, peeled
2 tablespoons (30 g) butter
¼ cup (63 ml) White Chicken Stock
   (page 251) or water
Salt
1 tablespoon sugar
1 bay leaf

Trim each turnip. Put them in a pan over medium-high heat with the butter. When the butter is melted, add the remaining ingredients. Cook until the turnips are tender, 5 to 10 minutes. Cool the turnips and set aside until ready to serve.

FOR THE BLACK TRUMPET MARMALADE

1½ ounces (45 g) fried duck skin,
   from the reserved breast skin
Grapeseed oil
3 ounces (90 g) finely minced shallots
1½ ounces (45 g) chopped and blanched
   black trumpet mushrooms
1½ ounces (45 g) almond flour
1½ tablespoons chopped chives
1 tablespoon chopped parsley
Salt and freshly ground black pepper
1 egg white

Preheat your oven to 300°F (175°C).

Put the duck skin on a sheet pan and bake it until browned and crisp, an hour or more.

Coat the bottom of a small sauté pan in the oil. Heat to medium high and fry the shallots until browned, about 2 to 5 minutes. Strain the shallots immediately and allow to cool and crisp.

Using a mortar and pestle, pound the shallot, fried skin, and black trumpet mushrooms until they are all thoroughly mixed to a paste. Add the almond flour, chives, parsley, salt and pepper to taste, and egg white, and mix with the pestle until combined. It can be stored in the refrigerator for 2 or 3 days.

FOR THE BANYULS JUS

¾ cup (180 ml) Veal Jus (page 254)
5 tablespoons (75 ml) Banyuls wine
   (or Madeira or port), reduced by half
2 tablespoons (30 g) butter
Salt and freshly ground black pepper

Combine the veal jus and wine in a small saucepan and bring to a simmer. Swirl in the butter, and season with salt and pepper.

TO FINISH

Salt and freshly ground black pepper
Butter
Juice of half a lemon (about
   1 tablespoon)

To finish the dish: Preheat your oven to 300°F (175°C).

Season the duck breasts with salt and pepper. Cook them in plenty of butter over low heat, basting them as you do, for a minute or so on each side. Put the duck in the oven, basting every 2 minutes and flipping each over as you do.

Remove the duck to a rack and allow it to rest for 5 minutes.

Preheat your broiler.

Meanwhile, sauté the stuffed pasta discs in butter until they're browned on each side. Warm the apples and turnips in a pan with a little butter. Reheat the jus.

Spread the black trumpet marmalade over the top of each breast (about 2 tablespoons/30 g for each breast). Broil for a minute or so, just until the top dries and takes on a lighter color.

Slice each breast widthwise into four thick pieces. Add the remaining components to the plates: the turnips, the pickled onions, and one wedge of apple. Then add the lemon juice to your Banyuls jus, and spoon onto the plate.

4

I call this "a la Ficelle," beef on a string—which often denotes meat cooked by turning on a string over a fire—because in France, one often poaches a piece of beef in a pot of stock that's already cooking; in order to remove it easily one would tie a string to the meat, hanging over the side of the pot. and then you used the string to pull it out of the pot. This is tenderloin very gently poached and served with a horseradish sauce, which is not too different from the rustic Alsatian version on page 94. In fact, this is very much like a refined version of our pot-au-feu. The garnish is up to you, but I highly recommend you don't skip the bone marrow toast (and don't forget that the marrow should soak overnight before being prepared).

FOR THE BEEF

2 (750 ml) bottles dry white wine, such as Riesling, Gruener Veltliner, or Sylvaner
4 sprigs thyme
1 sprig rosemary
1 small onion (80 g), cut into mirepoix
1 medium carrot (75 g), cut into mirepoix
½ stalk celery, cut into mirepoix
Sachet d'épices (3 tablespoons black peppercorns, 4 star anise, 2 tablespoons allspice, 6 cloves, 1 nutmeg, smashed, 1 tablespoon juniper berries, 3 long black Thai peppers, tied together in cheesecloth)
18 ounces (500 g) trimmed beef tenderloin (about 5 inches/12 cm) long, halved widthwise

To prepare the tenderloins, combine the wine, thyme, rosemary, onions, carrots, celery, and sachet d'épices in a saucepan. Bring the wine to a boil, cover, and reduce to a simmer. Cook for 15 minutes, then remove from the heat and allow the spices to steep for another 30 minutes (this can be done a day ahead and refrigerated).

Choose a pan that will accommodate the beef plus a rack or piece of foil placed at the bottom (the goal is to keep the meat from touching the bottom of the pan while also completely covering the meat with liquid).

Add the spiced wine and heat it to 175°F (80°C). Add the meat and bring the temperature of the liquid back up to 175°F (80°C). Maintain roughly that temperature for 20 to 25 minutes, until the tenderloins are medium rare, about 130°F (55°C). Remove to a rack for 5 to 10 minutes to rest. Reserve the cooking liquid to use in finishing the dish.

FOR THE HORSERADISH SAUCE

1 tablespoon butter
5 tablespoons (50 g) finely grated horseradish (or to taste, adding more if you like it spicy)
1 tablespoon sugar
Salt and freshly ground black pepper
Freshly grated nutmeg
1¾ cups (420 ml) beef stock or White Chicken Stock (page 251), reduced by half
1¼ cups (300 ml) dry Riesling, reduced to ⅓ cup (70 ml)
½ cup (120 ml) crème fraîche
Freshly grated nutmeg
Slurry (1 tablespoon cornstarch mixed with 1 or 2 tablespoons water; optional)

To make the sauce: In a saucepan over medium-high heat, melt the butter. Add the horseradish, stirring to cook it, 30 seconds or so. Add the sugar, season with salt and pepper, and cook another 30 to 60 seconds. Add the stock, the reduced Riesling, and the crème fraîche. Bring it to a boil, then reduce the heat to a simmer and cook for 10 to 15 minutes. Finish the sauce with a couple of gratings of nutmeg. If you'd like the sauce to be thicker, mix in the cornstarch slurry as you wish.

TO GARNISH (OPTIONAL)

8 pieces Bone Marrow Crouton (recipe follows)
2 to 3 large heirloom red or yellow beets, wrapped in foil and oven-baked until tender, peeled, and cut in batons
12 to 16 pearl onions, peeled, blanched and glazed
8 small German butterball potatoes, cooked in salted water, peeled and halved

To complete the dish: Slice each tenderloin in half, serving the cut side up of each on a plate with the horseradish sauce, garnishes of your choice, and a bone marrow crouton.

BONE MARROW CROUTON

Makes 8 toasts

6 ounces (180 g) bone marrow, soaked in ice water overnight
Salt and freshly ground black pepper
25 gratings nutmeg
2 tablespoons chopped chives
8 thin slices baguette, toasted
1 clove garlic

While the meat is resting, bring the cuisson, or cooking liquid, to a simmer and poach the marrow in it for a minute or two, just to cook the marrow. Remove it with a strainer, put it in a warm bowl, and season with salt, pepper, and the nutmeg. Stir in the chives. Rub the toasted baguette with the garlic clove. Top the garlic toast with the bone marrow and serve immediately with the beef.

FALLOW VENISON LOIN
WITH WALNUT CRUMBLE, SEASONAL VEGETABLES, AND SAUCE SALMIS

Serves 6

Game is an important part of Alsatian cuisine as it's one of the best parts of the country for hunting venison, hare, and game birds. Many people come to the region specifically to hunt. This dish is all about the venison and a fabulous sauce, which I mount with foie gras rather than butter. It makes a difference, but you can use butter instead, if you wish. The garnish can be whatever seasonal vegetables are best. This dish, with its rich game meat, reminds me of where I come from. We would have had a tougher cut, the shoulder, but for the restaurant I love the venison loin.

FOR THE VENISON

1½-pound (675 g) fallow venison loin or a smaller loin (or 4 ounces/110 g per person)

2 tablespoons toasted, pulverized juniper berries

Salt and freshly ground black pepper

6 to 8 sage leaves

8 ounces (250 g) thickly sliced bacon or fatback

Season the meat with the juniper berry powder, salt, and pepper, and place the sage along the top of the meat. Wrap the venison with the bacon or fatback and secure it with butcher's twine. Refrigerate for at least an hour to allow the seasoning to penetrate the meat.

FOR THE VENISON POACHING LIQUID

2 tablespoons grapeseed oil

1 small yellow onion (3 ounces/80 g), chopped

½ stalk celery, chopped

1 small carrot (2½ ounces/75 g), chopped

Salt

3 sprigs thyme

½ sprig rosemary

1 tablespoon black peppercorns

2 cloves

2 long peppercorns (use Sichuan or Tellicherry peppercorns, if unavailable)

3 star anise

⅓ of a nutmeg, smashed

2 teaspoons allspice berries

1 tablespoon juniper berries

2 bottles (1.5 liters) full-bodied red wine

In a 2-quart/liter saucepan over medium-high heat, add the oil then the onion, celery, and carrot and cook until the onion is tender and translucent. Season with salt and add the thyme, rosemary, black peppercorns, cloves, long peppercorns, star anise, nutmeg, allspice berries, and juniper berries. Pour in the wine, bring it to a simmer, and cook for 10 minutes. Allow the mixture to cool to room temperature. Strain it through a fine-mesh sieve into a clean pan.

TO FINISH THE VENISON

Poaching liquid (reserved from preparing the venison)

Butter as needed, for sautéing

5 or 6 sprigs thyme

1 or 2 cloves garlic, lightly smashed

To cook the venison, bring the poaching liquid to 160°F (71°C) and add the venison. Maintain that temperature for 20 minutes. Remove the meat from the wine, then remove the bacon or fatback and discard it. Pat the meat dry. In a sauté pan over medium-high heat, combine the butter, thyme, and garlic. When the butter froths, sauté the venison in it, basting continuously, until it's medium rare, 3 to 4 minutes. Allow to rest for 10 minutes.

recipe continues

FOR THE SAUCE

1 tablespoon grapeseed oil

1 tablespoon minced shallot

2 teaspoons green peppercorns, rinsed and smashed

1 tablespoon Dijon mustard

2 tablespoons Cognac

½ cup (125 ml) venison jus or Veal Jus (page 254)

1 cup (250 ml) red wine, reduced to 2 tablespoons

Salt and freshly ground black pepper

3 ounces (90 g) soft foie gras terrine (store-bought or see page 180), passed through a tamis or fine-mesh strainer

In a saucepan over medium-high heat, add the oil, then the shallots, and sweat them until they're translucent, then add the green peppercorns and Dijon mustard. Cook for 30 to 60 seconds, stirring. Add the Cognac and cook, stirring and flaming the alcohol. Add the jus and the reduced red wine and bring it to a simmer. Add salt and pepper. Just before serving, return the sauce to a simmer, then remove from the heat and whisk in the soft foie gras.

FOR THE CRUMBLE

5 ounces (150 g) walnuts, toasted and coarsely chopped

4 ounces (120 g) black prunes, minced

1 tablespoon gin

2 tablespoons cornstarch

Salt and freshly ground black pepper

Preheat your broiler.

Combine the walnuts and prunes. Add the gin and cornstarch and stir to mix well. Season with salt and pepper. Lay the mix on sheet tray lined with parchment paper or a Silpat. Broil until golden brown. Flip the mixture to brown the rest of it.

Turn the oven to 275°F (135°C) and bake the mixture for 20 more minutes. Let it cool, then break it apart into a crumble. This will make more than you need, but it keeps well in an airtight container and is a lovely snack to have in the kitchen.

TO GARNISH (OPTIONAL)

Celery root, poached until tender

Cooked chestnuts

Butternut Squash Puree (page 326)

Huckleberry marmalade or cranberry relish

Bok choy, braised in butter until tender

Spring onions, braised in butter until tender

Kohlrabi batons, wrapped in foil and roasted until tender (4 per plate)

Yellow beets, wrapped in foil and roasted until tender, cut into batons (3 per plate)

To serve, when the venison has rested, slice it and serve it on plates with your preferred garnishes and finish it with the sauce and the crumble, about 2 tablespoons (25 g) per serving.

MAPLE-BRINED BERKSHIRE PORK TENDERLOIN

WITH BUTTERNUT SQUASH PUREE, WALNUTS, AND MUSTARD-CURRY JUS

Serves 6 to 8

This is a lovely pork dish, a tenderloin briefly brined with cinnamon and star anise, that's gently cooked, then brushed with a sweet-savory glaze and rolled in nuts and minced guanciale for flavor and crunch. I serve it with Brussels sprouts (also enriched with more guanciale) and a small slab of bacon, since tenderloin is such a lean cut. I love mixing cultures in a dish. I of course became adept at using Asian flavors having worked with Jean-Georges for so long, and the mixture also reflects the melting pot of New York City. A walnut puree joins the walnuts on the pork and it's finished with some fennel pollen crackers. But what really makes this dish stand out is the mustard jus spiced with Thai red curry.

FOR THE FENNEL POLLEN TUILE

1 tablespoon soft butter
Pinch salt
2½ tablespoons all-purpose flour
½ teaspoon maple syrup
2 teaspoons orange juice
½ egg white
½ teaspoon fennel pollen
Fleur de sel
Freshly cracked pepper

Preheat your oven to 300°F (175°C).

Mix the butter, salt, and flour until well combined. Add the maple syrup and the orange juice and stir until well combined. Stir in the egg white to bring it together as a batter. Let the mix rest for about 30 minutes. Spread the batter on a half sheet pan lined with Silpat as thinly as possible. Sprinkle with the fennel pollen, fleur de sel, and pepper. Bake until lightly golden brown, 12 to 15 minutes. Allow it to cool before breaking it into 2-inch (5 cm) pieces, or as you wish.

FOR THE MUSTARD-CURRY JUS

1 small shallot, chopped
1 tablespoon chopped ginger
2 makrut lime leaves
2 tablespoons grapeseed oil
2 teaspoons Thai red curry paste
¾ cup (180 ml) Veal Jus (page 254)
1 ounce (30 g) guanciale, chopped
1 tablespoon butter
1 tablespoon whole-grain mustard
1 tablespoon smooth Dijon mustard
Juice from ½ lime

Combine the shallot, ginger, and makrut leaves in the oil in a saucepan over medium-high heat and cook until the shallots are tender. Stir in the curry paste. Deglaze with the veal jus and bring to a simmer. Strain the sauce through a fine-mesh sieve and add the guanciale. Let them infuse for 5 minutes or so, then blend with an immersion blender and strain again. Whisk in the butter and mustards and season with the lime juice.

FOR THE WALNUT COATING

4 tablespoons (60 ml) Chicken Jus (page 252)
2 tablespoons maple syrup
3 ounces (90 g) finely chopped guanciale, sautéed until tender (¾ cup)
3 ounces (90 g) toasted walnuts, finely chopped

Bring the jus and maple syrup to a simmer in a saucepan. Add the guanciale and walnuts, tossing to combine.

recipe continues

FOR THE BRINED PORK

½ cup (65 g) salt

1 cup (250 ml) maple syrup

1 cinnamon stick

3 star anise

1 tablespoon black peppercorns

2 sprigs sage

2 Berkshire pork tenderloins, cleaned of all fat and silver skins (you should have 1½ to 2 pounds/675 to 900 g), preferably tied with butcher's twine to help it maintain its shape

Butter, as needed for sautéing

4 or 5 sprigs thyme

2 cloves garlic, lightly smashed

¾ cup (180 ml) Butternut Squash Puree (page 326)

¾ cup (180 ml) Walnut Puree (page 327)

Warm Brussels Sprout Salad (recipe follows)

TO GARNISH (OPTIONAL)

6 ounces (175 g) applewood-smoked bacon, cut into cubes or slabs, roasted until tender

Celery root rounds, punched out with a fluted 1¾-inch cookie cutter, and cooked, braised until tender

2 tablespoons violet mustard (mustard made with deep red wine must, found online or in specialty food stores)

12 small cipollini onions, glazed

Microgreens or food-safe flowers

To make the brine, combine the salt, maple syrup, cinnamon stick, star anise, peppercorns, sage, and 1 quart/liter of water in a saucepan and bring it to a boil. Cool the brine at room temperature, then chill it in the refrigerator until ready to use. Add the pork loins and brine them for 1 hour.

To cook the pork, preheat your oven to 275°F (135°C). In a sauté pan over medium-high heat, add the butter, thyme, and garlic. When the butter is hot, add the tenderloins and sauté, basting them with the butter until they're colored on all sides. Put the pan in the oven and cook for about 10 minutes, until the pork is medium rare, about 130°F to 135°F (55°C to 57°C). Allow it to rest for 5 minutes.

Brush the pork with the mustard-curry jus and roll it in the nut mixture. Slice and serve on a spoonful of the butternut squash puree and a thin line of walnut puree. Place the Brussels sprouts, bacon, and remaining garnishes along it, if using. Finish the plate with the mustard-curry jus.

WARM BRUSSELS SPROUT SALAD

2 ounces (60 g) Ibérico ham or guanciale, minced

2 teaspoons grapeseed oil

2 tablespoons minced onion

1 tablespoon brunoised (very finely diced) carrot

1 tablespoon brunoised (very finely diced) celery

12 Brussels sprouts, trimmed and thinly sliced

Salt and freshly ground black pepper

Sherry vinegar

Sauté the ham or guanciale in the oil over medium-high heat. When it has begun to release its fat add the onion, carrot, and celery and sauté briefly, then add the Brussels sprouts and sauté until tender, 1 to 2 minutes. Season with salt, pepper, and sherry vinegar.

BEER-BRAISED PORK BELLY
WITH SAUERKRAUT, APPLE-GINGER SALAD, AND GINGER JUS

Serves 8

Pork belly with sauerkraut is practically a national dish in Alsace, and this is the upscale Alsace-Comes-to-New-York version: crispy skinned pork belly, enlivened with a ginger glaze, served on a bed of sauerkraut, and topped with a tangy, tart apple-ginger salad dressed with a lemon vinaigrette.

FOR THE BRINED PORK BELLY

1 cup (200 g) sugar

1 cup (132 g) salt

1 teaspoon juniper berries

2 teaspoons black peppercorns

4 sprigs thyme

2 bay leaves

½ teaspoon red pepper flakes

1 Granny Smith apple, cut into 8 slices, seeds removed

1 teaspoon coriander seeds

One 3-pound (1.35 kg) slab skin-on pork belly (preferably Berkshire)

Combine all the ingredients except the pork belly in a stockpot with 2 quarts/liters water, bring it to a boil, and stir until the sugar and salt have dissolved. Allow it to cool to room temperature, then refrigerate it until chilled. In a nonreactive container that will allow the pork to be completely submerged, combine the brine and the pork, weighing the pork down with a plate if necessary. Refrigerate for 36 hours.

TO COOK THE PORK

Grapeseed oil, for sautéing

3 quarts/liters dark beer

2 teaspoons black peppercorns

5 sprigs thyme

2 bay leaves

Preheat your oven to 350°F (175°C).

Remove the pork belly from the brine and pat it dry.

In a Dutch oven large enough to contain the pork in one layer (you can halve the pork if necessary) over medium-high heat, add enough oil to coat the bottom. When it's hot, add the pork belly and sear it on all sides until golden brown.

Remove the pork belly and deglaze the pot with the dark beer. Bring the beer to a boil and add the peppercorns, thyme, and bay leaves. Add the pork belly skin side up. Cover the pot and braise it in the oven for 3 hours or until fork tender. Remove the pork belly and place it skin side up on

a half sheet pan lined with a parchment paper. Put a piece of parchment on top, and place a second sheet pan on top, weighing it down with several cans so that the pork cools in a uniform shape. Refrigerate overnight.

Strain the braising liquid and refrigerate this as well.

When the pork is thoroughly chilled, divide it into equal portions (they should be between 3 and 3½ ounces/80 and 100 g each).

FOR THE GINGER JUS

Grapeseed oil, for sautéing

3 teaspoons peeled, minced ginger

1½ teaspoons minced shallot

½ cup (125 ml) balsamic vinegar

3 cups (750 ml) Chicken Jus (page 252)

3 cups (750 ml) reserved braising liquid from the pork belly

2 teaspoons honey

½ teaspoon sweet soy sauce

Slurry (2 tablespoons cornstarch mixed with 2 tablespoons water), as needed

1 tablespoon butter

In a saucepan over medium-high heat, add enough oil to coat the bottom of the pan. When the oil is hot, sauté the ginger until it is lightly caramelized (careful not to burn it). Lower the heat to medium, add the shallots, and cook them until they are translucent. Deglaze the pan with the vinegar and reduce until almost all the liquid has evaporated, then add the jus and braising liquid. Bring the liquid to a simmer and cook for about 40 minutes, then strain through a fine-mesh sieve into a clean saucepan. Return the liquid to a simmer and cook until it has reduced to a glaze consistency (about 1 cup/240 ml). Whisk in the honey and sweet soy sauce. Adjust the consistency with the slurry if necessary—it should have a good nappé consistency (you should be able to draw a line through the sauce on the back of a spatula). Whisk in the butter to finish the jus. The jus can be refrigerated or kept warm until needed.

FOR THE APPLE-GINGER SALAD AND VINAIGRETTE

2 tablespoons lemon juice

Salt and freshly ground black pepper

6 tablespoons (90 ml) olive oil

1 Granny Smith apple, seeded and julienned

1 (2-inch/5-cm) piece of ginger, peeled and cut in fine julienne

1 cup (40 g) loosely packed tatsoi

To make the vinaigrette, in a mixing bowl, add the lemon juice and season with salt and pepper. While whisking continuously, add the oil in a thin stream.

In a separate bowl, toss the julienned apple, ginger, and tatsoi. Dress with the lemon vinaigrette.

TO FINISH THE DISH

Grapeseed oil, for sautéing

Salt

3 cups (700 g) sauerkraut (page 60)

3 tablespoons butter

Preheat your oven to 350°F (175°C).

Put a heavy skillet over medium-high heat. When it's hot, add enough oil to coat the bottom of the pan. When the oil is hot, season the pork belly with salt, add it to the pan skin side down, and cook until the skin is crisp. Transfer the pork belly pieces to a tray or sizzle platter and put them in the oven for 10 minutes, or until heated through.

In the meantime, heat the sauerkraut with some butter in a pan, taste, and adjust the seasoning. Reheat the ginger jus.

When the pork belly is heated through, brush each piece with the ginger jus.

Place a line of sauerkraut on one side of each dinner plate. Place a piece of glazed pork belly on the other side, leaving about 1 inch (2.5 cm) in between, where you will drizzle the ginger jus. Finish with the apple-ginger salad.

LAMB RACK COOKED IN A HAYSTACK
WITH SWEET POTATO, ONION MARMALADE, CHICKPEAS, AND MERGUEZ

Serves 6

On the farm, cooking with hay is an old and common practice, so bringing this practice to Manhattan's fine-dining scene is a pleasure for me. We light the hay on fire, so that when we present the hay-wrapped lamb to the table, smoke fills the dining room with its fragrance. We even infuse the jus with hay. (In this recipe, I only call for veal jus. But at the restaurant we would roast lamb bones and simmer them in the veal jus for 20 minutes, then strain them through a chinois.) I think this deepens and helps define the lamb's flavor. We get our hay from an organic farmer at the Union Square Greenmarket. But you can buy it online (or even at pet stores—though you need to find organic hay).

We use cedarwood sheets to wrap the hay around the lamb. It's an effective method and makes for an appealing, natural-looking presentation in the dining room. The sheets are also available online. But you could tie the hay and lamb together using parchment paper, if you wanted to instead. The wrap insulates the meat from the oven's heat, finishing the cooking very slowly.

We remove every other bone in the rack for easier eating and presentation, but you could take the lamb off the bones entirely if you wanted, or just leave it as you get it from your butcher.

2 racks of lamb, cleaned and frenched (this can be done by your butcher, or see Note)

Salt and freshly ground black pepper

4 tablespoons (60 g) butter

1 bay leaf

Small bunch thyme

4 or 5 cloves garlic, lightly smashed

Organic hay (about 8 big handfuls)

1 cup (250 ml) White Chicken Stock (page 251)

3 cedarwood sheets or spruce-wood sheets (you'll need 2 but they sometimes break)

Butcher's twine

¾ cup (180 ml) Butternut Squash Puree (page 326)

Note: To French a lamb rack means to remove the layer of muscle and fat that extends from the chop to the end of the rib bones, and to clean those bones for an elegant appearance.

With a boning or paring knife, remove the top cap of muscle covering the chops by slicing along the seam and pulling away fat as you go. Make a crosswise cut an inch or so above the meat all the way across the fatty top side of the rib bones. Slip your blade under the crosswise cut, against the bone, and slice off the rectangular layer of fat, which should pull away from the ribs easily. Remove the strips of meat between the rib bones by cutting along the inner edges of the bones until you reach the crosswise cut. With a paring knife, carefully scrape each bone from the meat downward to remove the sinew and any remaining fragments of meat to obtain a clean white bone.

Season the lamb with salt and pepper. Sear in a sauté pan with the butter, bay leaf, thyme, and garlic, then cool. Put the entire contents of the pan into a zip-top bag with a big handful of hay and the chicken stock. Hold the bag under water to remove all the air and zip it shut. Using a sous vide machine, or carefully monitoring temperature on your stovetop, cook the lamb in a 135°F (57°C) water bath for 2½ hours and shock in an ice bath. Enclose the racks of lamb in hay, wrap them in the sheets of cedarwood, and then secure the package with butcher's twine. Chill until ready to finish the lamb on the stovetop.

FOR THE PEARL ONION MARMALADE

2 tablespoons (30 g) butter

4 ounces (120 g) red pearl onions, thinly sliced

2 teaspoons (9 g) brown sugar

2 tablespoons Madeira

2 teaspoons sherry vinegar

1 tablespoon (4 g) chopped toasted Marcona almonds

In a saucepan over medium-high heat, add 1 tablespoon of the butter then the onions, and sauté the onions until tender, a few minutes. Add the brown sugar and stir until it's mixed in, then add the Madeira and cook until most of the moisture has evaporated. Stir in the remaining butter to glaze the onions and finish them with the sherry vinegar. Fold in the almonds.

recipe continues

FOR THE ROASTED SWEET POTATOES

2 large sweet potatoes

Grapeseed oil, as needed

Salt

3 tablespoons butter

3 tablespoons hazelnut vinaigrette
   (2 parts hazelnut oil, 1 part sherry
   vinegar, whisked together)

Fleur de sel, as needed

Preheat your oven to 350°F (175°C).

Prick the outside of the sweet potatoes then lightly coat them in oil. Season with salt and roast until tender, about 1 hour. When they're cool, peel them and cut six ½-inch (1.25 cm) slices from their center. The remaining potato could be used to make puree, following the last steps for the Butternut Squash Puree (page 326).

FOR THE CHICKPEAS

½ cup (90 g) dried chickpeas, soaked
   in plenty of cold water overnight
   (or 1 cup/180 g good-quality canned
   chickpeas)

½ small onion

½ small carrot

1 bay leaf

Salt and freshly ground black pepper

2 to 3 tablespoons sherry vinegar

8 ounces (227 g) loose merguez or spicy
   Italian sausage, cooked

3 tablespoons chopped chives

Zest from 1 lemon

Drain the chickpeas, put them in a pot, and cover with water. Add the onion, carrot, bay leaf, and a healthy pinch of salt. Bring to a boil, then reduce to a simmer and cook until tender, 30 to 60 minutes. Season with more salt and the pepper as needed. Allow the chickpeas to cool completely in the cooking liquid, then strain, place them in a bowl, and toss them with the sherry vinegar. You can keep these stored in airtight container in the refrigerator for up to 2 days before serving.

FOR THE RED WINE–HARISSA VINAIGRETTE

¼ teaspoon minced garlic

1 teaspoon Dijon mustard

¼ teaspoon Aleppo or Espelette pepper

½ teaspoon harissa paste

¼ teaspoon herbes de Provence

4 tablespoons (60 ml) red wine vinegar

Salt and freshly ground black pepper

1 tablespoon olive oil

3 tablespoons grapeseed oil

Squeeze of lemon juice

Combine the garlic, mustard, Aleppo pepper, harissa, herbs de Provence, and vinegar and a pinch of salt. Whisk everything together to dissolve the salt. Then stream in the olive and grapeseed oil and whisk together again to make the vinaigrette. Season with lemon juice to taste. Check seasoning and add more salt and pepper if needed.

The lamb is lightly seared in a pan, then basted with butter, a bay leaf, thyme, and garlic. After it has cooled, it is packed in a ziptight bag with the same aromatics and a handful of organic hay, cooked sous-vide at 135°F (57°C) for 2½ hours, and then shocked in an ice bath.

FOR THE JUS TRANCHE (BROKEN JUS)

½ cup (125 ml) Veal Jus (page 254)
1 small handful organic hay
Salt and freshly ground black pepper
2 tablespoons butter
½ bunch thyme
3 cloves garlic, lightly smashed
2 tablespoons olive oil
Juice of ¼ lemon

Heat the jus over medium-high heat. To infuse it, add the hay and bring it to a simmer. Turn off the heat, let it steep for 20 minutes, and then strain. Season with salt and pepper to taste.

To finish the dish, preheat your oven to 300°F (150°C).

Bring the chilled lamb to room temperature on a baking sheet. Place in the oven for 30 to 40 minutes, until a cake tester inserted into the center feels warm on the bottom of your lip. Remove from the oven. (At this point, in the restaurant, we embed the lamb in hay on a platter and light the hay on fire so that it smokes fragrantly and present it to our guests before slicing and serving.)

Remove the lamb from the cedar and the hay. Brush off any hay that remains. In a sauté pan with the butter, sauté the lamb to brown it. Add several sprigs of thyme and a few smashed cloves of garlic. Cook and baste it for another 5 to 10 minutes, depending on the size of the eye, until the lamb is browned and cooked. Allow it to rest for 10 to 15 minutes before slicing. Reserve the butter from the pan.

Reheat the jus. Finish the jus with the browned butter from the pan you finished the lamb in. Add the olive oil, and stir it in.

Reheat the merguez sausage in a pan, then add the chickpeas. When they're warm, dress them with the chives, zest of the lemon, and red wine–harissa vinaigrette.

Sear the sweet potato discs in butter until nicely caramelized. Serve them brushed with the hazelnut vinaigrette and sprinkled with fleur de sel, then topped with the pearl onion marmalade. Serve the chickpea-sausage salad on the side.

Spoon some warm puree onto the plates. Slice and serve the lamb. Just before serving, add the lemon juice to the lamb jus and divide the jus among the plates. Be careful not to overwhisk the jus.

We add water to the hay to soften it up. To finish the lamb, we wrap the whole thing in hay, held together by a thin sheet of softened cedar, and gently heat it in the oven. Just before presenting it to the guest, we torch the hay to create a smoking effect, which turns heads in the dining room.

VENISON LOIN, PHEASANT, FOIE GRAS, AND BLACK TRUFFLE PIE

Serves 8

This is a very elegant presentation of a peasant-style dish, a meat pie. But it reminds me of when I was a teenager and trying to teach myself to cook by learning how to make *pâté en croûte*, those elegant French pâtés encased in a gorgeous, often ornately decorated crust. Here I combine pheasant breasts and venison, bound with a pheasant and mushroom mousseline made from the pheasant legs. We make our own puff pastry dough, with loads of butter, but you can find good-quality puff pastry at your local grocery. And, of course, a traditional pâte brisée dough would be fine as well. Use two 5- to 6-inch-diameter (12 to 15 cm) round molds, about 3½ inches (8.5 cm) tall. We use aluminum cans cut to the size we need—they make great molds! This is delicious and juicy on its own because of the foie gras, but it's especially lovely served with a jus or a mushroom cream sauce. You also might serve it on cooked spinach, squash puree, or with a small herb salad on the side.

FOR THE PHEASANT-MUSHROOM MOUSSELINE

Meat from 2 pheasant legs, trimmed of sinew, about 7 ounces (210 g), well chilled

1 egg white

½ cup (125 ml) heavy cream

2 ounces (120 g) white button mushrooms, diced

3½ ounces (105 g) black trumpet mushrooms, chopped

2 tablespoons (30 g) butter

2 tablespoons (18 g) chopped shallot

1 tablespoon chopped chervil

Salt and freshly ground black pepper

Combine the meat and the egg white in a food processor and blend until puréed. With the blade running, add the cream in a steady stream. Pass the mixture through a tamis and refrigerate.

Separately, sauté the button mushrooms and trumpet mushrooms in the butter with the shallot. Remove them from the heat and stir in the chervil. Season with salt and pepper. Refrigerate until the mushrooms are thoroughly chilled. Stir them into the chilled mousseline and season to taste.

FOR THE PÂTÉ

18 ounces (540 g) puff pastry

Egg wash (1 egg yolk mixed with 1½ teaspoons water)

Dried beans, for blind baking

8 large savoy cabbage leaves, blanched, shocked, and thoroughly dried

1 pheasant breast, cut into eight ¼-inch (6 mm) slices on the bias, lightly pounded to a uniform thickness

1 pound (455 g) venison loin, cut in eight ¼-inch (6 mm) slices, lightly pounded to a uniform thickness

7 ounces (210 g) foie gras, cut into eight thin slices

Salt and freshly ground black pepper

1½ ounces (45 g) black truffle, cut into eight thinly sliced pieces

Preheat your oven to 325°F (163°C).

Measure the circumference of your mold and cut two pieces of the dough that you can line the edges of your molds with. Use your mold to stamp out two circles of dough that will fill the bottoms of your molds. Line the two molds on the sides and bottoms with pastry. Brush the bottoms with the egg wash and connect the bottom dough pieces to the dough lining the edges of the molds. Dock the pastry with a fork. Line the molds with parchment and fill with dried beans. Bake them for about 15 minutes, then remove the paper and beans, and continue baking until the pastry is golden brown. Remove from the oven and let them cool.

Raise the temperature of the oven to 375°F (190°C).

Line the molds with the savoy cabbage, leaving plenty hanging over the edges, so that there will be enough extra cabbage to fold over the top after the mold is filled. Spread a thin layer of the mousse on the bottom of each mold. Season the pheasant, venison, and foie gras with salt and pepper to taste. Place a piece of pheasant breast on the mousse, and spread another layer of the mousseline on the pheasant. Put down a layer of foie gras, and top with a truffle. Spread more mousseline and repeat the layers until the pastry shell is filled. Top with the truffle slices. Fold the savoy cabbage over the top of the mold. Brush the edge of the pastry shell with the egg wash and top the pie with another layer of puff pastry. Cut a small hole in the top of the pie and decorate it as you wish.

Bake for 23 to 25 minutes, until golden brown. Allow them to rest for 15 minutes before cutting the pies into quarters and serving.

LIGHTLY SMOKED ROASTED BLACK ANGUS BEEF TENDERLOIN
WITH SUNCHOKE SOUFFLÉ AND PÉRIGOURDINE SAUCE

Serves 8

I love to serve venison in fall and winter, but even after the season has passed I miss it. So I thought, how can I achieve the effect of game using beef? I decided to lightly smoke the beef, which gives the meat a similar gamey, complex flavor. I serve it with sunchokes, which I love. Though they are so ubiquitous in Alsace, many of the older generation won't eat them because they're reminders of wartime shortages. But I bet even they wouldn't be able to resist them in this creamy soufflé. And the dish is finished with a classic sauce *périgourdine*, a veal stock–based sauce, flavored with the peelings of black truffle, which I love, in part, for the way it uses trim from the valuable truffle to such great effect. (A note about buying truffle jus. The label should include the Latin name for the truffle, *Tuber melanosporum*, which is the only way to know if it's true truffle juice, not a chemical substitute.)

I like to give the beef a coating of smoke, though without cooking it. You can use a smoking gun and smoke the beef in a container covered with plastic wrap or use a stovetop smoker, being careful not to overheat the beef.

FOR THE BEEF

1¾ pounds (800 g) black Angus beef tenderloin, trimmed of all sinew
Salt and freshly ground black pepper
Butter, for sautéing

Remove the tenderloin from the refrigerator at least an hour before smoking. Pat it dry and season it with salt and pepper. Smoke the loins for 40 minutes at room temperature. Wrap the loins with plastic immediately after that and refrigerate overnight.

FOR THE SOUFFLÉ

13 ounces (390 g) sunchokes, peeled and chopped
Half-and-half, as needed (enough to cover the sunchokes)
½ cup (125 ml) grapeseed oil
¾ cup (200 ml) heavy cream
1 cup (250 ml) milk, plus 4 ounces (120 ml)
1¼ teaspoons (5 g) carrageenan
2 teaspoons (4 g) agar
1 teaspoon salt

In a saucepan over medium heat, add the sunchokes and enough half-and-half to cover them. Simmer until they're tender. Puree them in a food processor, then pass them though a tamis or fine-mesh strainer.

In a saucepan over high heat, combine a generous ½ cup (130 ml) water with the oil, cream, and 1 cup (250 ml) of the milk. Bring it to a boil. Put the carrageenan and agar in a blender. Pour the hot liquid over them and blend. Put the mixture back in the pot and whisk in the remaining milk and the salt.

Whisk in ¾ cup (180 g) of the sunchoke puree.

Reheat when ready to use, then prepare an iSi canister with one charge.

FOR THE SAUCE

½ cup (125 ml) Madeira
1 cup (250 ml) port wine
2 tablespoons (30 g) butter
2 tablespoons (18 g) minced shallot
½ cup (125 ml) truffle jus, reduced to ¼ cup (60 ml)
¾ cup (180 ml) White Veal Stock (page 253)
3 tablespoons (40 g) finely chopped truffle (or truffle peelings)
Salt and freshly ground black pepper
Lemon juice
1 ounce (30 g) foie gras terrine (store-bought or see page 180)

Mix the Madeira and port in a saucepan and reduce it by three-quarters.

In a saucepan, combine the butter and shallots over medium-high heat and cook the shallot until it's tender. Add the truffle jus and bring the liquid to a boil. Add the veal stock and simmer to reduce to a sauce consistency. Add the chopped truffle. Season it to taste with salt, pepper, and lemon juice. Whisk in the foie gras. Keep warm or reheat when ready to serve.

FOR THE PANCETTA CRISPS

16 thin slices pancetta

Preheat your oven to 275°F (135°C).

Put the pancetta on a sheet pan lined with parchment paper. Cover the pancetta with another layer of parchment and put another sheet pan on top. Bake for 18 to 20 minutes or until the pancetta is crisp. These can be stored in an airtight container for 2 to 3 days.

To finish the dish, melt enough butter to coat a large sauté pan. Cut the meat into eight 3½-ounce (100 g) portions. Season them with salt and pepper. Sauté them, basting them with the butter, until they're medium rare, 130°F (55°C). Remove them to a rack to rest.

On each plate, fill a 4 by 2-inch (10 by 5 cm) ring mold halfway with the soufflé mix from the ICI canister. Let it rest for 2 minutes before removing the ring. Set the cooked filet on top of the soufflé and lay a pancetta crisp on the edge of it. Finish with the sauce.

BRAISED RABBIT LEG "PAUPIETTE"

WITH ROSEMARY-GARLIC STUFFING, WILD MUSHROOMS, AND CHERVIL SAUCE

Serves 6

My grandfather raised rabbits, usually about three hundred at a time. So we'd eat rabbit once a week. It was almost like roast chicken is here. I love rabbit and think it's an underused meat. This is a more elegant preparation, worthy of fine dining, but if you love to cook, eminently worth making at home. The legs are boned and filled with a rabbit farce, or stuffing, then braised, and served with mushrooms. It's a perfect fall dish.

8 rabbit legs, boned, soaked for 1 hour in an ice bath (to help them stay moist)

5½ ounces (165 g) fatback

Salt

2 small cloves garlic, smashed, and 1 clove minced

1 tablespoon finely chopped fresh rosemary

Pepper

15 gratings nutmeg, or to taste

6 tablespoons (90 ml) grapeseed oil

6 tablespoons (85 g) butter, plus more for basting the legs

2 medium shallots (1½ ounces/40 g), chopped

2 cups (500 ml) dry white wine

10 ounces (300 g) seasonal mushrooms (such as chanterelles, button mushrooms, black trumpets, oysters, or porcinis), cleaned

2 cups (500 ml) White Chicken Stock (page 251)

¾ cup (180 ml) heavy cream (optional)

Slurry (2 tablespoons cornstarch mixed with 2 tablespoons water)

2 tablespoons minced chervil

First make the farce (stuffing): Take 2 legs and pat them dry (the boned meat should weigh about 8 ounces/220 g). Combine the meat with the fatback and 2 teaspoons of salt. Pass it through the small die of a meat grinder. Put the ground meat in a bowl on ice. Add the rosemary and 30 grinds of black pepper. Stir well to keep combined. Keep it stored on ice or in the refrigerator while you prepare the rest of the legs.

Preheat your oven to 350°F (175°C).

Remove the remaining legs from the ice bath and pat them dry. Place them between parchment or plastic wrap, and pound them to a uniform thickness. Season with salt and pepper.

Put the farce (about 2½ tablespoons/50 grams per portion) into the center of the rabbit legs. Roll them into balls and tie them with butcher's twine.

In a Dutch oven over medium-high heat, add the grapeseed oil. When it's hot, sauté the stuffed legs until they're browned on all sides, a couple of minutes per side, adding a few tablespoons of butter as you do and basting them with it. Cover and put them in the oven for 15 minutes. Remove them to another oven-proof vessel, lower the oven temperature to 220°F (105°C), and keep them warm there while you finish the dish.

Pour off excess fat from the Dutch oven and put it over medium heat. Add 6 tablespoons (85 g) butter and the shallots, and cook the shallots until they're translucent. Add a little of the wine to deglaze the pan, and when it has cooked off, add the mushrooms and sauté until they begin to release their liquid. Season them with salt. Add the remaining wine and reduce it by half. Then add the stock and reduce it by half. Add the cream (if using). Bring to a simmer for a couple minutes. Taste for seasoning and adjust as necessary. Thicken the sauce with the cornstarch slurry as desired (the sauce should remain fairly loose).

FOR THE POTATOES

8 ounces (225 g) small fingerling potatoes

Salt

6 tablespoons (90 g) butter

Zest from 1 lemon

2 teaspoons minced parsley

Put the fingerling potatoes into a saucepan, cover with cold water, and add a hefty four-fingered pinch of salt. Put them over high heat and bring to a boil, then reduce the heat to a simmer and cook until tender, about 15 minutes.

Drain the potatoes. Slice the larger ones in half. Small ones can be left whole. Cover and keep warm until ready to serve.

To finish the dish, melt a few tablespoons of butter in a sauté pan and reheat the potatoes. Add the lemon zest and parsley just before serving.

Remove the rabbit from the oven, and remove the string. Cut each ball into 4 or 5 slices.

Add the chervil to the mushrooms. Spoon the mushrooms and plenty of the sauce into six deep plates or shallow bowls. Arrange the reheated potatoes around the mushrooms. Put a sliced stuffed leg on the mushrooms.

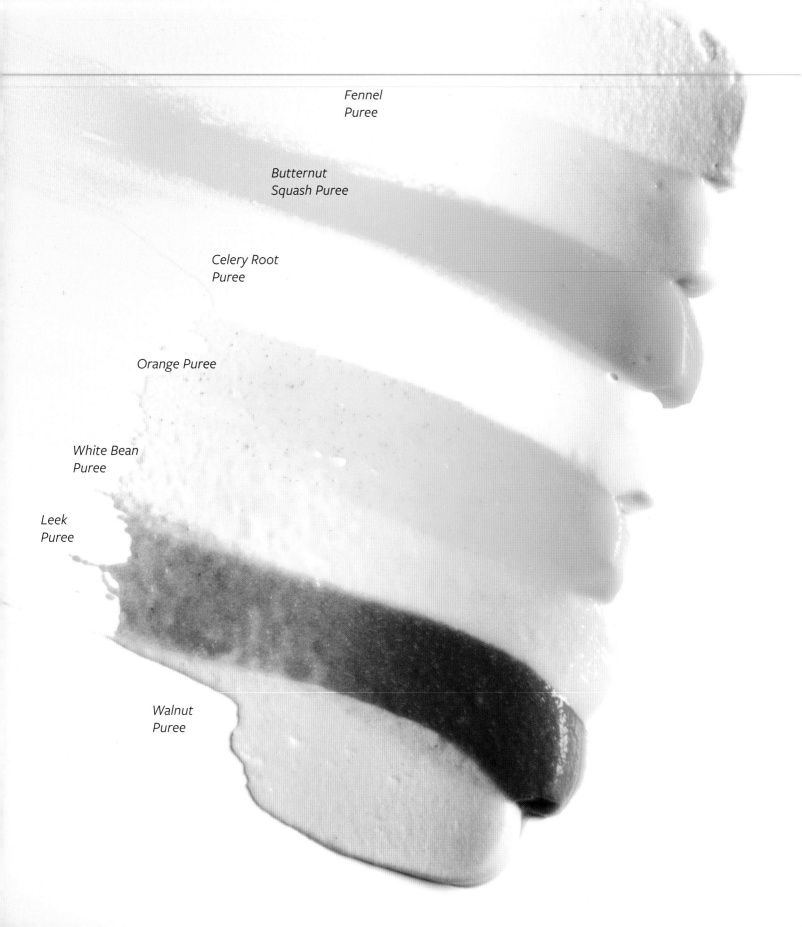

Cabbage
Puree

Fennel
Puree

Butternut
Squash Puree

Celery Root
Puree

Orange Puree

White Bean
Puree

Leek
Puree

Walnut
Puree

THE PUREES

I love purees because they reduce a vegetable to its essence, concentrating its flavor, while also giving the vegetable an elegant texture. While they are often white, a puree can also add a colorful dimension, the vivid orange of butternut squash or a green cabbage puree (yes, my love of cabbage endures here as well).

I often use them to link various elements in a dish, to harmonize disparate components. In the Halibut with Celery Root Puree, Hen of the Woods, and Riesling Cockle Sauce (page 264), I mix chopped hen of the woods into the puree to bring in a touch of earthiness that harmonizes with the larger roasted piece of mushroom—it brings the whole dish together.

In the Maple-Brined Berkshire Pork Tenderloin with Butternut Squash Puree, Walnuts, and Mustard-Curry Jus (page 309), the puree harmonizes and attenuates the nut flavor from the walnut and brings out more of the flavor of the pork, helping to layer flavors.

The cabbage puree has an earthy tone that smooths the rich iron-y flavor of the Squab and Foie Gras "Croustillant" with Roasted Salsify and Caramelized Ginger Jus (page 297).

Purees also have a practical purpose, especially important in the world of fine dining. They can hold main or heavier items in place on their fraught journey from the kitchen to the table.

But, again, the primary value of the puree is to concentrate the essence of a vegetable's or fruit's flavor, to link the various flavors, and to add a comforting and elegant texture to a complex dish.

CABBAGE PUREE

Makes 1 pint (480 ml)

2½ ounces (75 g) bacon, cut into large chunks

4 tablespoons (60 g) butter

1 shallot, thinly sliced

½ ounce (14 g) jalapeños, seeds removed, thinly sliced

1 (1 pound/455 g) savoy cabbage, thinly sliced

7 tablespoons (100 ml) White Chicken Stock (page 251)

1 ounce (30 g) baby spinach

In a saucepan over medium heat, render the bacon until it's crispy on all sides. Add the butter, shallot, and jalapeño and cook until soft. Add the cabbage and stir to cook the cabbage, until it's wilted. Add the chicken stock, cover, and simmer until the cabbage is soft, 10 to 15 minutes. Remove the bacon and blend the cabbage in a food processor until the mixture is smooth. Once smooth, blend in the spinach. Pass the mixture through a tamis or fine-mesh sieve. Transfer to a plastic pint container and refrigerate until ready to use. It can be refrigerated for up to 3 days, or frozen for up to 2 months.

FENNEL PUREE

Makes 1 pint (480 ml)

1 pound (455 g) fennel, outer leaves removed, thinly sliced

1 teaspoon fennel seeds, toasted

4 tablespoons (55 g) butter

Salt

½ cup (125 ml) heavy cream

In a saucepan over medium heat, combine the fennel and fennel seeds, and butter, adding a pinch of salt as you do. When the butter has melted and the fennel begins to cook, turn the heat to low, cover the pan, and cook until the fennel is tender, then remove the cover and continue to cook until all the liquid has evaporated. Add the cream and reduce until almost all the liquid has cooked off. Puree in a food processor and pass through a tamis or fine-mesh sieve. Transfer to a plastic pint container and refrigerate until ready to use. It can be refrigerated for up to 3 days, or frozen for up to 2 months.

recipes continue

BUTTERNUT SQUASH PUREE

Makes 1 pint (480 ml)

1 small butternut squash
2 tablespoons (30 g) brown butter
  (see Note)
2 sprigs thyme
Salt and freshly ground black pepper
2 tablespoons walnut oil
Sherry vinegar

Note: To make brown butter, put 3 or more tablespoons of butter in a pan over medium-high heat until it is melted and frothy. As the froth diminishes and the butter has turned a nutty brown, pour the butter into a ramekin until ready to use, or cover with plastic and store refrigerated for up to 1 week.

Preheat your oven to 375°F (190°C).

Halve the squash and season it with the brown butter, thyme, salt, and pepper. Bake on a parchment-lined sheet pan until completely tender, 45 minutes or so.

Scrape the squash into a food processor and puree. Transfer to a plastic pint container and refrigerate until ready to use. It can be refrigerated for up to 3 days, or frozen for up to 2 months.

Reheat to serve, seasoning it with the walnut oil and vinegar to taste.

CELERY ROOT PUREE

Makes 1 pint (480 ml)

⅓ cup (50 g) thinly sliced shallots
4 tablespoons (60 g) butter
Salt
10 ounces (300 g) celery root, thinly
  sliced
¾ cup plus 2 tablespoons (210 ml)
  heavy cream
1 sprig thyme
White pepper

In a saucepan over medium heat, cook the shallots in the butter, seasoning them with salt, until the shallots are tender but not browned. Add the celery root, reduce the heat to medium low, and cook until it's tender, 5 to 10 minutes. Add the cream and thyme, cover the pan, and simmer for 20 minutes. Remove the thyme and puree in a food processor until smooth. Season with salt and white pepper. Pass the puree through a tamis or fine-mesh sieve. Transfer to a plastic pint container and refrigerate until ready to use. It can be refrigerated for up to 3 days, or frozen for up to 2 months.

ORANGE PUREE

Makes 1½ cups (360 ml)

2 navel oranges
7 ounces (210 ml) fresh orange juice
1½ teaspoons salt
2 teaspoons sugar
4 ounces (120 ml) white balsamic vinegar
⅛ teaspoon (0.25 g) xanthan gum (for
  texture)
1½ tablespoons grapeseed oil

Preheat your oven to 350°F (175°C) on the convection setting (or 375°F/190°C in a conventional oven). Wrap the oranges in aluminum foil individually and put them on a quarter sheet pan (9 by 13 inches/23 by 33 cm). Roast, flipping the oranges once, until the peel is soft enough to pinch, about 1 hour 22 minutes. The oranges should be lightly roasted with no color.

Unwrap and cool to warm. If there are dark spots, cut them off. Quarter the oranges, then cut out the thick center leaving just ⅛ inch (3 mm) pulp on the peel. Discard the pulp. Dice the peel and transfer to a blender.

Add the juice, salt, and sugar and blend on high speed, scraping the bowl occasionally, until very smooth. With the machine running, add the vinegar. Reduce the speed to medium and add the xanthan gum, then drizzle in the oil. If you blend on too high a speed at the end, you'll trap air bubbles in the mixture.

Pass the mixture through a fine-mesh sieve into a bowl set over a larger bowl of ice and water. Stir until cool, then transfer to a plastic pint container and refrigerate until ready to use. It can be refrigerated for up to 3 days, or frozen for up to 2 months.

WHITE BEAN PUREE

Makes 1 pint (480 ml)

1 pound (450 g) dried coco beans or other
    white beans, such as navy or kidney
1 small carrot, peeled and cut in half
1 stalk celery, peeled and cut in half
1 small onion, peeled and quartered
1 bay leaf
1 sprig thyme
1 cup (250 ml) hot White Chicken Stock
    (page 251)
7 tablespoons (100 ml) aged Xeres
    (sherry) vinegar
⅔ cup (150 g) butter, cut into small dice
Salt and freshly ground black pepper

Put the beans in a large bowl and add 6½ cups (1.5 liters) cold water. Cover and let stand overnight.

Drain the beans and transfer to a large pot. Add enough cold water to cover them by 1 inch (2.5 cm). Add the carrot, celery, onion, bay leaf, and thyme. Bring to a boil, then reduce the heat to a simmer and cook until the beans are tender, 1½ to 2 hours. Add hot water if needed to keep the beans submerged by liquid.

Discard the carrot, celery, onion, bay leaf, and thyme. Transfer one-quarter of the beans to a container and add enough cooking liquid to cover them. Reserve the whole beans for serving.

Drain the remaining beans, then pass them through a food mill into a large pot to puree them (use a food processor if you don't have a food mill). Add the hot chicken stock a little at a time, folding it into the puree to blend. Repeat with the vinegar and then the butter, mixing until smooth. Season to taste with salt and pepper. Transfer to a plastic pint container and refrigerate until ready to use. It can be refrigerated for up to 3 days, or frozen for up to 2 months.

Reserve 1 cup of whole cooked beans in their cooking liquid if using as a garnish for the Chorizo-Crusted Cod (page 270).

LEEK PUREE

Makes 1 pint (480 ml)

1⅓ pounds (600 g) leeks, white and pale
    green parts only, cleaned and thinly
    sliced
2 cups baby spinach
4 tablespoons (60 g) butter
Salt and freshly ground black pepper
1 sprig thyme
1 bay leaf
2 ounces (60 g) Yukon gold potato, boiled
    until tender and warm

In a pot, sweat the leeks in the butter over medium heat. Season with salt and pepper. Add the thyme and bay leaf. Cover the pan, reduce the heat to low, and cook until the leeks are soft, 10 minutes or so. Uncover the pan and remove the thyme and bay leaf. Add the baby spinach and cook until almost all the liquid has evaporated. Puree in a food processor, adding the potato, until smooth. Season with salt and pepper. Pass it through a tamis or fine-mesh sieve. Transfer to a plastic pint container and refrigerate until ready to use. It can be refrigerated for up to 3 days, or frozen for up to 2 months.

WALNUT PUREE

Makes 1 pint (480 ml)

1 clove garlic, peeled and smashed
2 tablespoons (30 g) brown butter
    (see Note, page 326)
5 ounces (150 g) walnuts, toasted
¾ cup plus 2 tablespoons (210 ml)
    White Chicken Stock (page 251)
¾ cup (180 ml) heavy cream
2 tablespoons (30 g) butter
Sherry vinegar
Maple syrup

Sweat the garlic in the brown butter in a saucepan over medium heat. Add the walnuts, chicken stock, and cream and simmer for 1 hour. Put the walnut mixture with the butter into a mixer and blend until thoroughly pureed. Pass through a chinois or fine-mesh sieve and season it to taste with vinegar and maple syrup. Transfer to a plastic pint container and refrigerate until ready to use. We transfer this to a squeeze bottle for easy application on the plate. It can be refrigerated for up to 3 days, or frozen for up to 2 months.

DESSERTS

CHOCOLATE ÎLE
FLOTANTE
with Sicilian Pistachios
and Hazelnuts

331

CHILLED WHITE AND
YELLOW PEACH SOUP
with Beer and Lemon Verbena

332

CONCORD GRAPE
VACHERIN
with Concord Grape Sorbet,
Pistachio Ice Cream, and
Vanilla Chantilly

333

CARAMELITO PARFAIT
with Sesame Halva,
Horchata Panna Cotta,
and Yuzu Sorbet

337

CRÊPES FEUILLETINE
with Lemon Cream,
Ten-Flavor Sorbet, and
Pain d'Épices Linzer

339

BEER FRAPPE BRÛLÉE
with Apple Tatin and
Chamonix Biscuit

342

FIG CARPACCIO
with Nutmeg Tuile,
Passion Fruit Gelée, and
Olive Oil Ice Cream

344

BLACK FOREST
CRAQUELIN
with Vanilla Chantilly,
Sacher Biscuit, Cherry, and
Kirsch Sorbet

347

INTRODUCING MARC AUMONT

I love the simplicity of the Alsatian desserts (see the "Breads, Desserts, and Drinks" chapter starting on page 99). And although simple, the first dessert in the pages to follow—our version of the traditional Île Flotante and the Apple Tart a l'Alsacienne—can easily be made elegant enough to serve in a fine-dining restaurant. But I focus on the savory side at the restaurant and consider myself very lucky that chef Marc Aumont showed up when we were looking for a pastry chef to help us open the Modern. Marc had never worked in a restaurant before coming to the United States. For most of his life he worked at a bakery and chocolate shop in his hometown of Chamonix under his father, until he came to New York City in 2000.

You know right away when you're going to work well with someone. We had tryouts with several chefs, each of whom made three or four desserts meant to impress us. Marc made twenty-three. In truth, after tastes of just a few dishes, you have a good sense of a pastry chef's style and skill level, but his ambition and drive attracted us. We were from the same part of the world (Chamonix is a four-hour drive south from where I grew up). As it turned out, he lost his father when he was seventeen, the same age I lost my father. From this experience, I think we share a self-sufficiency and drive, which isn't desirable, given the tragedy, but it can serve a chef well in the long run. He became the opening pastry chef of the Modern in 2004 and we've been together ever since.

Except for the Chocolate Île Flotante (opposite) and Chilled White and Yellow Peach Soup (page 332), the desserts are all his (and his excellent pastry chef de cuisine, Priscilla Scaff-Mariani). Because of the precision required to make them successfully, we are only offering metric weights for the ingredients; it's fine to convert to imperial weights, but we don't recommend trying to make them using imperial volumes. Many rely on a few lesser-known ingredients. Trimoline and Cremodan, for example, are stabilizers for sorbets and ice creams that are used to keep the preparation smooth and creamy, preventing crystallization. You can buy them online or in a specialty food store.

Marc makes it a point not to mimic my food or make desserts that I would make. Dinner at Restaurant Gabriel Kreuther is a multi-course menu, so it lasts a couple of hours. And I love indulging guests in luxuries. But these can be heavy. So Chef Marc focuses on light desserts with dynamic flavors and varied textures. I hope you'll see this for yourself.

Karina Rendon working along with Marc Aumont during service, plating a mille feuille

CHOCOLATE ÎLE FLOTANTE
WITH SICILIAN PISTACHIOS AND HAZELNUTS

Serves 6 to 8

This is a more elegant version of the simple Île Flotante, often called oeuf à la neige, from Alsace (page 120), worthy of a four-star dining room. It follows the exact same method. I still prefer quenelling the meringue from spoons, but for a perfect shape, you could fill tin ramekins with the meringue, steam them, then unmold them and set them in the center of the chocolate sauce, topped with nuts and garnished with the micro basil leaves (basil goes beautifully in this dish—you could even whip a couple tablespoons of minced basil into the meringue for a stronger basil flavor).

FOR THE CHOCOLATE SAUCE

5 egg yolks
100 grams sugar
600 milliliters milk
150 milliliters heavy cream
100 grams 70% dark chocolate, pieces
   or chopped
125 milliliters Baileys Irish Cream
   or Kahlúa

Make the chocolate sauce: Combine the yolks and sugar in a bowl and whisk until it becomes frothy and the color becomes pale yellow. Bring the milk and cream to a simmer. Slowly add the milk and cream to the yolks while whisking. Return the mixture to the pan over medium heat and cook until the sauce thickens to a nappé consistency (you should be able to draw a line through the sauce on the back of a spatula). Remove from the heat and stir in the chocolate until it is completely melted and incorporated. Pour into a bowl set in ice and stir to cool it. Stir in the Baileys Irish Cream.

FOR THE MERINGUE

5 egg whites
1 pinch salt
100 grams sugar
2 tablespoons minced basil (optional)
60 grams pistachios, finely chopped
30 grams hazelnuts, toasted and finely
   chopped
Micro basil leaves, for garnish

Make the meringue: In a bowl, beat the egg whites with a pinch of salt until they become frothy, then add the sugar in thirds, whisking until you have soft peaks. Add the basil, if using.

Bring a pot of water to a simmer. Make large quenelles from the meringue and drop them into the water. (You should have 15 to 18 meringues.) They'll float. Cook for 15 to 20 seconds, then flip them to cook the other side for another 15 to 20 seconds. Remove them to a plate lined with paper towel. Mix the pistachios and hazelnuts together. Roll the meringues in the nuts.

To serve, ladle the chocolate sauce into six to eight bowls. Divide the meringues evenly among bowls. Garnish with micro basil leaves.

CHILLED WHITE AND YELLOW PEACH SOUP
WITH BEER AND LEMON VERBENA

Serves 6

Peaches and beer may sound like an unusual marriage, but the light lagers and pilsners of Alsace have a fruity flavor that brings out the sweetness of ripe stone fruit. A citrus duo along with lemon verbena make this light dessert even more refreshing for hot summer days.

5 large yellow peaches, pitted and cut
    into ½-inch (2.5 cm) wedges
5 large white peaches, pitted and cut into
    ½-inch (2.5 cm) wedges
480 ml light beer
1 vanilla bean, split lengthwise
100 g sugar
Juice of 1 lemon
Juice of 1 orange
1 small bunch lemon verbena or mint,
    tied with kitchen string, plus sliced
    leaves for garnish
Sliced almonds, toasted,
    for garnish

Combine the yellow and white peaches in a large bowl. Combine 2 cups (480 ml) water, the beer, vanilla, sugar, lemon juice, orange juice, and lemon verbena in a large saucepan. Bring to a boil, stirring to dissolve the sugar. Reduce the heat to a simmer and cook for 5 minutes to flavor the liquid with the aromatics.

Pour the liquid with its solids over the peaches. Refrigerate for 2 hours to infuse the peaches with the seasonings.

Discard the vanilla bean and lemon verbena. Divide the peaches and liquid among serving bowls. Garnish with the almonds and sliced lemon verbena leaves.

CONCORD GRAPE VACHERIN
WITH CONCORD GRAPE SORBET, PISTACHIO ICE CREAM, AND VANILLA CHANTILLY

Serves 6

This is a classic example of a light dessert with dramatic flavors that comes to the table looking like a celebration with two sculpturesque pieces of crisp meringue and a tart Concord grape sorbet. Before moving to New York, Marc had never worked with Concord grapes, this fruit hailing from Massachusetts, but he loves it now. The puree recipe alone is worth knowing, if you love this grape. It is so simple to make and it freezes well so it can be used all year long. He also adds a pistachio ice cream ("The American palate loves pistachio," he says). And it's finished with vanilla Chantilly cream, a whipped cream sweetened with confectioners' sugar and vanilla.

FOR THE PISTACHIO ICE CREAM
808 grams milk
48 grams milk powder
243 grams heavy cream
43 grams egg yolks
150 grams sugar
29 grams Trimoline
50 grams pistachio paste
6.5 grams Cremodan 30 Stabilizer

Combine the milk, milk powder, cream, yolks, three-quarters of the sugar, the Trimoline, and pistachio paste in a saucepan. Combine the remaining sugar and the Cremodan, and stir to combine.

Bring the milk mixture to 120°F (49°C) over medium-high heat. Stir in the sugar-Cremodan mixture. Continue heating until the milk mixture reaches 180°F (82°C). Maintain this temperature, stirring with a spatula, for 4 minutes to cook the eggs (a high temperature will result in a grainy texture).

Strain through a chinois into a bowl set in an ice bath. When the mixture is cool, refrigerate overnight.

Churn into ice cream according to your machine's instructions.

FOR THE VANILLA CHANTILLY
100 grams confectioners' sugar
1 vanilla bean
900 grams heavy cream

Put the sugar in a bowl.

Slice the vanilla along its length (don't slice it all the way through; keep the pod in one piece). Scrape the seeds off the pod and add them to the sugar. Add enough cream to make a smooth paste to avoid lumps. Slowly incorporate the remaining cream. (This can be covered and refrigerated until you're ready to whip it. If storing, include the pod.)

When ready to serve, whip the cream (removing the pod if you've included it) until it's fluffy.

FOR THE CONCORD GRAPE SORBET
167 grams sugar
42 grams glucose powder
4.6 grams Cremodan 64 Stabilizer
1 liter Concord Grape Puree (page 334)

In a saucepan, combine three-quarters of the sugar and 333 grams water over medium-high heat.

In a bowl, combine the remaining sugar, the glucose powder, and stabilizer, and whisk to distribute them.

Put the grape puree in a bowl.

When the sugar-water reaches 140°F (60°C), reduce the heat to medium and add the sugar-glucose-stabilizer mixture, whisking to avoid any lumps. Bring the water just to a boil and pour it through a chinois into the grape puree, and stir to combine. Allow it to cool, then cover and refrigerate overnight.

Churn into sorbet according to your machine's instructions.

FOR THE VANILLA MERINGUE
1 vanilla bean
414 grams egg whites
414 grams granulated sugar
166 grams confectioners' sugar

Preheat your oven to 175°F (79°C).

Slice the vanilla bean along its length (don't slice it all the way through; keep the pod in one piece), and scrape all the seeds out. Put the seeds and the pod in the bowl of a standing mixer, along with the egg whites and sugars.

Put water in a pot big enough to contain the mixing bowl over high heat. When it boils, reduce the heat to a simmer. Put the mixing bowl into the water, and whisk constantly until the mixture reaches 140°F (60°C), 5 to 10 minutes, to cook the egg whites and dissolve the sugar. (It should be hot enough to hold your finger in but feel the heat pinch.)

recipe continues

Put the bowl into the stand mixer with the whisk attachment. Whisk on medium speed to gentle peaks. The meringue should be shiny and smooth, thick as shaving cream.

On a large sheet pan lined with a Silpat, spread the meringue evenly across it to ⅛ to ¼ inch (3 to 6 mm) thick. Bake for about 2 hours, until stiff but pliable. Immediately remove the tray and cover with a sheet of parchment. Turn it over onto your work surface and, working quickly, peel the Silpat off. Lift the meringue and bend and fold it into a pleasing shape. Allow to cool.

When ready to serve, break off a large piece for the finished dessert. (You'll have more than you'll need for the dessert, but it makes a great snack, especially when dusted with chopped almonds, pistachios, or coconut.)

FOR THE GRAPE MERINGUE
80 grams egg whites
80 grams sugar
20 grams glucose syrup
400 grams Grape Puree (recipe follows)

Preheat your oven to 175°F (79°C).

Put the egg whites, sugar, and glucose syrup in the bowl of a standing mixer fitted with a whip attachment. Mix on medium speed until frothy and the ingredients are combined. Then slowly stream in the puree. Continue to mix until the puree is incorporated and the meringue has the consistency of shaving cream.

Spread a ½-inch-thick (1.25 cm) layer of the meringue on a large sheet pan lined with a Silpat. Bake for about 3 hours or until the meringue is set all the way through but still pliable. Immediately remove the tray and cover with a sheet of parchment. Turn it over onto your work surface and working quickly, peel the Silpat off. Lift the meringue and bend and fold it into a piece of modern art. Allow to cool.

When ready to serve, break off large pieces for the finished dessert. (You'll have more than you'll need for the dessert, but it makes a delicious snack.)

To compose the dessert, swipe a spoonful of grape puree across the plate. Break off two small pieces of vanilla meringue on which to set quenelles of ice cream and

sorbet and set them about an inch apart in the center of the plate. Put a dollop of Chantilly cream between them, a quenelle of sorbet on one, the ice cream on the other. Break off large pieces of both meringues and wedge them between the ice cream, Chantilly cream, and sorbet. Finish the plate with a few halves of sliced grapes.

CONCORD GRAPE PUREE

2 kilograms Concord grapes
200 grams sugar
2 lemons, cut in half

In a saucepan, combine all the ingredients over medium heat. Smash the grapes into the sugar to get them releasing their juices. Bring the pot to a simmer, stirring, and cook for a few minutes. Remove and discard the lemons. Blend the grapes thoroughly in a blender or with an immersion blender and pass them through a chinois into a bowl set in ice. Store and refrigerate (or freeze in an airtight container for up to 3 months) until needed.

Pastry chef Priscilla Scaff-Mariani, Marc's second-in-command

CARAMELITO PARFAIT
WITH SESAME HALVA, HORCHATA PANNA COTTA, AND YUZU SORBET

Serves 6

Created by pastry chef Priscilla Scaff-Mariani and her sous chef Lauren Young, this dish was inspired by sesame. Priscilla loves halva, a tahini brittle common in Jewish cuisine. We like to present a lot of cultures on any plate in our melting pot city. And there are all kinds of cultural influences in this dessert: the halva from the Middle East, the horchata from Latin America, a caramelized brioche from France, and yuzu from Asia. In Switzerland, chocolate with caramel flavor is especially popular, so there's that as well. We use a chocolate made by Felchlin called Caramelito. A citrus sorbet balances the rich flavors, and for crunch, there is both a sesame tuile and pieces of caramelized French toast.

FOR THE SESAME HALVA

600 grams sugar

85 grams glucose syrup

170 grams honey, preferably high-quality wildflower honey

684 grams tahini

6 grams fleur de sel

Put the sugar and glucose in a saucepan and add enough water so that the sugar resembles wet sand. Put the pan over medium-high heat and cook until the caramel reaches 347°F (190°C). Add the honey and return the pan to a simmer to melt the honey.

Put the tahini and fleur de sel in a mixing bowl. Pour the caramel in a thin stream into the tahini, folding it in using a spatula. Keep the caramel-tahini streaky, not fully homogenized. Pour the mixture onto a Silpat-lined sheet pan and quickly spread it about ¼ to ½ inch (6 mm to 1.25 cm) thick. Cool to room temperature. This can be covered and kept at room temperature for up to a week.

FOR THE HORCHATA PANNA COTTA

100 grams white rice

75 grams sesame seeds

60 grams sweetened condensed milk

¼ teaspoon ground cinnamon (preferably Saigon)

4 sheets silver gelatin, soaked in ice water until softened (see Note on page 172)

Combine the rice and sesame seeds with 472 grams water in a blender and blend for a few seconds to crack the rice and seeds. Refrigerate overnight.

Blend the rice and sesame water for 5 minutes. Strain through a fine-mesh sieve and discard the solids. Combine enough of this liquid (about one-third of the volume) with the condensed milk in a pan to melt it. Add the cinnamon and warm the mixture over medium heat until the milk disperses. Add it back to the rice liquid. This is your horchata.

Put one-quarter of the horchata in a saucepan over medium heat. When it's hot, add the gelatin and cook it until it dissolves. Add this back to the cold horchata. Pour this mixture into 2-inch (5 cm) ring molds, cover, and freeze (or it can be poured into a plastic-lined sheet pan and portioned in any shape you wish).

FOR THE CARAMELITO PARFAIT

225 grams milk

12 grams glucose

2.25 sheets silver gelatin, soaked in ice water until softened (see Note on page 172)

422 grams Caramelito chocolate

450 grams heavy cream

Combine milk and glucose in a small saucepan over medium-high heat and bring it to a simmer. Remove it from the heat and add the gelatin, wrung of any excess water. Stir until the gelatin is melted. Put the chocolate in a bowl and pour the hot milk over it. Let it sit for 2 minutes, then mix with an immersion blender until the ingredients are uniformly combined and become smooth and shiny, 1 minute or so. Add the cream while blending. Chill in the refrigerator overnight.

Once chilled, pipe the mixture into 2-inch (5 cm) ring molds and freeze (but again, the shape is up to you).

recipe continues

FOR THE YUZU SORBET

420 grams sugar

140 grams glucose powder

6 grams Cremodan 64 stabilizer

42 grams milk powder

225 grams lemon juice

375 grams yuzu juice

Combine roughly one-quarter of the sugar, the glucose powder, stabilizer, and milk powder in a bowl.

Put 791 grams water and the remaining sugar in a saucepan over medium heat. Once the water reaches 140°F (60°C), slowly whisk in the sugar mixture. Bring it to a boil, then pour it into a bowl set in an ice bath. When it's cool, add the lemon and yuzu juice.

Refrigerate the sorbet mixture, covered, overnight.

Churn according to your machine's instructions and return it to the freezer until needed.

FOR THE SESAME TUILE

60 grams milk

150 grams butter

60 grams glucose syrup

180 grams sugar

4 grams thermoreversible pectin (see page 154 for more information)

220 grams sesame seeds

Preheat your oven to 325°F (163°C).

Place the milk, butter, glucose, and three-quarters of the sugar in a small saucepan over medium-high heat. Combine the remaining sugar with the pectin. Bring the milk mixture just to a boil, remove from the heat, and add the pectin-sugar mixture. Return the pan to medium heat for 1 minute to activate the pectin. Then add the sesame seeds and mix until homogeneous. Remove the pan from the heat and let it cool. When it's cool enough to handle, put it into a piping bag. Cut a small hole, about ¼ inch, in the piping bag and pipe the mixture onto a Silpat-lined sheet pan in straight lines. Bake for 5 to 8 minutes.

Store in an airtight container for up to a week.

FOR THE SOAK

265 grams eggs

80 grams sugar

110 grams milk

175 grams heavy cream

Beans scraped from 1 vanilla bean pod

Combine the ingredients and blend.

FOR THE CARAMELIZED KOUGELHOPF OR BRIOCHE

6 portions of Kougelhopf (page 103) or brioche, cut in 1½ by 3-inch (4 by 7.5 cm) batons

300 g sugar

1 tablespoon butter

Leave the bread in the soak until it is saturated then set the pieces on a rack over a sheet pan. (Save the extra soak to make French toast, if you wish.)

Sprinkle one-quarter of the sugar in a sauté pan over medium heat. Once this sugar has melted, sprinkle another layer of sugar over it, repeating until you've caramelized all the sugar to a golden brown. Add the butter and stir it in.

When ready to prepare your dessert, cook your soaked bread in the caramel, coating all sides with the caramel, until the bread is warmed through, a few minutes.

To finish the dessert, cut a 2-inch (5 cm) disc of the halva for each plate. On top of this, lay one round of the panna cotta. Unmold and place the Caramelito parfait on top of this. And last, scoop one quenelle of the sorbet and place it on top of the parfait. Garnish with a piece of the sesame tuile and set a caramelized baton of kougelhopf or brioche on the side.

CRÊPES FEUILLETINE

WITH LEMON CREAM, TEN-FLAVOR SORBET, AND PAIN D'ÉPICES LINZER

Serves 6

This is another light dessert—crispy crêpes sandwiching bright lemon cream, a crunchy linzer cookie underneath, and sauce made from one of Marc's favorite fruits, the golden kiwi. Neither he nor I have much affection for the small green kiwis commonly available. But the big golden kiwis from New Zealand are soft and sweet and have a juice that pairs really well with both savory and sweet elements, like fish and chicken, or this crispy creamy napoleon. They're increasingly available in American stores, but green kiwis will work as well.

The lemon cream technique is critical. Too often cooks allow their lemon custard to become too hot, which overcooks the eggs and gives the cream an eggy flavor. Marc takes his lemon cream no higher than 180°F (83°C) and never above 185°F (85°C) and holds it there for 3 minutes, which cooks (and pasteurizes) the eggs and thickens the sauce. The technique can be used in any anglaise-like preparation. And another word about eggs—he puts hard-cooked yolks in the linzer dough (a trick he learned from pastry chef Pierre Hermé), which makes them delightfully crumbly.

FOR THE LEMON CREAM

375 grams eggs
450 grams sugar
Peels from 6 lemons (with as little pith as possible)
300 grams lemon juice
563 grams butter
1½ sheets silver gelatin, soaked in ice water until softened (see Note on page 172)

Place the eggs, sugar, lemon peel and juice, and butter in a bain-marie or bowl and set in simmering water with rings, foil, or a towel at the bottom to keep the metal from direct contact with the bowl and so that the water comes up to the level of the ingredients. Cook for 1 hour, stirring frequently.

Pour the lemon cream through a chinois into a bowl, add the gelatin (wrung of excess water), allowing it to dissolve for a minute, and then blend the mixture with an immersion blender for 10 to 15 minutes. Cover with plastic wrap, pressing it down onto the surface of the cream, and refrigerate overnight.

FOR THE CRÊPES

60 grams all-purpose flour
80 grams sugar
100 grams egg whites, at room temperature
40 grams butter, melted
600 grams warm water

Preheat your oven to 325°F (163°C).

Place the flour and sugar in a bowl and whisk. Then whisk in the egg whites until well combined. Add the melted butter, still whisking. Finally, whisk in the water until you have a loose pourable batter (it's so loose it should look like a pale slurry).

Ladle enough batter to fill 2-inch (5 cm) tart molds about ¼ inch deep.

Bake for about 15 minutes, until golden brown throughout. Take the crêpes out of the mold while still hot and flatten them with a heavy saucepan. Repeat with the remaining batter. This should be enough for 30 to 36 crêpes, or 5 to 6 crêpes per plate.

FOR THE LINZER BISCUIT

190 grams butter
33 grams confectioners' sugar
200 grams all-purpose flour
33 grams almond flour
5 grams baking powder
1 gram salt
10 grams ground cinnamon (preferably Saigon)
40 grams cooked egg yolks (from 2 or 3 hard-cooked eggs), sieved
10 grams dark rum

Preheat your oven to 325°F (163°C).

In the bowl of a standing mixer, cream your butter until very soft, then add the confectioners' sugar and mix to combine. Add the all-purpose flour, almond flour, baking powder, salt, and cinnamon. Once combined, add the egg yolks and continue to mix. Add the rum. Scrape down the bowl as necessary.

recipe continues

Turn the dough out onto parchment paper, cover with parchment, and roll to a thickness of about ⅛ inch (3 mm). Refrigerate, and when chilled cut out twelve 2-inch (5 cm) rounds. Feel free to make a couple of extra, due to any damage during handling. (This dough can also be frozen.) Place them on a Silpat-lined baking sheet and bake for 7 to 8 minutes, until the edges are golden brown.

If not using immediately, store in an airtight container for up to 1 week.

FOR THE TEN-FLAVOR TROPICAL FRUIT SORBET

16 grams lime juice
160 grams apricot puree
120 grams mango puree
120 grams banana puree
120 grams pineapple puree
120 grams passion fruit puree
220 grams sugar
1 long peppercorn (use Sichuan or Tellicherry peppercorns, if unavailable)
2 cinnamon sticks
2 star anise

Combine the lime juice and apricot puree in a bowl.

Combine the mango, banana, pineapple, and passion fruit purees with the sugar, peppercorn, cinnamon sticks, and star anise in a saucepan over medium heat, bring it to a simmer, and whisk to combine. Remove it from the heat and pour into the lime-apricot mixture. Cover and refrigerate overnight.

Strain and churn according to your machine's instructions.

FOR THE GARNISH

1 papaya
1 pineapple
1 mango
(or any fruits you like)
Simple syrup (1 ounce/30 grams sugar dissolved in 2 tablespoons/30 milliliters water) as needed, a tablespoon or so just to coat
Confectioners' sugar

Cut the fruit into a brunoise, or very small dice. You'll need about 2 tablespoons of brunoised fruit per dessert. You can create the ideal mixture based on your preferences, ideally 2 parts each of the mango and pineapple, and 1 part papaya (or any fruits you like).

FOR THE GOLDEN KIWI PUREE

10 golden kiwis, peeled and roughly chopped
2 tablespoons simple syrup (see above)

Combine the kiwis and simple syrup in a blender and puree until smooth.

To compose the dish, spread the kiwi puree in a large circle on each plate. Sprinkle the brunoised fruit around the perimeter.

Place a linzer cookie in the center (put a dot of lemon cream beneath it to prevent it from moving on the plate). Pipe lemon cream on top of the cookie. Top this with a second cookie and pipe more lemon cream on top. Repeat with four more layers of lemon cream and crêpes. Dust the top with a little confectioners' sugar and place a quenelle of sorbet beside it.

Note: The purees for the tropical fruit sorbet are often available in the frozen section of your supermarket. All are available on Amazon. We use the Boiron brand.

BEER FRAPPE BRÛLÉE
WITH APPLE TATIN AND CHAMONIX BISCUIT

Serves 6

This dessert is a spin on the classic French dessert tarte tatin—the apples are effectively cooked in a caramel sauce (Marc's favorite apple to cook with is the Granny Smith, by the way, but feel free to use whatever you like best). And just as in a proper tarte tatin, you have to use butter to make the caramel.

The Chamonix, not to be confused with Marc's birth town, is a kind of cake usually filled with orange marmalade and is almost as popular among kids in France as Twinkies or Hostess CupCakes are here. We combine a Chamonix-like cake with apple, and make the crème brûlée the old-fashioned way, like a traditional crème anglaise, tempering and then cooking the eggs—though Marc believes time and temperature are critical here; he brings the egg-cream-sugar mixture to between 80°C and 82°C (175°F to 180°F) and never above 85°C (185°F)—but this one is flavored with reduced beer, at my suggestion. We sprinkle sugar on top and brûlée it with a torch to serve.

FOR THE APPLE TATIN

400 grams sugar

75 grams butter

3 Granny Smith, Gala, or other good baking apples, cut into large chunks

Preheat your oven to 350°F (175°C).

Put the sugar in a large sauté pan over medium heat and cook until the sugar has melted (you can add the sugar in increments or make a caramel however you're used to doing it; Marc adds it all at once and stirs frequently). When the sugar has melted, stir in the butter and cook until you have a uniform caramel sauce.

Put the apples in an ovenproof vessel that contains them snugly and pour the caramel sauce over them (we use a third hotel pan, but you could use any ovenproof vessel in which the apples fit snuggly). Put a piece of parchment over the apples and weigh it down so that the apples remain submerged. Put the apples in the oven for 30 to 45 minutes, until they're thoroughly cooked and almost translucent.

Let them cool at room temperature (don't refrigerate) until you're ready to serve.

FOR THE CHAMONIX

168 grams eggs

200 grams sugar

182 grams all-purpose flour

3 grams baking powder

4 grams ground ginger

1 gram ground cloves

5 grams ground star anise

67 grams candied orange peel (you can purchase online and at select supermarkets and spice stores)

34 grams dark molasses

100 grams crème fraîche

67 grams butter, melted, plus more for the pan

Preheat your oven to 325°F (163°C).

Place the eggs and sugar in the bowl of a stand mixer fitted with a whip attachment. Whip on medium-high speed until light and fluffy, about 5 minutes.

Combine the flour, baking powder, ginger, cloves, and star anise, add them to the eggs, and mix on medium speed until it's all well combined. Add the candied orange peel, molasses, and crème fraîche, mixing and scraping down the sides as necessary. Stream in the melted butter to finish the batter.

Pour into a quarter sheet pan (9 by 13 inches/23 by 33 cm) lined with buttered parchment paper and bake for 15 minutes, or until cooked through (it should feel springy to the touch). Remove from the oven, allow to cool slightly, then cover with plastic wrap to retain moisture.

FOR THE BEER CRÈME BRÛLÉE

150 grams heavy cream

350 grams milk

85 grams sugar, plus more as needed for brûléeing

90 grams egg yolks

660 grams Belgian brown ale or other brown ale, reduced by two-thirds and cooled

50 grams Fernet Branca, or other amaro

Put the cream, milk, and 1 tablespoon of the sugar in a saucepan (the sugar will prevent dairy solids from sticking to the pan) over medium heat. Bring the mixture up just barely to a simmer.

Combine the yolks and remaining sugar (of the 85 grams) in a bowl and whisk to combine. Pour half the cream mixture into the eggs and whisk, then pour this mixture back into the pan and bring it to about 82°C (180°F). Hold it at about this temperature for 3 minutes or until it becomes thick enough that you can drag a finger across your spatula and retain the line.

Strain the mixture through a chinois into a bowl set in ice. Stir to cool it. Then stir in the beer and amaro. Refrigerate until needed.

To finish the dessert, cut the cake into a 1-inch (2.5 cm) dice or as you wish. Cut the apples into a 1-inch (2.5 cm) dice. Put a layer of apple in your serving vessels, followed by a few pieces of cake.

Fill an iSi gun with the crème brûlée and load it with one charge. Top the cake and apple with the beer crème brûlée. Sprinkle the top with sugar and caramelize it with a torch until crunchy.

FIG CARPACCIO
WITH NUTMEG TUILE, PASSION FRUIT GELÉE, AND OLIVE OIL ICE CREAM

Serves 6

This is Marc's ideal dessert: light and refreshing with a nice balance of fruit, one of his favorite ice creams, and a sweet-sour gelée. On top of that, it's very easy to prepare. We like to mix mission figs, honey figs, and tiger stripes when they're available. While you can prepare the ice cream as you would a traditional crème anglaise—heating the milk, creaming the sugar and yolks separately, tempering the yolks, and so on, Marc simplifies the process by combining the main ingredients and bringing the mixture to just below 85°C (185°F) for 3 minutes. This both pasteurizes the eggs and thickens the sauce. Here he flavors the ice cream with olive oil (use the very best available)—it's a neutral but beguiling preparation.

FOR THE FIGS

18 figs, ends cut off, cut lengthwise in ¼-inch-thick (6 mm) slices

Prepare twelve 7-inch-square (17 cm) pieces of parchment.

Lay the slices from three figs on one of the parchment pieces, overlapping in a roughly 4-inch (10 cm) circle. Cover them with a parchment square. Using a heavy pot, press down on the figs to flatten them to about ⅛ inch (3 mm) thick so they are perfectly flat. Remove the top piece. Using a 5-inch (12 cm) ring cutter, circular bowl, or template, cut the edges off so that you have a perfect circle. Re-cover with the parchment and freeze.

Repeat with the remaining figs for a total of six fig discs.

FOR THE NUTMEG TUILE

5 grams nutmeg
160 grams pastry flour
213 grams milk
80 grams butter
523 grams sugar
5 grams thermoreversible pectin
   (see page 154 for more information)

Sift the nutmeg and flour into a bowl.

Combine the milk, butter, and three-quarters of the sugar in a saucepan over high heat. Mix the remaining sugar and pectin together. Bring the milk and butter to a boil, then stir in the pectin-sugar mixture and bring the mixture to 104°C (220°F), then remove from the heat. Add the flour-nutmeg mixture, slowly, to avoid lumps. When it's incorporated, return it to the heat, bring to a boil, then remove it from the heat and let it sit for 5 minutes.

Ladle about ¼ cup (60 ml) of the batter onto a piece of parchment, cover it with another piece of parchment, and roll it to a thickness of about 1/16 inch (1.5 mm) and freeze. Repeat with the remaining tuile mixture. You will need three 5-inch (12 cm) tuile discs.

Preheat your oven to 325°F (163°C).

Remove the top layer of parchment from the tuile batter and bake for 8 to 10 minutes, until golden brown. Allow to cool, then cut 5-inch (12 cm) discs. Cut each disc in half and store in an airtight container until ready to plate the dessert.

FOR THE OLIVE OIL ICE CREAM

673 grams milk
18 grams heavy cream
7 egg yolks
135 grams sugar
17 grams good balsamic vinegar
40 grams extra-virgin olive oil

Prepare an ice bath.

Combine the milk, cream, yolks, and sugar in a saucepan over medium heat. Bring the mixture to 82°C (180°F). Hold it there—between 80°C and 85°C (175°F and 185°F)—for 3 minutes. Strain the mixture through a chinois into a bowl set in your ice bath. Stir until cooled, then stir in the vinegar. Cover and refrigerate overnight.

Add the olive oil and churn according to your machine's instructions.

FOR THE PASSION FRUIT GELÉE

273 grams passion fruit puree
26 grams sugar
Seeds from 1 vanilla bean pod
3 sheets silver gelatin, soaked in ice water until softened

Line a quarter sheet pan (9 by 13 inches/23 by 33 cm) with plastic wrap.

Combine the puree, sugar, and vanilla seeds in a saucepan over medium heat. Remove it from the heat and add the gelatin, squeezed of any excess water. Stir until it's dissolved. Allow the mixture to cool, then pour it into the sheet pan, cover with plastic, and freeze.

Turn the frozen gelée onto a cutting board and cut out three 5-inch (12 cm) discs, then cut these in half and refreeze them until needed.

FOR THE BALSAMIC REDUCTION SUGAR
200 grams good balsamic vinegar
275 grams sugar

In a saucepan over medium-high heat, bring the vinegar to a simmer and reduce to 50 grams. It should be reduced by three-quarters; it's for flavor, so exact precision is not critical, but feel free to weigh your reduction if you want to be exact. Combine the vinegar and sugar and mix until you have a uniform, darkened sandy mixture for garnishing the plate.

To finish the dessert, about a half hour before you want to serve the dessert, put a fig disc in the center of each plate. Put a half-circle of passion fruit gelée on top of each fig dish, aligning the edges.

To serve, place a semicircular tuile partially over the gelée, so that all three layers can be seen.

Place a quenelle of olive oil ice cream on the disc. Garnish the rim of the plate with some balsamic reduction sugar.

BLACK FOREST CRAQUELIN
WITH VANILLA CHANTILLY, SACHER BISCUIT, CHERRY, AND KIRSCH SORBET

Serves 6

This is an ode to my homeland, thanks to Marc. Alsace borders the Black Forest, where morello cherries grow and where the liqueur kirsch, a spirit made from those cherries, is said to have originated. This is an elaborate dessert with eight different components. No single component is difficult, and each one is delicious on its own, so you could choose to make some and not others, as you like. The cocoa nib tuile base is very versatile—you can swap in any crunchy texture you wish: peanuts, hazelnuts, sesame seed, pumpkin seed. The Sacher biscuits are in the style of the chocolate Austrian Sacher cake, though Marc uses almond paste, here and in most of the restaurant's cakes, for flavor and moisture.

FOR THE COCOA NIB TUILE

180 grams cocoa nibs

40 grams almonds, blanched, skins off

60 grams milk

150 grams butter

180 grams sugar

60 grams glucose syrup

2 grams thermoreversible pectin (see page 154 for more information)

Pulse the cocoa nibs in a food processor until they're roughly ground (but not into a powder). Do the same with the almonds, and combine the two.

Put the milk, butter, three-quarters of the sugar, and glucose in a small saucepan over high heat and bring to a boil.

Meanwhile, mix the remaining sugar with the pectin and stir to distribute the pectin. When the milk comes to a simmer, add the sugar-pectin mixture and boil for 1 to 2 minutes (to cook some of the water out). Stir in the ground cocoa nibs and almonds.

Pour 1 cup (240 ml) of the mixture between two sheets of parchment paper and with a rolling pin, spread the tuile until it is very thin, about 1⁄16 inch (1.5 mm) thick, and freeze.

Preheat your oven to 325°F (163°C).

Remove the tuile from the freezer, pull off the top layer of parchment, and bake for 8 to 10 minutes (don't overcook or it can be bitter). When the tuile has cooled enough so that it's pliable, cut it into 2½ by 5-inch (6 by 12 cm) rectangles, and roll them around a 1½-inch (4 cm) mold to create a cylinder (use a glass, jar, or rolling pin if you don't have molds). There will be more tuile batter left to roll out, but let this harden flat so that the cylinder stands up.

Alternatively, you can shape them over a rolling pin or PVC pipe for semicircles (how you plate the elements is up to you).

FOR THE CHERRY KIRSCH SORBET

667 grams cherry puree (we buy morello cherry puree)

100 grams sugar

28 grams glucose powder

10 grams sorbet stabilizer

22 grams lemon juice

23 grams kirsch

Place the cherry puree, 222 grams water, and three-quarters of the sugar in a medium saucepan. Combine the remaining sugar, the glucose powder, and stabilizer in a bowl. Bring the puree, water, and sugar to a simmer and slowly whisk in the sugar-glucose mixture. Bring to a boil.

Pour the sorbet base into a bowl or container and stir in the lemon juice and kirsch. Cover and refrigerate overnight.

Churn the next day according to your machine's instructions.

FOR THE CHOCOLATE FUDGE SAUCE

253 grams sugar

164 grams glucose syrup

38 grams butter

417 grams heavy cream

126 grams dark (70%) chocolate

2½ sheets silver gelatin, soaked in ice water until softened (see Note on page 172)

Place the sugar and glucose in a high-sided pan over medium heat, and stir to make a dry caramel. As the sugar melts and caramelizes, stir so that it cooks evenly.

Combine the butter and heavy cream in a saucepan. Bring it to a simmer, then remove it from the heat.

recipe continues

Once the caramel is a golden-brown caramel color, slowly add the hot cream mixture—careful, it will boil violently. Stir in the chocolate until it's well mixed.

Return the pan to the heat and bring the mixture to 103°C (215°F), then remove it from the heat and add the gelatin, squeezed of any excess water. Stir until the gelatin is melted, then strain through a chinois into a bowl and blend with a hand blender for 2 minutes, or until perfectly smooth. Refrigerate until chilled.

FOR THE SACHER BISCUIT

160 grams almond paste
100 grams egg yolks
55 grams whole eggs
90 grams confectioners' sugar
48 grams cocoa powder
48 grams pastry flour
150 grams egg whites
60 grams sugar
96 grams butter, melted

Preheat your oven to 350°F (175°C).

Place the almond paste in a mixing bowl with a paddle attachment and slowly add the yolks to make a paste—take your time to mix it slowly and thoroughly, a very important step. Once all yolks are added, add the whole eggs. Once the mixture is clump free and mixed well, add the confectioners' sugar, then switch to a whisk attachment, and whip for 15 minutes on medium-high speed.

Sift the cocoa powder and flour together and fold into the almond paste mixture.

In a clean bowl in a standing mixer, whip the egg whites to stiff peaks; it's best to start the eggs slowly on a low speed; this will result in a stronger meringue. Add a handful of sugar and continue mixing, then add the remaining sugar. Whip on high to incorporate all the sugar into the meringue.

Add a spoonful of the meringue into the almond paste-chocolate mixture to temper, then fold the rest of the meringue gently until all is well incorporated. Do this as delicately as possible.

Grease a half sheet pan (18 by 13 inches/ 46 by 33 cm) with melted butter, line with parchment paper, and then butter this. Pour the biscuit mixture into the tray and bake for 30 minutes, or until a paring knife inserted in the center comes out clean.

FOR THE VANILLA CHANTILLY

100 grams confectioners' sugar
1 vanilla bean
900 grams heavy cream

Put the sugar in a bowl.

Slice the vanilla bean along its length (don't slice it all the way through; keep the pod in one piece). Scrape the seeds off the pod and add them to the sugar. Add enough cream to make a smooth paste to avoid lumps. Slowly incorporate the remaining cream. (This can be covered and refrigerated until you're ready to whip it. If storing, include the pod.)

When ready to serve, whip the cream (removing the pod if you've included it) until it's fluffy.

FOR THE ALMOND CREAM GRANITA

40 grams almond paste
210 grams almond milk
Seeds from 1 vanilla bean pod
350 grams heavy cream
40 grams confectioners' sugar

Making the cocoa nib tuile: Cocoa nibs and almonds are cooked with milk, butter, sugar, and pectin, rolled between parchment, and baked.

Place the almond paste in a blender, turn it on, and slowly add the almond milk and vanilla seeds.

In a small pot, combine the heavy cream and confectioners' sugar over medium heat. When the sugar is melted, combine the cream mixture and the almond paste mixture, stirring until uniformly combined. Pour it into an airtight container. Let it cool and then freeze it overnight.

FOR THE CHOCOLATE FRAPPE (ANGLAISE METHOD)

555 grams milk

225 grams heavy cream

15 grams sugar

158 grams yolks

158 grams dark chocolate (70%), coarsely chopped

Combine the milk, cream, and half of the sugar in a saucepan.

In a bowl, combine the remaining sugar with the yolks and beat them until they're thick.

Over medium-high heat, bring the milk and cream to a simmer. Pour one-third of this into the yolks to temper them, whisking. Then pour the yolk mixture back into the saucepan. Return the pan to the stove over low heat and bring it to about 82°C (180°F) and hold it between 80°C and 85°C (175°F and 185°C) for 3 minutes. You should be able to draw a line across the back of a spatula with your finger when it is properly cooked.

Put your chocolate in a bowl and strain the custard through a chinois over the chocolate. Stir to combine until the chocolate is fully incorporated, then mix for several minutes with a hand blender. Allow it to cool and fill an iSi gun with one charge.

FOR THE CHERRY GELÉE

423 grams cherry puree

64 grams sugar

4 sheets silver gelatin, soaked in ice water until softened

Combine the puree and sugar in a pan over medium heat until it's hot enough to dissolve the sugar and the mixture begins to steam. Remove from the heat and add the gelatin, squeezed of excess water. Stir until the gelatin is dissolved. Put it into an airtight container and refrigerate overnight or until set.

FOR THE COCOA PUNCH

15 grams cocoa powder

100 grams simple syrup (50 g sugar dissolved in 50 ml water)

Combine 50 grams water, the cocoa powder, and simple syrup in a small saucepan and bring it to a simmer, stirring. Transfer it to a container and allow to cool until ready to serve. Warm it to serve.

To finish the dish, set the tuile cylinder in the center of the plate.

Cut small cylinders of biscuit using a ring cutter. Dip it in the cocoa punch and set it beside the tuile.

Add a few halved pieces of cherry to the plate for garnish. Put a small scoop of the cherry gelée on the plate. Drizzle chocolate-caramel fudge sauce over the biscuit.

Pipe Chantilly cream into the cylinder to fill it halfway. Put two more cherry halves on top of the cream. Fill the cylinder full with the chocolate frappe.

Scrape the almond granita until it's crumbly, and spoon a mound of this on the frappe.

Scoop a quenelle of the cherry sorbet and rest it on the biscuit.

While the tuile is still warm and pliable, it is cut and rolled into its cylindrical shape, an ingenious vessel for the Chantilly cream and chocolate frappe.

CAPTIONS FOR THE PHOTOGRAPHS OF ALSACE

Page 1: The Weiss River runs through the Village of Kaysersberg, birthplace of the 1952 Nobel Peace Prize winner Dr. Albert Schweitzer. His birth house is a museum worth a visit.

Pages 2–3: The valley of the Bruche, just south of Strasbourg, looking toward the village of Bellefosse and "Le Climont," a conical sandstone peak of the Vosges mountains, taken from Mont Saint-Jean. The small purplish blossoms in the foreground are wild heather bushes, a favorite of mine, a sign of independence and confidence, as they grow in places that are quite hard for any other flower to grow.

Page 5: View of the hill of Scharrach from the hill of Dangolsheim

Page 6: The abundant sunflowers in Alsace make sunflower oil one of the main cooking fats of the area, and they were the inspiration for the Fennel Panna Cotta with Cockles, Orange Emulsion, and Caviar (page 168).

Pages 8–9: A tractor path through the swathes of vineyards leading to the secluded little village of Niedermorschwihr, near Colmar. The town is known for the crooked spire of its church and, more importantly, for its pâtisserie shop, Maison Ferber, with its wide selection of confiture (jams).

Pages 96–97: The Weinhof, a typical old Alsatian farm building in the city of Colmar, dating to the fifteenth century, now a B&B

Pages 130–131: The three medieval castles of Ribeauvillé, overlooking their famous vineyards: the St. Ulrich (top), the Haut-Ribeaupierre (below left), and the Girsberg (below right)

Right: The Waldeck hamlet in the Bas-Rhin; part of the state park of the northern Vosges mountains

Page 365: Only a half-hour drive south of Strasbourg is Andlau, a charming village nestled in the vineyards, on the wine trail.

Page 366: A scenic mountain road near the town of Rombach-Le-Franc. Nearby is the castle of Haut-Kœnigsbourg, one of the most visited medieval castles in all of France, both for the castle itself and for the far-reaching views.

ACKNOWLEDGMENTS

All those years ago, when I was reading countless cookbooks as an apprentice holed up in one of the guest rooms at my uncle's country inn, it never occurred to me that one day I would be writing my own. While there were several key people directly involved in helping me put this book together, I want to first acknowledge those whose contributions were invaluable even before I became a chef.

My mother, Gabrielle. If it weren't for you, passing down your love of cooking and enjoying great food, this book would not exist. Every traditional recipe in these pages is a dish you cooked or we made together more times than I can count. You gave me a rare gift, one that I prize more than ever. You encouraged me to pursue my culinary dreams when everyone else tried to dissuade me. Thank you for your unconditional love and affection.

My father, Léon, who sadly left us way too early. I have him to thank for his unending support and the confidence he gave me to turn my passion into a vocation. And for passing along his love of foraging for mushrooms in the early mornings. He also taught me the importance of organically grown produce during a time when other farmers thought nothing of using fertilizers and pesticides.

My sister, Patricia Kreuther, and my brother Hervé Kreuther, for their support from afar and for taking care of our mother through difficult times, particularly when we lost our brother Marc. I couldn't have achieved all that I have during my years here in New York without the peace of mind of knowing you were all together, safe, at home in France.

My uncle Michel Kreuther. He taught me all the fundamentals a professional chef can dream of. Most important, he taught me a deep respect for the farmers, the products, and the profession of cooking itself. The years spent with him also taught me self-discipline, kindness, and calmness in a professional kitchen, a rare attribute at the time.

Chef Edmond Voltzenlogel, an Alsatian in Washington, DC, at Le Caprice during the eighteen months I worked there: He was pivotal in my cooking education at that stage, because he was a former culinary professor at the Ecole Hôteliere de Paris Lycee Jean Drouant. There was no Google at that time, so for me he was a walking, talking encyclopedia, as long as I picked his brain. The theoretical teachings he instilled in me are reflected throughout this book. I will be forever grateful to him.

Chef Franz Keller in Germany I have to thank for opening my mind to incorporating other cuisines from around the world into my flavor spectrum, particularly Asian and Italian methods and techniques.

With regard to the book you're reading, special thanks to executive editor Laura Dozier and publisher Michael Sand from Abrams for their amazing support during this whole process. Their vision determined how the first part of this book could dovetail with the second. I am deeply appreciative of their trust and patience during these unprecedented times. I would also like to thank senior managing editor Lisa Silverman, creative director Deb Wood, senior designer Danielle Youngsmith, associate director of production Denise LaCongo, senior director of marketing Jessica Weiner, and publicity manager Natasha Martin for their expertise.

This book would not have taken off without my literary agent, Jonah Straus. You had the vision to see the potential interest in my Alsatian heritage by combining the rustic food of Alsace into a contemporary book. I'll always be grateful for your intelligence, wit, friendship, and support.

My coauthor, Michael Ruhlman: Your knowledge and experience in translating the chef's world into manageable recipes for the home cook was invaluable guidance. Your love of food and technique and your enthusiasm for my homeland made working with you a pleasure. I'm glad I converted you to nutmeg! Your sense of humor, along with your friendship and the patience you exhibited with the myriad challenges we faced, was wonderful reassurance that, against all odds, we were on the right track and that there was a light at the end of the tunnel for this book.

Genevieve Ko: You have been a huge fan of my cooking since my days at the Modern, and I have you to thank for never giving up on the idea of writing a cookbook. You had the right approach for the proposal. Many thanks for all your contributions.

Chef Jean-Georges Vongerichten: You have been such an important and instrumental part of my career in this city. You are, after all, a fellow Alsatian at heart

The fairy-tale village of Riquewihr, surrounded by vineyards

and I appreciate that you've always looked out for me over the years. Thank you for giving me the opportunity at first to join you in your journey, but most important for appointing me to lead and run your kitchen with your full support and trust. You made me think outside the box and outside my comfort zone, to teach me more than cooking—to take risks, to listen to the guests, and, more than anything, to make things work on the business side. Your endless energy, yet down-to-earth personality, has always been an inspiration. Thank you.

Evan Sung, the photography wizard: Thank you for your mastery of the image, your love of food, and your great humor. This project, with the pandemic challenges that suddenly came into the mix, has made our collaboration unique in many ways, and unforgettable because of the protocols we had to take to safely achieve it.

Thank you, Joe Anthony, our chef de cuisine, for the planning work you did for the photo sessions. The passion you have for the plating artistry you love so much will be a true inspiration to the reader.

Justin Borah, our executive sous-chef: Thank you for the countless hours you cooked with me and Michael on every recipe test session. I couldn't have done it without you. You and Jordan Ottomanelli kept a tab on all the updates and edits and kept me and Michael on track with the conversions from metric to imperial.

William Cesark, our sous chef: Thank you. The time you took to collaborate and translate the detailed techniques you use to get the pâte de fruits right was essential to their inclusion in this book.

Jake Abbot, our sous chef: He has studied stock-making intensively and worked closely with Michael to scale down our restaurant recipes for this book. Thank you.

Agustin Garcia, sous chef and head butcher: Thanks to you for butchering many of the proteins for this book and for helping to gather the ingredients for the testing sessions. I can always rely on you and greatly appreciate all the hard work you do for the team behind the scenes.

Marc Aumont, our executive pastry chef: Thank you for contributing the lion's share of the dessert recipes, and for testing and plating them as well. Your exceptional talent and creativity are amazing, and the knowledge and friendship you bring to the team is second to none. What's more, your passion for educating and mentoring the younger generation of pastry professionals is admirable.

Priscilla Scaff-Mariani, our pastry chef: You are a brilliant chef in your own right. Thank you for your diligence in writing most of the modern dessert entries.

Todd Coleman, creative consultant: Thank you for all your marketing wisdom. It really doesn't get much better than you. I also want to give thanks to everyone else at Gabriel Kreuther, past and present, for running the restaurant while I was busy with this project: Angela Borah, Rodrigo Colin, Rachel Durboraw, Paul Lee, Robert Pugh, Nancy Schumann, Joseph Yi, Lauren Young, and many more . . .

I would also like to thank our investor group. I wanted to create a restaurant with a soul, one that transports you, and they have always supported me in this. They not only helped me to start a restaurant that reflected my vision, but stuck with me during the pandemic. Without them, we'd never have made it through.

Eben Dorros, my business partner, and our amazing interior decorating scout, his wife, Elizabeth Dorros: Thank you for your unconditional support, positive energy and spirit, and for believing in me. Eben, you're at the heart of everything we have achieved as a team, and I'm looking forward to the road ahead of us as we continue to grow our vision.

My remarkable wife, Patricia: You have been a tremendous asset throughout this entire project. Thank you for the many contributions you made, most notably the countless hours you devoted to acting as my sounding board during the development of the essays. As an avid reader, your grasp and knowledge of good storytelling convinced me of the importance of sharing my backstory, not just my recipes. Combined with your tireless editing and proofreading input, you made this book immeasurably better. Your support and love mean everything.

Last but not least, I want to thank all our guests. My heartfelt appreciation. Thanks to the unwavering loyalty you've shown throughout this pandemic, our restaurant family at Gabriel Kreuther has a very bright future. Thank you from the bottom of my heart.

INDEX

Editor: Laura Dozier
Managing Editor: Lisa Silverman
Designer: Danielle Youngsmith
Production Manager: Denise LaCongo

Library of Congress Control Number:
2021932499

ISBN: 978-1-4197-4782-3
eISBN: 978-1-64700-470-5

Printed and bound in China
10 9 8 7 6 5 4 3 2 1

Abrams books are available at special
discounts when purchased in quantity for
premiums and promotions as well as fund-
raising or educational use. Special editions
can also be created to specification. For
details, contact specialsales@abramsbooks.
com or the address below.

Abrams® is a registered trademark of Harry
N. Abrams, Inc.

ABRAMS The Art of Books
195 Broadway, New York, NY 10007
abramsbooks.com